Happy Gardening
to
Bonnie!

Love You!

Victoria
2001

AHS
GREAT
PLANT
GUIDE

AHS
GREAT
PLANT
GUIDE

A DORLING KINDERSLEY BOOK
www.dk.com

PROJECT EDITOR **Simon Maughan**

EDITOR **Tracie Lee**

ART EDITOR **Ursula Dawson**

MANAGING EDITOR **Louise Abbott**

MANAGING ART EDITOR **Lee Griffiths**

DTP DESIGN **Sonia Charbonnier**

PRODUCTION **Ruth Charlton**

PICTURE RESEARCH **Sam Ruston, Neale Chamberlain**

US PUBLISHING TEAM

SENIOR EDITOR **Ray Rogers**

EDITORIAL DIRECTOR **LaVonne Carlson**

PUBLISHER **Sean Moore**

CONSULTANT **Dr. H. Marc Cathey**

Published in the United States by
Dorling Kindersley, Inc., 95 Madison Avenue, New York, NY 10016

First published in Great Britain in 1998 by Dorling Kindersley
Publishers Limited, 9 Henrietta Street, London WC2E 8PS
This revised and expanded edition published 2000

2 4 6 8 10 9 7 5 3 1

Dorling Kindersley Publishing offers special discounts for bulk purchases for sales promotions or
premiums. Specific, large-quantity needs can be met with special editions, including personalized
covers, excerpts of existing guides, and corporate imprints. for more information, contact
Special Markets Department, Dorling Kindersley Publishing, Inc.,95 Madison Avenue, New York, NY 10016
Fax: 800-600-9098

Library of Congress Cataloging-in-Publication Data
AHS Great Plant Guide
p. cm.
Rev. ed. of: RHS good plant guide. 1998
ISBN 0-7894-7144-2 (alk. paper)
1. Landscape plants--United States. 2. Landscape gardening--United States.
3. Landscape plants. 4. Landscape gardening. I Title: Great Plant Guide
II American Horticultural Society III DK Publishing, Inc. IV RHS good plant guide
SB407 .A37 2001
635.9--dc21   00-058933

Color reproduction by GRB Editrice, Italy.
Printed and bound in Italy by L.E.G.O.

See our complete catalog at
www.dk.com

CONTENTS

INTRODUCTION

GARDENERS TODAY have plenty of choice when buying plants. Not only are plant breeders constantly producing new and exciting cultivars, but plants are now more widely available in garden centers and nurseries as well as in do-it-yourself superstores. In less traditional plant-buying situations, information and advice may not be readily available or reliable. It is perhaps no wonder, then, that gardeners sometimes find choosing the right plant a bewildering business. .

The *AHS Great Plant Guide* was conceived to help gardeners select outstanding and reliable plants for their garden, whatever their level of expertise and experience, and whatever the site. Because all of the plants in this book are suitable for some region of North America, however small or specialized, any gardener, even a novice, can choose plants from here with confidence.

However, these recommendations refer only to the plants themselves, and not to those who produce them. It is impossible to guarantee the

Ever-widening plant choice
Exotic flowers, such this blue poppy (Meconopsis grandis), may tempt the gardener, but check the conditions they require before buying.

quality of plants offered for sale by any nursery, garden center or store, and here gardeners must exercise a degree of common sense and good judgment in order to ensure that the individual plants they select and take home will thrive. The following pages include guidance on recognizing healthy, well-grown plants and bulbs, and they show how to choose them wisely and get them off to a good start.

CHOOSING FOR YOUR GARDEN

Selecting plants appropriate to your site and soil is essential, and each plant in the *A–Z of Plants* has its preferences indicated. Well prepared soil, fertilizing, mulching, and, in dry conditions, watering in the early stages are also important for the well-being of most plants (although in *The Planting Guide* you will find plants to grow in poor soil or dry sites). Entries in the *A–Z* include basic care for the plant concerned, along with specific hints and tips on topics such as pruning and siting, and on winter protection where hardiness is borderline. By following this advice, the plants you choose using the *AHS Great Plant Guide* should get off to a great start and continue to perform well.

Using the Guide

THE *AHS GREAT PLANT GUIDE* is designed to help you choose plants in two different ways.

The A–Z of Plants

Here, over 1,000 plants have full entries and are illustrated with photographs. This is the section to consult to find details about a plant, whether you are reading its name on a label or have noted it down from a magazine article or a television or radio broadcast. It will tell you what type of plant it is, how it grows, what its ornamental features are, where it grows and looks best, and how to care for it. For quick reference, symbols (right) summarize its main requirements.

The Planting Guide

This section provides "shopping lists" of plants for every purpose, whether practical, such as a group of plants for a damp, shady site, or for themed plantings, such as a selection of plants to attract birds into your garden. Page references are given to plants with entries and portraits elsewhere. Hundreds of plants not pictured are also recommended.

Plant sirens (facing page)
Garden centers and nurseries often feature new plants to tempt gardeners.

Symbols Used in the Guide

Soil Moisture Preferences/Tolerances
◊ Well-drained soil
◖ Moist soil
● Wet soil

Sun/Shade Preferences/Tolerances
☼ Full sun
☀ Partial shade: either dappled shade or shade for part of the day
☀ Full shade
Note: where two symbols appear from the same category, the plant is suitable for a range of conditions.

USDA Hardiness Zone Ranges
These are given (as Z6-9, for example) for all plants in this book, except for tender plants, for which the minimum temperature is given, and annuals (including some perennials commonly grown as annuals). Many subtropical plants that tolerate temperatures slightly below freezing are indicated as being hardy in Zones 10-11.

AHS Heat Zones
The 12 zones of the AHS Plant Heat-Zone map are based on the average number of days each year a given region experiences "heat days" – those days with temperatures over 86°F (30°C). Zones are given similarly to hardiness, except that the hottest zone is given first, for example H9-7.
All ranges given in this book are intended as approximate guides and should not be considered definitive.

THE PLANTS IN THE GUIDE

THE RANGE OF PLANTS – well over 2,000 – featured in the *AHS Great Plant Guide* has been carefully chosen to provide the best selection from among all the different types of plant, and for many of the situations for which plants may be required. Many of the plants in this book are readily available from local sources throughout North America, although gardeners in places not easily served by local nurseries and garden centers will need to do some research (including looking through mail-order catalogs, doing web searches, and networking with members of garden clubs and specialized plant societies) to track down many of these plants.

WHAT IS A GREAT PLANT?

Calling a plant "great" is, admittedly, the result of a combination of subjective and objective appraisals of a plant, whether on the part of an individual or a committee of experts. It must be remembered that a plant that performs exceedingly well as a great garden plant in one part of North America may be a miserable failure in the rest of the continent, or it may be a noxious weed. Similarly, any "great" plant put into a garden situation not to its liking will fail, if not immmediately, then eventually. The perception of an individual plant, genus, or even entire group of plants as "great" can also come and go upon the whims of current gardening trends and fads.

Geranium 'Kashmir White'
Plants that are versatile and easily grown are noteworthy for sheer garden value.

Camellia x williamsii 'Brigadoon'
Choice forms of familiar and unusual plants are in this book.

Hydrangea macrophylla 'Altona'
The best selections of many garden stalwarts are recommended.

Generally, though, a great garden plant that withstands the test of time will meet the following criteria:

• It is excellent for ornamental use, either outdoors (in the open ground or in a container) or under cover

• It is of good constitution, being neither frail and weak nor overly vigorous to the point of being invasive or weedy

• It is available in the horticultural trade, whether locally or through mail order

• It is not particularly susceptible to any pest or disease

• It does not require any highly specialized care other than providing the appropriate conditions for the type of plant or individual plant concerned (for example, acidic soil)

• It should not be subject to an unreasonable degree of reversion in its vegetative or floral characteristics.

To explain this last point simply, many plants with unusual characteristics differing from the species, such as double flowers or variegated leaves, have often been propagated from a single plant or part of a plant – a natural mutation or "sport" – that has appeared spontaneously. Plants bred from sports – especially when raised from seed – are liable to show only the normal leaf color or flower form. It takes several generations of careful and controlled propagation for the special feature to be stable enough for plants to be recognized and registered with a distinct cultivar name (which is usually chosen by the breeder) and then offered for sale. Many never retain the special feature when grown from seed and therefore can be reproduced only by vegetative methods such as cuttings or grafting.

Prunus laurocerasus
This evergreen is handsome year-round, both as a specimen shrub and as a hedge.

Anemone blanda 'White Splendour'
Floriferous cultivars for every site and season are included in this book.

Acer negundo 'Flamingo'
Plants that are grown for their variegated foliage should not be prone to excessive reversion.

NONPICTURED PLANTS

The Planting Guide section at the back of the book presents (in list form) hundreds of trees, shrubs, climbers, perennials, bulbs, and other plants that could not be pictured and that are suitable for a specific site or garden situation. These lists do not pretend to be exhaustive, but they do present a representative cross-section of plants to consider. The lists also contain plants that are pictured; these are cross-referenced to the appropriate pages.

In some categories of plant, notably annuals (particularly those for summer bedding, such as impatiens, petunias, and salvias) and in some perennial genera, new cultivars appear so rapidly, often superseding others offered for sale, that producers, retailers, and gardeners alike are hard pressed to keep up with developments. In order to give a wider choice in these somewhat underrepresented categories, the *AHS Great Plant Guide* includes, in *The Planting Guide*, selected cultivars that have proved their reliability over the years.

Putting plants to the test
Trials at public gardens and at display gardens at seed companies help select the best forms for gardeners.

FINDING PLANTS BY NAME

The botanical, or so-called "Latin," names for plants are used throughout this book, simply because these are the names that gardeners will find on plant tags and in publications. These names are also international, transcending any language barriers or regional variation.

To the uninitiated, plant nomenclature may seem confusing, and sometimes plant names appear to be very similar. It is important to recognize that plant nomenclature is by no means static; plant names, whether scientific or vernacular, are subject to constant revision. Sometimes this is in response to scholarly research, whereby a genus may be split up and given several new names (for example, the genus *Chrysanthemum* is now several genera); other times it is a marketing technique to create new interest for an already established plant. Some plants have synonyms – older or alternative names – by which they may sometimes be referred to: the *AHS Great Plant Guide* gives synonyms for a number of plants. A brief guide to plant nomenclature can be found on pages 24–25. Many common names for plants or plant types that feature in the *Guide* are also given, both in the *A–Z of Plants* and in the Index.

SHOPPING FOR GOOD PLANTS

THE FIRST STEP in ensuring that your garden will be full of healthy plants is to choose and buy carefully.

WHERE TO BUY

Plants can be found for sale in such a variety of situations today that there are no hard and fast rules. Generally, buy plants only when you feel sure that the plants offered are actually what they say they are, that they have been well grown, and they are not going to bring any pests and diseases into your garden.

PLANTS BY MAIL

Buying plants by mail order is one of the easiest (and most addictive!) ways of obtaining particular plants that you are eager to acquire. It gives you a huge choice, far greater than in most garden centers, and also gives you access to specialized nurseries that concentrate on certain plant groups or genera and that may not be open to visitors. Armed with a buyer's guide to nurseries, you can track down almost any specimen from the comfort of your own home, and provided that someone will be at home on the day it arrives, it should be delivered in perfect health. Mail-order nurseries are usually happy to replace any plant damaged in transit. Often, the plants will arrive with their roots surrounded with soil mix or peat (otherwise bare-root). They are best planted out soon after receipt.

WHEN TO BUY

Trees, shrubs, and roses that are available as bare-root specimens are almost always deciduous. Woody plants with roots balled and burlapped may be deciduous or evergreen. Many are available only in the dormant season; they are ideally purchased in late autumn or early spring and should be planted as soon as possible.

Container-grown plants are now extremely popular and are offered for sale throughout the planting season. However, the traditional planting times of spring and autumn, when conditions are not extreme, are still the best. Plants should not be put into near-freezing or baked, dry soil; instead, keep them in their containers until conditions improve.

In colder climates, reliably hardy plants can be planted in autumn. Spring is the time to put in plants of borderline hardiness and to buy bedding plants. Beware of buying them too early, however tempting they look after the dark, bare days of winter. Bedding sold in early and midspring is intended to be bought by people with greenhouses and cold frames, where plants can grow under cover until all danger of frost has passed. If you plant out bedding too early in the season, you risk losing it to late frost.

YOUR SHOPPING LIST

Whether you are starting a new garden from scratch, replacing a casualty, or simply wanting to add extra touches with some plants for a shady corner or for a half barrel,

Well-grown plants for sale
Healthy, clearly labeled plants in neat, well-kept surroundings are a good indication of excellent nursery care.

informed choice is the key to buying the right plants and to getting the very best and healthiest specimens.

There are many factors to consider about your garden (see pages 16–17) and, equally, buying tips that will help you make the best choice from the selection of plants offered (see pages 18–19). Many gardeners prefer to set out with specific plants in mind. However, no one could deny that impulse buys are one of gardening's great pleasures – and with the *AHS Great Plant Guide* at hand, you will be able to obtain just the right plants for your garden and avoid expensive mistakes.

CHOOSING THE RIGHT PLANTS

ALTHOUGH THERE ARE ways to get around many of plants' climatic and soil requirements, you will avoid extra work and expense by choosing plants well suited to the conditions your garden offers.

HARDINESS

Most of us garden in areas that experience frost and cold (including plenty of snow) in winter.

Choose plants that are generally known to be adapted to your area by checking the hardiness - and heat - zone ranges given in this book. Providing good growing conditions throughout the season helps promote survival, including appropriate winter and summer mulches such as pine boughs and light straw. Optimism is no substitute for action if plants are to survive in a particular region,

Extending the range
Container growing may be the answer for gardeners who covet plants with special soil needs, like these acid-loving azaleas, that their open gardens cannot meet.

yard, or microclimate, such as a low, poorly drained spot, an unusually hot and dry corner, or an exposed north-facing hillside.

Sun and Shade

It is well worth observing your garden to see how much sun areas receive at different times of the day and year. For good growth and the best display of features such as colored foliage, always match plants' sun and shade requirements.

Your Soil

Most plants tolerate soil that falls short of perfect, and many survive in conditions that are very far from ideal. It is always preferable – and far more labor-saving – to choose plants that suit your soil, rather than manipulate your soil to suit plants, by adding, for example, peat or lime. The effect never lasts and is now also considered environmentally inadvisable – local insects, birds and other fauna may be unable or unwilling to feed on plants to which they are unaccustomed. It is, however, important to add nutrients to the soil, and two aims can be achieved together if you add these not as powder or granules but as a mulch that will also improve soil texture, such as compost or manure.

Determining your soil acidity (or its reverse, alkalinity), measured by units known as pH values, is important. Most plants tolerate a broad range of pH values around neutral, but some groups have specifically evolved to be suited by soil that is either definitely acidic or definitely alkaline. There is no point to ignoring these soil preferences and trying to grow, for example, azaleas in an alkaline soil; they will not thrive. Choose plants that will enjoy your soil or, if you really covet some specialized plant groups, grow them in containers in a soil mix that meets their needs.

Drainage

The expression "well-drained yet moisture-retentive" is one of the most widely used yet seemingly baffling expressions in gardening. However, it is not such a contradiction in terms as it seems. What it applies to is a soil that in composition is not dominated by pebbles or grains of sand, which cannot hold water, nor clay, which binds up and retains water in a solid gluey mass. It is the presence of well-decomposed organic material that enables soil to hold moisture *and* air simultaneously, so that both are readily available to plants. Incorporating well-decomposed organic matter (see page 21) is the most useful way to improve soil texture, either for an entire area or as plants are planted.

CHOOSING A HEALTHY PLANT

TRY TO RESIST buying plants that are in poor condition, even if it is the sole example offered of a plant you really want. Nursing a pathetic specimen could take an entire growing season, during which time the plant will scarcely reward you, and with container-grown plants now so widely available it is likely that, later in the season, you will find a healthier specimen that you can plant right away. In practice, however, there are few gardeners that have never taken pity on a neglected or undernourished plant – but you must always harden your heart to those showing signs of pest infestation or disease. You risk importing problems that could spread to other plants.

WHAT TO BUY

Plants offered for sale should be clearly labeled, healthy, undamaged, and free from pests and diseases. Inspect the plant thoroughly for signs of neglect. With balled-and-burlapped plants, check that the root ball is firm and evenly moist, with the netting or burlap intact. Containerized plants should always have been raised in containers. Do not buy plants that appear to have been hastily uprooted from a nursery bed or field and potted up. There should be no sign of roots at the surface.

Look at the base of the pot for protruding roots, a sign that the plant is potbound (has been in its container for too long). Always lift the pot to make sure roots have not grown into the area beneath the pot, another sign of a badly potbound specimen. Crowded roots do not penetrate the surrounding soil readily after planting, and the plant will not establish well.

HEALTHY GROWTH

LEAVES ARE GLOSSY AND HEALTHY

EARLY PRUNING HAS PRODUCED AN ATTRACTIVE SHAPE

ROOTS ARE WELL GROWN BUT NOT CROWDED

Good specimen
This well-grown skimmia has a substantial root ball that is in good proportion to the bushy top growth.

Healthy bulb
A sound neck, tunic (the papery outer covering) and basal plate (where the roots grow) all recommend this bulb to the buyer.

SOUND, FIRM
BASAL PLATE

Poor specimen
The badly chopped neck, ragged tunic, discolored flesh, and wounded basal plate indicate poor harvesting and storage: the bulb will not do well.

INFECTION MAY ENTER
VIA WOUND

Strong top growth is another key factor. Avoid plants with pale or yellowing foliage, damaged shoot tips, or etiolated growth (soft, pale, overextended, and weak-looking shoots). Look at the soil surface: it should not be covered in weeds, mosses, or liverworts.

With herbaceous plants, small healthy specimens are cheaper than large ones and will soon grow once planted. Groups of three or five plants often look better than single specimens. With all types of herbaceous plants, including young annuals and bedding, pick out the stockiest, bushiest specimens, with (if appropriate) plenty of flower buds, rather than open flowers.

PLANT SHAPE AND FORM

When buying trees and shrubs, which are to make a long-lasting contribution to your garden, consider their shape as well as their good health. Choose plants with a well-balanced branch framework and with top growth that is in proportion to the rootball or pot. A stocky, multistemmed plant usually makes the best well rounded shrub, while young trees with a single trunk should have just that – and a good, straight, sound one, too – right from the start. A one-sided shrub may of course be acceptable for wall-training, but will put on more growth from the base, and thus cover space better, if its shoot tips are pruned after planting.

BUYING BULBS

Buy bulbs (see above) as if they were onions you were intending to cook with and eat – reject any that are soft, discolored, diseased, or damaged. While it is not ideal, there is no harm in buying bulbs that have begun to sprout a little, as long as the bulbs are planted soon afterward.

PREPARING THE SOIL

WHILE THE BEST plants for your garden are those suited to the growing conditions available, most soils can be improved to extend the range of plants that can be grown.

IDENTIFYING YOUR SOIL TYPE

Investigating your soil to discover just what its qualities are is one of the most useful things you can do to ensure thriving plants and successful gardening. Generally, the soil will be either sandy or have a clay texture, or somewhere between the two. If your soil has a light, loose texture and drains rapidly, it is probably sandy. Sandy soil has a rough, gritty feel when rubbed and makes a characteristic rasping, scraping sound against the blade of a spade. Although easy to dig, it is low in fertility. Clay soil is heavy, sticky, cold, easy to mold when wet, and can become waterlogged. It is difficult to work but is often very fertile. A good mix of the two – a "medium loam" – is ideal.

To further establish which plants will be best suited by the soil in your garden, you can determine its pH value (to what degree it is acidic or alkaline) and the levels of various nutrients it contains using very simple testing kits that are available at most garden centers.

CLEARING WEEDS

In a new garden, or if you are planting in a previously uncultivated area, your first task will be to clear away any debris and weeds. Pre-planting clearance of all weeds is essential, since they will compete with your plants for light, moisture, and nutrients. Where the ground is infested with perennial weeds, an alternative to laborious hand-clearing is to spray it during the season before planting with a systemic herbicide that will kill their roots. This is most effective when the weeds are growing strongly, usually in early summer. Although this may mean delaying planting, patience at this stage will be amply rewarded later. Repeat applications may be needed.

Isolated perennial weeds can be forked out carefully, removing all root fragments. Annual weeds may be hoed or sprayed off immediately before planting.

WORKING THE SOIL

Digging or forking over the soil helps break down compacted areas and increase aeration, which encourages good plant growth. The deeper you dig the better, but never bring poor-quality subsoil up to the surface: plants need all the nourishment that the darker, more

Digging with ease
The correct tools and technique make digging more comfortable, and safer for your back. Test the weight and height of a spade before buying, and always keep your back straight when using it.

Forking over
Drive the fork into the ground, then lift and turn the fork over to break up and aerate soil Spread a layer of organic matter over the soil first so that it is incorporated into the soil as you work.

nutritious topsoil can give them. If you need to dig deeply, remove the topsoil, fork over the subsoil, then put the topsoil back in.

Dig heavy clay soils in late autumn. The weathering effects of frost and cold over the winter will help improve the soil's texture by breaking it down into smaller pieces. Avoid digging when the soil is wet; this will damage the soil structure. It will save work if you incorporate soil amendments as you go.

ADDING SOIL AMENDMENTS

Digging and forking will improve soil texture to some extent, but to really bring a soil to life, the addition of a soil amendment is invaluable The drainage, aeration, fertility and moisture-holding properties of most soil types can be improved simply by adding well-rotted organic matter. This is best done in the season before planting, to allow the soil to settle. Well-rotted manure, compost, and leafmold enhance the moisture retention of a sandy soil and improve nutrient levels. Applied regularly, they improve the structure of clay soil. Clay soils can be further opened up by the addition of coarse sand to a depth of at least 12in (30cm). Organic mulches of bark, cocoa shells, or wood chips are also eventually broken down into the soil.

PLANTING OUT

WHATEVER YOU ARE planting, make sure that you give your plants a really promising start. Careful planting saves both time and money, and well-chosen plants positioned in optimum conditions will perform well and should resist attack from pests and diseases.

PREPLANTING PLANNING

Before planting, check the potential heights and spreads of plants to ensure that you leave the correct distances between them. When designing plant groups, consider different plants' season of interest, including their appearance in winter.

WHEN TO PLANT

In most areas, the best planting seasons are autumn and spring. Autumn planting allows plants to establish quickly before the onset of winter, since the soil is still warm and moist enough to permit root growth. Spring planting is better in cold areas for plants that are not reliably hardy.

Perennials can be planted at any time of the year, except during extreme conditions. They should grow rapidly and usually perform well within their first year. To reduce stress on a perennial when planting during dry or hot weather, prune off

Basic planting
Soak plants well in a bucket of water. Position the plant so that the root ball surface is flush with soil level, then fill around the sides.

Settling the soil
Backfill the hole, gently firming the soil to ensure good contact with the roots. Water in well, then add a layer of mulch over the root area.

its flowers and the largest leaves before planting. In full, hot sun, shade the plant for a few days.

PLANTING TECHNIQUES

For container-grown or balled-and-burlapped plants, dig a hole about twice the size of the rootball. If necessary, water the hole in advance to ensure that the surrounding soil is thoroughly moist. Carefully remove the plant from its pot and gently tease out the roots with your fingers. Check that the plant is at the correct depth, then backfill the hole with a mix of compost, fertilizer, and soil. Firm the soil, then water thoroughly to settle it around the roots. Apply a mulch around, but not touching, the plant base to aid moisture retention and suppress weeds.

For bare-root plants, the planting technique is essentially the same, but it is vital that the roots never dry out before replanting. Dig holes in advance, and if there is any delay in planting, heel the plants in or store in moist sand or compost until conditions are more suitable. Bare-root plants need a planting hole wide enough to accommodate their roots when fully spread. The hole must be at least deep enough to ensure the final soil level will be the same as it was in the pot or nursery. After planting, press the soil gently to firm.

WALL SHRUBS AND CLIMBERS

Always erect supports before planting. Plant wall shrubs and climbers at least 10in (25cm) from walls and fences so that the roots are not in a rain shadow, and lean the plant slightly inward toward the wall. Fan out the main shoots and attach them firmly to their support. Shrubs and nonclinging climbers will need further tying in as they grow; the shoots of twining climbers may also need gentle guidance.

ANNUALS AND BEDDING

In order to ensure that these plants look their best for the little time that they are in flower, it is essential that they are well planted. A moist soil and regular deadheading are keys to success. Bedding plants need regular feeding throughout the growing season, especially in containers, but many annuals flower best in soil that is not overly fertile. Many annuals are available as seedling "plugs," which should be grown on under cover. When planted, the well-developed root system suffers little damage, ensuring rapid growth.

PLANTING BULBS

In general, bulbs can be planted at between three and five times their own depth. Plant small bulbs quite shallowly; those of bigger plants such as large tulips more deeply.

UNDERSTANDING PLANT NAMES

THROUGHOUT THE *AHS Great Plant Guide*, all plants are listed by their current botanical names. The basic unit of plant classification is the species, with a two-part name correctly given in italic text: the first part is the genus, and the second part is the species name, or "epithet."

GENUS

A group of one or more plants that share a wide range of characteristics, such as *Chrysanthemum* or *Rosa*, is known as a genus. A genus name is quite like a family name, because it is shared by a group of individuals that are all closely related. Hybrid genera (crosses between plants derived from two genera, such as x *Cupressocyparis*), are denoted by the x symbol before the genus name.

SPECIES

A group of plants capable of breeding together to produce similar offspring are known as a species. In a two-part botanical name, the species epithet distinguishes a species from other plants in the same genus, rather like a given name. A species epithet usually refers to a particular feature of that species, such as *tricolor* (of three colors), or it may refer to the person who first discovered the plant.

SUBSPECIES, VARIETY, AND FORMA

Naturally occurring variants of a species – subspecies, variety, or forma – are given an additional name in italics, prefixed by "subsp.," "var.," or "f.". All of these are

Genus/Species
Malus floribunda *is in the same genus as apples. Its species name means "mass of flowers."*

Variety
Dictamnus albus *var.* purpureus *has purplish flowers instead of the white of the species.*

Hybrid
The x *symbol after the genus name in* Osmanthus x burkwoodii *denotes its hybrid status.*

concerned with minor subdivisions of a species, differing slightly in their botanical structure or appearance.

HYBRIDS

If different species within the same genus are cultivated together, they may cross-breed, giving rise to hybrids sharing attributes of both parents. This process is exploited by gardeners who wish to combine the valued characteristics of two distinct plants. The new hybrid is then increased by propagation. An example is *Camellia* x *williamsii*, which has the parents *C. japonica* and *C. saluensis*.

CULTIVARS

Variations of a species that are selected or artificially raised are given a vernacular name. This appears in single quotation marks

after the species name. Some cultivars are also registered with trademark names, often used commercially instead of the valid cultivar name. If the parentage is obscure or complex, the cultivar name may directly follow the generic name – *Iris* 'Muse's Visit'. In a few cases, particularly roses, the plant is known by a popular selling name, which is not the correct cultivar name; here, the popular name comes before the cultivar name, as in *Rosa* BONICA 'Meidomonac'.

GROUPS AND SERIES

Several very similar cultivars may, for convenience, be classified in named Groups or Series that denote their similarities. Sometimes, they can be a deliberate mixture of cultivars of the same overall character but with flowers in different colors.

Cultivar
The species parentage of plants like Osteospermum *'Buttermilk' is complex and therefore not given.*

Cultivar of species
Ophiopogon planiscapus *'Nigrescens' is an unusual form cultivated for its black leaves.*

Seed series
Antirrhinum *Sonnet Series is a mixture of brightly colored cultivars for summer bedding.*

THE
A–Z OF
PLANTS

ATTRACTIVE AND RELIABLE plants for every
garden, and for every part of the garden,
can be found in this section. However
much their ornamental features and
season(s) of interest appeal to you, always
check hardiness, eventual size, and site
and soil requirements before you buy.

ABELIA 'EDWARD GOUCHER'

This semi-evergreen shrub with arching branches bears glossy, dark green leaves that are bronze when young. Trumpet-shaped, lilac-pink flowers appear from summer to autumn. Like most abelias, it is suitable for a sunny border.

CULTIVATION *Grow in well-drained, fertile soil, in sun with shelter from cold winds. Remove dead or damaged growth in spring, cutting some of the older stems back to the ground after flowering to promote new growth.*

☼ ◊ Z7-9 H9-1   ‡5ft (1.5m) ↔6ft (2m)

ABELIA FLORIBUNDA

An evergreen shrub with arching shoots, from which tubular, bright pink-red flowers hang in profuse clusters in early summer. The leaves are oval and glossy dark green. Ideal for a sunny border. Where marginally hardy, grow in a sheltered position or provide a deep winter mulch .

CULTIVATION *Grow in well-drained, fertile soil, in full sun with shelter from cold, drying winds. Prune older growth back after flowering, removing any dead or damaged growth in spring.*

☼ ◊ Z8-11 H12-8 ‡10ft (3m) ↔12ft (4m)

ABELIA × *GRANDIFLORA*

A rounded, semi-evergreen shrub bearing arching branches. Cultivated for its attractive, glossy dark green leaves and profusion of fragrant, pink-tinged white flowers that are borne from mid-summer to autumn. Suitable for a sunny border.

CULTIVATION *Grow in well-drained, fertile soil, in full sun with shelter from cold, drying winds. Prune back older growth back after flowering, and remove damaged growth in spring.*

☼ ◊ Z6-9 H9-1   ↕10ft (3m) ↔12ft (4m)

ABUTILON 'KENTISH BELLE'

A semi-evergreen shrub bearing dark purple-brown shoots and slender, arching branches. The large, bell-shaped flowers, which hang from the branches during summer and autumn, are apricot-yellow and red. The leaves are shallowly lobed and dark green. Where marginally hardy, provide shelter, warmth, and support by training against a warm wall.

CULTIVATION *Grow in well-drained, fertile soil, in sun. Prune annually in late winter to preserve a well-spaced, healthy framework.*

☼ ◊ Z8-10 H12-1   ↔ to 8ft (2.5m)

ABUTILON MEGAPOTAMICUM

The trailing abutilon is a semi-evergreen shrub bearing pendulous, bell-shaped, red and yellow flowers from summer to autumn. The oval leaves are bright green and heart-shaped at the base. Where marginal or not hardy, train against a warm wall or grow in a conservatory.

CULTIVATION *Best in well-drained, moderately fertile soil, in full sun. Remove any wayward shoots during late winter or early spring.*

☼ ◊ Z8-10 H12-1   ↕↔ 6ft (2m)

ABUTILON VITIFOLIUM 'VERONICA TENNANT'

A fast-growing, upright, deciduous shrub that may attain the stature of a small, bushy tree. Masses of large, bowl-shaped flowers hang from the thick, gray-felted shoots in early summer. The softly gray-hairy leaves are sharply toothed. 'Tennant's White', with pure white flowers, is also recommended.

CULTIVATION *Grow in well-drained, moderately fertile soil, in full sun. Prune young plants after flowering to encourage a good shape; do not prune established plants.*

☼ ◊ Z8-9 H12-1   ↕15ft (5m) ↔8ft (2.5m)

ACAENA MICROPHYLLA

This summer-flowering, mat-forming
perennial bears heads of small, dull
red flowers with spiny bracts that
develop into decorative burrs. The
finely divided, mid-green leaves are
bronze-tinged when young and
evergreen through most winters.
Good for a rock garden, trough, or
raised bed.

CULTIVATION *Grow in well-drained soil,
in full sun or partial shade. Pull out
rooted stems around the main plant to
restrict spread.*

☼-◐ ◊ Z6-8 H8-6 ‡2in (5cm) ↔ 6in (15cm)

ACANTHUS SPINOSUS

Bear's breeches is a striking,
architectural perennial bearing long,
arching, dark green leaves that have
deeply cut and spiny edges. From
late spring to mid-summer, pure
white, two-lipped flowers with
purple bracts are borne on tall,
sturdy stems; they are good for
cutting and drying. Grow in a
spacious border.

CULTIVATION *Best in deep, well-drained,
fertile soil, in full sun or partial shade.
Provide plenty of space to display its
architectural merits.*

☼-◐ ◊ Z5-9 H9-5 ‡5ft (1.5m)
↔ 24in (60cm)

ACER GRISEUM

The paperbark maple is a slow-growing, spreading, deciduous tree valued for its peeling orange-brown bark. The dark green leaves, divided into three leaflets, turn orange to red and scarlet in autumn. Tiny yellow flowers are carried in hanging clusters during early or mid-spring, followed by brown, winged fruits.

CULTIVATION *Grow in moist but well-drained, fertile soil, in sun or partial shade. In summer only, remove shoots that obscure the bark on the trunk and lower parts of the main branches.*

☼ ◐ ◊ Z4-8 H10-3   ↔ 30ft (10m)

ACER GROSSERI
VAR. *HERSII*

This variety of the snakebark maple with boldly green- and white-streaked bark is a spreading to upright, deciduous tree. The three-lobed, triangular, bright green leaves turn orange or yellow in autumn. Hanging clusters of tiny, pale yellow flowers appear in spring, followed by pink-brown, winged fruits.

CULTIVATION *Grow in moist but well-drained, fertile soil, in full sun or partial shade. Shelter from cold winds. Remove shoots that obscure the bark on the trunk and main branches in summer.*

☼ ◐ ◊ Z5-7 H8-5   ↔ 50ft (15m)

ACER JAPONICUM
'ACONITIFOLIUM'

A deciduous, bushy tree or large shrub bearing deeply lobed, mid-green leaves that turn brilliant dark red in autumn. It is very free-flowering, producing upright clusters of conspicuous, reddish purple flowers in mid-spring, followed by brown, winged fruits. 'Vitifolium' is similar, not so free-flowering but with fine autumn color.

CULTIVATION *Grow in moist but well-drained, fertile soil, in partial shade. Where marginally hardy, mulch around the base in autumn. Remove badly placed shoots in summer only.*

☼ ◊ Z5-7 H8-3 ‡15ft (5m) ↔ 20ft (6m)

ACER NEGUNDO
'FLAMINGO'

Round-headed, deciduous tree with pink-margined, oval leaflets which turn white in summer. With regular pruning it can be grown as a shrub; this also produces larger leaves with an intensified color. Flowers are tiny and inconspicuous. Plain-leaved var. *violaceum* has glaucous shoots and long tassels of violet flowers.

CULTIVATION *Grow in any moist but well-drained, fertile soil, in full sun or partial shade. For larger leaves and a shrubby habit, cut back to a framework every 1 or 2 years in winter. Remove any branches with all-green leaves.*

☼ ◊ Z5-8 H8-3 ‡50ft (15m) ↔ 30ft (10m)

JAPANESE MAPLES (*ACER PALMATUM*)

Cultivars of *Acer palmatum*, the Japanese maple, are mostly small, round-headed, deciduous shrubs, although some, such as 'Sango-kaku', will grow into small trees. They are valued for their delicate and colorful foliage, which often gives a beautiful display in autumn. The leaves of 'Butterfly', for example, are variegated gray-green, white, and pink, and those of 'Osakazuki' turn a brilliant red before they fall. In mid-spring, hanging clusters of small, reddish purple flowers are produced, followed by winged fruits later in the season. Japanese maples are excellent for gardens of any size.

CULTIVATION *Grow in moist but well-drained, fertile soil, in sun or partial shade. Restrict pruning and training to young plants only; remove badly placed or crossing shoots in summer to develop a well-spaced branch network. Keep pruning to a minimum on established plants.*

☼☀ ◊ Z5-8 H8-2

1 ↕↔ 15ft (5m)

2 ↕ 10ft (3m) ↔ 5ft (1.5m)

3 ↕ 6ft (2m) ↔ 10ft (3m)

4 ↕ 6ft (2m) ↔ 10ft (3m)

1 *Acer palmatum* 'Bloodgood' **2** *A. palmatum* 'Butterfly'
3 *A. palmatum* 'Chitoseyama' **4** *A. palmatum* 'Garnet'

5 ↕ 15ft (5m) ↔ 12ft (4m)

MORE CHOICES

'Burgundy Lace' Very
deeply cut red-purple
leaves, 12ft (4m) tall
and widely spreading

var. *coreanum* 'Korean
Gem' Green leaves
turning crimson-scarlet
in autumn.

var. *dissectum* 'Crimson
Queen' (see p.556)

var. *dissectum* (see
p.630)

var. *dissectum* 'Inabe-
Shidare' Deeply divided
purple-red leaves.

'Seiryū' (see p.630)

6 ↕ ↔ 30ft (6m)

7 ↕ ↔ 5ft (1.5m)

8 ↕ 20ft (6m) ↔ 15ft (5m)

5 *A. palmatum* 'Linearilobum' **6** *A. palmatum* 'Osakazuki'
7 *A. palmatum* 'Red Pygmy' **8** *A. palmatum* 'Sango-kaku' (*syn.* 'Senkaki')

ACER PENSYLVANICUM 'ERYTHROCLADUM'

This striped maple is an upright, deciduous tree. Its leaves are bright green, turning clear yellow in autumn. In winter, brilliant pink or red young shoots make a fiery display; they become orange-red with white stripes as they mature. Hanging clusters of small, greenish yellow flowers in spring are followed by winged fruits. Best grown as a specimen tree.

CULTIVATION *Grow in fertile, moist but well-drained soil in sun or part shade. Remove crossing or damaged shoots in summer only.*

☼ ◑ ◊ Z3-7 H7-1 ‡40ft (12m) ↔30ft (10m)

ACER PLATANOIDES 'CRIMSON KING'

Like *Acer platanoides*, the Norway maple, this cultivar is a large, spreading, deciduous tree. It is grown for its dark red-purple leaves, which deepen to dark purple as they mature. The foliage is preceded in spring by clusters of small, red-tinged yellow flowers. These develop into winged fruits. A colorful specimen tree.

CULTIVATION *Grow in fertile, moist but well-drained soil, in sun or partial shade. Prune in summer only, to remove any crossing, crowded, or unhealthy growth.*

☼ ◑ ◊ Z3-7 H7-1 ‡80ft (25m) ↔50ft (15m)

ACER PLATANOIDES 'DRUMMONDII'

This is a much smaller, more spreading deciduous tree than the Norway maple, and is as broad as it is tall. Its leaves have a wide, pale green to cream margin and color well in autumn. In spring, clusters of yellow flowers appear; from these later develop winged fruits. An attractive specimen tree for a medium-sized garden.

CULTIVATION *Grow in fertile, moist but well-drained soil, in sun or partial shade. Prune in summer only, to remove any crossing, crowded, or unhealthy growth.*

☼ ◐ ◊ Z3-7 H7-1 ↕↔30–40ft (10–12m)

ACER PSEUDOPLATANUS 'BRILLIANTISSIMUM'

This small, slow-growing cultivar of sycamore maple is a spreading, deciduous tree with a dense head. It bears colorful, five-lobed leaves that turn from salmon-pink to yellow then dark green as they mature. Hanging clusters of tiny, yellow-green flowers appear in spring, followed by winged fruit. An attractive maple for smaller gardens.

CULTIVATION *Grow in any soil, in sun or partial shade. Tolerates exposed sites. Prune in summer to develop well-spaced branches and a clear trunk.*

☼ ◐ ◊ Z4-7 H7-1 ↕20ft (6m) ↔25ft (8m)

ACER RUBRUM 'OCTOBER GLORY'

This cultivar of the red, or swamp, maple is a round-headed to open-crowned, deciduous tree with glossy dark green foliage, turning bright red in early autumn. The upright clusters of tiny red flowers in spring are followed by winged fruits. A fine specimen tree for a larger garden.

CULTIVATION *Grow in any fertile, moist but well-drained soil, although best autumn color is seen in acidic soil. Choose a site with full sun or in partial shade, and restrict pruning to summer to remove any crossing or congested branches*

☼ ◑ ◊ Z3-9 H9-1 ‡70ft (20m) ↔30ft (10m)

ACER TATARICUM SUBSP. *GINNALA*

The Amur maple is a rounded, bushy, deciduous tree with slender, arching branches and glossy bright green leaves, very deeply lobed; in autumn, these become a deep, rich bronze-red. In spring, it bears upright clusters of cream flowers, from which develop red, winged fruits. Best as a specimen tree.

CULTIVATION *Grow in any fertile, moist but well-drained soil, in full sun or in partial shade. Restrict pruning to summer to remove any crossing or congested branches, if necessary.*

☼ ◊ Z3-7 H7-1 ‡30ft (10m) ↔25ft (8m)

ACHILLEA AGERATIFOLIA

This small yarrow is a fast-growing, creeping perennial, forming mats of silvery, hairy leaf rosettes above which, in summer, small white flowerheads stand on upright stems. Grow at the front of a sunny border or in a rock or scree garden, or in planting spaces in a paved area

CULTIVATION *Grow in any moderately fertile, free-draining soil, in sun. Divide plants that have spread too widely or become straggly in spring or autumn. Deadhead to encourage further flowers*

☼ ◊ Z3-9 H9-1   ↕2–3in (5–8cm)
↔to 18in (45cm)

ACHILLEA 'CORONATION GOLD'

This cultivar of yarrow is a clump-forming perennial that bears large, flat heads of golden yellow flowers from mid-summer to early autumn. The luxuriant, evergreen, fernlike leaves are silver-gray, complementing the flower color (contact may aggravate skin allergies). Excellent for a mixed or herbaceous border, and for cutting and drying.

CULTIVATION *Grow in moist but well-drained soil in an open site in full sun. Divide large or congested clumps to maintain vigor.*

☼ ◊◊ Z3-9 H9-1   ↕30–36in (75–90cm)
↔18in (45cm)

ACHILLEA FILIPENDULINA 'GOLD PLATE'

This strong-growing, clump-forming and upright, evergreen perennial is similar to *A.* 'Coronation Gold' (p.39), but taller, with gray-green leaves. The flat-headed clusters of bright golden yellow flowers are borne on strong stems from early summer to early autumn; they make good cut flowers. Grow in a mixed or herbaceous border. Contact with the foliage may aggravate skin allergies.

CULTIVATION *Grow in moist but well-drained soil in an open, sunny site. To maintain good performance, divide clumps when large and congested.*

☼ ◊◊ Z3-9 H9-1 ‡4ft (1.2m) ↔18in (45cm)

ACHILLEA × LEWISII 'KING EDWARD'

This woody-based, low mound-forming perennial bears pale yellow flowerheads in dense, flat-headed clusters in early summer. They fade as they age, but attractively so. The serrated, semi-evergreen leaves are narrow, fernlike, and soft gray-green. It looks well in a wildflower or rock garden. Contact with the foliage may aggravate skin allergies.

CULTIVATION *Grow in moist but well-drained soil in an open site in full sun. Divide clumps every 3 years or so to maintain vigor.*

☼ ◊◊ Z4-8 H8-1 ‡3–5in (8–12cm) ↔9in (23cm or more)

ACHILLEA 'MOONSHINE'

A clump-forming, evergreen
perennial with narrow, feathery,
gray-green leaves. Light yellow
flowerheads with slightly darker
centers appear from early summer to
early autumn in flattish clusters; they
dry well for arrangements. Excellent
for mixed borders and for informal,
wild or cottage-style plantings.

CULTIVATION *Grow in well-drained soil
in an open, sunny site. Divide every 2
or 3 years in spring to maintain vigor.*

☼ ◊ Z4-8 H9 2　　‡ ↔ 24in (60cm)

ACHILLEA TOMENTOSA

The woolly yarrow is a mat-forming
perennial that bears dense, flat-
headed clusters of lemon yellow
flowerheads from early summer to
early autumn. The woolly, gray-
green leaves are narrow and fernlike. Tolerant of dry conditions, it
suits a wildflower or rock garden,
or grow near the front of a border.
The flowers dry well. Contact with
foliage may aggravate skin allergies.

CULTIVATION *Grow in moist but well-
drained soil in an open, sunny site. To
maintain good flowering, divide clumps
when they become large and congested.*

☼ ◊◊ Z4-8 H8-1　　‡ to 14in (35cm)
　　　　　　　　　　↔ 18in (45cm)

ACONITUM 'BRESSINGHAM SPIRE'

A compact perennial producing very upright spikes of hooded, deep violet flowers from mid-summer to early autumn. The leaves are deeply divided and glossy dark green. Ideal for woodland or borders in partial or dappled shade. For lavender flowers on a slightly taller plant, look for *A. carmichaelii* 'Kelmscott'. All parts of these plants are poisonous.

CULTIVATION *Best in cool, moist, fertile soil, in partial shade, but will tolerate most soils and full sun. The tallest stems may need staking.*

☼ ☀ ◖ Z3-7 H8-3 ‡36–39in (90–100cm) ↔12in (30cm)

ACONITUM 'SPARK'S VARIETY'

This upright perennial is taller than 'Bressingham Spire' (above) bearing spikes of hooded, deep violet flowers that are clustered together on branched stems; these are borne in mid- and late summer. The rich green leaves are deeply divided. Like all monkhoods, it is ideal for woodland gardens or shaded sites. All parts of the plant are poisonous.

CULTIVATION *Grow in cool, moist soil, in partial or deep shade. Taller stems may need staking. Divide and replant every third year in autumn or late winter to maintain vigor.*

☼ ☀ ◖ Z3-7 H8-3 ‡5ft (1.5m) ↔18in (45cm)

ACTINIDIA KOLOMIKTA

A vigorous, deciduous climber with large, deep green leaves that are purple-tinged when young and develop vivid splashes of white and pink as they mature. Small, fragrant, white flowers appear in early summer. Female plants produce small, egg-shaped, yellow-green fruits, but only if a male plant is grown nearby. Train against a wall or up into a tree.

CULTIVATION *Best in well-drained, fertile soil. For best fruiting, grow in full sun with protection from strong winds. Tie in new shoots as they develop, and remove badly placed shoots in summer.*

☼ ◊ Z5-8 H12-1   ‡15ft (5m)

ADIANTUM PEDATUM

A deciduous relative of the maidenhair fern bearing long, mid-green fronds up to 14in (35cm) tall. These have glossy dark brown or black stalks that emerge from creeping rhizomes. There are no flowers. *A. aleuticum* is very similar and also recommended; var. *subpumilum* is a dwarf form of this fern, only 6in (15cm) tall. Grow in a shady border or light woodland.

CULTIVATION *Best in cool, moist soil, in deep or partial shade. Remove old or damaged fronds in early spring. Divide and replant rhizomes every few years.*

☼☀ ◊ Z3-8 H8-1 ‡↔ 12–16in (30–40cm)

ADIANTUM VENUSTUM

The Himalayan maidenhair fern has black-stalked, triangular, mid-green fronds, beautifully divided into many small leaflets. The new foliage is bright bronze-pink when it emerges in late winter to early spring from creeping rhizomes. It is evergreen above 14°F (−10°C). Decorative groundcover for a woodland garden or shady border.

CULTIVATION *Grow in moderately fertile, moist but well-drained soil in partial shade. Remove old or damaged fronds in spring, and divide the rhizomes every few years in early spring.*

☀ ◐◊ Z5-8 H8-3 ‡6in (15cm) ↔indefinite

AEONIUM HAWORTHII

A succulent subshrub with slender branches, each crowned by a neat rosette of bluish green, fleshy leaves with red margins. Clusters of pale yellow to pinkish white flowers are borne in spring. It is a popular pot plant for conservatories and porches.

CULTIVATION *Under glass, grow in standard cactus soil mix in filtered light, and allow the mix to dry out between waterings. Outdoors, grow in moderately fertile, well-drained soil in partial shade. Minimum temperature 50°F (10°C).*

☀ ◊ H12-11 ‡↔24in (60cm)

AEONIUM 'ZWARTKOP'

An upright, succulent subshrub with few branches, each tipped by a rosette of black-purple leaves. Large, pyramid-shaped clusters of bright yellow flowers appear in late spring. Makes an unusually colored pot plant. *A. arboreum* 'Atropurpureum' is similarly striking.

CULTIVATION *Grow in standard cactus soil mix in filtered light under glass, allowing the mix to dry out between waterings. Outdoors, grow in reasonably fertile, well-drained soil in partial shade. Minimum temperature 50°F (10°C).*

☀ ◊ H12–11 ↕↔to 6ft (2m)

AESCULUS CARNEA 'BRIOTII'

This cultivar of red horsechestnut is a spreading tree, admired in early summer for its large, upright cones of dark rose-red flowers. The dark green leaves are divided into 5–7 leaflets. The flowers are followed by spiny fruits. For larger gardens, look for the sunrise horsechestnut, *A. x. neglecta* 'Erythroblastos', to 30ft (10m), or the red buckeye, *A. pavia*, to 15ft (5m).

CULTIVATION *Grow in deep, fertile, moist but well-drained soil in full sun or partial shade. Remove dead, diseased or crossing branches during winter.*

☀☀ ◊◊ Z7-8 H8-5 ↕70ft (20m) ↔50ft (15m)

AESCULUS PARVIFLORA

A large, thicket-forming, deciduous shrub, closely related to the horse-chestnut, that bears large-lobed, dark green leaves. The foliage is bronze when young, turning yellow in autumn. Upright white flowerheads, up to 12in (30cm) tall, appear in mid-summer, followed by smooth-skinned fruits.

CULTIVATION *Grow in moist but well-drained, fertile soil, in sun or partial shade; it will not grow in wet ground. If necessary, restrict spread by pruning stems to the ground after leaf fall.*

☼◑ ◊◊ Z5-9 H8-4 ‡10ft (3m) ↔15ft (5m)

AETHIONEMA 'WARLEY ROSE'

A short-lived, evergreen or semi-evergreen, compact shrub bearing clusters of bright pink, cross-shaped flowers in late spring and early summer. The small, narrow leaves are blue-gray. For flowers of a much paler pink, look for *A. grandiflorum*, very similar if a little taller. Aethionemas are ideal for a rock garden or on a wall.

CULTIVATION *Best in well-drained, fertile, alkaline soil, but tolerates poor, acidic soils. Choose a site in full sun.*

☼ ◊ Z7-9 H9-7 ‡↔ 6–8in (15–20cm)

AGAPANTHUS CAMPAN-ULATUS SUBSP. *PATENS*

A vigorous, clump-forming perennial bearing round heads of bell-shaped, light blue flowers on strong, upright stems during late summer and early autumn. The narrow, strap-shaped, grayish green leaves are deciduous. Useful in borders or large containers.

CULTIVATION *Grow in moist but well-drained, fertile soil or soil mix, in full sun. Water freely when in growth, and sparingly in winter.*

☼ ◊ Z7-10 H12-8 ‡18in (45cm) ↔12in (30cm)

AGAPANTHUS CAULESCENS

A clump-forming perennial with leeklike stems bearing large, rounded, open flowerheads of bell-shaped, violet-blue flowers. These appear from mid-summer to early autumn above the strap-shaped, mid-green, deciduous leaves. Very useful perennial that can also be container-grown in climates where it is not hardy.

CULTIVATION *Grow in moist but well-drained, fertile soil or soil mix, in full sun. Minimum temperature 35°F (2°C).*

☼ ◊ H12-1 ‡4ft (1.2m) ↔24in (60cm)

AGAVE VICTORIAE-REGINAE

A frost-tender, succulent perennial bearing basal rosettes of triangular, dark green leaves with white marks. The central leaves curve inward, each tipped with a brown spine. Upright spikes of creamy white flowers appear in summer. A good specimen plant: where not hardy, grow in containers for summer display, taking it under cover for winter shelter.

CULTIVATION *Best in sharply drained, moderately fertile, slightly acidic soil, or standard cactus soil mix. Site in full sun. Minimum temperature 35°F (2°C).*

☼ ◊ H12-5   ‡↔ to 20in (50cm)

AJUGA REPTANS 'ATROPURPUREA'

An excellent evergreen perennial for groundcover, spreading freely over the soil surface by means of rooting stems. Dark blue flowers are borne in whorls along the upright stems during late spring and early summer. The glossy leaves are deep bronze-purple. *A. reptans* 'Catlin's Giant' has similarly colored leaves. Invaluable for border edging under shrubs and vigorous perennials.

CULTIVATION *Best in moist but well-drained, fertile soil, but tolerates most soils. Site in sun or partial shade.*

☼☀ ◊◊ Z3-9 H8-2 ‡6in (15cm) ↔3ft (1m)

AJUGA REPTANS 'BURGUNDY GLOW'

A low-growing, creeping, evergreen perennial groundcover with partly hairy stems carrying attractive, silvery green leaves that are suffused deep wine-red. Dark blue flowers are borne in tall, spikelike whorls in late spring and early summer.

CULTIVATION *Best in any moist, fertile soil in partial shade, but will tolerate poor soils, even in full shade.*

:☼::☼: ◊ Z3-9 H8 2 ‡6in (15cm) ↔3ft (1m)

ALCHEMILLA MOLLIS

Lady's mantle is a drought-tolerant, clump-forming, tallish perennial groundcover that produces sprays of tiny, bright greenish yellow flowers from early summer to early autumn; these are ideal for cutting and dry well for winter arrangements. The pale green leaves are rounded with crinkled edges. It looks well in a wildflower garden; for a rock garden, *A. erythropoda* is similar but smaller, with blue-tinged leaves.

CULTIVATION *Grow in any moist but well-drained, organic soil, in an open, sunny site. Deadhead soon after flowering; it self-seeds very freely.*

:☼: ◊◊ Z4-7 H7-1 ‡24in (60cm) ↔30in (75cm)

TALL ORNAMENTAL ONIONS (*ALLIUM*)

These onions grown for garden display are bulbous perennials from the genus *Allium*; their attractive flowerheads are excellent for a mixed border, especially grouped together. The tiny summer flowers are usually massed into dense, rounded or hemispherical heads – like those of *A. giganteum* – or they may hang loosely, like the yellow flowers of *A. flavum*. When crushed, the strap-shaped leaves release a pungent aroma; they are often withered by flowering time. The seedheads tend to dry out intact, standing well into autumn and continuing to look attractive. Some alliums self-seed and will naturalize.

CULTIVATION *Grow in fertile, well-drained soil in full sun to simulate their dry native habitats. Plant bulbs 2–4in (5–10cm) deep in autumn; divide and replant older clumps at the same time or in spring. Where marginally hardy, provide a thick winter mulch for* A. cristophii *and* A. caeruleum.

☼ ◊ Zones vary H12-1

1 ‡3ft (1m) ↔ 6in (15cm)

MORE CHOICES

A carinatum subsp. *pulchellum* Purple flowers, 12–18in (30–45cm) tall.

A. cernuum 'Hidcote' Nodding pink flowers.

A. hollandicum Purplish pink flowers, 3ft (1m) tall, very similar to 'Purple Sensation'.

2 ‡24in (60cm) ↔ 1in (2.5cm)

1 *Allium* 'Beau Regard' Z6-8 **2** *A. caeruleum* Z4-10

3 ‡12–24in (30–60cm) ↔ 7in (18cm)

5 ‡5–6ft (1.5m–2m) ↔0

4 ‡ to 14in (35cm) ↔ 2in (5cm)

6 ‡4ft (1.2m) ↔ 6in (15cm)

7 ‡32in (80cm) ↔ 8in (20in)

8 ‡3ft (1m) ↔ 3in (7cm)

3 *A. cristophii* Z5-8 4 *A. flavum* Z4-10 5 *A. giganteum* Z6-10 6 *A.* 'Gladiator' Z6-8
7 *A.* 'Globemaster' Z6-10 8 *A. hollandicum* 'Purple Sensation' Z4-9

SMALL ORNAMENTAL ONIONS (*ALLIUM*)

These alliums are summer-flowering, bulbous perennials for the front of a border or rock garden. They form clumps as they establish; some, such as *A. moly*, will self-seed. The flowers are borne in clustered heads which may be large or small; those of *A. karataviense* can be 3in (8cm) across, despite its small stature. Flower colors range from bright gold to purple, blue, and pale pink. The seedheads are attractive, too, lasting well into winter. The strap-shaped leaves are often withered by flowering time. Those of ornamental chives, such as *A. schoenopraesum* 'Pink Perfection' and the very similar 'Black Isle Blush', are edible.

CULTIVATION *Best in well-drained, organic soil in full sun. Plant bulbs 2–4in (5–10cm) deep in autumn; divide and replant old or crowded clumps in autumn or spring. Provide a thick, dry winter mulch for A.* karataviense *where marginally hardy.*

☼ ◊ Zones vary H12-1

1 ↕ 4–10in (10–25cm) ↔ 4in (10cm)

2 ↕ 6–10in (15–25cm) ↔ 2in (5cm)

3 ↕ 2–8in (5–20cm) ↔ 1¼in (3cm)

4 ↕ 12–24in (30–60cm) ↔ 2in (5cm)

1 *Allium karataviense* Z5-9 **2** *A. moly* Z3-9 **3** *A. oreophilum* Z4-9
4 *A. schoenoprasum* 'Pink Perfection' Z3-9

ALNUS GLUTINOSA 'IMPERIALIS'

This attractive cultivar of the black alder is a broadly conical tree with deeply dissected, lobed, mid-green leaves. Groups of yellow-brown catkins emerge in late winter, followed by small oval cones in summer. This is a beautiful foliage tree, particularly good close to water because it tolerates poor, wet soil.

CULTIVATION *Thrives in any moderately fertile, moist but not waterlogged soil, in full sun. Prune after leaf fall, if necessary, to remove any damaged or crossing branches.*

☼ ◊ Z3-7 H7-1 ‡80ft (25m) ↔15ft (5m)

ALOE VARIEGATA

The partridge-breast aloe, a stemless succulent, forms clumps of narrow, fleshy leaves, dark green with white edges and horizontal white bands. Clusters of hanging pink or scarlet flowers may form in summer. For a desert garden in areas with a min. temp. of 50°F (10°C), or grow as a house or container plant. Smaller than the plain-leaved *Aloe vera*, it is more manageable in a pot.

CULTIVATION *Under glass, grow in well-drained potting mix in a sunny, well-ventilated position. Water sparingly during winter. Outdoors, grow in fertile, well-drained soil in full sun.*

☼ ◊ H12-11 ‡8in (20cm) ↔indefinite

ALONSOA WARSCEWICZII

This species of maskflower is a compact, bushy perennial, grown for its bright scarlet, sometimes white, flowers. These are on display from summer to autumn amid the dark green leaves. Useful as summer bedding or in a mixed border, it also provides good cut flowers.

CULTIVATION *Outdoors, grow in any fertile, well-drained soil in full sun, or in soil-based potting mix if grown in a container. Water moderately.*

☼ ◊ Z10–11 H12-10 ‡18–24in (45–60cm)
↔12in (30cm)

ALOYSIA TRIPHYLLA

The lemon verbena is cultivated for its strongly lemon-scented, bright green foliage, used for culinary purposes or in potpourri. Pick and dry the leaves in summer before flowering. Tiny, pale lilac to white flowers are borne in slender clusters in late summer on this deciduous shrub. Where hardy, grow in a sunny border; elsewhere, grow in a cool greenhouse.

CULTIVATION *Grow in well-drained, poor, dry soil in full sun. Mulch well where marginal for winter protection. Cut back to a low framework each spring to maintain a good shape.*

☼ ◊ Z8–11 H12-8 ‡↔6ft (2m)

ALSTROEMERIA LIGTU HYBRIDS

These summer-flowering, tuberous perennials produces heads of widely flared flowers that are considerably varied in color from white to shades of pink, yellow or orange, often spotted or streaked with contrasting colors. The mid-green leaves are narrow and twisted. Ideal for a sunny mixed or herbaceous border. The cut flowers are good for indoor arrangements.

CULTIVATION *Grow in moist but well-drained, fertile soil, in full sun. Mulch thickly where marginally hardy. Leave undisturbed to form clumps.*

☼ ◊ Z7-10 H12-7 ‡20in (50cm) ↔30in (75cm)

AMELANCHIER X *GRANDIFLORA* 'BALLERINA'

A spreading, deciduous tree grown for its profusion of white spring flowers and colorful autumn foliage. When young, the glossy leaves are tinted bronze, becoming mid-green in summer, then red and purple in autumn. The sweet, juicy fruits are red at first, ripening to purplish black in summer. They can be eaten if cooked and are attractive to birds.

CULTIVATION *Grow in moist but well-drained, fertile, neutral to acidic soil, in full sun or partial shade. Allow shape to develop naturally; only minimal pruning is necessary, in winter.*

☼☀ ◊◊ Z5-8 H8-3 ‡20ft (6m) ↔25ft (8m)

AMELANCHIER LAMARCKII

A many-stemmed, upright, deciduous shrub bearing leaves that are bronze when young, maturing to dark green in summer, then brilliant red and orange in autumn. Hanging clusters of white flowers are produced in spring. The ripe, purple-black fruits that follow are edible when cooked and are attractive to birds. Also known as *A. canadensis*.

CULTIVATION *Grow in moist but well-drained, organic, neutral to acidic soil, in sun or partial shade. Develops its shape naturally with only minimal pruning when dormant in winter.*

☼ ◐ ◊◊ Z5-8 H9-3 ‡30ft (10m) ↔40ft (12m)

ANAPHALIS TRIPLINERVIS 'SOMMERSCHNEE'

A clump-forming perennial carrying pale gray-green, white-woolly leaves. The tiny yellow flowerheads, surrounded by brilliant white bracts, appear during mid- and late summer in dense clusters; they are excellent for cutting and drying. Provides good foliage contrast in borders that are too moist for the majority of other gray-leaved plants.

CULTIVATION *Grow in any reasonably well-drained, moderately fertile soil that does not dry out in summer. Choose a position in full sun or partial shade.*

☼ ◐ ◊ Z3-8 H8-3 ‡32–36in (80–90cm) ↔18–24in (45–60cm)

ANCHUSA AZUREA 'LODDON ROYALIST'

An upright, clump-forming perennial that is much-valued in herbaceous borders for its spikes of intensely dark blue flowers. These are borne on branching stems in early summer, above the lance-shaped and hairy, mid-green leaves that are arranged at the base of the stems. For a rock garden, *A. cespitosa* looks similar in miniature, only 2–4in (5–10cm) tall.

CULTIVATION *Grow in deep, moist but well-drained, fertile soil in sun. Often short-lived, but easily propagated by root cuttings. If growth is vigorous, staking may be necessary.*

☼ ◊ Z3-8 H8-1 ↕36in (90cm) ↔24in (60m)

ANDROSACE CARNEA SUBSP. *LAGGERI*

An evergreen, cushion-forming perennial that bears small clusters of tiny, cup-shaped, deep pink flowers with yellow eyes, in late spring. The pointed, mid-green leaves are arranged in small, tight rosettes. Rock jasmines grow wild in alpine turf and rock crevices, making them ideal for rock gardens or troughs. *A. sempervivoides* has scented flowers, ideal for a raised bed.

CULTIVATION *Grow in moist but sharply drained, gritty soil, in full sun. Provide a topdressing of grit or gravel to keep the stems and leaves dry.*

☼ ◊ Z4-7 H7-1 ↕2in (5cm) ↔6in (15cm)

ANDROSACE LANUGINOSA

A mat-forming, evergreen perennial producing compact heads of flat, small pink flowers with dark pink or greenish yellow eyes, in mid- and late summer. The deep gray-green leaves are borne on trailing, reddish green stems, which are covered in silky hairs. Thrives in scree gardens, raised beds, or troughs.

CULTIVATION *Grow in gritty, moist but well-drained soil. Choose a site in full sun. In areas with wet winters, provide protection under some sort of cover.*

☼ ◊ Z5-7 H7-3   ‡to 4in (10cm)
                     ↔to 12in (30cm)

ANEMONE BLANDA 'WHITE SPLENDOUR'

A spreading, spring-flowering perennial that soon forms clumps of stems growing from knobby tubers. The solitary, upright, flattish white flowers, with pink-tinged undersides, are borne above oval, dark green leaves divided into delicately lobed leaflets. Excellent for naturalizing in sunny or shaded sites with good drainage. Mix it with 'Radar', with white-centered magenta flowers, or 'Ingramii', with deep blue flowers.

CULTIVATION *Grow in well-drained soil that is rich in organic matter. Choose a position in full sun or partial shade.*

☼☼ ◊ Z4-8 H9-3   ‡↔ 6in (15cm)

ANEMONE HUPEHENSIS
'HADSPEN ABUNDANCE'

Upright, woody-based, late-flowering border perennial that spreads by shoots growing from the roots. Reddish pink flowers, with petal margins that gradually fade to white, are borne on branched stems during mid- and late summer. The deeply divided, long-stalked, dark green leaves are oval and sharply toothed. *A. hupehensis* 'Prinz Heinrich' is similar but spreads more vigorously.

CULTIVATION *Grow in moist, fertile, organic soil, in sun or partial shade. Provide a mulch where marginal.*

☼☀ ◊◊ Z4-8 H9-3 ‡24–36in (60–90cm)
↔16in (40cm)

ANEMONE × HYBRIDA
'HONORINE JOBERT'

This upright, woody-based perennial with branched, wiry stems is an invaluable long-flowering choice for late summer to mid-autumn, when single, cupped white flowers, with pink-tinged undersides and golden yellow stamens, are borne above divided, mid-green leaves. (For pure white flowers without a hint of pink, look for 'Géante des Blanches'.) It can be invasive.

CULTIVATION *Grow in moist but well-drained, moderately fertile, organic soil, in sun or partial shade.*

☼☀ ◊◊ Z4-8 H9-3 ‡4–5ft (1.2–1.5m)
↔indefinite

ANEMONE NEMOROSA 'ROBINSONIANA'

A vigorous, carpeting perennial that produces masses of large, star-shaped, pale lavender-blue flowers on maroon stems from spring to early summer, above deeply divided, mid-green leaves that die down in midsummer. Excellent for underplanting or a woodland garden; it naturalizes with ease. 'Allenii' has deeper blue flowers; choose 'Vestal' for white flowers.

CULTIVATION *Grow in loose, moist but well-drained soil that is rich in organic matter, in light, dappled shade.*

☀ ◊ Z4-8 H8-1   ‡3–6in (8–15cm)
↔12in (30cm) or more

ANEMONE RANUNCULOIDES

This spring-flowering, spreading perennial is excellent for naturalizing in damp woodland gardens. The large, solitary, buttercup-like yellow flowers are borne above the "ruffs" of short-stalked, rounded, deeply lobed, fresh green leaves.

CULTIVATION *Grow in moist but well-drained, organic soil, in semi-shade or dappled sunlight. Tolerates drier conditions when dormant in summer.*

☀ ◊◊ Z4-8 H8-1   ‡2–4in (5–10cm)
↔to 18in (45cm)

ANTENNARIA MICROPHYLLA

A mat-forming, semi-evergreen perennial carrying densely white-hairy, spoon-shaped, gray-green leaves. In late spring and early summer, heads of small, fluffy, rose-pink flowers are borne on short stems. Use in a rock garden, as a low groundcover at the front of a border, or in crevices in walls or paving. The flowerheads dry well for indoor decoration.

CULTIVATION *Best in well-drained soil that is no more than moderately fertile. Choose a position in full sun.*

☼ ◊ Z5-9 H9 ‡2in (5cm) ↔ 18in (45cm)

ANTHEMIS PUNCTATA SUBSP. *CUPANIANA*

A mat-forming, evergreen perennial that produces a flush of small but long-lasting, daisylike flowerheads in early summer, and a few blooms later on. The white flowers with yellow centers are borne singly on short stems, amid dense, finely cut, silvery gray foliage that turns dull gray-green in winter. Excellent for border edges.

CULTIVATION *Grow in well-drained soil, in a sheltered, sunny position. Cut back after flowering to maintain vigor.*

☼ ◊ Z6-9 H7-1 ‡12in (30cm) ↔ 18in (45cm)

ANTIRRHINUM
SONNET SERIES

Snapdragons are short-lived
perennials best grown as annuals.
The Sonnet Series produces upright
spikes of fragrant, two-lipped flowers
in a broad range of colors, available
mixed or in single shades, from
early summer into autumn. Planted
in groups, the deep green leaves on
woody-based stems are barely
visible. Excellent for cut flowers or
summer bedding.

CULTIVATION *Grow in sharply drained,
fertile soil, in full sun. Deadhead whole
flower spikes to prolong flowering.*

☀ ◊ Z7-9 H9-1 ‡12–24in (30–60cm)
↔12in (30cm)

AQUILEGIA VULGARIS
'NIVEA'

An upright, vigorous, clump-forming
perennial, sometimes sold as
'Munstead's White', bearing leafy
clusters of nodding, short-spurred,
pure white flowers in late spring
and early summer. Each grayish
green leaf is deeply divided into
lobed leaflets. Attractive in light
woodland or in a herbaceous
border; plant with soft blue
Aquilegia 'Hensol Harebell' for a
luminous mix in light shade.

CULTIVATION *Best in moist but well-
drained, fertile soil. Choose a position
in full sun or partial shade.*

☀◐ ◊ Z3-8 H8-1 ‡36in (90cm) ↔18in (45cm)

AQUILEGIA VULGARIS 'NORA BARLOW'

This upright, vigorous perennial is much valued for its leafy clusters of funnel-shaped, double, pompon flowers. These are pink and white with pale green petal tips and appear from late spring to early summer. The grayish green leaves are deeply divided into narrow lobes. Nice in herbaceous borders and cottage garden-style plantings.

CULTIVATION *Grow in moist but well-drained, fertile soil. Position in an open, sunny site.*

☼ ◊ Z3-8 H7-1 ‡36in (90cm) ↔18in (45cm)

ARABIS PROCURRENS 'VARIEGATA'

A mat-forming, evergreen or semi-evergreen perennial bearing loose clusters of cross-shaped white flowers on tall, slender stems during late spring. The narrow, mid-green leaves, arranged into flattened rosettes, have creamy white margins and are sometimes pink tinged. Useful in a rock garden.

CULTIVATION *Grow in any well-drained soil, in full sun. Remove completely any stems with plain green leaves.*

☼ ◊ Z5-8 H8-1 ‡2–3in (5–8cm) ↔12–16in (30–40cm)

ARALIA ELATA 'VARIEGATA'

The variegated Japanese angelica tree is deciduous, with a beautiful, exotic appearance. The large leaves are divided into 80 or more leaflets, irregularly edged with creamy white. Flat clusters of small white flowers appear in late summer and early autumn, followed by round, black fruits. Suitable for a shady border or wooded streambank in a large garden, and less prone to suckering than the plain-leaved *Aralia elata*.

CULTIVATION *Grow in fertile, organic, moist soil, in sun or part shade. Remove any branches with all-green foliage in summer. Needs a sheltered site; strong winds can damage leaves.*

☼ ◐ ◖ Z4-9 H9-1   ↕ ↔ 15ft (5m)

ARAUCARIA HETEROPHYLLA

The Norfolk Island pine is a grand, cone-shaped conifer valued for its geometrical shape and unusual branches of whorled foliage. The scalelike leaves are tough, light green. There are no flowers. An excellent, fast-growing, wind-tolerant tree for coastal sites; in cold climates, it can be grown as a conservatory plant.

CULTIVATION *Grow in moderately fertile, moist but well-drained soil in an open site with shelter from cold, drying winds. Tolerates partial shade when young.*

☼ ◖◖ Z9-10 H11-10 ↕ 80–150ft (25–45m)
↔ 20–25ft (6–8m)

ARBUTUS X *ANDRACHNOIDES*

This strawberry tree is a broad, sometimes shrubby tree, with peeling, red-brown bark. The mid-green leaves are finely toothed and glossy. Clusters of small white flowers are borne from autumn to spring, only rarely followed by fruits. Excellent for a large shrub border, or as a specimen tree.

CULTIVATION *Grow in fertile, well-drained soil rich in organic matter, in a sheltered but sunny site. Protect from cold winds, even when mature, and keep pruning to a minimum, in winter if necessary. It tolerates alkaline soil.*

☼ ◊ Z8 9 H9-8　　　↕↔25ft (8m)

ARBUTUS MENZIESII

The madrone is a spreading tree with beautiful, peeling, red-brown bark. Its dark green leaves are glossy and toothed. In early summer, the tree is covered with upright clusters of pure white flowers, followed by warty, orange-red, small spherical fruits that ripen in the next growing season. A good tree for a large shrub border or woodland where there is acidic soil.

CULTIVATION *Grow in fertile, organic, well-drained, acidic soil in a sheltered site in full sun. Protect from cold winds. Keep pruning to a minimum, in winter if necessary.*

☼ ◊ Z7-9 H9-7　　　↕↔50ft (15m)

ARBUTUS UNEDO

The strawberry tree is a spreading, evergreen tree with attractive, rough, shredding, red-brown bark. Hanging clusters of small, urn-shaped white flowers, which are sometimes pink-tinged, open during autumn as the previous season's strawberry-like red fruits ripen. The glossy deep green leaves are shallowly toothed. Excellent for a large shrub border, with shelter from wind.

CULTIVATION *Best in well-drained, fertile, organic, acidic soil. Tolerates slightly alkaline conditions. Choose a sheltered site in sun. Prune low branches in spring, but keep to a minimum.*

☼ ◊ Z7-9 H9-4   ‡↔ 25ft (8m)

ARENARIA MONTANA

This sandwort is a low-growing, spreading, vigorous, evergreen perennial freely bearing shallowly cup-shaped white flowers in early summer. The small, narrowly lance-shaped, grayish green leaves on wiry stems form loose mats. Easily grown in wall or paving crevices, or in a rock garden.

CULTIVATION *Grow in sandy, moist but sharply drained, poor soil, in full sun. Must have adequate moisture.*

☼ ◊ Z3-5 H5-1   ‡¾–2in (2–5cm)
                    ↔12in (30cm)

ARGYRANTHEMUM 'JAMAICA PRIMROSE'

A bushy, evergreen perennial that bears daisylike, primrose-yellow flowerheads with darker yellow centers throughout summer above fernlike, grayish green leaves. Where not hardy, grow as summer bedding or in containers, bringing under cover for the winter. 'Cornish Gold' – shorter, with flowers of a deep yellow – is also recommended.

CULTIVATION *Grow in well-drained, fairly fertile soil or soil mix, in a warm, sunny site. Pinch out shoot tips to encourage bushiness.*
Min. temp. 35°F (2°C).

☼ ◊ H12-10 ↕3½ft (1.1m) ↔3ft (1m)

ARGYRANTHEMUM 'VANCOUVER'

This compact, summer-flowering, evergreen subshrub is valued for its double, daisylike pink flowerheads with rose-pink centers and fernlike, gray-green leaves. Suits a mixed or herbaceous border; where marginal, grow as summer bedding or in containers that can be sheltered over winter.

CULTIVATION *Grow in well-drained, fairly fertile soil, in sun. Pinch out growing tips to encourage bushiness. Minimum temperature 35°F (2°C).*

☼ ◊ H12-1 ↕36in (90cm) ↔32in (80cm)

ARMERIA JUNIPERIFOLIA

This tiny, hummock-forming, evergreen subshrub bears small, purplish pink to white flowers that are carried in short-stemmed, spherical clusters during late spring. The small, linear, gray-green leaves are hairy and spine-tipped and are arranged in loose rosettes. Native to mountain pastures and rock crevices, it is ideal for a rock garden or trough. Also known as *A. caespitosa*.

CULTIVATION *Grow in well-drained, poor to moderately fertile soil, in an open position in full sun.*

☼ ◊ Z5-7 H8-4   ↕2–3in (5–8cm) ↔to 6in (15cm)

ARMERIA JUNIPERIFOLIA 'BEVAN'S VARIETY'

A compact, cushion-forming, evergreen subshrub that bears small, deep rose-pink flowers. These are carried in short-stemmed, rounded clusters during late spring, over the loose rosettes of small and narrow, pointed, gray-green leaves. Suits a rock garden or trough; for the front of the border, look for *Armeria* 'Bee's Ruby' (H7-5), a similar plant growing to 12in (30cm) tall, with chivelike flowerheads.

CULTIVATION *Grow in well-drained, poor to moderately fertile soil. Choose an open site in full sun.*

☼ ◊ Z5-7 H8-4   ↕2in (5cm) ↔6in (15cm)

ARTEMISIA ABSINTHIUM 'LAMBROOK SILVER'

A clump-forming, woody-based, evergreen perennial cultivated for its mass of ferny, aromatic, silvery gray foliage. The closely related 'Lambrook Mist' (H8-1) is very similar, if slightly less hardy. The grayish yellow flowerheads in late summer are of little ornamental value. Suitable for a rock garden or border, but shelter is needed if grown in an exposed site.

CULTIVATION *Grow in well-drained, fertile soil, in full sun. Short-lived on poorly drained soils. Cut to the base in autumn to maintain a compact habit.*

☼ ◊ Z4-8 H12-8 ‡30in (75cm) ↔24in (60cm)

ARTEMISIA LUDOVICIANA 'SILVER QUEEN'

An upright, bushy, clump-forming, semi-evergreen perennial bearing narrow, downy leaves, sometimes jaggedly toothed; silvery white when young, they become greener with age. White-woolly plumes of brown-yellow flowers are borne from mid-summer to autumn. Indispensable in a silver-themed border. 'Valerie Finnis' (H9-1) is also worthy; its leaves have more deeply cut edges.

CULTIVATION *Grow in well-drained soil, in an open, sunny site. Cut back in spring for best foliage effect.*

☼ ◊ Z4-9 H12-8 ‡30in (75cm) ↔24in (60cm) or more

ARTEMISIA 'POWIS CASTLE'

A vigorous, shrubby, woody-based perennial forming a dense, billowing clump of finely cut, aromatic, silver-gray leaves. Sprays of insignificant, yellow-tinged silver flowerheads are borne in late summer. Excellent in a rock garden or border.

CULTIVATION *Grow in well-drained, fertile soil, in full sun. Will die back in heavy, poorly drained soils and may be short-lived. Cut to the base in autumn to maintain a compact habit.*

☀ ◊ Z7-9 H12-8 ‡24in (60cm) ↔36in (90cm)

ASPARAGUS DENSIFLORUS 'MYERSII'

This asparagus fern is an arching, trailing, evergreen perennial forming spires of narrow, feathery, leaflike, light green stems. In warm climates, it bears clusters of small, pink-tinged white flowers in summer, followed by bright red berries. In cold areas, it is better grown under cover and makes an impressive conservatory specimen or a much smaller house- or hanging basket plant.

CULTIVATION *Grow in moist but well-drained, fertile soil, in partial shade. Minimum temperature 35°F (2°C).*

☀ ◊ H12-1 ‡24–36in (60–90cm) ↔3–4ft (1–1.2m)

ASPLENIUM SCOLOPENDRIUM

The hart's tongue fern has irregular crowns of shuttlecock-like, tongue-shaped, leathery, bright green fronds, to 16in (40cm) long. Heart-shaped at the bases, they often have wavy margins, markedly so in the cultivar 'Crispum Bolton's Nobile'. On the undersides of mature fronds, rust-colored spore cases are arranged in a herringbone pattern. Good in alkaline soil.

CULTIVATION *Grow in moist but well-drained, organic, preferably alkaline soil with added grit, in partial shade.*

☼ ◊◊ Z6-8 H8-6 ↕18–28in (45–70cm)
↔24in (60cm)

ASTER ALPINUS

This spreading, clump-forming perennial is grown for its mass of daisylike, purplish blue or pinkish purple flowerheads with deep yellow centers. These are borne on upright stems in early and mid-summer above short-stalked, narrow, mid-green leaves. A low-growing aster, it is suitable for the front of a border or in a rock garden. Several outstanding cultivars are available.

CULTIVATION *Grow in well-drained, moderately fertile soil, in sun. Mulch annually after cutting back in autumn.*

☼ ◊ Z5-7 H9-1 ↕10in (25cm) ↔18in (45cm)

ASTER AMELLUS 'KING GEORGE'

A clump-forming, bushy perennial bearing loose clusters of large, daisy-like, violet-blue flowerheads with yellow centers that open from late summer to autumn. The rough, mid-green leaves are hairy and lance-shaped. An invaluable late-flowering border plant; other recommended cultivars include 'Framfieldii' (lavender-blue flowers), 'Jacqueline Genebrier' (bright red-purple), and 'Veilchenkönigen' (deep purple).

CULTIVATION *Grow in open, well-drained, moderately fertile soil, in full sun. Thrives in alkaline conditions.*

☼ ◊ Z5-8 H9-1   ‡↔ 18in (45cm)

ASTER 'ANDENKEN AN ALMA PÖTSCHKE'

This vigorous, upright, clump-forming perennial carries sprays of large, daisylike, bright salmon-pink flowerheads with yellow centers from late summer to mid-autumn, on stiff stems above rough, stem-clasping, mid-green leaves. Good for cutting, or in late-flowering displays. *A. novae-angliae* 'Harrington's Pink' is very similar, with paler flowers.

CULTIVATION *Grow in moist but well-drained, fertile, well-cultivated soil, in sun or semi-shade. Divide and replant every third year to maintain vigor and flower quality. May need staking.*

☼☀ ◊ Z4-8 H8-1 ‡4ft (1.2m) ↔24in (60cm)

ASTER × *FRIKARTII*
'MÖNCH'

This upright, bushy perennial provides a continuous show of long-lasting, daisylike, lavender-blue flowerheads with orange centers during late summer and early autumn. The dark green leaves are rough-textured and oblong. A useful plant for adding cool tones to a late summer or autumn display, as is the very similar 'Wunder von Stäfa'.

CULTIVATION *Best in well-drained, moderately fertile soil. Position in an open, sunny site. Mulch annually after cutting back in late autumn.*

☼ ◊ Z5-8 H9-1   ↕28in (70cm)
↔14–16in (35–40cm)

ASTER LATERIFOLIUS
'HORIZONTALIS'

A clump-forming, freely branching perennial bearing clusters of daisy-like, sometimes pink-tinged white flowerheads with darker pink centers, from mid-summer to mid-autumn. The slender, hairy stems bear small, lance shaped, mid-green leaves. An invaluable late-flowerer for a mixed border.

CULTIVATION *Grow in moist but well-drained, moderately fertile soil, in partial shade. Keep moist in summer.*

☼ ◊ Z4-8 H9-1 ↕24in (60cm) ↔12in (30cm)

ASTER 'LITTLE CARLOW'

A clump-forming, upright perennial that produces large clusters of daisy-like, violet-blue flowers with yellow centers, in early and mid-autumn. The dark green leaves are oval to heart-shaped and toothed. Valuable for autumn displays; the flowers cut and dry very well. Closely related to *A. cordifolius* 'Chieftain' (mauve flowers) and 'Sweet Lavender' (Z5-8, H8-3).

CULTIVATION *Best in moist, moderately fertile soil, in partial shade, but tolerates well-drained soil, in full sun. Mulch annually after cutting back in late autumn. May need staking.*

☼ ☀ ◊◊ Z5-8 H9-1   ‡36in (90cm)
↔18in (45cm)

ASTILBE × *ARENDSII* 'FANAL'

A leafy, clump-forming perennial grown for its long-lasting, tapering, feathery heads of tiny, dark crimson flowers in early summer; they later turn brown, keeping their shape well into winter. The dark green leaves, borne on strong stems, are divided into several leaflets. Grow in a damp border or woodland garden, or use for waterside plantings. 'Brautschleier' is similar, with creamy white flower plumes.

CULTIVATION *Grow in moist, fertile, preferably organic soil. Choose a position in full sun or partial shade.*

☼ ☀ ◊ Z4-9 H9-1 ‡24in (60cm) ↔18in (45cm)

ASTILBE × *CRISPA* 'PERKEO'

A summer-flowering, clump-forming perennial, low-growing compared with other astilbes, that bears small, upright plumes of tiny, star-shaped, deep pink flowers. The stiff, finely cut, crinkled, dark green leaves are bronze-tinted when young. Suitable for a border or rock garden; the flowers color best in light shade. 'Bronce Elegans' is another good, compact astilbe for where space is limited.

CULTIVATION *Grow in reasonably moist, fertile soil that is rich in organic matter. Choose a position in partial shade.*

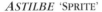 Z4-8 H8-1 ‡8in (15–20cm) ↔6in (15cm)

ASTILBE 'SPRITE'

A summer-flowering, leafy, clump-forming dwarf perennial that is suitable for waterside plantings. The feathery, tapering plumes of tiny, star-shaped, shell pink flowers arch elegantly over a mass of broad, mid-green leaves composed of many narrow leaflets. *Astilbe* 'Deutschland' Z4-9, H9-1) has the same arching (as opposed to upright) flower plumes, in cream.

CULTIVATION *Grow in reliably moist, fertile soil that is rich in organic matter. Choose a site in a partial shade.*

☼ ◗ Z4-8 H8-2 ‡20in (50cm) ↔3ft (1m)

ASTILBE 'STRAUSSENFEDER'

A vigorous, clump-forming perennial that bears loose, arching sprays of rich coral-pink flowers in late summer and early autumn; the flowerheads turn brown when dry, and persist into winter. The dark green leaves, divided into oval leaflets, are bronze-tinted when young. Ideal for damp borders, bog gardens, or waterside plantings. Sometimes called 'Ostrich Plume'.

CULTIVATION *Grow in moist, fertile, rich soil, in sun or partial shade. Requires ample moisture in the growing season. Apply an annual mulch in spring of organic matter to hold water in the soil.*

☼ ☀ ◊ Z4-9 H8-2 ‡36in (90cm) ↔24in (60cm)

ASTRANTIA MAXIMA

Sometimes known as Hattie's pincushion, this mat-forming perennial produces domed, rose-pink flowerheads with star-shaped collars of papery, greenish pink bracts, on tall stems during summer and autumn. The mid-green leaves are divided into three toothed lobes. Flowers are good for cutting and drying for use in cottage-style arrangements.

CULTIVATION *Grow in any moist, fertile, preferably organic soil, in sun or semi-shade. Tolerates drier conditions.*

☼ ☀ ◊◊ Z5-8 H7-1 ‡24in (60cm) ↔12in (30cm)

ASTRANTIA MAJOR
'SUNNINGDALE VARIEGATED'

A clump-forming perennial bearing
attractive, deeply lobed, basal leaves
that have unevenly variegated,
creamy yellow margins. From early
summer, domes of tiny, green or
pink, often deep purple-red flowers
with star-shaped collars of pale pink
bracts, are carried on wiry stems.
Thrives in a moist border, woodland
garden, or on a stream bank.

CULTIVATION *Grow in any moist but
well-drained, fertile soil. Needs full sun
to obtain the best leaf coloring.*

☼ ◊ Z4-7 H7-1   ‡12–36in (30–90cm)
                      ↔18in (45cm)

ATHYRIUM FILIX-FEMINA

The lady fern has much divided,
light green, deciduous fronds that
are borne like upright shuttlecocks,
about 3ft (1m) long, arching
outward with age. Frond dissection
is very varied, and the stalks are
sometimes red-brown. Useful for
shaded sites, such as a woodland
garden. Its cultivars 'Frizelliae'
and 'Vernoniae' have unusual,
distinctive fronds.

CULTIVATION *Grow in moist, fertile,
neutral to acidic soil enriched with leaf
mold or compost. Choose a shaded,
sheltered site.*

☼ ◊ Z4-9 H9-1   ‡to 4ft (1.2m)
                      ↔24–36in (60–90cm)

AUCUBA JAPONICA 'CROTONIFOLIA' (FEMALE)

This variegated form of Japanese laurel is a rounded, evergreen shrub with large, glossy, dark green leaves boldly speckled with golden yellow. Upright clusters of small purplish flowers are borne in mid-spring, followed by red berries in autumn. Ideal for dense, semi-formal hedging.

CULTIVATION *Grow in any but water-logged soil, in full sun for best foliage color, or in shade. Plant with male cultivars to ensure good fruiting. Tolerates light pruning at any time; cut back in spring to promote bushiness.*

☼☀ ◊◊ Z6-10 H12-6   ↕↔ 10ft (3m)

AURINIA SAXATILIS

An evergreen perennial that forms dense clusters of bright yellow flowers in late spring that give rise to its common name, gold dust. The flowers of its cultivar 'Citrinus', also recommended, are a more lemony yellow. The oval, hairy, gray-green leaves are arranged in clumps. Ideal for rock gardens, walls, and banks. Also sold as *Alyssum saxatilis*.

CULTIVATION *Grow in moderately fertile soil that is reliably well drained, in a sunny site. Cut back after flowering to maintain compactness.*

☼ ◊ Z4-8 H8-1 ↕8in (20cm) ↔12in (30cm)

BALLOTA PSEUDODICTAMNUS

An evergreen subshrub that forms mounds of rounded, yellow-gray-green leaves on upright, white-woolly stems. Whorls of small, white or pinkish white flowers, each enclosed by a pale green funnel, are produced in late spring and early summer.

CULTIVATION *Grow in poor, very well-drained soil, in full sun with protection from excessive winter moisture. Cut back in early spring to keep compact.*

☼ ◊ Z7-9 H9-7 ‡18in (45cm) ↔24in (60cm)

BAPTISIA AUSTRALIS

Blue false indigo is a gently spreading, upright perennial with a long season of interest. The bright blue-green leaves, on gray-green stems, are divided into three oval leaflets. Spikes of indigo-blue flowers, often flecked white or cream, open throughout early summer. The dark gray seed pods can be dried for winter decoration.

CULTIVATION *Grow in deep, moist but well-drained, fertile, preferably neutral to acidic soil, in full sun. Once planted, it is best left undisturbed.*

☼ ◊ Z3-9 H9-2 ‡5ft (1.5m) ↔24in (60cm)

BEGONIAS WITH DECORATIVE FOLIAGE

These perennial begonias are typically grown as annuals for their large, usually asymmetrical, ornamental leaves that are available in a variety of colors. For example, there are lively leaves of 'Merry Christmas' outlined with emerald green, or there is the more subtle, dark green, metallic foliage of *B. metallica*. Some leaves are valued for their unusual patterns; *B. masoniana* is appropriately known as the iron-cross begonia. Under the right conditions, 'Thurstonii' may reach shrublike proportions, but most,

like 'Munchkin', are more compact. Grow as summer bedding, in a conservatory, or as house plants.

CULTIVATION *Grow in fertile, well-drained, neutral to acidic soil or soil mix, in light dappled shade. Promote compact, leafy growth by pinching out shoot tips during the growing season. When in growth, feed regularly with a nitrogen-rich fertilizer. Minimum temperature 59°F (15°C).*

☀ ◊ H12-1

1 ↕ ↔ 2ft (60cm)

2 ↕ 20in (50cm) ↔ 18in (45cm)

1 *Begonia listada* **2** *B. masoniana*

3 ↕8in (25cm) ↔ 12in (30cm)

5 ↕8in (20cm) ↔ 10in (25cm)

4 ↕36in (90cm) ↔ 24in (60cm)

6 ↕30cm (12in) ↔ 45cm (18in)

7 ↕6ft (2m) ↔ 18in (45cm)

8 ↕8in (20cm) ↔ 10in (25cm)

3 *B.* 'Merry Christmas' **4** *B. metallica* **5** *B.* 'Munchkin'
6 *B.* 'Silver Queen' **7** *B.* 'Thurstonii' **8** *B.* 'Tiger Paws'

FLOWERING BEGONIAS

Usually grown outdoors as annuals, these bold-flowered begonias are very variable in size and shape, offering a range of summer uses to the gardener. For specific information on growth habit, check the label or ask advice when buying. Upright or compact begonias, such as 'Pin Up' or the Olympia series, are ideal for summer bedding; for containers and hanging baskets, there are pendulous or trailing varieties such as 'Illumination Orange'. Begonias can also be grown as house plants. The flowers also come in a wide variety of sizes and colors; they are either single or double and appear in loose clusters throughout summer.

CULTIVATION *Fertile, organic, neutral to acidic soil or soil mix with good drainage. Flowers are best in partial shade; they suffer in direct sun. When in growth, give a balanced fertilizer. Many will not survive below 59°F (15°C).*

☀ ◊ H12-1

1 ‡ to 18in (45cm) ↔ to 14in (35cm)

2 ‡↔ to 16in (40cm)

3 ‡8in (20cm) ↔ 8–9in (20–22cm)

4 ‡24in (60cm) ↔ 12in (30cm)

1 *B.* 'Alfa Pink' **2** *Begonia* 'All Round Dark Rose Green Leaf'
3 *B.* 'Expresso Scarlet' **4** *B.* 'Illumination Orange'

5 ‡to14in (35cm) ↔ to 12in (30cm)

6 ‡30in (75cm) ↔ 24in (60cm)

7 ‡↔ 12in (30cm)

8 ‡↔ to 8in (20cm)

9 ‡24in (60cm) ↔ 18in (45cm)

10 ‡10in (25cm) ↔ 8in (20cm)

11 ‡30in (75cm) ↔ 18in (45cm)

5 *B.* 'Inferno Apple Blossom' **6** *B.* 'Irene Nuss' **7** *B.* 'Nonstop'
8 *B.* 'Olympia White' **9** *B.* 'Orange Rubra' **10** *B.* 'Pin Up'
11 *B. sutherlandii*

BELLIS PERENNIS 'POMPONETTE'

This double-flowered form of the English daisy is usually grown as a biennial for spring bedding. Pink, red, or white flowerheads with quill-shaped petals appear from late winter to spring, above the dense clumps of spoon-shaped, bright green leaves. 'Dresden China' and 'Rob Roy' are other recommended selections.

CULTIVATION *Grow in well-drained, moderately fertile soil, in full sun or partial shade. Deadhead to prolong flowering and to prevent self-seeding.*

☼☀ ◊ Z4-8 H8-1 ‡↔ 4–8in (10–20cm)

BERBERIS DARWINII

The Darwin barberry is a vigorous, arching, evergreen shrub that carries masses of small, deep golden orange flowers on spiny stems from mid- to late spring; these are followed by blue berries in autumn. The leaves are glossy dark green and spiny. Use as a vandal-resistant or barrier hedge.

CULTIVATION *Grow in any but water-logged soil, in full sun or partial shade with shelter from cold, drying winds. Trim after flowering, if necessary.*

☼☀ ◊◊ Z7-9 H9-4 ‡10ft (3m) or more
↔10ft (3m)

BERBERIS × *OTTAWENSIS* 'SUPERBA'

This spiny, rounded, deciduous, spring-flowering shrub bears clusters of small, pale yellow, red-tinged flowers that are followed by red berries in autumn. The red-purple leaves turn crimson before they fall. Effective as a specimen shrub or in a mixed border.

CULTIVATION *Grow in almost any well-drained soil, preferably in full sun Thin out dense growth in mid-winter.*

☼ ◊◊ Z5-9 H8-3　　　↕↔ 8ft (2.5m)

BERBERIS × *STENOPHYLLA* 'CORALLINA COMPACTA'

While *Berberis stenophylla* is a large, arching shrub, ideal for informal hedging, this cultivar of it is tiny: a small, evergreen shrub bearing spine-tipped, deep green leaves on arching, spiny stems. Quantities of tiny, light orange flowers appear from mid-spring, followed by small, blue-black berries.

CULTIVATION *Best in fertile, organic soil that is reliably drained, in full sun. Cut back hard after flowering.*

☼ ◊ Z6-9 H9-6　　　↕↔ to 12in (30cm)

BERBERIS THUNBERGII
'BAGATELLE'

A very compact, spiny, spring-flowering, deciduous shrub with deep red-purple leaves that turn orange and red in autumn. The pale yellow flowers are followed by glossy red fruits. Good for a rock garden. *B. thunbergii* 'Atropurpurea Nana', (also sold as 'Crimson Pygmy'), is another small purple-leaved barberry, to 24in (60cm) tall.

CULTIVATION *Grow in well-drained soil, in full sun for best flower and foliage color. Thin out dense, overcrowded growth in mid- to late winter.*

☼ ◊ Z5-8 H8-3 ‡12in (30cm) ↔16in (40cm)

BERBERIS THUNBERGII
'ROSE GLOW'

A compact, spiny, deciduous shrub with reddish purple leaves that gradually become flecked with white as the season progresses. Tiny, pale yellow flowers appear in mid-spring, followed by small red berries. Good as a barrier hedge.

CULTIVATION *Grow in any but water-logged soil, in full sun or partial shade. Cut out any dead wood in summer.*

☼◐ ◊◊ Z5-8 H8-3 ‡6ft (2m) or more ↔6ft (2m)

BERBERIS VERRUCULOSA

A slow-growing, compact, spring-flowering barberry that makes a fine evergreen specimen shrub. The cup-shaped, golden yellow flowers are carried amid the spine-tipped, glossy dark green leaves on spiny, arching stems. Oval to pear-shaped black berries develop in autumn.

CULTIVATION *Best in well-drained, organic, fertile soil, in full sun. Keep pruning to a minimum.*

☼ ◊ Z6-9 H9-4 ↔ 5ft (1.5m)

BERBERIS WILSONIAE

A very spiny, semi-evergreen, arching shrub forming dense mounds of gray-green foliage that turns red and orange in autumn. Clusters of pale yellow flowers in summer are followed by coral-pink to pinkish red berries. Makes a good barrier hedge. Avoid seed-grown plants; they may be inferior hybrids.

CULTIVATION *Grow in any well-drained soil, in sun or partial shade. Flowering and fruiting are best in full sun. Thin out dense growth in mid-winter.*

☼◑ ◊ Z6-9 H9-4 ‡3ft (1m) ↔6ft (2m)

BERGENIA 'BALLAWLEY'

This clump-forming, evergreen perennial, one of the first to flower in spring, bears bright crimson flowers that are carried on sturdy red stems. The leathery, oval leaves turn bronze-red in winter. Suits a woodland garden, or plant in groups to edge a mixed border. *B. cordifolia* 'Purpurea' has similarly colored leaves, with deep magenta flowers.

CULTIVATION *Grow in any well-drained soil, in full sun or light shade. Shelter from cold winds. Mulch in autumn.*

☼ ☀ ◊◊ Z3-8 H8-1   ↕to 24in (60cm)
                            ↔24in (60cm)

BERGENIA 'SILBERLICHT'

An early-flowering, clump-forming, evergreen perennial bearing clusters of cup-shaped white flowers, often flushed pink, in spring. (For pure white flowers on a similar plant, look for 'Bressingham White', or for deep pink, 'Morgenröte'.) The mid-green leaves are leathery, with toothed margins. Good under-planting for shrubs, which give it some winter shelter.

CULTIVATION *Grow in any well-drained soil, in full sun or partial shade. Shelter from cold winds to avoid foliage scorch. Provide a mulch in autumn.*

☼ ☀ ◊◊ Z3-8 H8-1   ↕12in (30cm)
                            ↔20in (50cm)

BETULA NIGRA

The river birch is a tall, conical to
spreading, deciduous tree with
glossy, mid- to dark green, diamond-
shaped leaves. It has shaggy, red-
brown bark that peels in layers on
young trees; on older specimens, the
bark becomes blackish or gray-white
and develops cracks. Yellow-brown
male catkins are conspicuous in
spring. Makes a fine specimen tree.
'Heritage' is a superior selection.

CULTIVATION *Grow in moist but well-
drained, moderately fertile soil, in full
sun. Remove any damaged, diseased,
or dead wood in late autumn.*

☼ ◊ Z4-9 H7-2 ‡60ft (18m) ↔40ft (12m)

BETULA PENDULA
'YOUNGII'

Young's weeping birch is a
deciduous tree with an elegant,
weeping habit. The yellow-brown
male catkins appear in early spring
before the triangular leaves; the
foliage turns golden yellow in
autumn. An attractive tree for a
small garden, more dome-shaped
than 'Tristis' or 'Laciniata', other
popular weeping birches, growing
wider than it is tall.

CULTIVATION *Any moist but well-
drained soil, in an open, sunny site.
Keep pruning to a minimum; remove
any shoots on the trunk in late autumn.*

☼ ◊ Z2-7 H7-1 ‡25ft (8m) ↔30ft (10m)

BETULA UTILIS VAR. *JACQUEMONTII*

The West Himalayan birch is an open, broadly conical, deciduous tree with smooth, peeling white bark. Catkins are a feature in early spring, and the dark green leaves turn rich golden yellow in autumn. Plant where winter sun will light up the bark, particularly brilliantly white in the cultivars 'Silver Shadow', 'Jermyns', and 'Grayswood Ghost'.

CULTIVATION *Grow in any moist but well-drained soil, in sun. Remove any damaged or dead wood from young trees in late autumn; once established, keep pruning to a minimum.*

☼ ◊ Z5-7 H7-3 ‡50ft (15m)↔23ft (7.5m)

BIDENS FERULIFOLIA

This clump-forming, spreading, short-lived perennial is generally grown as an annual. A profusion of star-shaped, bright golden yellow flowers are borne over a long period from mid-spring until the first frosts. The leaves are fresh green and finely divided. Ideal for trailing over the edges of hanging baskets and other containers.

CULTIVATION *Grow in moist but well-drained, fairly fertile soil or soil mix, in sun. Short-lived, but easily propagated by stem cuttings in autumn.*

☼ ◊◊ Z8-10 H12-8 ‡to 12in (30cm)
↔indefinite

BRACHYGLOTTIS
'SUNSHINE'

A bushy, mound-forming, evergreen shrub bearing oval leaves that are silvery gray when young, becoming dark green with white-felted undersides as they develop. Daisylike yellow flowers appear from early to mid-summer. Some gardeners prefer it as a foliage plant, pinching or snipping off the flower buds before they open. Thrives in coastal sites.

CULTIVATION *Grow in any well-drained soil, in a sunny, sheltered site. Trim back after flowering. Responds well to hard pruning in spring.*

☼ ◊ Z9-10 H10-8   ‡3–5ft (1–1.5m)
↔6ft (2m) or more

BRACTEANTHA
BRIGHT BIKINI SERIES

These strawflowers are upright annuals or short-lived perennials with papery, double flowers in red, pink, orange, yellow, and white from late spring to autumn. The leaves are gray-green. Use to edge a border, or grow in a windowbox; flowers are long-lasting and cut and dry well. For single colors rather than a mixture, try 'Frosted Sulphur' (lemon yellow), 'Silvery Rose', and 'Reeves Purple'.

CULTIVATION *Grow in moist but well-drained, moderately fertile soil. Choose a position in full sun.*

☼ ◊ Z10-11 H12-1   ‡↔12in (30cm)

BRUNNERA MACROPHYLLA 'HADSPEN CREAM'

This clump-forming perennial with attractive foliage is ideal as a groundcover in borders and among deciduous trees. In mid- and late spring, upright clusters of small, bright blue flowers appear above heart-shaped leaves, plain green in *Brunnera macrophylla*, but with irregular, creamy white margins in this attractive cultivar.

CULTIVATION *Grow in moist but well-drained, organic soil. Choose a position that is cool and lightly shaded.*

☼ ◑◒ Z3-7 H7-1 ‡18in (45cm) ↔24in (60cm)

BUDDLEJA ALTERNIFOLIA

A dense, deciduous shrub carrying slender, arching branches. Fragrant, lilac-purple flowers are produced in neat clusters during early summer among the narrow, gray-green leaves. Makes a good wall shrub or can be trained with a single, clear trunk as a striking specimen tree. Attractive to beneficial insects.

CULTIVATION *Best in alkaline soil but can be grown in any soil that is well drained, in full sun. Cut stems back to strong buds after flowering; responds well to hard pruning in spring.*

☼ ◊ Z6-9 H10-4 ‡↔ 12ft (4m)

BUDDLEJA DAVIDII

All cultivars of *B. davidii*, the butterfly bush, are fast-growing, deciduous shrubs with a wide range of flower colors. As the popular name suggests, the flowers attract butterflies and other beneficial garden insects in profusion. The long, arching shoots carry lance-shaped, mid- to gray-green leaves, up to 10in (25cm) long. Conical clusters of bright, fragrant flowers, usually about 12in (30cm) long, are borne at the end of arching stems from summer to autumn; those of 'Royal Red' are the largest, up to 20in (50cm) long. These shrubs respond well to hard pruning in spring, which keeps them a compact size for a small garden.

CULTIVATION *Grow in well-drained, fertile soil, in sun. Restrict size and encourage better flowers by pruning back hard to a low framework each spring. To prevent self-seeding, cut spent flowerheads back to a pair of leaves or sideshoots; this may also result in a second period of bloom.*

☼ ◊ Z6-9 H10-4

1 ↕ 10ft (3m) ↔ 15ft (5m)

2 ↕ 10ft (3m) ↔ 15ft (5m)

3 ↕ 10ft (3m) ↔ 15ft (5m)

1 *B. davidii* 'Empire Blue' **2** *B. davidii* 'Royal Red' **3** *B. davidii* 'White Profusion'

BUDDLEJA GLOBOSA

The orange ball tree is a deciduous or semi-evergreen shrub bearing, unusually for a buddleja, round clusters of tiny, orange-yellow flowers that appear in early summer. The lance-shaped leaves are dark green with woolly undersides. This large shrub is prone to becoming bare at the base and does not respond well to pruning, so grow toward the back of a mixed border.

CULTIVATION *Best on well-drained, alkaline soil, in a sunny position with shelter from cold winds. Pruning should be kept to a minimum, or the next year's flowers will be lost.*

☼ ◊ Z7-9 H9-6 ↕↔ 15ft (5m)

BUDDLEJA 'LOCHINCH'

A compact, deciduous shrub, very similar to a *Buddleja davidii* (see p. 93), bearing long spikes of lilac-blue flowers from late summer to autumn. The leaves are downy and gray-green when young, becoming smooth and developing white-felted undersides as they mature. Very attractive to butterflies.

CULTIVATION *Grow in any well-drained, moderately fertile soil, in sun. Cut back all stems close to the base each year as the buds begin to swell in spring.*

☼ ◊ Z6-9 H9-6 ↕ 8ft (2.5m) ↔ 10ft (3m)

BUXUS SEMPERVIRENS 'ELEGANTISSIMA'

This variegated form of the common boxwood is a rounded, dense, evergreen shrub bearing small and narrow, glossy bright green leaves edged with cream. The flowers are of little significance. Responding well to trimming, it is very good as an edging plant or for use as a low hedge. 'Latifolia Maculata' is also variegated, with yellow leaf markings.

CULTIVATION *Grow in any well-drained soil, in sun or light shade. Trim in spring and summer; overgrown shrubs respond well to hard pruning in late spring.*

☼◑ ◊ Z6-8 H8-6   ‡↔ 5ft (1.5m)

BUXUS SEMPERVIRENS 'SUFFRUTICOSA'

A very dense, slow-growing boxwood bearing small, evergreen, glossy, bright green leaves. Widely used as an edging plant or for clipping into precise shapes. During late spring or early summer, inconspicuous but fragrant flowers are produced. Excellent as a hedge.

CULTIVATION *Grow in any well-drained, fertile soil, in sun or semi-shade. The combination of dry soil and full sun can cause scorching. Trim hedges in summer; overgrown specimens can be pruned hard in late spring.*

☼◑ ◊ Z6-8 H9-4   ‡3ft (1m) ↔5ft (1.5m)

CALENDULA
'FIESTA GITANA'

This dwarf pot marigold is a bushy, fast-growing annual that produces masses of usually double flower-heads in pastel orange or yellow, including bicolors, mostly in spring and autumn. The leaves are hairy and aromatic. Excellent for cutting, bedding, and containers.

CULTIVATION *Grow in well-drained, poor to moderately fertile soil, in full sun or partial shade. Deadhead regularly to prolong flowering.*

☼☀ ◊ annual H6-1   ‡to 12in (30cm)
↔12–18in (30–45cm)

CALLICARPA BODINIERI
VAR. *GIRALDII* 'PROFUSION'

An upright, deciduous shrub grown mainly for its long-lasting autumn display of shiny, beadlike, deep violet berries. The large, pale green, tapering leaves are bronze when they emerge in spring, and pale pink flowers appear in summer. Brings a long season of interest to a shrub border; for maximum impact, plant in groups..

CULTIVATION *Grow in any well-drained, fertile soil, in full sun or dappled shade. Cut back hard in spring to remove winter kill and to keep compact .*

☼☀ ◊ Z6-8 H8-6 ‡10ft (3m) ↔ 8ft (2.5m)

CALLISTEMON CITRINUS 'SPLENDENS'

This attractive cultivar of the crimson bottlebrush is an evergreen shrub, usually with arching branches. Dense spikes of brilliant red flowers appear in spring and summer, amid the gray-green, lemon-scented leaves, which are bronze-red when young. Grow at the base of a sunny wall to give some protection from cold.

CULTIVATION *Best in well-drained, fertile, neutral to acidic soil, in full sun. Pinch out tips young of young plants to promote bushiness. Tolerates hard pruning in spring.*

☼ ◊ Z10-11 H10-8   ‡6–25ft (2–8m)
↔5–20ft (1.5–6m)

CALLISTEPHUS MILADY SUPER MIXED

This sturdy, partially wilt-resistant mixture of variably colored, fast-growing annuals is ideal for use in bedding and containers. The double, rounded flowerheads, borne from late summer to autumn, are pink, red, scarlet, blue, or white. The leaves are mid-green and toothed.

CULTIVATION *Grow in moist but well-drained, fertile, neutral to alkaline soil, in a sheltered, sunny site. Deadhead regularly to prolong flowering.*

☼ ◊◊ annual H12-1   ‡to 12in (30cm)
↔10in (25cm)

CALLUNA VULGARIS

Cultivars of *C. vulgaris* are upright to spreading, fine-leaved heathers. They make excellent evergreen groundcover plants if weeds are suppressed before planting. Dense spikes of bell-shaped flowers appear from mid-summer to late autumn, in shades of red, purple, pink, or white; 'Kinlochruel' is quite distinctive with its double white flowers in long clusters. Seasonal interest is extended into winter by cultivars with colored foliage, such as 'Robert Chapman' and 'Beoley Gold'. Heathers are very attractive to bees and other beneficial insects and make good companions to dwarf conifers.

CULTIVATION *Best in well-drained, organic, acidic soil, in an open, sunny site, to recreate their native moorland habitats. Trim off flowered shoots in early spring with shears; remove overly long shoots wherever possible, cutting back to their point of origin below the flower cluster.*

☼ ◊ Z5-7 H7-5

3 ‡10in (25cm) ↔ 16in (40cm)

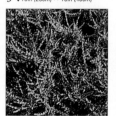

1 ‡10in (25cm) ↔ 14in (35cm)   **2** ‡14in (35cm) ↔ to 30in (75cm)   **4** ‡10in (25cm) ↔ 26in (65cm)

1 *C. vulgaris* 'Beoley Gold' **2** *C. vulgaris* 'Darkness' **3** *C. vulgaris* 'Kinlochruel'
4 *C. vulgaris* 'Robert Chapman'

CALTHA PALUSTRIS

The marsh marigold is a clump-forming, aquatic perennial that thrives in a bog garden or at the margins of a stream or pond. Cup-shaped, waxy, bright golden yellow flowers appear on tall stems in spring, above the kidney-shaped, glossy green leaves. For cheerful double flowers, look for the cultivar 'Flore Pleno'.

CULTIVATION *Best in boggy, rich soil, in an open, sunny site. Tolerates root restriction in aquatic containers in water no deeper than 9in (23cm), but prefers shallower conditions.*

☼ ◑ Z3-7 H7-1　‡4–16in (10–40cm)
　　　　　　　　↔18in (45cm)

CAMELLIA 'INSPIRATION'

A dense, upright, evergreen shrub or small tree bearing masses of saucer-shaped, semidouble, deep pink flowers from mid-winter to late spring. The dark green leaves are oval and leathery. Good for the back of a border or as a specimen shrub.

CULTIVATION *Best in moist but well-drained, fertile, neutral to acidic soil, in partial shade with shelter from cold, drying winds. Mulch around the base with shredded bark. After flowering, prune back young plants to encourage a bushy habit and a balanced shape.*

☼ ◐◑ Z7-8 H8-7　‡12ft (4m) ↔6ft (2m)

CAMELLIA JAPONICA

These long-lived and elegant, evergreen shrubs or small trees for gardens with acidic soil are very popular in shrub borders, woodland gardens, or standing on their own in the open ground or in containers. The oval leaves are glossy and dark green; they serve to heighten the brilliance of the single to fully double flowers in spring. Single and semidouble flowers have a prominent central boss of yellow stamens. Most flowers are suitable for cutting, but blooms may be spoiled by late frosts.

CULTIVATION *Grow in moist but well-drained, organic, acidic soil in partial shade. Choose a site sheltered from early morning sun, cold winds, and late frosts. Do not plant too deeply; the top of the root ball must be level with the firmed soil. Maintain a mulch 2–3in (5–7cm) deep of leaf mold or shredded bark. Little pruning is necessary, although moderate trimming of young plants will help produce a balanced shape.*

☀ ◊◊ Z7-8 H8-7

1 ‡15ft (5m) ↔ 25ft (8m)   **2** ‡28ft (9m) ↔ 25ft (8m)   **3** ‡28ft (9m) ↔ 25ft (8m)

4 ‡6ft (2m) ↔ 3ft (1m)   **5** ‡28ft (9m) ↔ 25ft (8m)   **6** ‡28ft (9m) ↔ 25ft (8m)

1 *Camellia japonica* 'Adolphe Audusson' **2** 'Alexander Hunter' **3** 'Berenice Boddy'
4 'Bob's Tinsie' **5** 'Coquettii' **6** 'Elegans'

MORE CHOICES

'Akashigata' Deep pink
flowers.

'Bob Hope' Dark red.

'C. M. Hovey' Crimson-
scarlet

'Doctor Tinsley' Pinkish
white.

'Grand Prix' Bright red
with yellow stamens

'Hagoromo' Pale pink

'Masayoshi' White with
red marbling.

'Miss Charleston' Ruby
red.

'Nuccio's Gem' White.

7 ‡ 28ft (9m) ↔ 25ft (8m)

8 ‡ 28ft (9m) ↔ 25ft (8m)

9 ‡ 28ft (9m) ↔ 25ft (8m)

10 ‡ 28ft (9m) ↔ 25ft (8m)

11 ‡ 28ft (9m) ↔ 25ft (8m)

12 ‡ 28ft (9m) ↔ 25ft (8m)

13 ‡ 28ft (9m) ↔ 25ft (8m)

14 ‡ 28ft (9m) ↔ 25ft (8m)

7 *Camellia japonica* 'Gloire de Nantes' **8** 'Guilio Nuccio' **9** 'Jupiter' (*syn.* 'Paul's Jupiter')
10 'Lavinia Maggi' **11** 'Mrs D. W. Davis' **12** 'R. L. Wheeler' **13** 'Rubescens Major'
14 'Tricolor'

CAMELLIA 'LASCA BEAUTY'

An open, upright shrub greatly valued for its very large, semi-double, pale pink flowers, which appear in mid-spring. They stand out against the dark green foliage. Grow in a cool greenhouse, and move outdoors to a partially shaded site in early summer where not hardy.

CULTIVATION *Grow in acidic potting mix in bright filtered light. Water freely with soft water when in growth; more sparingly in winter. Apply a balanced fertilizer once in mid-spring and again in early summer.*

☀ ◊◊ Z7-8 H8-7 ‡6–15ft (2–5m) ↔5–10ft (1.5–3m)

CAMELLIA 'LEONARD MESSEL'

This spreading, evergreen shrub with oval, leathery, dark green leaves is one of the hardiest camellias available. It produces an abundance of large, flattish to cup-shaped, semidouble, clear pink flowers from early to late spring. Exccllent in a shrub border.

CULTIVATION *Best in moist but well-drained, fertile, neutral to acidic soil. Position in semi-shade with shelter from cold, drying winds. Maintain a mulch of shredded bark or leafmold around the base. Pruning is rarely necessary.*

☀ ◊◊ Z7-8 H8-7 ‡12ft (4m) ↔10ft (3m)

CAMELLIA
'MANDALAY QUEEN'

This large, widely branching shrub
bears deep rose-pink, semidouble
flowers in spring. The broad,
leathery leaves are dark green. Best
grown in a cool greenhouse, but
move it outdoors in summer.

CULTIVATION *Best in acidic potting mix
with bright, filtered light. Water freely
with soft water when in growth, more
sparingly in winter. Apply a balanced
fertilizer in mid-spring and again in
early summer.*

☼ ◊◊ Z7-8 H8-7   ↕ to 50ft (15m)
↔15ft (5m)

CAMELLIA SASANQUA
'NARUMIGATA'

An upright shrub or small tree
valued for its late display of fragrant,
single-petaled white flowers in mid-
to late autumn. The foliage is dark
green. Makes a good hedge, though
where marginally hardy it does
better against a warm, sunny wall.
C. sasanqua 'Crimson King' is a very
similar shrub, with red flowers.

CULTIVATION *Grow in moist but well-
drained, organic, acidic soil, and
maintain a thick mulch. Choose a site
in full sun or partial shade, with shelter
from cold winds. Tolerates hard
pruning after flowering.*

☼◌ ◊◊ Z7-8 H8-7 ↕20ft (6m)↔10ft (3m)

CAMELLIA × WILLIAMSII

Cultivars of *C. × williamsii* are strong-growing, evergreen shrubs that are much valued for their bright, lustrous foliage and the unsurpassed elegance of their roselike flowers that range from pure white to crimson.

Most flower in mid- and late spring, although 'Anticipation' and 'Mary Christian' begin to flower in late winter. These plants make handsome specimens for a cool conservatory or shrub border, and 'J.C. Williams', for example, can be trained against a wall.

Avoid sites exposed to morning sun to prevent damage to buds and flowers.

CULTIVATION *Best in moist but well-drained, acidic to neutral soil, in partial shade. Shelter from frost and cold winds, and mulch with shredded bark. Prune young plants after flowering to promote bushiness; wall-trained shrubs should be allowed to develop a strong central stem.*

☀ ◊◊ Z7-8 H8-7

1 ↕12ft (4m) ↔ 6ft (2m)

2 ↕10ft (3m) ↔ 8ft (2.5m)   **3** ↕15ft (5m) ↔ 8ft (2.5m)

1 *C. × williamsii* 'Anticipation'   **2** *C. × williamsii* 'Brigadoon'   **3** *C. × williamsii* 'Donation'

4 ↕↔ 12ft (4m)

5 ↕ 12ft (4m) ↔ 8ft (2.5m)

6 ↕ 12ft (4m) ↔ 8ft (2.5m)

7 ↕ 12ft (4m) ↔ 8ft (2.5m)

8 ↕ 12ft (4m) ↔ 8ft (2.5m)

9 ↕↔ 10ft (3m)

4 *C.* x *williamsii* 'George Blandford' 5 *C.* x *williamsii* 'Joan Trehane'
6 *C.* x *williamsii* 'J.C. Williams' 7 *C.* x *williamsii* 'Mary Christian' 8 *C.* x *williamsii* 'Saint Ewe'
9 *C.* x *williamsii* 'Water Lily'

CAMPANULA COCHLEARIIFOLIA

Fairies' thimbles is a low-growing, rosette-forming perennial bearing, in mid-summer, abundant clusters of open, bell-shaped, mauve-blue or white flowers. The bright green leaves are heart-shaped. It spreads freely by means of creeping stems and can be invasive. Particularly effective if allowed to colonize areas of gravel, paving crevices, or the tops of dry walls.

CULTIVATION *Prefers moist but well-drained soil, in sun or partial shade. To restrict spread, pull up unwanted plants.*

☼ ◐ ◊ Z5-7 H7-4 ↕to 3in (8cm)
↔to 20in (50cm) or more

CAMPANULA GLOMERATA 'SUPERBA'

A fast-growing, clump-forming perennial carrying dense heads of large, bell-shaped, purple-violet flowers in summer. The lance-shaped to oval, mid-green leaves are arranged in rosettes at the base of the plant and along the stems. Excellent in herbaceous borders or informal, cottage-style gardens.

CULTIVATION *Best in moist but well-drained, neutral to alkaline soil, in sun or semi-shade. Cut back after flowering to encourage a second flush of flowers.*

☼ ◐ ◊◊ Z3-8 H8-1 ↕30in (75cm)
↔3ft (1m) or more

CAMPANULA LACTIFLORA 'LODDON ANNA'

An upright, branching perennial producing sprays of large, nodding, bell-shaped, soft lilac-pink flowers from mid-summer above mid-green leaves. Makes an excellent border perennial but may need staking in an exposed site. Mixes well with the white-flowered 'Alba', or the deep purple 'Prichard's Variety'.

CULTIVATION *Best in moist but well-drained, fertile soil, in full sun or partial shade. Trim after flowering to encourage a second, although less profuse, flush of flowers*

☼ ◑ ◊◊ Z5-7 H7-5 ‡4–5ft (1.2–1.5m)
↔24in (60cm)

CAMPANULA PORTENSCHLAGIANA

The Dalmatian bellflower is a robust, mound-forming, evergreen perennial with long, bell-shaped, deep purple flowers from mid- to late summer. The leaves are toothed and mid-green. Good in a rock garden or on a sunny bank. May become invasive. *Campanula poschkarskyana* can be used in a similar way; look for the recommended cultivar 'Stella'.

CULTIVATION *Best in moist but well-drained soil, in sun or partial shade. Very vigorous, so plant away from smaller, less robust plants.*

☼ ◑ ◊ Z4-7 H7-1 ‡to 6in (15cm)
↔20in (50cm) or more

CAMPSIS × TAGLIABUANA 'MADAME GALEN'

Woody-stemmed climber that will cling with aerial roots against a wall, fence, or pillar, or up into a tree. From late summer to autumn, clusters of trumpet-shaped, orange-red flowers open among narrow, toothed leaves. For yellow flowers, choose *C. radicans* f. *flava*.

CULTIVATION *Prefers moist but well-drained, fertile soil, in a sunny, sheltered site. Tie in new growth until the allotted space is covered by a strong framework. Prune back hard each winter to promote bushiness.*

☼ ◊◊ Z5-9 H9-4   ‡30ft (10m) or more

CARDIOCRINUM GIGANTEUM

The giant lily is a spectacular, summer-flowering, bulbous perennial with trumpet-shaped white flowers that are flushed with maroon-purple at the throats. The stems are thick and the leaves broadly oval and glossy green. It needs careful siting and can take up to seven years to bloom. Grow in woodland or in a sheltered border in shade.

CULTIVATION *Best in deep, moist but well-drained, reliably cool, organic soil, in semi-shade. Intolerant of hot or dry conditions. Slugs can be a problem.*

☼ ◊ Z7-9 H9-7   ‡5–12ft (1.5–4m)
↔18in (45cm)

CAREX ELATA 'AUREA'

Bowles' golden sedge is a colorful, tussock-forming, deciduous perennial for a moist border, bog garden, or the margins of a pond or stream. The bright leaves are narrow and golden yellow. In spring and early summer, small spikes of relatively inconspicuous, dark brown flowers are carried above the leaves. Often sold as *C.* 'Bowles' Golden'.

CULTIVATION *Grow in moist or wet, reasonably fertile soil. Position in full sun or partial shade.*

☀☀ ◐◐ Z5-9 H9-3   ‡to 28in (70cm)
↔18in (45cm)

CAREX OSHIMENSIS 'EVERGOLD'

A very popular, evergreen, variegated sedge, bright and densely tufted with narrow, dark green, yellow-striped leaves. Spikes of tiny, dark brown flowers are borne in mid- and late spring. Tolerates freer drainage than many sedges and is suitable for a mixed border.

CULTIVATION *Needs moist but well drained, fertile soil, in sun or partial shade. Remove dead leaves in summer.*

☀☀ ◐ Z6-9 H9-4   ‡12in (30cm)
↔14in (35cm)

CARPENTERIA CALIFORNICA

This summer-flowering, evergreen shrub bears large, fragrant, white flowers with showy yellow stamens. The glossy, dark green leaves are narrowly oval. It is suitable for wall-training, which overcomes its sometimes sprawling habit. Where marginally hardy, protect it by growing it on a sheltered wall.

CULTIVATION *Grow in well-drained soil, in full sun with shelter from cold winds. In spring, remove branches that have become exhausted by flowering, cutting them back to their bases.*

☼ ◊ Z8-9 H12-8   ↕ ↔6ft (2m)

CARYOPTERIS X CLANDONENSIS 'HEAVENLY BLUE'

A compact, upright, deciduous shrub grown for its clusters of intensely dark blue flowers that appear in late summer and early autumn. The irregularly toothed leaves are gray-green.

CULTIVATION *Grow in well-drained, moderately fertile, light soil, in full sun. Prune all stems back hard to low buds in late spring. A woody framework will develop, which should not be cut into.*

☼ ◊ Z6-9 H9-4   ↕↔ 3ft (1m)

CASSIOPE 'EDINBURGH'

A heatherlike, upright, evergreen shrub producing nodding, bell-shaped flowers in spring; these are white with small, greenish brown outer petals. The scalelike, dark green leaves closely overlap along the stems. Good in a rock garden (not among limestone) or a peat bed. *C. lycopoides* (Z7 8, H8-7) has very similar flowers but is mat-forming, almost prostrate, only 3in (8cm) tall.

CULTIVATION *Grow in reliably moist, organic, acidic soil, in partial shade. Trim after flowering.*

☀ ◊ Z2-6 H6-1   ↔ to 10in (25cm)

CEANOTHUS ARBOREUS 'TREWITHEN BLUE'

A vigorous, spreading, evergreen shrub valued for its profusion of fragrant, mid-blue flowers in spring and early summer. The leaves are dark green and rounded. Where marginally hardy, grow against a wall; otherwise, this is suitable for a large, sheltered border

CULTIVATION *Grow in well-drained, fertile soil, in full sun with shelter from cold, drying winds. Tip-prune young plants in spring. Once established, prune only to shape, after flowering.*

☀ ◊ Z9-10 H10-8 ↕20ft (6m) ↔25ft (8m)

CEANOTHUS 'AUTUMNAL BLUE'

A vigorous, evergreen shrub that produces a profusion of tiny but vivid, rich sky blue flowers from late summer to autumn. The leaves are broadly oval and glossy dark green. One of the hardiest of the evergreen ceanothus, it is suitable in an open border as well as for informal training on walls; especially where marginally hardy.

CULTIVATION *Grow in well-drained, moderately fertile soil, in full sun with shelter from cold winds. Tip-prune young plants in spring, and trim established plants after flowering.*

☼ ◊ Z9-10 H10-8   ↕↔ 10ft (3m)

CEANOTHUS 'BLUE MOUND'

This mound-forming, late spring-flowering ceanothus is an evergreen shrub carrying masses of rich dark blue flowers. The leaves are finely toothed and glossy dark green. Ideal as a groundcover, for cascading over banks or low walls, or in a large, sunny rock garden. *Ceanothus* 'Burkwoodii' and 'Italian Skies' can be used similarly.

CULTIVATION *Grow in well-drained, fertile soil, in full sun. Tip-prune young plants and trim established ones after flowering, in mid-summer.*

☼ ◊ Z9-10 H10-8   ↕5ft (1.5m) ↔6ft (2m)

CEANOTHUS × DELILEANUS 'GLOIRE DE VERSAILLES'

This deciduous ceanothus is a fast-growing shrub. From mid-summer to early autumn, large spikes of tiny, pale blue flowers are borne amid broadly oval, finely toothed, mid-green leaves. 'Topaze' (Z9-10, H10-8) is similar, with dark blue flowers. They benefit from harder annual pruning than evergreen ceanothus.

CULTIVATION *Grow in well-drained, fairly fertile, light soil, in sun. Tolerates alkaline soil. In spring, shorten the previous year's stems by half or more, or cut right back to a low framework.*

☼ ◊ Z7-10 H10-8　↔5ft (1.5m)

CEANOTHUS THYRSIFLORUS VAR. REPENS

This low and spreading ceanothus is a mound-forming, evergreen shrub bearing rounded clusters of tiny blue flowers in late spring and early summer. The leaves are dark green and glossy. A good shrub to clothe a sunny or slightly shaded bank, provide the protection of a warm, sunny site where marginal.

CULTIVATION *Best in light, well-drained, fertile soil, in sun or light shade. Trim back after flowering to keep compact.*

☼◐ ◊ Z8-10 H10-8　↕3ft (1m) ↔8ft (2.5m)

CERATOSTIGMA PLUMBAGINOIDES

A spreading, woody-based, sub-shrubby perennial bearing clusters of brilliant blue flowers in late summer. The oval, bright green leaves, carried on upright, slender red stems, become red-tinted in autumn. Good for a rock garden, and also suitable as a groundcover.

CULTIVATION *Grow in light, moist but well-drained, moderately fertile soil. Choose a sheltered site in full sun. Cut back stems to the ground in late winter or early spring.*

☼ ◊ Z6-9 H9-6   ‡to 18in (45cm)
                              ↔to 12in (30cm) or more

CERATOSTIGMA WILLMOTTIANUM

The Chinese plumbago is an open and spreading, deciduous shrub bearing pale to mid-blue flowers during late summer and autumn. The roughly diamond-shaped, mid-green leaves turn red in autumn. Dies back in cold winters, but usually regenerates in spring. Good for a sheltered mixed border.

CULTIVATION *Grow in any fertile soil, including dry soil, in full sun. In mid-spring, cut out all dead wood and shorten the remaining stems to a low, woody framework.*

☼ ◊ Z6-9 H9-6   ‡3ft (1m) ↔(1.5m)

CERCIS SILIQUASTRUM

The Judas tree is a handsome, broadly spreading, deciduous tree that gradually develops a rounded crown. Clusters of pealike, bright pink flowers appear on the previous year's wood, either before or with the heart-shaped leaves in mid-spring. The foliage is bronze when young, maturing to dark blue-green, then to yellow in autumn. Flowering is best after a long, hot summer.

CULTIVATION *Grow in deep, reliably well-drained, fertile soil, in full sun or light dappled shade. Prune young trees to shape in early summer, removing any frost-damaged growth.*

☼☀ ◊ Z6-9 H9-6   ↔ 30ft (10m)

CHAENOMELES SPECIOSA
'MOERLOOSEI'

A fast-growing and wide-spreading, deciduous shrub bearing large white flowers, flushed dark pink, in early spring. Tangled, spiny branches bear oval, glossy dark green leaves. The flowers are followed in autumn by apple-shaped, aromatic, yellow-green fruits. Use as a free-standing shrub or train against a wall.

CULTIVATION *Grow in well-drained, moderately fertile soil, in full sun for best flowering, or light shade. If wall-trained, shorten sideshoots to 2 or 3 leaves in late spring. Free-standing shrubs require little pruning.*

☼☀ ◊ Z5-8 H8-5 ↕8ft (2.5m) ↔15ft (5m)

CHAENOMELES × SUPERBA 'CRIMSON AND GOLD'

This spreading, deciduous shrub bears masses of dark red flowers with conspicuous golden yellow anthers from spring until summer. The dark green leaves appear on the spiny branches just after the first bloom of flowers; these are followed by yellow-green fruits. Useful as a groundcover or low hedging.

CULTIVATION *Grow in well-drained, fertile soil, in sun. Trim lightly after flowering; shorten sideshoots to 2 or 3 leaves if grown against a wall.*

☼ ◊ Z5-8 H9-4   ‡3ft (1m) ↔6ft (2m)

CHAENOMELES × SUPERBA 'PINK LADY'

A rounded, deciduous shrub with spiny, spreading branches that bear cup-shaped, dark pink flowers from early spring. The glossy, dark green leaves appear after the first bloom of flowers; aromatic, yellow-green fruits follow in autumn. Grow against a wall for extra protection.

CULTIVATION *Grow in any but water-logged soil, in full sun or partial shade. Trim back after flowering, as necessary. If grown against a wall, shorten side-shoots to 2 or 3 leaves, in summer.*

☼ ◊◊ Z5-8 H9-4   ‡5ft (1.5m) ↔6ft (2m)

LAWSON CYPRESSES *(CHAMAECYPARIS LAWSONIANA)*

Cultivars of *C. lawsoniana* are popular evergreen conifers, available in many different shapes, sizes, and foliage colors. All have red-brown bark and dense crowns of branches that droop at the tips. The flattened sprays of dense, aromatic foliage, occasionally bearing small, rounded cones, make the larger types of Lawson cypress very suitable for thick hedging, such as bright blue-gray 'Pembury Blue', or golden yellow 'Lane'. Use compact cultivars in smaller gardens such as 'Ellwoodii' (to 10ft/3m)

and 'Ellwood's Gold'; dwarf upright types such as 'Chilworth Silver' make eye-catching feature plants for containers, rock gardens, or borders.

CULTIVATION *Grow in moist but well-drained soil, in sun. They tolerate alkaline soil but not exposed sites. Trim regularly from spring to autumn; do not cut into older wood. To train as formal hedges, pruning must begin on young plants.*

☼ ◊ Z5-9 H9-3

1 ↕ 5ft (1.5m) ↔ 24in (60cm) **2** ↕ to 130ft (40m) ↔ to 15ft (5m) **3** ↕ to 50ft (15m) ↔ 6-15ft (2–5m)

1 *C. lawsoniana* 'Ellwood's Gold' **2** *C. lawsoniana* 'Lane' **3** *C. lawsoniana* 'Pembury Blue'

CHAMAECYPARIS NOOTKATENSIS 'PENDULA'

This large and drooping conifer develops a gaunt, open crown as it matures. Hanging from the arching branches are evergreen sprays of dark green foliage with small, round cones that ripen in spring. Its unusual habit makes an interesting feature for a large garden.

CULTIVATION *Best in full sun, in moist but well-drained, neutral to slightly acidic soil; will also tolerate dry, alkaline soil.* .

☼ ◊◊ Z4-7 H7-1   ‡to 100ft (30m)
↔to 25ft (8m)

CHAMAECYPARIS OBTUSA 'NANA GRACILIS'

This dwarf form of Hinoki cypress is an evergreen, coniferous tree with a dense pyramidal habit. The aromatic, rich green foliage is carried in rounded, flattened sprays, bearing small cones that ripen to yellow-brown. Useful in a large rock garden, particularly to give Oriental style. 'Nana Aurea' (Z5-8, H8-3) looks very similar but grows to only half the size.

CULTIVATION *Grow in moist but well-drained, neutral to slightly acidic soil, in full sun. Also tolerates dry, alkaline soil. Regular pruning is not necessary.*

☼ ◊ Z4-8 H8-1   ‡10ft (3m) ↔6ft (2m)

CHAMAECYPARIS OBTUSA 'TETRAGONA AUREA'

This cultivar of Hinoki cypress, with golden to bronze-yellow, evergreen foliage, is a conical, coniferous tree. The aromatic foliage, carried in flattened sprays on upward-sweeping stems, is greener in the shade, and bears small green cones that ripen to brown. Grow as a specimen tree.

CULTIVATION *Best in moist but well-drained, neutral to slightly acidic soil. Tolerates alkaline conditions. For the best foliage color, position in full sun. No regular pruning is required.*

☼ ◊ Z4-8 H7-1 ‡30ft (10m) ↔10ft (3m)

CHAMAECYPARIS PISIFERA 'BOULEVARD'

A broad, evergreen conifer that develops into a conical tree with an open crown. The soft, blue-green foliage is borne in flattened sprays with angular green cones, maturing to brown. Very neat and compact in habit; this makes an excellent specimen tree for poorly drained, damp soil.

CULTIVATION *Grow in reliably moist, preferably neutral to acidic soil, in full sun. No regular pruning is required.*

☼ ◊◊ Z4-8 H8-1 ‡30ft (10m) ↔15ft (5m)

CHIMONANTHUS PRAECOX 'GRANDIFLORUS'

Wintersweet is a vigorous, upright, deciduous shrub grown for the fragrant flowers borne on its bare branches in winter; on this cultivar they are large, cup-shaped, and deep yellow with maroon stripes inside. The leaves are mid-green. Suitable for a shrub border or for training against a sunny wall.

CULTIVATION *Grow in well-drained, fertile soil, in a sunny, sheltered site. Best left unpruned when young so that mature flowering wood can develop. Cut back flowered stems of wall-trained plants in spring.*

☼ ◊ Z7-9 H9-7   ‡12ft (4m) ↔10ft (3m)

CHIONODOXA LUCILIAE

Glory of the snow is a small, bulbous perennial bearing star-shaped, clear blue flowers with white eyes in early spring. The glossy green leaves are usually curved backward. Grow in a sunny rock garden, or naturalize under deciduous trees. Sometimes referred to as *C. gigantea* of gardens. *C. forbesii* (Z3-9, H9-1) is very similar, with more erect leaves.

CULTIVATION *Grow in any well-drained soil, with a position in full sun. Plant bulbs 3in (8cm) deep in autumn.*

☼ ◊ Z3-9 H9-1 ‡6in (15cm) ↔1¼in (3cm)

CHOISYA TERNATA

Mexican orange blossom is a fast-growing, rounded, evergreen shrub valued for its attractive foliage and fragrant flowers. The aromatic, dark green leaves are divided into three. Clusters of star-shaped white flowers appear in spring. A fine, pollution-tolerant shrub for town gardens, but prone to frost damage in exposed sites. 'Aztec Pearl' is similar, its flowers perhaps not quite as fragrant.

CULTIVATION *Grow in well-drained, fairly fertile soil, in full sun. Naturally forms a well-shaped bush without pruning. Cutting back flowered shoots encourages a second flush of flowers.*

☼ ◊ Z8-10 Z10-8   ↨↔ 8ft (2.5m)

CHOISYA TERNATA 'SUNDANCE'

This slower-growing, bright yellow-leaved variety of Mexican orange blossom is a compact, evergreen shrub. The aromatic leaves, divided into three leaflets, are a duller yellow-green if positioned in shade. Flowers are rare.

CULTIVATION *Best in well-drained, fertile soil, in full sun for the best leaf color. Provide shelter from cold winds. Trim wayward shoots in summer, removing any frost-damaged shoots in spring.*

☼ ◊ Z8-10 H10-8   ↨↔ 8ft (2.5m)

GARDEN CHRYSANTHEMUMS

These upright, bushy perennials are a mainstay of the late border, with bright, showy flowerheads traditionally used for display and cutting. The lobed or feathery leaves are aromatic and bright green. They flower from late summer to mid-autumn, depending on the cultivar; very late-flowering cultivars are best raised under glass in colder climates (see p.125). The flower form, often many-petaled, varies from the daisylike 'Pennine Alfie' to the blowsy, reflexed blooms of 'George Griffith'.

Lift in autumn and store over winter in frost-free conditions. Plant out after any risk of frost has passed.

CULTIVATION *Grow in moist but well-drained, neutral to slightly acidic soil enriched with well-rotted manure, in a sunny, sheltered site. Stake tall flower stems. Apply a balanced fertilizer when in growth, until flower buds begin to show.*

☀ ◊◊ Z3-9 H9-1

1 ↕4ft (1.2m) ↔ 30in (75cm)   **2** ↕4ft (1.2m) ↔ 30in (75 cm)   **3** ↕3ft (1m) ↔ 24-30in (60–75cm)

4 ↕20in (50cm) ↔ 10in (25cm)   **5** ↕↔ 24in (60cm)   **6** ↕3½ft (1.1m) ↔ 24-30 in (60–75cm)

1 *Chrysanthemum* 'Amber Enbee Wedding' **2** *C.* 'Amber Yvonne Arnaud'
3 *C.* 'Angora' **4** *C.* 'Bravo' **5** *C.* 'Bronze Fairie' **6** *C.* 'Cherry Nathalie'

7 ‡3½ft (1m) ↔ 24–30 in (60–75cm)

8 ‡30in (90cm) ↔ 12in (30cm)

9 ‡4½–5ft (1.3–1.5m) ↔ 30in (75cm)

10 ‡4ft (1.2m) ↔ 30in (75cm)

11 ‡30in (90cm) ↔ 12in (30cm)

12 ‡24in (60cm) ↔ 12in (30cm)

13 ‡30in (90cm) ↔ 12in (30cm)

14 ‡4ft (1.2m) ↔ 30in (75cm)

15 ‡4ft (1.2m) ↔ 30in (75cm)

7 *C.* 'Eastleigh' **8** *C.* 'Flo Cooper' **9** *C.* 'George Griffiths' **10** *C.* 'Madeleine'
11 *C.* 'Mancetta Bride' **12** *C.* 'Mavis' **13** *C.* 'Myss Madi' **14** *C.* 'Pennine Alfie'
15 *C.* 'Pennine Flute'

16 ↕28in (70cm) ↔ 10in (30cm)

17 ↕25in (65cm) ↔ 12in (30cm)

18 ↕4ft (1.2m) ↔ 24–30in (60–75cm)

19 ↕3ft (1m) ↔ 18in (45cm)

20 ↕4ft(1.2m) ↔ 30in (75cm)

21 ↕↔ 24in (30–60cm)

22 ↕4ft (1.2m) ↔ 24-30in (60–75cm)

23 ↕34in (85cm) ↔ 18in (45cm)

MORE CHOICES

'Margaret' Pink, with
reflexed petals.
'Max Riley' Yellow.
'Pennine Signal' Scarlet.
'Yellow Pennine Oriel'
Sprays of small yellow
flowers.

24 ↕4ft (1.2m) ↔ 30in (75cm)

25 ↕4ft (1.2m) ↔ 24-30in (60–75cm)

16 *Chrysanthemum* 'Pennine Lace' **17** *C.* 'Pennine Marie' **18** *C.* 'Pennine Oriel'
19 *C.* 'Primrose Allouise' **20** *C.* 'Purple Pennine Wine' **21** *C.* 'Salmon Fairie'
22 *C.* 'Salmon Margaret' **23** *C.* 'Southway Swan' **24** *C.* 'Wendy' **25** *C.* 'Yvonne Arnaud'

LATE-FLOWERING CHRYSANTHEMUMS

This group of herbaceous perennials comes into flower from autumn into winter, which means that the protection of a greenhouse during this time is essential in cold areas. None can tolerate frost, but they can be moved outdoors during summer. The showy flowerheads come in a wide range of shapes and sizes and are available in a blaze of golds, bronzes, yellows, oranges, pinks, and reds. Protection from the elements enables perfect blooms for exhibition to be nurtured.

Grow late-flowering chrysanthemums in containers or in a greenhouse border.

CULTIVATION *Best in a good soil-based potting mix, kept slightly moist at all times, in bright, filtered light. Stake plants as they grow, and give liquid fertilizer until flower buds begin to form. Ensure adequate ventilation and a min. temp. of 50°F (10°C). In frost-free areas, grow outdoors in fertile, moist but well-drained soil in full sun.*

☼ ◊◊ Z3-9 H9-1

1 ↕4ft (1.2m) ↔ 24in (60cm)

3 ↕4½ft (1.4m) ↔ 24in (60cm)

2 ↕5ft (1.5m) ↔ 24in (60cm)

MORE CHOICES

'Apricot Shoesmith Salmon'
'Bronze Cassandra'
'Dark Red Mayford Perfection'
'Pink Gin' Light purple.
'Rose Mayford Perfection'
'Rynoon' Light pink.

4 ↕4ft (1.2m) ↔ 30-39in (75–100cm)

5 ↕4ft (1.2m) ↔ 24-30in (60–75cm)

1 *Chrysanthemum* 'Beacon' **2** *C.* 'Golden Cassandra'
3 *C.* 'Roy Coopland' **4** *C.* 'Satin Pink Gin' **5** *C.* 'Yellow John Hughes'

CIMICIFUGA RACEMOSA

Black snakeroot is a clump-forming perennial that produces long spikes of strongly scented, tiny white flowers in mid-summer. The dark green leaves are broadly oval to lance-shaped. Plant in a bog garden, moist border, or light woodland *C. simplex* 'Elstead' (Z4-8, H8-1) does not have the scent problem but is much less imposing, to only 3ft (1m) tall.

CULTIVATION *Grow in reliably moist, fertile, preferably organic soil, in partial shade. Provide clumps with support, using ring stakes or similar.*

☀ ◑ ◊ Z3-8 H8-1   ‡4–7ft (1.2–2.2m)
↔24in (60cm)

CISTUS × AGUILARII 'MACULATUS'

This fast-growing, evergreen shrub bears large, solitary white flowers for a few weeks in early and mid-summer. At the center of each flower is a mass of bright golden yellow stamens surrounded by five crimson blotches. The lance-shaped leaves are sticky, aromatic, and bright green. Excellent on a sunny bank or in containers.

CULTIVATION *Grow in well-drained, poor to moderately fertile soil, in a sunny, sheltered site. Tolerates alkaline soil. If necessary, trim lightly (not hard) in early spring or after flowering.*

☀ ◊ Z9-10 H10-8   ‡↔4ft (1.2m)

CISTUS × HYBRIDUS

A dense, spreading shrub producing
white flowers with yellow blotches
at the centers. These are borne singly
or in clusters of two or three during
late spring and early summer. The
aromatic leaves are wrinkled, oval,
and dark green. Suitable for a shrub
border or rock garden; it benefits
from the protection of a wall where
marginally hardy. Sometimes known
as *C.* × *corbariensis*.

CULTIVATION *Grow in well-drained,
poor to moderately fertile soil, in a
sheltered site in full sun. Tolerates
alkaline soil. If necessary, trim lightly
after flowering, but do not prune hard.*

☼ ◊ Z8-10 H8-1　‡3ft (1m) ↔5ft (1.5m)

CISTUS × PURPUREUS

This summer-flowering, rounded,
evergreen shrub bears few-flowered
clusters of dark pink flowers with
maroon blotches at the base of each
petal. The dark green leaves are
borne on upright, sticky, red-flushed
shoots. Good in a large rock garden,
on a sunny bank, or in a container.

CULTIVATION *Grow in well-drained,
poor to moderately fertile soil. Choose a
sheltered site in full sun. Tolerates
alkaline soil. Can be trimmed lightly
after flowering; avoid hard pruning.*

☼ ◊ Z9-10 H10-8　‡↔3ft (1m)

EARLY-FLOWERING CLEMATIS

The early-flowering species clematis are valued for their showy displays during spring and early summer. They are generally deciduous climbers with mid- to dark green, divided leaves. The flowers of the earliest species to bloom are usually bell-shaped; those of the later *C. montana* types are either flat or saucer-shaped. Flowers are often followed by decorative seedheads. Many clematis, especially *C. montana* types, are vigorous and will grow very quickly, making them ideal for covering featureless or unattractive walls. Allowed to grow through deciduous shrubs, they may flower before their host comes into leaf.

CULTIVATION *Grow in well-drained, fertile, organic soil, in full sun or semi-shade. The roots and base of the plant should be shaded. Immediately after flowering, tie in young growth carefully and prune out shoots that exceed the allotted space.*

☼☼ ◊ Z6-9 H9-6

1 ‡6–10ft (2–3m) ↔ 1.5m (5ft)

2 ‡2–3m (6–10ft) ↔ 5ft (1.5m)

3 ‡30ft (10m) ↔ 12ft (4m)

MORE CHOICES

C. alpina 'White Columbine' White flowers.

C. alpina 'Helsingborg' Deep blue and brown

C. cirrhosa var. *balearica* and *C. cirrhosa* 'Freckles' Cream flowers speckled with pinkish brown. Z7-9

4 ‡30ft (10m) ↔ 6-10ft (2–3m)

5 ‡15ft (5m) ↔ 6-10ft (2–3m)

1 *Clematis alpina* 'Frances Rivis' 2 *C. macropetala* 'Markham's Pink'
3 *C. montana* f. *grandiflora* 4 *C. montana* var. *rubens* 5 *C. montana* var. *rubens* 'Tetrarose'

MID-SEASON CLEMATIS

The mid-season, mainly hybrid clematis are twining and deciduous climbers, bearing an abundance of stunning flowers throughout the summer months. Their flowers are large, saucer-shaped, and outward-facing, with a plentiful choice of shapes and colors. Toward the end of the summer, blooms may darken. The leaves are pale to mid-green and divided into several leaflets. Mid-season clematis look very attractive scrambling through other shrubs, especially if they bloom before or after their host. Topgrowth may be damaged in severe winters, but plants are usually quick to recover.

CULTIVATION *Grow in well-drained, fertile, organic soil, with the roots in shade and the heads in sun. Pastel flowers may fade in sun; better in semi-shade. Mulch in late winter, avoiding the immediate crown. Cut back older stems to strong buds in late winter, and tie in young growth carefully.*

☼◑ ◊ Z4-9 H9-1

1 ↕8ft (2.5m) ↔ 3ft (1m)

2 ↕8ft (2.5m) ↔ 3ft (1m)

3 ↕6–10ft (2–3m) ↔ 3ft (1m)

1 *Clematis* 'Bees' Jubilee' **2** *C.* 'Doctor Ruppel' **3** *C.* 'Elsa Späth'

5 ‡to 10ft (3m) ↔ 3ft (1m)

6 ‡8ft (2.5m) ↔ 3ft (1m)

7 ‡8ft (2.5m) ↔ 3ft (1m)

8 ‡10ft (3m) ↔ 3ft (1m)

9 ‡8ft (2.5m) ↔ 3ft (1m)

10 ‡10ft (3m) ↔ 3ft (1m)

11 ‡8ft (2.5m) ↔ 3ft (1m)

12 ‡6–10ft (2–3m) ↔ 3ft (1m)

5 *C.* 'Fireworks' **6** *C.* 'Gillian Blades' **7** *C.* 'H. F. Young' **8** *C.* 'Henryi'
9 *C.* 'Lasurstern' **10** *C.* 'Marie Boisselot' **11** *C.* 'Miss Bateman' **12** *C.* 'Nelly Moser'

13 ‡6–10ft (2–3m) ↔ 3ft (1m)

14 ‡6–10ft (2–3m) ↔ 3ft (1m)

15 ‡6ft (2m) ↔ 3ft (1m)

16 ‡6ft (2m) ↔ 3ft (1m)

MORE CHOICES

'Lord Nevill' Deep blue
flowers with purple-red
anthers.

'Mrs Cholmondely'
Lavender; brown anthers.

'Will Goodwin' Pale blue
with yellow anthers.

17 ‡6–10ft (2–3m) ↔ 3ft (1m)

18 ‡6–10ft (2–3m) ↔ 3ft (1m)

13 *C.* 'Niobe' **14** *C.* 'Richard Pennell' **15** *C.* 'Royalty'
16 *C.* 'Silver Moon' **17** *C.* 'The President' **18** *C.* 'Vyvyan Pennell'

LATE-FLOWERING CLEMATIS

Many large-flowered hybrid clematis flower from mid- to late summer, when the season for the *C. viticella* types, characterized usually by smaller but more profuse flowers, also begins. These are followed by other late-flowering species. They may be deciduous or evergreen, with an enormous variety of flower and leaf shapes and colors. Many, like 'Perle d'Azur', are vigorous and will cover large areas of wall or disguise unsightly buildings. Some develop decorative, silvery-gray seedheads that last well into winter. With the exception of 'Bill Mackenzie', most look good when trained up into small trees.

CULTIVATION *Grow in organic, fertile soil with good drainage, with the base in shade and the upper part in sun or partial shade. Mulch in late winter, avoiding the crown. Each year in early spring, cut back hard before growth begins.*

☼◐ ◊ Z6-9

1 ‡12ft (4m) ↔ 5ft (1.5m)

2 ‡22ft (7m) ↔ 6–10ft (2–3m)

3 ‡8ft (2.5m) ↔ 5ft (1.5m)

1 *C.* 'Alba Luxurians' 2 *C.* 'Bill Mackenzie' 3 *C.* 'Duchess of Albany'

4 ‡6–10ft (2–3m) ↔ 3ft (1m)

5 ‡10–15ft (3–5m) ↔ 5ft (1.5m)

6 ‡10ft (3m) ↔ 3ft (1m)

7 ‡10ft (3m) ↔ 5ft (1.5m)

8 ‡10ft (3m) ↔ 3ft (1m)

9 ‡10ft (3m) ↔ 3ft (1m)

10 ‡10ft (3m) ↔ 3ft (1m)

11 ‡10ft (3m) ↔ 3ft (1m)

12 ‡20 (6m) ↔ 10ft (3m)

4 *C.* 'Comtesse de Bouchaud' **5** *C.* 'Etoile Violette' **6** *C.* 'Jackmanii' **7** *C.* 'Madame Julia Correvon' **8** *C.* 'Minuet' **9** *C.* 'Perle d'Azur' **10** *C.* 'Venosa Violacea' **11** *C. viticella* 'Purpurea Plena Elegans' **12** *C. rehderiana*

CLIANTHUS PUNICEUS

Lobster claw is an evergreen, woody-stemmed, climbing shrub with scrambling shoots. Drooping clusters of clawlike, brilliant red flowers appear in spring and early summer. (The cultivar 'Albus' has pure white flowers.) The mid-green leaves are divided into many oblong leaflets. Suitable for wall-training. It grows nicely under glass where not hardy.

CULTIVATION *Grow in well-drained, fairly fertile soil, in sun with shelter from wind. Pinch-prune young plants to promote bushiness; otherwise, keep pruning to a minimum.*

☼ ◊ Z7-11 H12-7 ‡12ft(4m) ↔10ft (3m)

CODONOPSIS CONVOLVULACEA

A slender, herbaceous, summer-flowering climber with twining stems that bears delicate, bell- to saucer-shaped, soft blue-violet flowers. The leaves are lance-shaped to oval and bright green. Grow in a herbaceous border or woodland garden, scrambling through other plants.

CULTIVATION *Grow in moist but well-drained, light, fertile soil, ideally in dappled shade. Provide support or grow through neighboring shrubs. Cut to the base in spring.*

☼ ◊◊ Z7-9 H9-7 ‡to 6ft(2m)

COLCHICUM SPECIOSUM 'ALBUM'

While *Colchicum speciosum*, the autumn crocus, has pink flowers, this cultivar is white. A cormous perennial, it produces thick, weather-resistant, goblet-shaped, snow-white blooms in autumn; its narrow, mid-green leaves appear in spring and die down in early summer. Grow at the front of a border, at the foot of a bank, or in a rock garden. All parts are highly toxic if ingested.

CULTIVATION *Grow in moist but well-drained soil, in full sun. Plant bulbs in late summer, 4in (10cm) below the surface of soil that is deep and fertile.*

☼ ◊ Z4-9 H9-1 ‡7in (18cm) ↔4in (10cm)

CONVALLARIA MAJALIS

Lily-of-the-valley is a creeping perennial bearing small, very fragrant white flowers that hang from arching stems in late spring or early summer. The narrowly oval leaves are mid- to dark green. An excellent groundcover plant for woodland gardens and other shady areas, although it will spread rapidly under suitable conditions.

CULTIVATION *Grow in reliably moist, fertile, organic, leafy soil in deep or partial shade. Topdress with leaf mold in autumn.*

☼☼ ◊ Z2-7 H7-1 ‡9in (23cm) ↔indefinite

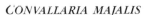

CONVOLVULUS CNEORUM

This compact, rounded, evergreen shrub bears masses of funnel-shaped, shining white flowers with yellow centers that open from late spring to summer. The narrowly lance-shaped leaves are silvery green. Excellent as a larger plant in a rock garden, or on a sunny bank. Where not hardy, grow in a container and move into a cool greenhouse in winter.

CULTIVATION *Grow in gritty, very well-drained, poor to moderately fertile soil, in a sunny, sheltered site. Trim back after flowering, if necessary.*

☼ ◊ Z8-10 H10-8 ↔36in (90cm)

CONVOLVULUS SABATIUS

A small, trailing perennial bearing trumpet-shaped, vibrant blue-purple flowers from summer into early autumn. The slender stems are clothed with small, oval, mid-green leaves. Excellent in crevices between rocks; where marginally hardy, it is best grown in containers with shelter under glass during the winter. Sometimes seen as *C. mauritanicus.*

CULTIVATION *Grow in well-drained, gritty, poor to moderately fertile soil. Provide a sheltered site in full sun.*

☼ ◊ Z8-9 H9-8 ‡6in (15cm) ↔20in (50cm)

CORDYLINE AUSTRALIS 'ALBERTII'

This New Zealand cabbage palm is a palmlike, evergreen tree carrying lance-shaped, matte green leaves with red midribs, cream stripes, and pink margins. Clusters of creamy white flowers appear on mature specimens in summer, followed by white or blue-tinted berries. Where not hardy, grow in a large container for standing out during the warmer months.

CULTIVATION *Best in well-drained, fertile soil or soil mix, in sun or partial shade. Remove dead leaves and cut out faded flower stems as necessary.*

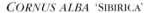

☼☀◑ ◊ Z10-11 H12-1 ‡30ft (10m) ↔12ft (4m)

CORNUS ALBA 'SIBIRICA'

A deciduous shrub that is usually grown for the winter effect of its bright coral-red, bare young stems. Small clusters of creamy white flowers appear in late spring and early summer amid oval, dark green leaves that turn red in autumn. Particularly effective in a waterside planting or any situation where the winter stems show off well.

CULTIVATION *Grow in any moderately fertile soil, in sun. For the best stem effect, cut back hard and feed every spring once established, although this will be at the expense of the flowers.*

☼ ◊◊ Z2-8 H8-1 ↔ 10ft (3m)

CORNUS ALBA 'SPAETHII'

A vigorous and upright, deciduous shrub bearing bright green, elliptic leaves that are margined with yellow. It is usually grown for the effect of its bright red young shoots in winter. In late spring and early summer, small clusters of creamy white flowers appear amid the foliage. Very effective wherever the stems show off well in winter.

CULTIVATION *Grow in any moderately fertile soil, preferably in full sun. For the best stem effect, but at the expense of any flowers, cut back hard and feed each year in spring, once established.*

☼ ◊◊ Z2-8 H8-1   ↔ 10ft (3m)

CORNUS CANADENSIS

The creeping dogwood is a superb groundcover perennial for under-planting a shrub border or wood-land garden. Flower clusters with prominent white bracts appear above the oval, bright green leaves during late spring and early summer. These are followed by round, bright red berries.

CULTIVATION *Best in moist, acidic, leafy soil in partial shade. Divide plants in spring or autumn to restrict spread or increase plants.*

☼ ◊ Z2-7 H7-1   ↕ 6in (15cm) ↔ indefinite

CORNUS KOUSA
VAR. *CHINENSIS*

This broadly conical, deciduous tree with flaky bark is valued for its dark green, oval leaves that turn an impressive, deep crimson-purple in autumn. The early summer flowers have long white bracts, fading to red-pink. An effective specimen tree, especially in a woodland setting. *C. kousa* 'Satomi' has even deeper autumn color and pink flower bracts.

CULTIVATION *Best in well-drained, fertile, organic, neutral to acidic soil, in full sun or partial shade. Keep pruning to a minimum.*

☼ ◐ ◊ Z5-8 H8-4 ‡22ft (7m) ↔15ft (5m)

CORNUS MAS

The Cornelian cherry is a vigorous and spreading, deciduous shrub or small tree. Clusters of small yellow flowers provide attractive late winter color on the bare branches. The oval, dark green leaves turn red-purple in autumn, giving a display at the same time as the fruits ripen to red. Particularly fine as a specimen tree for a woodland garden.

CULTIVATION *Tolerates any well-drained soil, in sun or partial shade. Pruning is best kept to a minimum.*

☼ ◐ ◊ Z5-8 H8-4 ‡↔ 15ft (5m)

CORNUS STOLONIFERA 'FLAVIRAMEA'

This vigorous, deciduous shrub makes a bright display of its bare yellow-green young shoots in winter, before the oval, dark green leaves emerge in spring. Clusters of white flowers appear in late spring and early summer. The leaves redden in autumn. Excellent in a bog garden or in wet soil near water.

CULTIVATION *Grow in reliably moist soil, in full sun. Restrict spread by cutting out 1 in 4 old stems annually. Prune all stems hard and feed each year in early spring for the best display of winter stems.*

☼ ◑ Z2-8 H8-1   ‡6ft (2m) ↔12ft (4m)

CORREA BACKHOUSEANA

The Australian fuchsia is a dense, spreading, evergreen shrub with small clusters of tubular, pale red-green or cream flowers during late autumn to late spring. The hairy, rust-red stems are clothed with oval, dark green leaves. Where not hardy, grow against a warm wall or over-winter in frost-free conditions. *Correa* 'Mannii', with red flowers, is also recommended.

CULTIVATION *Grow in well drained, fertile, acidic to neutral soil, in full sun. Trim back after flowering, if necessary.*

☼ ◑ Z9-10 H10-8   ‡3–6ft (1–2m)
↔5–8ft (1.5–2.5m)

CORTADERIA SELLOANA 'AUREOLINEATA'

This pampas grass, with rich yellow-margined, arching leaves that age to dark golden yellow, is a clump-forming, evergreen perennial. Feathery plumes of silvery flowers appear on tall stems in late summer. The flowerheads can be dried for decoration. Also known as 'Gold Band'.

CULTIVATION *Grow in well-drained, fertile soil, in full sun. In late winter, cut out all dead foliage and remove the previous year's flower stems: wear gloves to protect hands from the sharp foliage.*

☼ ◊ Z7-10 H12-7   ‡to 7ft (2.2m)
                  ↔5ft (1.5m) or more

CORTADERIA SELLOANA 'SUNNINGDALE SILVER'

This sturdy pampas grass is a clump-forming, evergreen, weather-resistant perennial. In late summer, silky plumes of silvery cream flowers are borne on strong, upright stems above the narrow, arching, sharp-edged leaves. Where marginal, protect the crown with a winter mulch.

CULTIVATION *Grow in well-drained, fertile, not too heavy soil, in full sun. Remove old flower stems and any dead foliage in late winter: wear gloves to protect hands from the sharp foliage.*

☼ ◊ Z7-10 H12-7   ‡10ft (3m) or more
                  ↔to 8ft (2.5m)

CORYDALIS SOLIDA 'GEORGE BAKER'

A low, clump-forming, herbaceous perennial bearing upright spires of deep salmon-rose flowers. These appear in spring above the delicate, finely cut, grayish green leaves. Excellent in a rock garden or in an alpine house.

CULTIVATION *Grow in sharply drained, moderately fertile soil or soil mix. Site in full sun, but tolerates some shade.*

☼ ◊ Z5-7 H7-5   ‡to 10in (25cm)
↔to 8in (20cm)

CORYLOPSIS PAUCIFLORA

This deciduous shrub bears hanging, catkinlike clusters of small, fragrant, pale yellow flowers on its bare branches during early to mid-spring. The oval, bright green leaves are bronze when they first emerge. Often naturally well-shaped, it makes a beautiful shrub for sites in dappled shade. The flowers may be damaged by frost.

CULTIVATION *Grow in moist but well-drained, orrganic, acidic soil, in partial shade with shelter from wind. Allow room for the plant to spread. The natural shape is easily spoiled, so prune only to remove dead wood.*

☼ ◊◊ Z6-9 H9-6 ‡5ft (1.5m) ↔8ft (2.5m)

CORYLUS AVELLANA 'CONTORTA'

The corkscrew hazel is a deciduous shrub bearing strongly twisted shoots that are particularly striking in winter; they can also be useful in flower arrangements. Winter interest is enhanced later in the season with the appearance of pale yellow catkins. The mid-green leaves are almost circular and toothed.

CULTIVATION *Grow in any well-drained, fertile soil, in sun or semi-shade. Once established, the twisted branches tend to become congested and may split, so thin out in late winter.*

☼☀ ◊ Z3-9 H9-1   ↔ 50ft (15m)

CORYLUS MAXIMA 'PURPUREA'

The purple filbert is a vigorous, open, deciduous shrub that, left unpruned, will grow into a small tree. In late winter, purplish catkins appear before the rounded, purple leaves emerge. The edible nuts ripen in autumn. Effective as a specimen tree, in a shrub border, or as part of a woodland planting.

CULTIVATION *Grow in any well-drained, fertile soil, in sun or partial shade. For the best leaf effect, but at the expense of the nuts, cut back hard in early spring.*

☼☀ ◊ Z4-9 H9-2 ↕20ft (6m) ↔15ft (5m)

COSMOS BIPINNATUS
'SONATA WHITE'

A branching but compact annual bearing single, saucer-shaped white flowers with yellow centers from summer to autumn at the tips of upright stems. The leaves are bright green and feathery. Excellent for exposed gardens. The flowers are good for cutting.

CULTIVATION *Grow in moist but well-drained, fertile soil, in full sun. Deadhead to prolong flowering.*

☼ ◐◐ annual H12-1   ↕↔ 12in (30cm)

COTINUS COGGYGRIA
'ROYAL PURPLE'

This deciduous shrub is grown for its rounded, red-purple leaves that turn a brilliant scarlet in autumn. Smokelike plumes of tiny, pink-purple flowers are produced on older wood, but only in areas with long, hot summers. Good in a shrub border or as a specimen tree, where space permits, plant in groups.

CULTIVATION *Grow in moist but well-drained, fairly fertile soil, in full sun or partial shade. For the best foliage effect, cut back hard to a framework of older wood each spring, before growth begins.*

☼☀ ◐◐ Z5-8 H8-3   ↕↔ 15ft (5m)

COTINUS 'GRACE'

A fast-growing, deciduous shrub
or small tree carrying oval, purple
leaves that turn a brilliant,
translucent red in late autumn. The
smokelike clusters of tiny, pink-
purple flowers appear in abundance
only during hot summers. Effective
on its own or in a border. For green
leaves during the summer but
equally brilliant autumn foliage
color, look for *Cotinus* 'Flame'.

CULTIVATION *Grow in moist but well-
drained, reasonably rich soil, in sun or
partial shade. The best foliage is seen
after hard pruning each spring, just
before new growth begins.*

☼☀ ◊◊ Z5-8 H8-4 ‡20ft (6m) ↔15ft (5m)

COTONEASTER ATROPURPUREUS 'VARIEGATUS'

This compact, low-growing shrub,
sometimes seen as *C. horizontalis*
'Variegatus', has fairly inconspicuous
red flowers in summer, followed in
autumn by a bright display of orange-
red fruits. The small, oval, white-
margined, deciduous leaves also
give autumn color, turning pink and
red before they drop. Effective as a
groundcover or in a rock garden.

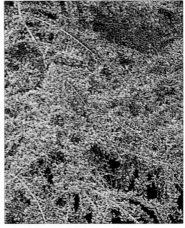

CULTIVATION *Grow in well-drained,
moderately fertile soil, in full sun.
Tolerates dry soil and partial shade.
Pruning is best kept to a minimum.*

☼☀ ◊ Z5-7 H7-5 ‡18in (45cm) ↔36in (90cm)

COTONEASTER CONSPICUUS 'DECORUS'

A dense, mound-forming, evergreen shrub that is grown for its shiny red berries. These ripen in autumn and will often persist until late winter. Small white flowers appear amid the dark green leaves in summer. Good in a shrub border or under a canopy of deciduous trees.

CULTIVATION *Grow in well-drained, moderately fertile soil, ideally in full sun, but tolerates shade. If necessary, trim lightly to shape after flowering.*

☼☀ ◊ Z6-8 H8-6   ↕5ft (1.5m)
↔6–8ft (2–2.5m)

COTONEASTER HORIZONTALIS

A deciduous shrub with spreading branches that form a herringbone pattern. The tiny, pinkish white flowers, which appear in summer, are attractive to bees. Bright red berries ripen in autumn, and the glossy, dark green leaves redden before they fall. Good as a ground-cover, but most effective when grown flat up against a wall.

CULTIVATION *Grow in any but water-logged soil. Site in full sun for the best berries, or in semi-shade. Keep pruning to a minimum; if wall-trained, shorten outward-facing shoots in late winter.*

☼☀ ◊◊ Z5-7 H7-5   ↕3ft (1m) ↔5ft (1.5m)

COTONEASTER LACTEUS

This dense, evergreen shrub has arching branches that bear clusters of small, cup-shaped, milky white flowers from early to mid-summer. These are followed by brilliant red berries in autumn. The oval leaves are dark green and leathery, with gray-woolly undersides. Ideal for a wildlife garden, since it provides food for bees and birds; also makes a good windbreak or informal hedge.

CULTIVATION *Grow in well-drained, fairly fertile soil, in sun or semi-shade. Trim hedges lightly in summer, if necessary; keep pruning to a minimum.*

☼ ◑ ◊ Z7-9 H9-7   ↔ 12ft (4m)

COTONEASTER SIMONSII

An upright, deciduous or semi-evergreen shrub with small, cup-shaped white flowers in summer. The bright orange-red berries that follow ripen in autumn and persist well into winter. Autumn color is also seen in the glossy leaves, which redden from dark green. Good for hedging and can also be clipped fairly hard to a semi-formal outline.

CULTIVATION *Grow in any well-drained soil, in full sun or partial shade. Clip hedges to shape in late winter or early spring, or allow to grow naturally.*

☼ ◑ ◊ Z6-8 H8-6   ↕10ft(3m) ↔6ft (2m)

COTONEASTER STERNIANUS

This graceful, evergreen or semi-evergreen shrub bears arching branches that produce clusters of pink-tinged white flowers in summer, followed by a profusion of large, orange-red berries in autumn. The gray-green leaves have white undersides. Good grown as a hedge.

CULTIVATION *Grow in any well-drained soil, in sun or semi-shade. Trim hedges lightly after flowering, if necessary; pruning is best kept to a minimum.*

☼ ☀ ◊ Z7-9 H9-7 ↕↔ 10ft (3m)

COTONEASTER X *WATERERI* 'JOHN WATERER'

A fast-growing, evergreen or semi-evergreen shrub or small tree valued for the abundance of red berries that clothe its branches in autumn. In summer, clusters of white flowers are carried among the lance-shaped, dark green leaves. Good on its own or at the back of a shrub border.

CULTIVATION *Grow in any but water-logged soil, in sun or semi-shade. When young, cut out any badly placed shoots to develop a framework of well-spaced branches. Thereafter, keep pruning to an absolute minimum.*

☼ ☀ ◊◊ Z6-8 H8-6 ↕↔ 15ft (5m)

CRAMBE CORDIFOLIA

A tall, clump-forming, vigorous
perennial grown for its stature and
its fragrant, airy, billowing sprays of
small white flowers, which are very
attractive to bees. These are borne
on strong stems in summer above
the large, elegant, dark green leaves.
Magnificent in a mixed border, but
allow plenty of space.

CULTIVATION *Grow in any well-drained,
preferably deep, fertile soil, in full sun
or partial shade. Provide shelter from
strong winds.*

☼ ◑ ◊ Z6-9 H9-6 ‡8ft (2.5m) ↔5ft (1.5m)

CRATAEGUS LAEVIGATA 'PAUL'S SCARLET'

This rounded, thorny, deciduous
tree is valued for its long season
of interest. Abundant clusters of
double, dark pink flowers appear
from late spring to summer, followed
in autumn by small red fruits. The
leaves, divided into three or five
lobes, are a glossy mid-green.
Particularly useful for a city, coastal,
or exposed garden. The very similar
'Rosea Flore Pleno' (Z5-8, H8-4)
makes a good substitute.

CULTIVATION *Grow in any but water-
logged soil, in full sun or partial shade.
Pruning is best kept to a minimum.*

☼ ◑ ◊◊ Z5-8 H8-5 ‡↔25ft (8m)

CRATAEGUS × *LAVALLEI* 'CARRIEREI'

This vigorous hawthorn is a broadly spreading, semi-evergreen tree with thorny shoots and leathery green leaves that turn red in late autumn and persist into winter. Flattened clusters of white flowers appear in early summer, followed in autumn by round, red fruits that persist into winter. Tolerates pollution, so it is good for an urban garden. Often offered as simply *C.* × *lavallei*.

CULTIVATION *Grow in any but water-logged soil, in full sun or partial shade. Pruning is best kept to a minimum.*

☀️☼ ◊◊ Z5-7 H7-4 ‡22ft (7m) ↔30ft (10m)

CRINODENDRON HOOKERIANUM

The lantern tree is an upright, evergreen shrub, so-called because of its large, scarlet to carmine-red flowers that hang from the upright shoots during late spring and early summer. The leaves are narrow and glossy dark green. It dislikes alkaline soils.

CULTIVATION *Grow in moist but well-drained, fertile, organic, acidic soil, in partial shade with protection from cold winds. Tolerates a sunny site if the roots are kept cool and shaded. Trim lightly after flowering, if necessary.*

☀️ ◊ Z9-10 H10-8 ‡20ft (6m) ↔15ft (5m)

CRINUM × *POWELLII* 'ALBUM'

A sturdy, bulbous perennial bearing clusters of up to ten large, fragrant, widely flared, pure white flowers on upright stems in late summer and autumn. *C.* × *powellii* is equally striking, with pink flowers. The strap-shaped leaves, to 5ft (1.5m) long, are mid-green and arch over. Where marginal, choose a sheltered site and protect the dormant bulb over winter with a deep, dry mulch.

CULTIVATION *Grow in deep, moist but well-drained, fertile, organic soil in full sun with shelter from frost and cold, drying winds.*

☼ ◊ Z7-10 H10-7 ‡5ft (1.5m) ↔12in (30cm)

CROCOSMIA × *CROCOSMIIFLORA* 'SOLFATERRE'

This clump-forming perennial produces spikes of funnel-shaped, apricot-yellow flowers on arching stems in mid-summer. The bronze-green, deciduous leaves are strap-shaped, emerging from swollen corms at the base of the stems. Excellent in a border; the flowers are good for cutting.

CULTIVATION *Grow in moist but well-drained, fertile, organic soil, in full sun. Provide a dry mulch over winter.*

☼ ◊ Z6-9 H9-6 ‡24–28in (60–70cm) ↔3in (8cm)

CROCOSMIA 'LUCIFER'

A robust, clump-forming perennial
with swollen corms at the base of
the stems. These give rise to pleated,
bright green leaves and, in summer,
arching spikes of upward-facing red
flowers. Particularly effective at the
edge of a shrub border or by water.

CULTIVATION *Grow in moist but well-
drained, moderately fertile, organic soil.
Site in full sun or dappled shade.*

☀☀ ◊◊ Z6-9 H9-6 ‡3–4ft (1–1.2m)
↔3in (8cm)

CROCOSMIA MASONIORUM

A robust, late-summer-flowering
perennial bearing bright vermilion,
upward-facing flowers. These are
carried above the dark green foliage
on arching stems. The flowers and
foliage emerge from a swollen, bulb-
like corm. Thrives in coastal gardens.
Where marginally hardy, grow in the
shelter of a warm wall.

CULTIVATION *Best in moist but well-
drained, fairly fertile, organic soil, in
full sun or partial shade. In cold areas,
provide a dry winter mulch.*

☀☀ ◊ Z7-9 H9-7 ‡4ft (1.2m) ↔3in (8cm)

SPRING-FLOWERING CROCUS

Spring-flowering crocus are indispensable dwarf perennials, since they bring a welcome splash of early spring color into the garden. Some cultivars of *C. sieberi*, such as 'Tricolor' or 'Hubert Edelstein', bloom even earlier, in late winter. The goblet-shaped flowers emerge from swollen, underground corms at the same time as or just before the narrow, almost upright foliage. The leaves are mid-green with silver-green central stripes and grow markedly as the blooms fade. Very effective in drifts at the front of a mixed or herbaceous border, or in massed plantings in rock gardens or raised beds.

CULTIVATION *Grow in gritty, well-drained, poor to moderately fertile soil, in full sun. Water freely during the growing season, and apply a low-nitrogen fertilizer each month. C. corsicus must be kept completely dry over summer. Can be naturalized under the right growing conditions.*

☼ ◊ Z3-8 H8-1 (corsicus Z6-9 H9-6)

3 ↕2–3in (5–8cm) ↔ 1in (2.5cm)

2 ↕3in (7cm) ↔ 2 in (5cm)

1 ↕3-4in (8–10cm) ↔ 1½in (4cm)

4 ↕2–3in (5–8cm) ↔ 1in (2.5cm)

5 ↕2–3in (5–8cm) ↔ 1in (2.5cm)

1 *C. corsicus* **2** *C. chrysanthus* 'E.A. Bowles' **3** *C. sieberi* 'Albus'
4 *C. sieberi* 'Tricolor' **5** *C. sieberi* 'Hubert Edelstein'

AUTUMN-FLOWERING CROCUS

These crocus are invaluable for their late-flowering, goblet-shaped flowers with showy interiors. They are dwarf perennials with underground corms that give rise to the foliage and autumn flowers. The leaves are narrow and mid-green with silver-green central stripes, appearing at the same time or just after the flowers. All types are easy to grow in the right conditions and look excellent when planted in groups in a rock garden. Rapid-spreading crocus, such as *C. ochroleucus*, are useful for naturalizing in grass or under deciduous shrubs. *C. banaticus* is effective planted in drifts at the front of a border, but do not allow it to become swamped by larger plants.

CULTIVATION *Grow in gritty, well-drained, poor to moderately fertile soil, in full sun. Reduce watering during the summer for all types except* C. banaticus, *which prefers damper soil and will tolerate partial shade.*

☼ ◊ Z3-8 H8-1(ochro. Z5-8 H8-4)

1 ↕4in (10cm) ↔ 2in (5cm)

2 ↕4in (10cm) ↔ 2in (5cm)

3 ↕2½–3in (6–8cm) ↔ 2in (5cm)

4 ↕3in (8cm) ↔ 1in (2.5cm)

5 ↕2in (5cm) ↔ 1in (2.5cm)

6 ↕4–5in (10–12cm) ↔ 1½in (4cm)

1 *C. banaticus* **2** *C. goulimyi* **3** *C. kotschyanus*
4 *C. medius* **5** *C. ochroleucus* **6** *C. pulchellus*

CRYPTOMERIA JAPONICA 'ELEGANS COMPACTA'

This small, slow-growing conifer looks good in a heather bed or rock garden with other dwarf conifers. It has feathery sprays of slender, soft green leaves, which turn a rich bronze-purple in winter. Mature trees usually have a neat cone shape. *C. elegans* 'Bandai-Sugu' is very similar but grows to only 6ft (2m).

CULTIVATION *Grow in any well-drained soil, in full sun or partial shade. Needs no formal pruning, but to renovate ungainly trees, cut back to within 28in (70cm) of ground level, in spring.*

 ☼☀ ◊ Z6-9 H9-6 ↕6–12ft (2–4m)
↔6ft (2m)

CUPHEA IGNEA

The cigar flower is a spreading, evergreen shrub or subshrub grown as an annual in colder climates. It bears small, slender, dark orange-red flowers over a long period from spring to autumn, amid the lance-shaped, dark green leaves. In frost-free areas grow in a shrub border; otherwise, treat as a bedding plant or grow in a cool conservatory.

CULTIVATION *Grow in well-drained, moderately fertile soil or soil mix, in full sun or partial shade. Pinch-prune young plants to encourage bushiness. Minimum temperature 35°F (2°C).*

☼☀ ◊ H12-1 ↕12–30in (30–75cm)
↔12–36in (30–90cm)

x *CUPRESSOCYPARIS LEYLANDII* 'HAGGERSTON GREY'

This popular cultivar of the Leyland cypress is a fast-growing coniferous tree with a tapering, columnar shape. It has dense, gray-green foliage and will establish quickly planted as a screen or windbreak.

CULTIVATION *Grow in deep, well-drained soil in full sun or partial shade. Needs no formal pruning, unless grown as a hedge, when it should be trimmed 2 or 3 times during the growing season.*

☼ ◐ ◊ Z6-9 H9-4   ↕to 120ft (35m) ↔to 15ft (5m)

CYANANTHUS LOBATUS

A spreading, mat-forming perennial grown for its late summer display of bright blue-purple, broadly funnel-shaped flowers, on single stems with hairy brown calyces. The leaves are fleshy and dull green, with deeply cut lobes. Perfect in a rock garden or trough.

CULTIVATION *Grow in poor to moderately fertile, moist but well-drained soil, preferably neutral to slightly acidic, and rich in organic matter. Choose a site in partial shade.*

☼ ◐◊ Z6-7 H7-6   ↕2in (5cm) ↔12in (30cm)

CYCAS REVOLUTA

The Japanese sago palm is a robust cycad – a slow-growing tree with a palmlike appearance. Large leaves, up to 5ft (1.5m) long, are divided into glossy leaflets. Flowers and fruit are rare in container-grown plants, but it makes an excellent foliage, house, or conservatory plant that can be brought outside in summer.

CULTIVATION *Grow in a mix of equal parts soil, compost, and coarse bark, with added grit, charcoal, and slow-release fertilizer. Provide full light, with shade from hot sun, and moderate humidity. Water sparingly in winter. Minimum temperature 45°F (7°C).*

☼ ◐◐ H12-9 ↔3–6ft (1–2m)

CYCLAMEN CILICIUM

A tuberous perennial valued for its slender, nodding, white or pink flowers, borne in autumn and often into winter among patterned, rounded or heart-shaped, mid-green leaves. This elegant plant needs a warm and dry summer, when it is dormant, and in cool-temperate climates it may be better grown in a cool greenhouse, or under trees or shrubs, to avoid excessive summer moisture.

CULTIVATION *Grow in moderately fertile, well-drained soil enriched with organic matter, in partial shade. Mulch annually with leafmold after flowering when the leaves wither.*

☼ ◐ Z5-9 H9-4 ↕2in (5cm) ↔3in (8cm)

CYCLAMEN COUM
PEWTER GROUP

This winter- to spring-flowering,
tuberous perennial is excellent for
naturalizing beneath trees or shrubs.
The compact flowers have upswept
petals that vary from white to shades
of pink and carmine-red. These
emerge from swollen, underground
tubers at the same time as the
rounded, silver-green leaves. Provide
a deep, dry mulch where marginal.

CULTIVATION *Grow in gritty, well-
drained, fertile soil that dries out in
summer, in sun or light shade. Mulch
annually when the leaves wither.*

☀️◐ ◊ Z5-9 H9-4   ‡2–3in (5–8cm)
↔4in (10cm)

CYCLAMEN HEDERIFOLIUM

An autumn-flowering, tuberous
perennial bearing shuttlecock-like
flowers that are pale to deep pink
and flushed deep maroon at the
mouths. The ivylike leaves, mottled
with green and silver, appear after
the flowers from a swollen, underground tuber. It self-seeds freely,
forming extensive colonies under
trees and shrubs, especially where
protected from summer rainfall.

CULTIVATION *Grow in well-drained,
fertile soil, in sun or partial shade.
Mulch each year after the leaves wither.*

☀️◐ ◊ Z8-9 H9-7   ‡4–5in (10–13cm)
↔6in (15cm)

CYNARA CARDUNCULUS

The cardoon is a clump-forming, statuesque, late-summer-flowering perennial that looks very striking in a border. The large, thistlelike purple flowerheads, which are very attractive to bees, are carried above the deeply divided, silvery leaves on thick, gray-woolly stems. The flowerheads dry well for indoor display and are very attractive to bees. When blanched, the leaf stalks can be eaten.

CULTIVATION *Grow in any well-drained, fertile soil, in full sun with shelter from cold winds. For the best foliage effect, remove the flower stems as they emerge.*

☼ ◊ Z7-9 H9-7 ↕5ft (1.5m) ↔4ft (1.2m)

CYTISUS BATTANDIERI

Pineapple broom develops a loose and open-branched habit. It is a semi-evergreen shrub bearing dense clusters of pineapple-scented, bright yellow flowers from early to midsummer. The silver-gray leaves, divided into three, make an attractive backdrop to herbaceous and mixed plantings. Best by a sunny wall in cold areas. The cultivar 'Yellow Tail' is recommended.

CULTIVATION *Grow in any well-drained, not too rich soil, in full sun. Very little pruning is necessary, but old wood can be cut out after flowering to be replaced with strong, young growth. Resents transplanting.*

☼ ◊ Z7-9 H9-7 ↕↔ 15ft (5m)

CYTISUS × BEANII

This low-growing and semi-trailing, deciduous, spring-flowering shrub carries an abundance of pealike, rich yellow flowers on arching stems. The leaves are small and dark green. It is a colorful bush for a rock garden or raised bed and is also effective if allowed to cascade over a wall. *Cytisus × ardoinei* (Z6-8, H8-6) is similar but slightly less spreading where space is limited.

CULTIVATION *Grow in well-drained, poor to moderately fertile soil, in full sun. Trim lightly after flowering, but avoid cutting into old wood.*

☼ ◊ Z7-8 H8-7 ‡24in (60cm) ↔3ft (1m)

CYTISUS × PRAECOX 'ALLGOLD'

This compact, deciduous shrub is smothered by a mass of pealike, dark yellow flowers from mid- to late spring. The tiny, gray-green leaves are carried on arching stems. Suitable for a sunny shrub border or large rock garden. 'Warminster' is very similar, with paler, cream yellow flowers.

CULTIVATION *Grow in well-drained, acidic to neutral soil, in sun. Pinch out the growing tips to encourage bushiness, then cut back new growth by up to two-thirds after flowering; avoid cutting into old wood. Replace old, leggy specimens.*

☼ ◊ Z6-9 H9-6 ‡4ft (1.2m) ↔5ft (1.5m)

DABOECIA CANTABRICA 'BICOLOR'

This straggling, heatherlike shrub bears slender spikes of urn-shaped flowers from spring to autumn. They are white, pink, or beet-red, sometimes striped with two colors. The leaves are small and dark green. Good in a heather bed or among other acidic-soil-loving plants. 'Waley's Red', with glowing magenta flowers, is also recommended.

CULTIVATION *Best in sandy, well-drained, acidic soil, in full sun; tolerates neutral soil and some shade. Clip lightly in early spring to remove spent flowers; do not cut into old wood.*

☼◑ ◊ Z6-8 H8-6 ‡18in (45cm) ↔24in (60cm)

DABOECIA CANTABRICA 'WILLIAM BUCHANAN'

This vigorous, compact, heatherlike shrub bears slender spikes of bell-shaped, purple-crimson flowers from late spring to mid-autumn. The narrow leaves are dark green above with silver-gray undersides. Good with other acidic-soil-loving plants, or among conifers in a rock garden. Try planting with 'Silverwells', more ground-hugging, with white flowers.

CULTIVATION *Grow in well-drained, sandy, acidic to neutral soil, preferably in sun, but tolerates light shade. Trim in early to mid-spring to remove flowers, but do not cut into old wood.*

☼◑ ◊ Z6-8 H8-6 ‡18in (45cm) ↔24in (60cm)

DAHLIAS

Dahlias are showy, deciduous perennials, grown as annuals in cold climates, with swollen underground tubers that must be stored in frost-free conditions in climates with cold winters. They are valued for their massive variety of brightly colored flowers that bloom from mid-summer to autumn, when many other plants are past their best. The leaves are mid- to dark green and divided. Very effective in massed plantings, wherever space allows: in small gardens, choose from a variety of dwarf types to fill gaps in border displays, or grow in containers. The flowers are ideal for cutting.

CULTIVATION *Best in well-drained soil, in sun. Where not hardy, lift tubers and store over winter. Plant out tubers once the danger of frost has passed. Feed with high-nitrogen fertilizer every week in early summer. Taller varieties need staking. Deadhead to prolong flowering.*

☼ ◊ Z8-11 H12-1

1 ‡3½ft (1.1m) ↔ 18in (45cm)

2 ‡3½ft (1.1m) ↔ 24in (60cm)

3 ‡24in (60cm) ↔ 18in (45cm)

4 ‡4ft (1.2m) ↔ 24in (60cm)

5 ‡3½ft (1.1m) ↔ 24in (60cm)

1 *D.* 'Bishop of Llandaff' **2** *D.* 'Clair de Lune'
3 *D.* 'Fascination' (dwarf) **4** *D.* 'Hamari Accord' **5** *D.* 'Conway'

6 ↕1.2m (4ft) ↔ 60cm (24in)

7 ↕1.1m (3½ft) ↔ 60cm (24in)

8 ↕1.2m (4ft) ↔ 60cm (24in)

9 ↕3ft (1m) ↔ 18in (45cm)

10 ↕↔ 18–20in (45–50cm)

11 ↕3½ft (1.1m) ↔ 24in (60cm)

12 ↕3½ft (1.1m) ↔ 24in (60cm)

13 ↕24in (60cm) ↔ 18in (45cm)

14 ↕4ft (1.2m) ↔ 24in (60cm)

15 ↕4ft (1.2m) ↔ 24in (60cm)

6 *D.* 'Hamari Gold' 7 *D.* 'Hillcrest Royal' 8 *D.* 'Kathryn's Cupid' 9 *D.* 'Rokesley Mini'
10 *D.* 'Sunny Yellow' (dwarf) 11 *D.* 'So Dainty' 12 *D.* 'Wootton Cupid'
13 *D.* 'Yellow Hammer' (dwarf) 14 *D.* 'Zorro' 15 *D.* 'Wootton Impact'

DAPHNE BHOLUA
'GURKHA'

An upright, deciduous shrub bearing clusters of strongly fragrant, tubular, white and purplish pink flowers on its bare stems in late winter. They open from deep pink-purple buds and are followed by round, black-purple fruits. The lance-shaped leaves are leathery and dark green. A fine plant for a winter garden. All parts are highly toxic if ingested.

CULTIVATION *Grow in well-drained but moist soil, in sun or semi-shade. Mulch to keep the roots cool. Best left unpruned.*

☼☀ ◊ Z8-9 H7-3   ‡6–12ft (2–4m) ↔5ft (1.5m)

DAPHNE PETRAEA
'GRANDIFLORA'

A very compact, slow-growing, evergreen shrub bearing clusters of fragrant, deep rose-pink flowers in late spring. The spoon-shaped leaves are leathery and glossy dark green. Ideal for a sheltered rock garden. All parts of the plant are highly toxic.

CULTIVATION *Grow in reasonably moist but well-drained, fairly fertile, organic soil, in sun or semi-shade. Regular pruning is not necessary.*

☼☀ ◊ Z5-7 H7-3   ‡4in (10cm) ↔10in (25cm)

DAPHNE TANGUTICA RETUSA GROUP

These dwarf forms of *D. tangutica*, sometimes listed simply as *D. retusa*, are evergreen shrubs valued for their clusters of very fragrant, white to purple-red flowers that are borne during late spring and early summer. The lance-shaped leaves are glossy and dark green. Useful in a variety of sites, such as a large rock garden, shrub border, or mixed planting. All parts are toxic.

CULTIVATION *Grow in well-drained, moderately fertile, organic soil that does not dry out, in full sun or dappled shade. Pruning is not necessary.*

☼☀◐ ◊ Z7-9 H9-7　　　↕↔ 30in (75cm)

DARMERA PELTATA

A handsome, spreading perennial, sometimes included in the genus *Peltiphyllum*, that forms an imposing, umbrella-like clump with large, round, mid-green leaves, to 24in (60cm) across, that turn red in autumn. The foliage appears after the compact clusters of star-shaped, white to bright pink, spring flowers. Ideal for a bog garden or by the edge of a pond or stream.

CULTIVATION *Grow in reliably moist, moderately fertile soil, in sun or partial shade; tolerates drier soil in shade.*

☼☀◐ ◊ Z5-9 H9-4　　↕6ft (2m) ↔3ft (1m)

DELPHINIUMS

Delphiniums are clump-forming perennials cultivated for their towering spikes of spectacular spikes of, shallowly cup-shaped, spurred, single or double flowers. These appear in early to mid-summer and are available in a range of colors from creamy whites through lilac-pinks and clear sky blues to deep indigo-blue. The toothed and lobed, mid-green leaves are arranged around the base of the stems. Grow tall delphiniums in a mixed border or island bed with shelter to prevent them from being blown over in strong winds; shorter ones do well in a rock garden. The flowers are good for cutting.

CULTIVATION *Grow in well-drained, fertile soil, in full sun. For quality blooms, feed weekly with a balanced fertilizer in spring, and thin out the young shoots when they reach 3in (7cm) tall. Most cultivars need staking. Remove spent flower spikes, and cut back all growth in autumn.*

☼ ◊ Z3-7 H7-1

1 ‡5½ft (1.7m) ↔ 24-36in (60–90cm)   **2** ‡6ft (2m) ↔ 24-36in (60–90cm)   **3** ‡5½ft (1.7m) ↔ 24-36in (60–90cm

1 *Delphinium* 'Blue Nile'   **2** *D.* 'Bruce'   **3** *D.* 'Cassius'

4 ‡ to 6ft (2m) ↔ 24–36in (60–90cm)

‡ to 5ft (1.5m) ↔ 24-36in (60–90cm) **5**

6 ‡ 5½ft (1.7m) ↔ 24-36in (60–90cm

7 ‡ 6ft (2m) ↔ 24-36in (60–90cm)

8 ‡ 5½ft (1.7m) ↔ 24-36in (60–90cm)

4 *D.* 'Claire' **5** *D.* 'Conspicuous'
6 *D.* 'Emily Hawkins' **7** *D.* 'Fanfare' **8** *D.* 'Giotto'

MORE CHOICES

'Blue Dawn' Pinkish blue flowers with brown eyes.

'Constance Rivett' White.

'Faust' Cornflower blue with indigo eyes.

'Fenella' Deep blue with black eyes.

'Gillian Dallas' White.

'Loch Leven' Mid-blue with white eyes.

'Michael Ayres' Violet.

'Min' Mauve veined with deep purple, brown eyes.

'Oliver' Light blue/mauve with dark eyes.

'Spindrift' Cobalt blue with cream eyes.

'Tiddles' Slate blue.

9 ↕ to 6ft (2m) ↔ 24–36in (60–90cm)   **10** ↕ to 5ft (1.5m) ↔ 24–36in (60–90cm)   **11** ↕ 5ft (1.5m) ↔ 24–36in (60–90cm)

9 *D.* 'Kathleen Cooke' **10** *D.* 'Langdon's Royal Flush' **11** *D.* 'Lord Butler'

12 ‡6ft (2m) ↔ 30in (75cm)

13 ‡5ft (1.5m) ↔ 24–36in (60–90cm)

14 ‡to 5ft (1.5m) ↔ 24–36in (60–90cm)

17 ‡4ft (1.2m) ↔ 24–36in (60–90cm)

15 ‡to 5ft (1.5m) ↔ 30in (75cm)

16 ‡5ft (1.5m) ↔ 24–36in (60–90cm)

18 ‡5½ft (1.7m) ↔ 24–36in (60–90cm)

12 *D.* 'Mighty Atom' **13** *D.* 'Our Deb' **14** *D.* 'Rosemary Brock' **15** *D.* 'Sandpiper'
16 *D.* 'Sungleam' **17** *D.* 'Thamesmead' **18** *D.* 'Walton Gemstone'

DEUTZIA ×
ELEGANTISSIMA
'ROSEALIND'

This compact, rounded, deciduous
shrub bears profuse clusters of
small, deep carmine-pink flowers.
These are carried from late spring
to early summer amid the oval, dull
green leaves. Very suitable for a
mixed border.

CULTIVATION *Grow in any well-drained,
fertile soil that does not dry out, in full
sun or partial shade. Tip-prune when
young to encourage bushiness; after
flowering, thin out by cutting some
older stems back to the ground.*

☼ ◐ ◊ Z6-8 H8-6 ↕4ft (1.2m) ↔5ft (1.5m)

DEUTZIA × HYBRIDA
'MONT ROSE'

A dense, upright shrub, very similar
to *D.* × *elegantissima* 'Rosealind'
(above), but with smaller flower
clusters. These consist of small, star-
shaped, light pink or pinkish purple
flowers, borne in early summer amid
the narrow, dark green, deciduous
leaves. Good as a specimen shrub
or in a mixed border.

CULTIVATION *Grow in any fertile, well-
drained but not too dry soil. Best in
sun, but tolerates light shade. Tip-prune
on planting; in subsequent years, prune
young shoots below the flowered wood.*

☼ ◐ ◊ Z6-8 H8-6 ↕↔4ft (1.2m)

BORDER CARNATIONS (*DIANTHUS*)

This group of *Dianthus* are annuals or evergreen perennials of medium height, suitable for mixed or herbaceous borders. They are grown for their mid-summer flowers, which are good for cutting. Each flower stem bears five or more double flowers to 3in (8cm) across, with no fewer than 25 petals. These may be of one color only, as in 'Golden Cross'; gently flecked, like 'Grey Dove'; or often with white petals margined and striped in strong colors. Some have clove-scented flowers. The linear leaves of all carnations are blue-gray or gray-green with a waxy bloom.

CULTIVATION *Ideal in well-drained, neutral to alkaline soil enriched with well-rotted manure or compost; apply a balanced fertilizer in spring. Plant in full sun. Provide support in late spring using thin stakes or twigs, or wire rings. Deadhead to prolong flowering and maintain a compact plant habit.*

☼ ◊ Z7-10 H10-7

1 ↕ 18–24in (45–60cm) ↔ 18in (45cm)   **2** ↕ 18–24in (45–60cm) ↔ 18in (45cm)   **3** ↕ 18–24in (45–60cm) ↔ 18in (45cm)

4 ↕ 18–24in (45–60cm) ↔ 18in (45cm)   **5** ↕ 8–24in (45–60cm)1 ↔ 18in (45cm)   **6** ↕ 18–24in (45–60cm) ↔ 18in (45cm)

1 *Dianthus* 'David Russell' **2** *D.* 'Devon Carla' **3** *D.* 'Golden Cross'
4 *D.* 'Grey Dove' **5** *D.* 'Ruth White' **6** *D.* 'Spinfield Wizard'

PINKS (*DIANTHUS*)

Summer-flowering pinks belong, like carnations, to the genus *Dianthus* and are widely grown for their charming, often clove-scented flowers and narrow, blue-gray leaves. They flower profusely over long periods; when cut, the stiff-stemmed blooms last exceptionally well. Thousands are available, usually in shades of pink, white, carmine, salmon, or mauve with double or single flowers; they may be plain (self), marked with a contrasting color or laced around the margins. Most are excellent border plants; tiny alpine pinks such as 'Pike's Pink' and magenta 'Joan's Blood' are well suited to a rock garden or raised bed.

CULTIVATION *Best in well-drained, neutral to alkaline soil, in an open, sunny site. Alpine pinks need very sharp drainage. Feed with a balanced fertilizer in spring. Deadhead all types to prolong flowering and to maintain a compact habit.*

☼ ◊ Z5-9 H9-1

1 ‡10–18in (25–45cm) ↔ 16in (40cm)

2 ‡10–18in (25–45cm) ↔ 16in (40cm)

3 ‡10–18in (25–45cm) ↔ 16in (40cm)

4 ‡10–18in (25–45cm) ↔ 16in (40cm)

5 ‡10–18in (25–45cm) ↔ 16in (40cm)

6 ‡10–18in (25–45cm) ↔ 16in (40cm)

1 *Dianthus* 'Becky Robinson' 2 *D.* 'Devon Pride' 3 *D.* 'Doris'
4 *D.* 'Gran's Favourite' 5 *D.* 'Haytor White' 6 *D.* 'Houndspool Ruby'

7 ‡10–18in (25–45cm) ↔ 16in (40cm)

8 ‡3–4in (8–10cm) ↔ 8in (20cm)

9 ‡10–18in (25–45cm) ↔ 16in (40cm)

10 ‡10–18in (25–45cm) ↔ 16in (40cm)

11 ‡10–18in (25–45cm) ↔ 16in (40cm)

12 ‡10–18in (25–45cm) ↔ 16in (40cm)

MORE CHOICES

D. alpinus The original
alpine pink, with pale-
flecked pink flowers.
D. alpinus 'Joan's
Blood' Dark-centered
deep pink flowers.
'Bovey Belle' Clove-
scented, fuchsia-pink.
'Coronation Ruby'
Clove-scented, warm
pink flowers with ruby
markings.
'Inschriach Dazzler'
Alpine pink with
fringed carmine flowers.
'Valda Wyatt' Clove-
scented, double
lavender flowers.

13 ‡3–4in (8–10cm) ↔ 18in (20cm)

14 ‡10–18in (25–45cm) ↔ 16in (40cm)

15 ‡10–18in (25–45cm) ↔ 16in (40cm)

16 ‡10–18in (25–45cm) ↔ 16in (40cm)

7 *D.* 'Kathleen Hitchcock' **8** *D.* 'La Bourboule' **9** *D.* 'Monica Wyatt' **10** *D.* 'Natalie Saunders'
11 *D.* 'Oakwood Romance' **12** *D.* 'Oakwood Splendour' **13** *D.* 'Pike's Pink'
14 *D.* 'Suffolk Pride' **15** *D.* 'Trisha's Choice' **16** *D.* 'White Joy'

DIASCIA BARBERAE 'BLACKTHORN APRICOT'

A mat-forming perennial bearing loose spikes of apricot flowers. These are produced over a long period from summer to autumn above the narrowly heart-shaped, mid-green leaves. Good in a rock garden, at the front of a mixed border, or on a sunny bank. *D. barberae* 'Fisher's Flora' and 'Ruby Field' are also recommended.

CULTIVATION *Grow in moist but well-drained, fertile soil, in full sun. Where not hardy, overwinter young plants under glass.*

☼ ◊ Z8-9 H9-8   ↕10in (25cm)
↔to 20in (50cm)

DIASCIA RIGESCENS

This trailing perennial is valued for its tall spires of salmon-pink flowers. These appear above the mid-green, heart-shaped leaves during summer. Excellent in a rock garden or raised bed, or at the front of a border. Where marginally hardy, grow at the base of a warm, sunny wall.

CULTIVATION *Grow in moist but well-drained, fertile, organic soil. Site in full sun. Where marginally hardy, overwinter young plants under glass.*

☼ ◊ Z7-9 H9-7 ↕12in (30cm) ↔20in (50cm)

DICENTRA SPECTABILIS

Bleeding heart is an elegant, mound-forming perennial. In spring, it bears rows of distinctive hanging, red-pink, heart-shaped flowers on arching stems. The leaves are deeply cut and mid-green, and they die back completely in early summer. A beautiful plant for a shady border or woodland garden.

CULTIVATION *Grow in reliably moist, fertile, organic, neutral or slightly alkaline soil. Prefers a site in partial shade, but it tolerates full sun.*

☼ ◐ ◊ Z3–9 H9–1 ↕18in (45cm) ↔3ft (1m)

DICENTRA SPECTABILIS 'ALBA'

This white-flowered form of bleeding heart is otherwise very similar to the species (above), so to avoid possible confusion, purchase plants during the flowering period. The leaves are deeply cut and light green, and the heart-shaped flowers are borne along arching stems in spring.

CULTIVATION *Grow in reliably moist but well-drained soil that is enriched with well-rotted organic matter. Prefers partial shade, but tolerates full sun.*

☼ ◐ ◊ Z3–9 H9–1 ↕18in (45cm) ↔3ft (1m)

DICENTRA 'STUART BOOTHMAN'

A spreading perennial that bears heart-shaped pink flowers along the tips of arching stems during late spring and summer. The very finely cut foliage is fernlike and gray-green. Very attractive for a shady border or woodland planting.

CULTIVATION *Best in moist but well drained, organic, neutral to slightly alkaline soil, in partial shade. Divide and replant clumps in early spring, after the leaves have died down.*

☀◐ ◊◊ Z3-9 H9-1 ‡12in (30cm) ↔16in (40cm)

DICTAMNUS ALBUS

Gas plant is a tall, woody-based perennial that suits both mixed and herbaceous borders. Dense spikes of star-shaped, fragrant white flowers appear above the lemon-scented, light green foliage in early summer. The aromatic oils produced by the flowers and ripening seedpods can be ignited in very still, hot weather, hence the common name.

CULTIVATION *Grow in well-drained, fertile soil, in sun or partial shade. Does not respond well to root disturbance, so avoid transplanting.*

☀☀ ◊ Z3-8 H8-1 ‡16–36in (40–90cm) ↔24in (60cm)

DICTAMNUS ALBUS VAR. *PURPUREUS*

This purple-flowered perennial is otherwise identical to the species (see facing page, below). Upright spikes of flowers are borne in early summer, above the highly aromatic, light green leaves. Striking in a mixed or herbaceous border.

CULTIVATION *Grow in any dry, well-drained, moderately fertile soil, in full sun or partial shade.*

 ☼ ◑ ◊ Z3-8 H8-1 ‡16–36in (40–90cm) ↔24in (60cm)

DIGITALIS GRANDIFLORA

The yellow foxglove is a short-lived, evergreen perennial producing upright spikes of tubular, pale yellow flowers from early to mid-summer. The leaves are oval and mid-green. Smaller and more subtle than many cultivated foxgloves, it looks attractive in woodland gardens or "natural" plantings.

CULTIVATION *Grow in moist but well-drained soil that is not allowed to dry out. Site in partial shade. Self-seeds freely, so deadhead after flowering to prevent unwanted seedlings.*

☼ ◊◊ Z3-8 H8-1 ‡3ft (1m) ↔18in (45cm)

DIGITALIS X *MERTONENSIS*

An evergreen, clump-forming, short-lived perennial grown for its spires of flared, strawberry pink flowers that are borne from late spring to early summer. The leaves are dark green and lance-shaped. A beautiful plant for mixed or herbaceous borders or woodland plantings. The dusky pink cultivar 'Raspberry' is also recommended.

CULTIVATION *Best in moist but well-drained soil, in partial shade, but tolerates full sun and dry soil.*

☼:☀: ◊◊ Z3-8 H8-1   ↕36in (90cm)
↔12in (30cm)

DIGITALIS PURPUREA
F. *ALBIFLORA*

This ghostly form of the common foxglove is a tall biennial producing robust, stately spires of tubular, pure white flowers during summer. The coarse, lance-shaped leaves are bright green. A lovely addition to a woodland garden or mixed border. May be sold as *D. purpurea* 'Alba'.

CULTIVATION *Grow in moist but well-drained soil, in partial shade, but also tolerates dry soil in full sun.*

☼:☀: ◊◊ Z4-8 H8-1   ↕3–6ft (1–2m)
↔24in (60cm)

DODECATHEON MEADIA F. *ALBUM*

This herbaceous perennial is valued for its open clusters of creamy white flowers with strongly reflexed petals. These are borne on arching stems during mid- to late spring, above the rosettes of oval, pale green, toothed leaves. Suits a woodland or shady rock garden, flowering is followed by a period of dormancy. *D. dentatum* (Z5-7 H7 5) is similar but is only half the height; it is ideal for a small rock garden.

CULTIVATION *Grow in moist, organic soil, in partial shade. May be prone to slug and snail damage in spring.*

☀ ◊ 7.4-8 H8-1 ‡16in (40cm) ↔10in (25cm)

DRYOPTERIS FILIX-MAS

The male fern is a deciduous foliage perennial forming large clumps of lance-shaped, mid-green fronds that emerge from a thick, scaly crown in spring. Ideal for a shady border or corner, by the side of a stream or pool, or in woodland. 'Cristata', with crested fronds, is a handsome cultivar.

CULTIVATION *Grow in reliably moist, organic soil. Site in partial shade with shelter from cold, drying winds.*

☀ ◊ Z6-8 H8-6 ‡↔ 3ft (1m)

DRYOPTERIS WALLICHIANA

Wallich's wood fern is a deciduous foliage perennial with a strongly upright, shuttlecock-like habit. The fronds are yellow-green when they emerge in spring, becoming dark green in summer. A fine architectural specimen for a moist, shady site.

CULTIVATION *Best in damp soil that is rich in organic matter. Choose a sheltered position in partial shade.*

☀☼◐ Z10-11 H12-10 ‡3ft(1m) ↔30in (75cm)

ECCREMOCARPUS SCABER

The Chilean glory flower is a fast-growing, scrambling climber with clusters of brilliant orange-red, tubular flowers in summer. The leaves are divided and mid-green. Grow as a short-lived perennial to clothe an arch or pergola, or up into a large shrub. Where not hardy, use as a trailing annual.

CULTIVATION *Grow in free-draining, fertile soil, in a sheltered, sunny site. Cut back to within 12–24in (30–60cm) of the base in spring.*

☀◐ Z10-11 H12-10 ‡6ft (2m) ↔8in (20cm)

ECHEVERIA AGAVOIDES

A lovely, star-shaped, succulent perennial forming rosettes of chunky, sharply pointed, pale green leaves. Clusters of yellow-tipped red flowers appear above the foliage in spring and early summer. Usually grown in a conservatory or as a houseplant where not hardy, but where it is hardy, it will form clumps in a succulent border.

CULTIVATION *Grow in well-drained, fairly fertile soil, or standard cactus soil mix, in sun. Keep barely moist in winter; increase watering in spring. Minimum temperature 35°F (2°C).*

☼ ◊ H12-1 ‡6in (15cm)
↔12in (30cm) or more

ECHINOPS RITRO

This globe thistle is a compact perennial forming clumps of eye-catching flowerheads, metallic blue at first, turning a brighter blue as the flowers open. The leathery green leaves have white-downy under-sides. Excellent for a wild garden. The flowers dry well if cut before fully open. *E. bannaticus* 'Taplow Blue' (Z5-9 H9-4) makes a good substitute for *E. ritro*, although it may grow a little taller.

CULTIVATION *Grow in well-drained, poor to moderately fertile soil. Site in full sun, but tolerates partial shade. Deadhead to prevent self-seeding.*

☼◑ ◊ Z3-9 H9-1 ‡24in (60cm) ↔18in (45cm)

ELAEAGNUS × *EBBINGEI* 'GILT EDGE'

A large, dense, evergreen shrub grown for its oval, dark green leaves that are edged with rich golden yellow. Inconspicuous yet highly scented, creamy white flowers are produced in autumn. Makes an excellent, fast-growing, well-shaped specimen shrub; it can also be planted as an informal hedge.

CULTIVATION *Grow in well-drained, fertile soil, in full sun. Dislikes very alkaline soil. Trim to shape in late spring; completely remove any shoots with plain green leaves as soon as seen.*

☼ ◊ Z7-10 H12-7   ↔ 12ft (4m)

ELAEAGNUS PUNGENS 'MACULATA'

This large, evergreen foliage shrub bears oval, dark green leaves that are generously splashed in the centre with dark yellow. Small but very fragrant flowers are produced from mid-autumn, followed by red fruits. Tolerates coastal conditions.

CULTIVATION *Best in well-drained, fairly fertile soil, in sun. Dislikes very alkaline soil. Trim lightly in spring, as needed. Remove completely any shoots with plain green leaves as soon as seen.*

☼ ◊ Z7-9 H9-7   ↕ 12ft (4m) ↔ 15ft (5m)

ELAEAGNUS 'QUICKSILVER'

A fast-growing shrub with an open habit bearing small yellow flowers in summer, followed by yellow fruits. The silver, deciduous leaves are lance-shaped and are carried on silvery shoots. Makes an excellent specimen shrub, or it can be planted to great effect with other silver-leaved plants. May be known as *E. angustifolia* var. *caspica*.

CULTIVATION *Grow in any but alkaline soil that is fertile and well-drained, in full sun. Tolerates dry soil and coastal winds. Keep pruning to a minimum.*

☼ ◊ Z3-8 H8-1 ↔ 12ft (4m)

ENKIANTHUS CAMPANULATUS

A spreading, deciduous shrub grown for its dense, hanging clusters of bell-shaped, creamy yellow flowers in late spring. The dull green leaves turn to a fine orange red autumn display. Suits an open site in a woodland garden; can become treelike with age. *E. cernuus* var. *rubens*, (Z6-8, H8-6) with deep pink flowers, is more suited to a small garden, at only 8ft (2.5m) tall.

CULTIVATION *Grow in reliably moist but well-drained, peaty or organic, acidic soil. Best in full sun, but tolerates some shade. Keep pruning to a minimum.*

☼◑ ◊◊ Z5-8 H8-4 ↕↔ 12–15ft (4–5m)

EPIMEDIUM × *PERRALCHICUM*

A robust, clump-forming, evergreen perennial that produces spikes of delicate, bright yellow flowers above the glossy dark green foliage in mid- and late spring. The leaves are tinged bronze when young. Very useful as a groundcover under trees or shrubs.

CULTIVATION *Grow in moist but well-drained, moderately fertile, organic soil in partial shade. Provide shelter from cold, drying winds.*

☀ ◊◊ Z5-9 H9-2 ‡16in (40cm) ↔24in (60cm)

EPIMEDIUM × *RUBRUM*

A compact perennial bearing loose clusters of pretty crimson flowers with yellow spurs, in spring. The divided leaves are tinted bronze-red when young, aging to mid-green, then reddening in autumn. Clump together to form drifts in a damp, shady border or woodland garden. *E. grandiflorum* 'Rose Queen' is very similar.

CULTIVATION *Grow in moist but well-drained, moderately fertile, organic soil, in partial shade. Cut back old, tattered foliage in late winter so that the flowers can be seen in spring.*

☀ ◊◊ Z4-8 H8-1 ‡↔ 12in (30cm)

EPIMEDIUM X *YOUNGIANUM* 'NIVEUM'

A clump-forming perennial that bears dainty clusters of small white flowers in late spring. The bright green foliage is bronze-tinted when young and, despite being deciduous, persists well into winter. Makes a good groundcover in damp, shady borders and woodland areas.

CULTIVATION *Grow in moist but well-drained, fertile, organic soil, in partial shade. In late winter, cut back old, tattered foliage so that the new flowers can be seen in spring.*

☼ ◊◊ Z5-9 H9-5   ↕8–12in (20–30cm)
↔12in (30cm)

ERANTHIS HYEMALIS

Winter aconite is one of the earliest spring-flowering bulbs, bearing buttercup-like, bright yellow flowers. These sit on a ruff of light green leaves, covering the ground from late winter until early spring. Ideal for naturalizing beneath deciduous trees and large shrubs, as is 'Guinea Gold', with similar flowers and bronze-green leaves.

CULTIVATION *Grow in moist but well-drained, fertile soil that does not dry out in summer. Best in dappled shade.*

☼ ◊◊ Z4-9 H9-1   ↕3in (8cm) ↔2in (5cm)

ERICA ARBOREA
VAR. *ALPINA*

This tree heath is an upright shrub, much larger than other heathers, densely clothed with clusters of small, honey-scented white flowers from late winter to late spring. The evergreen leaves are needlelike and dark green. A fine centerpiece for a heather garden.

CULTIVATION *Grow in well-drained, ideally sandy, acidic soil, in an open, sunny site. Tolerates alkaline conditions. Cut back young plants in early spring by about two-thirds to promote bushy growth; in later years, pruning is unnecessary. Tolerates hard renovation pruning.*

☼ ◊ Z9-10 H10-9   ‡6ft (2m) ↔3ft (1m)

ERICA × *VEITCHII*
'EXETER'

An upright, open, evergreen shrub that bears masses of highly scented, tubular to bell-shaped white flowers from mid-winter to spring. The needlelike leaves are bright green. Good in a large rock garden with conifers or as a focal point among low-growing heathers.

CULTIVATION *Grow in sandy soil that is well-drained, in sun. Best in acidic soil, but tolerates slightly alkaline conditions. When young, cut back by two-thirds in spring to encourage a good shape; reduce pruning as the plant gets older.*

☼ ◊ Z8-9 H9-8   ‡6ft (2m) ↔26in (65cm)

EARLY-FLOWERING ERICAS

The low-growing, early flowering heaths are evergreen shrubs valued for their urn-shaped flowers in winter and spring. The flowers come in white and a wide range of pinks, bringing invaluable early interest during the winter months. This effect can be underlined by choosing cultivars with colorful foliage; *E. erigena* 'Golden Lady', for example, has bright golden yellow leaves, and *E. carnea* 'Foxhollow' carries yellow, bronze-tipped foliage that turns a deep orange in cold weather. Excellent as a groundcover, either in groups of the same cultivar or with other heathers and dwarf conifers.

CULTIVATION *Grow in open, well-drained, preferably acidic soil, but tolerate alkaline conditions. Choose a site in full sun. Cut back flowered stems in spring to remove most of the previous year's growth; cultivars of* E. erigena *may be scorched by frost, so remove any affected growth in spring.*

☼ ◊ Z5-7 H7-5

1 ‡6in (15cm) ↔ 10in (25cm)

2 ‡6in (15cm) ↔ 16in (40cm)

3 ‡6in (15cm) ↔ 18in (45cm)

4 ‡6in (15cm) ↔ 14in (35cm)

5 ‡12in (30cm) ↔ 24in (60cm)

6 ‡12in (30cm) ↔ 16in (40cm)

1 *E. carnea* 'Ann Sparkes' 2 *E. carnea* 'Foxhollow' 3 *E. carnea* 'Springwood White'
4 *E. carnea* 'Vivellii' 5 *E.* x *darleyensis* 'Jenny Porter' 6 *E. erigena* 'Golden Lady'

LATE-FLOWERING ERICAS

Mostly low and spreading in form, the summer-flowering heaths are fully hardy, evergreen shrubs. They look well on their own or mixed with other heathers and dwarf conifers. Flowers are borne over a very long period; *E.* x *stuartii* 'Irish Lemon' starts in late spring, and cultivars of *E. ciliaris* and *E. vagans* bloom well into autumn. Their season of interest can be further extended by choosing types with colorful foliage; the young shoots of *E. williamsii* 'P.D. Williams' are tipped with yellow in spring, and the golden foliage of *E. cinerea* 'Windlebrooke' turns a deep red in winter.

CULTIVATION *Grow in well-drained, acidic soil, although* E. vagans *and* E. williamsii *tolerate alkaline conditions. Choose an open site in full sun. Prune or shear lightly in early spring, cutting back to strong shoots below the flower clusters.*

☼ ◊ ciliaris Z8-9; cinerea Z6-8; vagans Z7-9; all others Z5-7; H5-8

1 ↕9in (22cm) ↔ 35cm (14in)

2 ↕to 16in (40cm) ↔ 18in (45cm)

3 ↕8in (20cm) ↔ 20in (50cm)

4 ↕10in (25cm) ↔ 20in (50cm)

5 ↕6in (15cm) ↔ 18in (45cm)

1 *E. ciliaris* 'Corfe Castle' 2 *E. ciliaris* 'David McClintock'
3 *E. cinerea* 'Eden Valley' 4 *E. cinerea* 'C.D. Eason' 5 *E. cinerea* 'Windlebrooke'

6 ‡10in (25cm) ↔ 18in (45cm)

7 ‡10in (25cm) ↔ 20in (50cm)

8 ‡8in (20cm) ↔ 12in (30cm)

9 ‡12in (30cm) ↔ 20in (50cm)

10 ‡10in (25cm) ↔ 20in (50cm)

11 ‡12in (30cm) ↔ 18in (45cm)

12 ‡6in (15cm) ↔ 12in (30cm)

13 ‡8in (20cm) ↔ to 34in (85cm)

14 ‡12in (30cm) ↔ 18in (45cm)

6 *E. cinerea* 'Fiddler's Gold' **7** *E.* × *stuartii* 'Irish Lemon' **8** *E. tetralix* 'Alba Mollis'
9 *E. vagans* 'Birch Glow' **10** *E. vagans* 'Lyonesse' **11** *E. vagans* 'Mrs. D.F. Maxwell'
12 *E. vagans* 'Valerie Proudley' **13** *E. watsonii* 'Dawn' **14** *E.* × *williamsii* 'P.D. Williams'

ERIGERON KARVINSKIANUS

This carpeting, evergreen perennial with gray-green foliage produces an abundance of yellow-centered, daisylike flowerheads in summer. The outer petals are initially white, maturing to pink and purple. Ideal for wall crevices or cracks in paving. Sometimes sold as *E. mucronatus*.

CULTIVATION *Grow in well-drained, fertile soil. Choose a site in full sun, ideally with some shade at midday.*

☼ ◊ Z5-7 H7-4   ‡6–12in (15–30cm) ↔3ft (1m) or more

ERINUS ALPINUS

The fairy foxglove is a tiny, short-lived, evergreen perennial producing short spikes of pink, purple, or white, daisylike flowers in late spring and summer. The lance- to wedge-shaped leaves are soft, sticky, and mid-green. Ideal for a rock garden or in crevices in old walls. 'Mrs Charles Boyle' is a recommended cultivar.

CULTIVATION *Grow in light, moderately fertile soil that is well-drained. Tolerates semi-shade, but best in full sun.*

☼☼ ◊ Z4-7 H7-1 ‡3in (8cm) ↔4in (10cm)

ERYNGIUM ALPINUM

This spiky, upright, thistlelike perennial bears cone-shaped, purple-blue flowerheads in summer; these are surrounded by prominent, feathery bracts. The deeply toothed, mid-green leaves are arranged around the base of the stems. An excellent textural plant for a sunny garden. The flowerheads can be cut, and they dry well for arrangements.

CULTIVATION *Grow in free-draining but not too dry, poor to moderately fertile soil, in full sun. Choose a site not prone to excessive winter moisture.*

☼ ◊ Z5-8 H8-4 ‡28in (70cm) ↔18in (45cm)

ERYNGIUM × OLIVERIANUM

An upright, herbaceous perennial bearing cone-shaped, bright silver-blue flowerheads with a flat ring of silvery, daggerlike bracts around the base, produced from mid-summer to early autumn, above spiny-toothed, dark green leaves. Longer-lived than its parent *E. giganteum*, and an essential architectural addition to a dry, sunny border with a theme of silver- or gray-leaved plants.

CULTIVATION *Grow in free-draining, fairly fertile soil, in full sun. Choose a site without excessive winter moisture.*

☼ ◊ Z5-8 H8-4 ‡36in (90cm) ↔18in (45cm)

ERYNGIUM × TRIPARTITUM

This delicate but spiky, upright perennial bears conelike heads of tiny, metallic blue flowers in late summer and autumn. The flowerheads sit on a ring of pointed bracts and are carried above rosettes of gray-green foliage on the tips of wiry, blue-tinted stems. The flowers dry well if cut before fully open.

CULTIVATION *Grow in free-draining, moderately fertile soil. Choose a position not prone to excessive winter moisture, in full sun. Trim lightly after flowering to prevent legginess.*

☼ ◊ Z5-8 H8-5 ‡24–36in (60–90cm)
↔ 20in (50cm)

ERYSIMUM 'BOWLES' MAUVE'

This vigorous, shrubby wallflower is one of the longest-flowering of all perennials. It forms a rounded, evergreen bush of narrow, gray-green leaves and produces dense spikes of small, four-petaled, rich mauve flowers all year, most freely in spring and summer. An excellent border plant that benefits from the shelter of a warm wall where not fully hardy.

CULTIVATION *Grow in any well-drained, preferably alkaline soil, in full sun. Trim lightly after flowering to keep compact. Often short-lived, but easily propagated by cuttings in summer.*

☼ ◊ Z7-10 H12-6 ‡30in (75cm) ↔24in (60cm)

ERYSIMUM CHEIRI 'HARPUR CREWE'

A short-lived, upright, and bushy evergreen perennial that brings long-lasting spring color to the front of a warm, sunny border or raised bed. Spikes of sweetly scented, bright yellow flowers are borne from late winter to early summer above the narrow, gray-green leaves. May be sold as *Cheiranthus* 'Harpur Crewe'.

CULTIVATION *Grow in well-drained, poor to moderately fertile, preferably alkaline soil, in full sun. Trim lightly after flowering to prevent legginess. Usually dies after just a few years but is easily propagated by cuttings in summer.*

☼ ◊ Z5-8 H7-1 ‡12in (30cm) ↔24in (60cm)

ERYSIMUM 'WENLOCK BEAUTY'

A bushy, evergreen perennial that produces clusters of bluish pink and salmon, bronze-shaded flowers from early to late spring. The lance-shaped leaves are softly hairy and mid-green. Good for early-season color in a sunny rock garden or dry wall; where marginally hardy, choose a warm, sheltered spot.

CULTIVATION *Grow in poor or fairly fertile, ideally alkaline soil that has good drainage, in full sun. Trim lightly after flowering to keep compact.*

☼ ◊ Z5-8 H8-5 ‡↔ 18in (45cm)

ERYTHRONIUM 'PAGODA'

This very vigorous, clump-forming, bulbous perennial is related to the dog's tooth violet, *E. dens-canis*, and, like it, looks good planted in groups under deciduous trees and shrubs. Clusters of pale sulfur yellow flowers droop from slender stems in spring above the large, oval, bronze-mottled, glossy dark green leaves.

CULTIVATION *Grow in moist but well-drained soil rich in organic matter. Choose a position in partial shade.*

☼ ◊◊ Z4–9 H9–8   ↕6–14in (15–35cm)
                      ↔4in (10cm)

ESCALLONIA 'APPLE BLOSSOM'

A compact, evergreen shrub carrying dense, glossy dark foliage and, from early to mid-summer, a profusion of small, pink-flushed white flowers. Valuable in a shrub border, it can also be grown as a hedge, barrier, or windbreak. Very useful in coastal areas, if prevailing winds are not harshly cold. *E.* 'Donard Seedling', also usually readily available, looks similar, and is a little hardier.

CULTIVATION *Grow in any well-drained, fertile soil, in full sun. In especially cold areas, shelter from wind. Cut out old or damaged growth after flowering.*

☼ ◊ Z8–9 H9–8   ↕↔ 8ft (2.5m)

ESCALLONIA 'IVEYI'

A vigorous, upright, evergreen shrub
bearing large clusters of fragrant,
pure white flowers from mid- to late
summer. The rounded leaves are
glossy dark green. Grow in a shrub
border, or use as a hedge where
winters are reliably mild; the foliage
often takes on bronze tints in cold
weather, but choose a sheltered
position where marginally hardy.

CULTIVATION *Grow in any fertile soil
with good drainage, in full sun with
shelter from cold, drying winds. Remove
damaged growth in autumn, or in
spring if flowering finishes late.*

☀ ◊ Z8-9　　　　　↔ 10ft (3m)

ESCALLONIA 'LANGLEYENSIS'

This graceful, semi-evergreen shrub
produces abundant clusters of small,
rose-pink flowers. These are borne
from early to mid-summer above the
oval, glossy bright green leaves.
Thrives in relatively mild coastal
gardens as an informal hedge or in
a shrub border.

CULTIVATION *Best in well-drained,
fertile soil, in a sunny site. Protect from
cold, drying winds where marginal.
Cut out dead or damaged growth after
flowering; old plants can be renovated
by hard pruning in spring.*

☀ ◊ Z8-9　　　‡6ft (2m) ↔10ft (3m)

ESCHSCHOLZIA CAESPITOSA

A tufted annual bearing a profusion of scented, bright yellow flowers in summer. The blue-green leaves are finely divided and almost thread-like. Suitable for a sunny border, rock garden, or gravel patch. The flowers close up in dull weather.

CULTIVATION *Grow in well-drained, poor soil. Choose a site in full sun. For early flowers the following year, sow seed directly outdoors in autumn.*

☼ ◊ annual H9-2 ‡↔ to 6in (15cm)

ESCHSCHOLZIA CALIFORNICA

The California poppy is a mat-forming annual with cup-shaped flowers borne on slender stems throughout summer. Colors are mixed, including white, red, or yellow, but most are usually orange. The cultivar 'Dali' flowers in scarlet only. The leaves are finely cut and grayish green. Grow in a sunny border or rock garden; the flowers last well when cut.

CULTIVATION *Best in light, poor soil with good drainage, in full sun. For early flowers the following year, sow seed directly outdoors in autumn.*

☼ ◊ annual H9-2 ‡12in (3cm) ↔6in (15cm)

EUCALYPTUS GUNNII

The cider gum is a vigorous,
evergreen tree useful as a fast-
growing feature in a new garden.
The new yellow- to grayish green
bark is revealed in late summer as
the old, whitish green layer is shed.
Young plants have rounded, gray-
blue leaves; on adult growth they
are lance-shaped. Protect where
marginally hardy with a winter
mulch, especially when young.

CULTIVATION *Grow in well-drained,
fertile soil, in sun. To keep compact, and
for the best display of young foliage, cut
back hard each spring.*

☼ ◊ Z8-10 H10-8 ↕30–80ft (10–25m)
↔20–50ft (6–15m)

EUCALYPTUS PAUCIFLORA SUBSP. *NIPHOPHILA*

The snow gum is a handsome,
silvery, evergreen tree with open,
spreading branches and attractively
peeling, white and gray bark. Young
leaves are oval and dull blue-green;
on mature stems they are lance-
shaped and deep blue-green. The
flowers are less significant. Popularly
grown as a shrub, pruned back hard
at regular intervals.

CULTIVATION *Grow in well-drained,
fertile soil, in full sun. For the best
display of young foliage, cut back hard
each year in spring.*

☼ ◊ Z8-10 H10-8 ↕↔ to 20ft (6m)

EUCRYPHIA X *NYMANSENSIS* 'NYMANSAY'

A columnar, evergreen tree that bears clusters of large, fragrant, glistening white flowers with yellow stamens. These are borne in late summer to early autumn amid the oval, glossy dark green leaves. Makes a magnificent flowering specimen tree; best in mild and damp, frost-free climates.

CULTIVATION *Grow in well-drained, reliably moist soil, preferably in full sun with shade at the roots, but will tolerate semi-shade. Shelter from cold winds. Remove damaged growth in spring.*

☼ ◊◊ Z8-9 H9-8 ‡50ft (15m) ↔15ft (5m)

EUONYMUS ALATUS

The burning bush is a dense, deciduous shrub with winged stems, much valued for its spectacular autumn display; small purple and red fruits split to reveal orange seeds as the oval, deep green foliage turns to scarlet. The flowers are much less significant. Excellent in a shrub border or light woodland. The fruits are poisonous. 'Compactus' is a dwarf version of this shrub, only half its height.

CULTIVATION *Grow in any well-drained, fertile soil. Tolerates light shade, but fruiting and autumn color are best in full sun. Keep pruning to a minimum.*

☼☼ ◊ Z4-9 H9-1 ‡6ft (2m) ↔10ft (3m)

EUONYMUS EUROPAEUS
'RED CASCADE'

A treelike, deciduous shrub that produces colorful autumn foliage. Inconspicuous flowers in early summer are followed by rosy red fruits that split to reveal orange seeds. The oval, mid-green leaves turn scarlet-red at the end of the growing season. The fruits are toxic.

CULTIVATION *Grow in any fertile soil with good drainage, but thrives on alkaline soil. Tolerates light shade, but fruiting and autumn color are best in full sun. Two or more specimens are required to guarantee a good crop of fruits. Very little pruning is necessary.*

☀◐ ◊ Z4-7 H7-1 ↕10ft (3m) ↔8ft (2.5m)

EUONYMUS FORTUNEI
'EMERALD 'N' GOLD'

A small and scrambling, evergreen shrub that will climb if supported. The bright green, oval leaves have broad, bright golden yellow margins and take on a pink tinge in cold weather. The spring flowers are insignificant. Use to fill gaps in a shrub border, or wall-train.

CULTIVATION *Grow in any but water-logged soil. The leaves color best in full sun, but tolerates light shade. Trim in mid-spring. Trained up a wall, it may reach a height of up to 15ft (5m).*

☀◐ ◊◊ Z5-9 H9-3 ↕24in (60cm) or more ↔36in (90cm)

EUONYMUS FORTUNEI 'SILVER QUEEN'

A compact, upright or scrambling, evergreen shrub that looks most effective when grown as a climber against a wall or up into a tree. The dark green leaves have broad white edges that become pink-tinged in prolonged cold. The greenish white flowers in spring are insignificant.

CULTIVATION *Grow in any but water-logged soil, in sun or light shade. Leaf color is best in full sun. Trim shrubs in mid-spring. Allowed to climb, it can grow up to 20ft (6m) tall.*

☀️◐ ◊◊ Z5-9 H9-5 ‡8ft (2.5m) ↔5ft (1.5m)

EUPHORBIA AMYGDALOIDES VAR. ROBBIAE

Mrs. Robb's bonnet, also known simply as *E. robbiae*, is a spreading, evergreen perennial bearing open heads of yellowish green flowers in spring. The long, dark green leaves are arranged in rosettes at the base of the stems. Particularly useful in shady areas. Can be invasive.

CULTIVATION *Grow in well-drained but moist soil, in full sun or partial shade. Tolerates poor, dry soil. Dig up invasive roots to contain spread. The milky sap can irritate skin.*

☀️◐ ◊◊ Z6-9 H9-6 ‡30–32in (75–80cm) ↔12in (30cm)

EUPHORBIA CHARACIAS

A shrubby, evergreen perennial that
forms clumps of narrow, dark blue-
green leaves. Large, rounded heads
of dark-eyed, pale yellowish green
flowers are carried at the tips of the
upright stems in spring and early
summer. A dramatic structural plant,
bringing long-lasting color to a
spacious Mediterranean-style garden.
Often damaged by severe cold.

CULTIVATION *Grow in well-drained,
light soil, in full sun with shelter from
cold winds. Cut the flowered stems back
to the base in autumn; wear gloves,
since the milky sap can irritate skin.*

☼ ◊ Z7-10 H12-7   ↕↔ 4ft (1.2m)

EUPHORBIA CHARACIAS
SUBSP. *WULFENII*
'JOHN TOMLINSON'

This billowing, shrubby perennial
bears larger flowerheads than the
species (above). The flowers are
bright yellow green, without dark
eyes, and are borne in rounded
heads above the narrow, gray-
green leaves. Where marginally
hardy, it is best grown at the base
of a warm, sunny wall.

CULTIVATION *Grow in light soil that has
good drainage, in full sun. Shelter from
cold winds. Cut the flowered stems back
to the base in autumn; wear gloves,
since the milky sap can irritate skin.*

☼ ◊ Z7-10 H12-7   ↕↔ 4ft (1.2m)

EUPHORBIA × *MARTINII*

This upright, clump-forming, evergreen subshrub bears spikes of yellow-green flowers with very distinctive, dark red nectar glands. These are carried on red-tinged shoots from spring to mid-summer, above lance-shaped, mid-green leaves that are often tinged purple when young. A choice plant with an architectural look for a hot, dry site.

CULTIVATION *Grow in well-drained soil, in a sheltered, sunny site. Deadhead after flowering, wearing gloves to protect hands from the milky sap that may irritate skin.*

☼ ◊ Z7-10 H12-7   ↕↔3ft (1m)

EUPHORBIA MYRSINITES

A small, evergreen perennial bearing sprawling stems that are densely clothed with a spiral arrangement of fleshy, elliptic, blue-green leaves. Clusters of yellow-green flowers brighten the tips of the stems in spring. Excellent in a dry, sunny rock garden, or trailing over the edge of a raised bed.

CULTIVATION *Grow in well-drained, light soil, in full sun. Deadhead after flowering; it self-seeds freely. Wear gloves to avoid contact with the milky sap, which is a potential skin irritant.*

☼ ◊ Z5-8 H8-5   ↕4in (10cm)
                    ↔to 12in (30cm)

EUPHORBIA POLYCHROMA

This evergreen perennial forms a neat, rounded clump of softly hairy, mid-green foliage. It is covered with clusters of brilliant greenish yellow flowers over long periods in spring. Excellent with spring bulbs, in a border or light woodland. Tolerates a wide range of soil types. Its cultivar 'Major' grows a little taller.

CULTIVATION *Grow in either well-drained, light soil, in full sun, or moist, organic soil, in light dappled shade. Deadhead after flowering. The milky sap can irritate skin.*

☼☀ ◊◊ Z4-9 H9-1 ‡16in (40cm)
↔24in (60cm)

EUPHORBIA SCHILLINGII

This vigorous, clump-forming perennial that, unlike many euphorbias, dies back in winter, bears clusters of long-lasting, yellowish green flowers from mid-summer to mid-autumn. The lance-shaped leaves are dark green and have pale green or white central veins. Ideal for lighting up a wood-land planting or shady wild garden.

CULTIVATION *Grow in reliably moist, organic soil, in light dappled shade. Deadhead after flowering. The milky sap can irritate skin.*

☼ ◊ Z7-9 H9-7 ‡3ft (1m) ↔12in (30cm)

EXOCHORDA X *MACRANTHA* 'THE BRIDE'

A dense, spreading, deciduous shrub grown for its gently arching habit and abundant clusters of fragrant, pure white flowers. These are borne in late spring and early summer amid the oval, fresh green leaves. An elegant foil to other plants in a mixed border.

CULTIVATION *Grow in any well-drained soil, in full sun or light dappled shade. Does not like shallow, alkaline soil. Very little pruning is necessary.*

☼◑ ◊ Z5-9 H9-5 ‡6ft (2m) ↔10ft (3m)

FALLOPIA BALDSCHUANICA

Russian vine, sometimes still included in *Polygonum*, is an extremely vigorous, woody-stemmed, deciduous climber that bears hanging clusters of tiny, pink-tinted white flowers during summer and autumn. The leaves are oval and mid-green. Use to cover unsightly buildings or in a wild garden where there is plenty of space. In other situations, it can be difficult to control.

CULTIVATION *Grow in any well-drained, poor to moderately fertile soil, in sun or partial shade. Flowering is best in sun. Cut back as necessary in early spring.*

☼ ◊ Z5-9 H9-5 ‡40ft (12m)

FARGESIA NITIDA

Fountain bamboo is a slow-growing perennial that forms a dense clump of upright, dark purple-green canes. In the second year after planting, cascades of narrow, dark green leaves are produced from the top of the clump. Handsome in a wild garden; to restrict spread, grow in a large container. May be sold as *Sinarundinaria nitida*. *F. murielae* (Z8-10 H10-8) is equally attractive, similar but with yellow stems and brighter leaves.

CULTIVATION *Grow in reliably moist, fertile soil, in light dappled shade. Shelter from cold, drying winds.*

☼ ◖ Z7-10 H10-7   ↕to 15ft (5m)
                              ↔15ft (5m) or more

X *FATSHEDERA LIZEI*

The tree ivy is a mound-forming, evergreen shrub cultivated for its large, handsome, glossy dark green, ivylike leaves. Small white flowers appear in autumn. Excellent in shady areas; where marginally hardy, grow in a sunny, sheltered site. Given support, it can be trained against a wall; it also makes a fine house- or conservatory plant. Look for cream-edged 'Variegata'.

CULTIVATION *Best in moist but well-drained, fertile soil, in sun or partial shade. No regular pruning is required. Tie in to grow against a support.*

☼☼ ◖◖ Z8-10 H10-8   ↕4–6ft (1.2–2m)
                               ↔10ft (3m)

FATSIA JAPONICA

The Japanese aralia is a spreading, evergreen shrub grown for its large, palm-shaped, glossy green leaves. Broad, upright clusters of rounded, creamy white flowerheads appear in autumn. An excellent architectural plant for a shady border. Tolerates atmospheric pollution and thrives in sheltered city gardens. 'Variegata' has cream-edged leaves.

CULTIVATION *Grow in any well-drained soil, in sun or shade. Provide shelter from cold winds and hard frosts, especially when young. Little pruning is necessary, except to cut out wayward shoots and damaged growth in spring.*

☼☼ ◊ Z8-10 H10-8 ↔ 5–12ft (1.5–4m)

FELICIA AMELLOIDES 'SANTA ANITA'

This blue daisy, with white-marked, bright green foliage, is a rounded, evergreen subshrub. Large, daisylike flowers, with blue petals and bright yellow centers, open from late spring to autumn. Good in a sunny rock garden or in hanging baskets or other containers. Best treated as an annual in cold climates. There is a selection with variegated leaves, also recommended.

CULTIVATION *Grow in well-drained, fairly fertile soil, in sun. Pinch-prune to encourage bushiness, and deadhead to prolong flowering.*

☼ ◊ Z11 H12-1 ↔ 12–24in (30–60cm)

FESTUCA GLAUCA
'BLAUFUCHS'

This bright blue fescue is a densely tufted, evergreen, perennial grass. It is excellent in a border or rock garden as a foil to other plants. Spikes of not particularly striking, violet-flushed, blue-green flowers are borne in early summer, above the foliage. The narrow, bright blue leaves are its chief attraction.

CULTIVATION *Grow in dry, well-drained, poor to moderately fertile soil, in sun. For the best foliage color, divide and replant clumps every 2 or 3 years.*

☼ ◊ Z4-8 H8-1   ‡↔12in (30cm)

FILIPENDULA PURPUREA

An upright, clump-forming perennial that looks well planted in groups to form drifts of elegant, dark green foliage. Feathery clusters of red-purple flowers are carried above the leaves on purple-tinged stems in summer. Suitable for a waterside planting or bog garden; can also be naturalized in damp woodland.

CULTIVATION *Grow in reliably moist, moderately fertile, organic soil, in partial shade. Can be planted in full sun where the soil does not dry out.*

☼☀ ◊◊ Z4-9 H9-1 ‡4ft (1.2m) ↔24in (60cm)

FILIPENDULA RUBRA 'VENUSTA'

A vigorous, upright perennial that produces feathery plumes of tiny, soft pink flowers on tall branching stems in mid-summer. The large, dark green leaves are jaggedly cut into several lobes. Excellent in a bog garden, in moist soil by the side of water, or in a damp wild garden.

CULTIVATION *Grow in reliably moist, moderately fertile soil, in partial shade. Thrives in wet or boggy soil, where it will tolerate full sun.*

☼ ◑◑ Z3-9 H9-1   ↕6–8ft (2–2.5m)
                           ↔4ft (1.2m)

FORSYTHIA X *INTERMEDIA* 'LYNWOOD'

A vigorous, deciduous shrub with upright stems that arch slightly at the tips. Its golden yellow flowers appear in profusion on bare branches in early spring. Mid-green, oval leaves emerge after flowering. A reliable shrub for a mixed border or as an informal hedge: particularly effective with spring bulbs. The flowering stems are good for cutting.

CULTIVATION *Grow in well-drained, fertile soil, in full sun. Tolerates partial shade, although flowering will be less profuse. On established plants, cut out some old stems after flowering.*

☼◐ ◊ Z6-9 H9-6   ↕↔ 10ft (3m)

FORSYTHIA SUSPENSA

This upright, deciduous shrub,
sometimes called golden bell, is less
bushy than *F. x intermedia* (see
facing page, below), with more
strongly arched stems. It is valued
for the nodding, bright yellow
flowers that open on its bare
branches from early to mid-spring.
The leaves are oval and mid green.
Good planted on its own, as an
informal hedge, or in a shrub border.

CULTIVATION *Best in well-drained,
fertile soil, ideally in full sun; flowering
is less spectacular in shade. Cut out
some of the older stems on established
plants after flowering.*

☼ ◑ ◊ Z6-8 H8-6   ↔ 10ft (3m)

FOTHERGILLA MAJOR

This slow-growing, upright shrub
bears spikes of bottlebrush-like,
fragrant white flowers in late spring.
It is also valued for its blaze of
autumn foliage. The deciduous
leaves are glossy dark green in
summer, then turn orange, yellow,
and red before they fall. An
attractive addition to a shrub border
or in light woodland.

CULTIVATION *Best in moist but well-
drained, acidic, organic soil. Choose a
position in full sun for the best flowers
and autumn color. Requires very little
pruning.*

☼ ◊◊ Z5-8 H8-5   ↕8ft (2.5m) ↔6ft (2m)

FREMONTODENDRON 'CALIFORNIA GLORY'

A vigorous, upright, semi-evergreen shrub producing large, cup-shaped, golden yellow flowers from late spring to mid-autumn. The rounded leaves are lobed and dark green. Excellent for wall-training; where marginally hardy, grow against walls that receive plenty of sun.

CULTIVATION *Best in well-drained, poor to moderately fertile, neutral to alkaline soil, in sun. Shelter from cold winds. Best with no pruning, but wall-trained plants can be trimmed in spring.*

☼ ◊ Z8-10 H12-8 ‡20ft (6m) ↔12ft (4m)

FRITILLARIA ACMOPETALA

This bulbous perennial is grown for its drooping, bell-shaped, pale green flowers that are stained red-brown on the insides. They appear singly or in clusters of two or three in late spring, at the same time as the narrow, blue-green leaves. Suitable for a rock garden or sunny border.

CULTIVATION *Grow in fertile soil that has good drainage, in full sun. Divide and replant bulbs in late summer.*

☼ ◊ Z6-8 H8-6 ‡to 16in (40cm) ↔2–3in (5–8cm)

FRITILLARIA MELEAGRIS

The snake's head fritillary is a bulbous perennial that naturalizes well in grass where summers are cool and damp. The drooping, bell-shaped flowers are pink, pinkish purple, or white, and are strongly checkered. They are carried singly or in pairs during spring. The narrow leaves are gray-green. There is a white-flowered form, f. *alba*, which is also recommended.

CULTIVATION *Grow in any moist but well-drained, organic soil in full sun or light shade. Divide and replant bulbs in late summer.*

☼ ◑ ◊◊ Z3-8 H8-1 ‖ 12in (30cm)
↔ 2–3in (5–8cm)

FRITILLARIA PALLIDIFLORA

In late spring, this robust, bulbous perennial bears bell-shaped, foul-smelling flowers above the gray-green, lance-shaped leaves. They are creamy yellow with green bases, checkered brown-red inside. Suits a rock garden or border in areas with cool, damp summers. Naturalizes easily in damp meadows.

CULTIVATION *Grow in moist but well-drained, moderately fertile soil, in sun or partial shade. Divide and replant bulbs in late summer.*

☼ ◑ ◊◊ Z5-8 H8-1 ‖ 16in (40cm)
↔ 2–3in (5–8cm)

HARDIER FUCHSIAS

The hardier fuchsias are wonderfully versatile shrubs: as well as being useful in mixed borders and as flowering hedges, they can be trained as espaliers or fans against warm walls, or grown as free-standing standards or pillars. Hanging flowers, varying in form from single to double, appear throughout summer and into autumn. Where marginally hardy, these fuchsias will lose some or all of their topgrowth during winter. They are fast to recover, however, and most will retain their leaves if overwintered in a cool greenhouse or temperatures stay above 39°F (4°C).

CULTIVATION *Grow in well-drained but moist, fertile soil. Choose a position in sun or semi-shade with shelter from cold winds. Provide a deep winter mulch. Pinch-prune young plants to encourage a bushy habit. In early spring, remove winter-damaged stems; cut back healthy growth to the lowest buds.*

☀☀ ◊◊ Z7-9 H12-1

1 ↕↔30–36in (75–90cm)

2 ↕12in (30cm) ↔ 18in (45cm)

3 ↕↔3–3½ft (1–1.1m)

4 ↕6–10ft (2–3m) ↔ 3-6ft (1–2m)

5 ↕↔6–12in (15–30cm)

6 ↕ to 10ft (3m) ↔ 6-10ft (2–3m)

1 *F.* 'Genii' **2** *F.* 'Lady Thumb' **3** *F.* 'Mrs. Popple'
4 *F.* 'Riccartonii' **5** *F.* 'Tom Thumb' **6** *F. magellanica* 'Versicolor'

TENDER FUCHSIAS

The tender fuchsias are flowering shrubs that require at least some winter protection in cold climates. The compensation for this extra care is an increased range of beautiful summer flowers for the garden, greenhouse, and conservatory. All can be grown out of doors in the summer months and make superb patio plants when grown in containers, whether pinch-pruned into dense bushes or trained as columns or standards. Where not hardy, shelter tender fuchsias in a greenhouse or cool conservatory over the winter months; the tender species fuchsias, including 'Thalia', need a minimum temperature of 50°C (10°C) at all times.

CULTIVATION *Grow in moist but well-drained, fertile soil or soil mix, in sun or partial shade. Pinch-prune young plants to promote bushiness, and trim after flowering to remove spent blooms. Prune back to an established framework in early spring.*

☼◑ ◐◗ Z8-10 H10-8 (mostly)

1 ↕↔ 12–24in (30–60cm)

2 ↕ to 24in (60cm) ↔ to 18in (45cm)

3 ↕ to 12ft (4m) ↔ 3–4ft (1–1.2m)

1 *Fuchsia* 'Annabel' **2** *F.* 'Billy Green' (Z11 H12-1) **3** *F. boliviana* var. *alba* (Z11 H12-1)

4 ↕ ↔ 18–30in (45–75cm) **5** ↕ to 36in (90cm) ↔ to 30in (75cm) **6** ↕ to 36in (90cm) ↔ to 24in (60cm)

7 ↕ 5ft (1.5m) ↔ to 32in (80cm) **8** ↕ to 18in (45cm) ↔ to 24in (60cm) **9** ↕ to 18in (75cm) ↔ to 24in (60cm)

4 *Fuchsia* 'Celia Smedley' **5** *F.* 'Checkerboard' **6** *F.* 'Coralle'
7 *F. fulgens* **8** *F.* 'Joy Patmore' **9** *F.* 'Leonora'

10 ↕↔ 12–24in (30–60cm)

11 ↕ to 18in (45cm) ↔ 18in (45cm)

12 ↕ to 30in (75cm) ↔ to 24in (60cm)

14 ↕ to 24in (60cm) ↔ 30in (75cm)

15 ↕↔ 18–36in (45–90cm)

13 ↕ 24in (60cm) ↔ 18in (45cm)

MORE CHOICES

'Brookwood Belle' Cerise and white flowers
'Pacquesa' Red and red-veined white.
'Winston Churchill' Lavender and pink.

10 *F.* 'Mary' **11** *F.* 'Nellie Nuttall' **12** *F.* 'Royal Velvet'
13 *F.* 'Snowcap' **14** *F.* 'Swingtime' **15** *F.* 'Thalia'

TRAILING FUCHSIAS

Fuchsia cultivars with a trailing or spreading habit are the perfect plants to have trailing over the edge of a tall container, windowbox, or hanging basket, where their pendulous flowers will be shown to great effect. They bloom continuously throughout summer and into early autumn and can be left in place undisturbed right up until the end of the season. After this, they are best discarded and new plants bought the following year. An alternative, longer-lived planting is to train trailing fuchsias into attractive weeping standards for container plantings, but they must be kept frost-free in winter.

CULTIVATION *Grow in fertile, moist but well-drained soil or soil mix, in full sun or partial shade. Shelter from cold, drying winds. Little pruning is necessary, except to remove wayward growth. Regularly pinch out the tips of young plants to encourage bushiness and a well-balanced shape.*

☼☀ ◊◊ Z8-10 H10-8

1 ‡6–12in (15–30cm) ↔ 18in (45cm)

2 ‡6–12in (15–30cm) ↔ 18in (45cm)

3 ‡18in (45cm) ↔ 24in (60cm)

4 ‡to 24in (60cm) ↔ 30in (75cm)

1 *F.* 'La Campanella' **2** *F.* 'Golden Marinka' **3** *F.* 'Jack Shahan' **4** *F.* 'Lena'

GAILLARDIA 'DAZZLER'

A bushy, short-lived perennial that bears large, daisylike flowers over a long period in summer. These have yellow-tipped, bright orange petals surrounding an orange-red center. The leaves are soft, lance-shaped, and mid-green. Effective in a sunny, mixed or herbaceous border; the flowers are good for cutting.

CULTIVATION *Grow in well-drained, not too fertile soil, in full sun. May need staking. Often short-lived, but can be reinvigorated by division in winter.*

☼ ◊ Z3-8 H8-3   ↕24–34in (60–85cm)
↔ 18in (45cm)

GALANTHUS ELWESII

This robust snowdrop is a bulbous perennial that produces slender, honey-scented, pure white flowers in late winter, above the bluish green foliage. The inner petals have green markings. Good for borders and rock gardens; naturalizes easily in light woodland.

CULTIVATION *Grow in moist but well-drained, organic soil that does not dry out in summer. Choose a position in partial shade.*

☼ ◊◊ Z3-9 H9-3   ↕4–6in (10–15cm)
↔3in (8cm)

GALANTHUS 'MAGNET'

This tall snowdrop is a vigorous bulbous perennial bearing drooping, pear-shaped, pure white flowers during late winter and early spring; the inner petals have a deep green, V-shaped mark at the tips. The strap-shaped, gray-green leaves are arranged around the base of the plant. Good for naturalizing in grass or in a woodland garden.

CULTIVATION *Grow in moist but well-drained, fertile soil that does not dry out in summer. Choose a position in partial shade.*

☼ ◊◊ Z4-9 H9-1 ‡8in (20cm) ↔3in (8cm)

GALANTHUS NIVALIS 'FLORE PLENO'

This double-flowered form of the common snowdrop, *G. nivalis*, is a robust, bulbous perennial. Drooping, pear-shaped, pure white flowers appear from late winter to early spring, with green markings on the tips of the inner petals. The narrow leaves are gray-green. Good for naturalizing under deciduous trees or shrubs.

CULTIVATION *Grow in reliably moist but well-drained, fertile soil, in light shade. Divide and replant every few years after flowering to maintain vigor.*

☼ ◊◊ Z3-9 H9-1 ‡↔4in (10cm)

GALANTHUS 'S. ARNOTT'

This honey-scented snowdrop, which has even larger flowers than 'Magnet' (facing page, above), is a fast-growing, bulbous perennial. Nodding, pear-shaped, pure white flowers appear in late winter to early spring and have a green, V-shaped mark at the tip of each inner petal. The narrow leaves are gray-green. Good for a rock garden or raised bed. 'Atkinsii' is also recommended, similar to this one.

CULTIVATION *Grow in moist but well-drained, fertile soil, in dappled shade. Keep reliably moist in summer. Divide and replant clumps after flowering.*

☼ ◊◊ Z4-9 H9-1 ‡8in (20cm) ↔3in (8cm)

GARRYA ELLIPTICA 'JAMES ROOF'

This silk-tassel bush is an upright, evergreen shrub, becoming treelike with age. It is grown for its long, silver-gray catkins, which dangle from the branches in winter and early spring. The leaves are dark sea green and have wavy margins. Excellent in a shrub border, against a shady wall, or as hedging; tolerates coastal conditions.

CULTIVATION *Grow in well-drained, moderately fertile soil, in full sun or partial shade. Tolerates poor, dry soil. Trim after flowering, as necessary.*

☼☼ ◊ Z8-10 H10-8   ‡↔12ft (4m)

GAULTHERIA MUCRONATA 'MULBERRY WINE' (FEMALE)

This evergreen, spreading shrub, sometimes included in *Pernettya*, is much valued for its autumn display of large, rounded, magenta to purple berries that show off well against the toothed, glossy dark green leaves. Small white flowers are borne throughout summer.

CULTIVATION *Grow in reliably moist, peaty, acidic to neutral soil, in partial shade or full sun. Plant close to male varieties to ensure a reliable crop of berries. Chop away spreading roots with a spade to restrict the overall size.*

☼ ◐ ◗ Z8-9 H9-8　↔ 4ft (1.2m)

GAULTHERIA MUCRONATA 'WINTERTIME' (FEMALE)

An evergreen, spreading shrub, sometimes included in the genus *Pernettya*, bearing large, showy white berries that persist well into winter. Small white flowers are borne from late spring into early summer. The glossy dark green leaves are elliptic to oblong and toothed.

CULTIVATION *Grow in reliably moist, acidic to neutral, peaty soil. Best in light shade, but tolerates sun. Plant close to male varieties to ensure a good crop of berries. Dig out spreading roots as necessary to restrict the overall size.*

☼ ◐ ◗ Z8-9 H9-8　↔ 4ft (1.2m)

GAULTHERIA PROCUMBENS

Checkerberry is a creeping shrub that bears drooping, urn-shaped, white or pink flowers in summer, followed by aromatic scarlet fruits. As these usually persist until spring, they give winter color. The glossy, dark green leaves have a strong fragrance when crushed, giving the plant its other common name, wintergreen. Good groundcover in shade.

CULTIVATION *Grow in acidic to neutral, peaty, moist soil in partial shade; full sun is tolerated only where the soil is always moist. Trim after flowering.*

 ☀ ◐ Z3-8 H8-1　‡6in (15cm)
↔3ft (1m) or more

GAURA LINDHEIMERI

A tall, clump-forming perennial with basal leaves and slender stems. From late spring to autumn, it bears loose spires of pinkish white buds that open in the morning into white flowers. A graceful plant for a mixed border, tolerating both heat and drought.

CULTIVATION *Grow in fertile, moist but well-drained soil, ideally in full sun, but some part-day shade is tolerated. If necessary, divide clumps in spring.*

☀ ◐◐ Z6-9 H9-6　‡to 5ft (1.5m)
↔36in (90cm)

GAZANIAS

These useful summer bedding plants are vigorous, spreading perennials usually grown as annuals. They are cultivated for their long display of large and very colorful, daisylike flowers. They close in dull or cool weather. Flowers may be orange, white, golden yellow, beige, bronze, or bright pink, often with striking contrasting central zones of one or two other colors. Hybrid selections with variously colored flowerheads are also popular. The lance-shaped leaves are dark green with white-silky undersides. Gazanias grow well in containers and tolerate coastal conditions.

CULTIVATION *Grow in light, sandy, well-drained soil in full sun. Remove old or faded flowerheads to prolong flowering. Water freely during the growing season. The plants will die back on arrival of the first frosts.*

☼ ◊ Z8-11 H12-1

MORE CHOICES

G. Chansonette Series Mixed colors, zoned in a contrasting shade.

G. Mini-star Series Mixed or single zoned colors.

G. Talent Series Mixed or single colors.

1 ‡8in (20cm) ↔ 10in (25cm)

2 ‡8in (20cm) ↔ 10in (25cm)

5 ‡8in (20cm) ↔ 10in (25cm)

4 ‡8in (20cm) ↔ 10in (25cm)

3 ‡8in (20cm) ↔ 10in (25cm)

1 *Gazania* 'Aztec' **2** *G.* 'Cookei' **3** *G.* 'Daybreak Garden Sun'
4 *G.* 'Michael' **5** *G. rigens* var. *uniflora*

GENISTA AETNENSIS

The Mount Etna broom is an upright, almost leafless, deciduous shrub that is excellent on its own or at the back of a border in hot, dry situations. Masses of fragrant, pea-like, golden yellow flowers cover the weeping, mid-green stems during mid-summer.

CULTIVATION *Grow in well-drained, light, poor to moderately fertile soil, in full sun. Keep pruning to a minimum; old, straggly plants are best replaced.*

☼ ◊ Z9-10 H12-9   ‡↔ 25ft (8m)

GENISTA LYDIA

This low, deciduous shrub forms a mound of arching, prickle-tipped branches that are covered with yellow, pealike flowers in early summer. The small, narrow leaves are blue-green. Ideal for hot, dry sites such as a rock garden or raised bed.

CULTIVATION *Grow in well-drained, light, poor to moderately fertile soil, in full sun. Keep pruning to a minimum; old, straggly plants are best replaced.*

☼ ◊ Z6-9 H9-6   ‡24in (60cm) ↔3ft (1m)

GENISTA TENERA 'GOLDEN SHOWER'

This graceful cultivar of broom is a deciduous shrub with slender shoots and narrow gray-green leaves. It is valued for its mass of fragrant, bright yellow flowers that appear in profusion during the first half of summer. It is usually grown in a shrub or mixed border.

CULTIVATION *Grow in light, poor to moderately fertile, well-drained soil, in full sun. Trim in late winter or early spring, but do not cut back to old wood.*

☀ ◊ Z9-10 H10-9   ↕10ft (3m)
                         ↔15ft (5m)

GENTIANA ACAULIS

The trumpet gentian is a mat-forming, evergreen perennial that bears large, trumpet-shaped, vivid deep blue flowers in spring. The leaves are oval and glossy dark green. Good in a rock garden, raised bed, or trough; thrives in areas with cool, wet summers.

CULTIVATION *Grow in reliably moist but well-drained, organic soil, in full sun or partial shade. Protect from hot sun in areas with warm, dry summers.*

☀ ☀ ◊◊ Z5-8 H8-5   ↕3in (8cm)
                         ↔to 12in (30cm)

GENTIANA ASCLEPIADEA

The willow gentian is an arching, clump-forming perennial producing trumpet-shaped, dark blue flowers in late summer and autumn; these are often spotted or striped with purple on the insides. The leaves are lance-shaped and fresh green. Suitable for a border or large rock garden.

CULTIVATION *Grow in moist, fertile, organic soil. Best in light shade, but tolerates sun if the soil is reliably moist.*

☀ ◑ Z6-9 H9-6 ‡24–36in (60–90cm)
↔18in (45cm)

GENTIANA SEPTEMFIDA

This late-summer-flowering gentian is a spreading to upright, clump-forming herbaceous perennial. Clusters of narrowly bell-shaped, bright blue flowers with white throats are borne amid the oval, mid-green leaves. Good for a rock garden or raised bed; thrives in cool, moist summers. The variety var. *lagodechiana*, also recommended, has just one flower per stem.

CULTIVATION *Grow in moist but well-drained, organic soil, in full sun or partial shade. Protect from hot sun in areas with warm, dry summers.*

☀☀ ◐◑ Z6-8 H8-6 ‡6–8in (15–20cm)
↔12in (30cm)

SMALL HARDY GERANIUMS

The low-growing members of the genus *Geranium* (not to be confused with pelargoniums; see pages 319–321) are versatile plants, useful not only at the front of borders but also in rock gardens or as a groundcover. These evergreen perennials are long-lived and undemanding, tolerating a wide range of sites and soil types. The lobed and toothed leaves are often variegated or aromatic. In summer, they bear typically saucer-shaped flowers ranging in color from white through soft blues such as 'Johnson's Blue' to the intense pink of *G. cinereum* var. *caulescens*, often with contrasting veins, eyes, or other markings.

CULTIVATION *Grow in sharply drained, organic soil, in full sun. Feed with a balanced fertilizer every month during the growing season. Remove withered flower stems and old leaves to encourage fresh growth later in the season.*

☼ ◊ Z4-8 H9-1

1 ‡ to 18in (45cm) ↔ 3ft (1m) or more   **2** ‡ to 6in (15cm) ↔ to 12in (30cm)

1 *G.* 'Ann Folkard' **2** *G. cinereum* 'Ballerina'

3 ↕ to6in (15cm) ↔ to 12in (30cm)

4 ↕ to18in (45cm) ↔ indefinite

5 ↕ to 6in (15cm) ↔ 20in (50cm)

6 ↕ 12in (30cm) ↔ 24in (60cm)

7 ↕ to 18in (45cm) ↔ 30in (75cm)

8 ↕ to 12in (30cm) ↔ to 3ft (1m)

9 ↕ 12in (30cm) ↔ 4ft (1.2m)

3 *G. cinereum* var. *subcaulescens* **4** *G. clarkei* 'Kashmir White' **5** *G. dalmaticum*
6 *G. himalayense* 'Gravetye' **7** *G.* 'Johnson's Blue' **8** *G.* × *riversleaianum* 'Russell Prichard'
9 *G. wallichianum* 'Buxton's Variety'

LARGE HARDY GERANIUMS

The taller, clump-forming types of hardy perennial geranium – not to be confused with pelargoniums (see pages 319–321) – make effective, long-lived border plants or fillers among shrubs, requiring a minimum of attention. They are especially suited to cottage garden plantings and between roses. Their lobed, evergreen leaves may be colored or aromatic and give a long season of interest. Throughout summer, this is heightened by an abundance of saucer-shaped flowers in white and shades of blue, pink, and purple. Markings on flowers vary from the dramatic, contrasting dark eyes of *G. psilostemon* to the delicate venation of *G. sanguineum* var. *striatum*.

CULTIVATION *Best in well-drained, fairly fertile soil, in full sun or partial shade, but tolerant of any soil that is not waterlogged. Remove old leaves and withered flower stems to encourage new growth.*

☼ ☀ ◊◊ Z4-8 H9-1

1 ‡18in (45cm) ↔ 24in (60cm)

2 ‡↔ 24in (60cm)

3 ‡20in (50cm) ↔ 24in (60cm)

1 *G. endressii* **2** *G.* x *magnificum* **3** *G. macrorrhizum* 'Ingwersen's Variety'

4 ↕ ↔ 24in (60cm)

5 ↕ ↔ 24in (60cm)

6 ↕ ↔ 12in (30cm)

8 ↕ 24in (60cm) ↔ 36in (90cm)

7 ↕ 4in (10cm) ↔ 12in (30cm)

9 ↕ 24in (60cm) ↔ 36in (90cm)

4 *G. pratense* 'Mrs. Kendall Clark' 5 *G. psilostemon* (syn. *G. armenum*) 6 *G. renardii*
7 *G. sanguineum* var. *striatum* 8 *G. sylvaticum* 'Mayflower' 9 *G.* x *oxonianum* 'Wargrave Pink'

GEUM 'LADY STRATHEDEN'

A clump-forming perennial bearing double, bright yellow flowers on arching stems over a long period in summer. The mid-green leaves are large and lobed. An easy, long-flowering plant for brightening up a mixed or herbaceous border. The taller 'Fire Opal' (Z5-9 H9-4) is closely related, with reddish orange flowers on purple stems.

CULTIVATION *Grow in moist but well-drained, fertile soil, in full sun. Avoid sites that become waterlogged in winter.*

☼ ◑◑ Z5-9 H9-5 ‡16–24in (40–60cm)
↔24in (60cm)

GEUM MONTANUM

A small, clump-forming perennial grown for its solitary, cup-shaped, deep golden yellow flowers. These are produced in spring and early summer above large, lobed, dark green leaves. Excellent for a rock garden, raised bed, or trough.

CULTIVATION *Grow in well-drained, preferably gritty, fertile soil, in full sun. Will not tolerate waterlogging in winter.*

☼ ◑ Z4-8 H8-3 ‡6in (15cm) ↔12in (30cm)

GILLENIA TRIFOLIATA

An upright, graceful perennial that forms clumps of olive green leaves that turn red in autumn. Delicate white flowers with slender petals are borne on wiry red stems in summer. Effective in a shady border or light woodland; the cut flowers last well.

CULTIVATION *Grow in moist but well drained, fertile soil. Best in partial shade, but tolerates some sun if shaded during the hottest part of the day.*

☼ ◐ ◊◊ Z5-9 H9-5 ‡3ft (1m) ↔24in (60cm)

GLADIOLUS CALLIANTHUS

An upright cormous perennial that bears strongly scented white flowers with purple-red throats. These hang from elegant stems during summer above fans of narrow, mid green leaves. Ideal for mixed borders; the flowers are suitable for cutting.

CULTIVATION *Grow in fertile soil, in full sun. Plant on a layer of sand to improve drainage. Where not hardy, lift the corms when the leaves turn yellow-brown, remove off the leaves, and store the corms in frost-free conditions.*

☼ ◊ Z8-10 H12-1 ‡28–39in (70–100cm) ↔2in (5cm)

GLADIOLUS COMMUNIS
SUBSP. *BYZANTINUS*

In late spring, this upright, cormous perennial produces a blaze of magenta flowers with purple-marked lips. These are arranged in spikes above fans of narrow, mid-green leaves. An elegant subject for a mixed or herbaceous border; the flowers are good for cutting.

CULTIVATION *Grow in fertile soil in full sun. Plant corms on a bed of sharp sand to improve drainage. Benefits from a light but deep winter mulch where marginally hardy..*

☼ ◊ Z8-10 H12-1 ‡3ft (1m) ↔3in (8cm)

GLEDITSIA TRIACANTHOS
'SUNBURST'

This fast-growing honeylocust is a broadly conical, deciduous tree valued for its beautiful foliage and light canopy. The finely divided leaves are bright gold-yellow when they emerge in spring, maturing to dark green, then yellowing again before they fall. A useful, pollution-tolerant tree for a small garden.

CULTIVATION *Grow in any well-drained, fertile soil, in full sun. Prune only to remove dead, damaged or diseased wood, from late summer to mid-winter.*

☼ ◊ Z3-7 H7-1 ‡40ft (12m) ↔30ft (10m)

GOMPHRENA HAAGEANA 'STRAWBERRY FAYRE'

An upright, bushy annual bearing brilliant red flowerheads throughout summer to early autumn. These are carried on upright stems above narrow, mid-green leaves that are covered with white hairs when young. Good for summer bedding; the flowers can also be cut, drying well for winter decoration. For bronze flowers on a similar plant, look for 'Amber Glow'.

CULTIVATION *Grow in any moderately fertile soil with good drainage. Choose a position in full sun.*

☀ ◊ annual H12-1 ‡30–32in (75–80cm)
↔to 12in (30cm)

GUNNERA MANICATA

A massive, clump-forming perennial that produces the largest leaves of most any garden plant, to 6ft (2m) long. These are rounded, lobed, sharply toothed, and dull green, with thick, prickly stalks. Spikes of tiny, greenish red flowers appear in summer. An imposing plant by water or in a bog garden. Provide protection where marginally hardy..

CULTIVATION *Best in permanently moist, fertile soil, in full sun or partial shade. Shelter from cold winds. Protect from frost by folding the dead leaves over the dormant crown before winter.*

☀◐ ◊◊ Z7-10 H12-7 ‡8ft (2.5m)
↔10–12ft (3–4m) or more

GYMNOCALYCIUM ANDREAE

This prickly cactus forms clusters of spherical, dark blue-green or black-green stems with warty ribs and pale yellow-white spines. Bright yellow flowers are borne in early summer. Ideal for a cactus garden; must be grown in a heated greenhouse where not hardy.

CULTIVATION *Best in sharply drained, poor soil, or standard cactus soil mix, in sun. Keep dry in winter. Minimum temperature 35–50°F (2–10°C).*

☼ ◊ H12-10   ‡2½in (6cm) ↔6in (15cm)

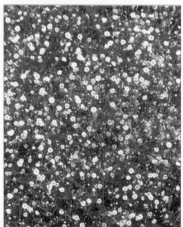

GYPSOPHILA PANICULATA
'BRISTOL FAIRY'

This herbaceous perennial forms a mound of slightly fleshy, lance-shaped, blue-green leaves on very slender, wiry stems. The profusion of tiny, double white flowers in summer forms a cloudlike display. Very effective cascading over a low wall or as a foil to more upright, sharply defined flowers.

CULTIVATION *Grow in well-drained, deep, moderately fertile, preferably alkaline soil, in full sun. Resents being disturbed after planting.*

☼ ◊ Z4-9 H9-4   ‡↔ to 4ft (1.2m)

GYPSOPHILA
'ROSENSCHLEIER'

A mound-forming perennial, also sold as 'Rosy Veil' or 'Veil of Roses', bearing trailing stems that look great cascading over a low wall. In summer, tiny, double white flowers that age to pale pink are borne in airy sprays, forming a dense cloud of blooms. The slightly fleshy leaves are lance-shaped and blue-green. The flowers dry well for decoration.

CULTIVATION *Grow in well-drained, deep, moderately fertile, preferably alkaline soil. Choose a position in full sun. Resents root disturbance.*

☼ ◊ Z4-9 H9-3 ‡50cm (20in) ↔1m (3ft)

HAKONECHLOA MACRA
'AUREOLA'

This colorful grass is a deciduous perennial that forms a clump of narrow, arching, bright yellow leaves with cream and green stripes. They flush red in autumn and persist well into winter. Reddish brown flower spikes appear in late summer. A versatile plant that can be used in a border, rock garden, or containers.

CULTIVATION *Grow in moist but well-drained, fertile, organic soil. Leaf color is best in partial shade, but it tolerates full sun.*

☼◑ ◊◊ Z5-9 H9-5 ‡14in (35cm) ↔16in (40cm)

x *HALIMIOCISTUS SAHUCII*

A compact shrub that forms mounds of linear, dark green leaves with downy undersides. Masses of saucer-shaped white flowers are produced throughout summer. Good in a border, at the base of a warm wall, or in a rock garden.

CULTIVATION *Best in freely draining, poor to moderately fertile, light, gritty soil, in a sunny site. Shelter from excessive winter moisture.*

☼ ◊ Z8-9 H9-8 ‡18in (45cm) ↔36in (90cm)

x *HALIMIOCISTUS WINTONENSIS* 'MERRIST WOOD CREAM'

A spreading, evergreen shrub bearing creamy yellow flowers with red bands and yellow centers in late spring and early summer. The lance-shaped leaves are gray-green. Good at the front of a mixed border or at the foot of a warm wall. Also suits a raised bed or rock garden.

CULTIVATION *Grow in freely draining, poor to moderately fertile soil, in full sun. Choose a position protected from excessive winter moisture.*

☼ ◊ Z7-9 H9-7 ‡24in (60cm) ↔36in (90cm)

HALIMIUM LASIANTHUM

A spreading bush with clusters of saucer-shaped, golden yellow flowers in late spring and early summer. Each petal normally has a brownish red mark at the base. The foliage is gray-green. Halimiums flower best in regions with long, hot summers, and this one is suited to a coastal garden.

CULTIVATION *Best in well-drained, moderately fertile sandy soil in full sun, with shelter from cold, drying winds. Established plants dislike being moved. Trim after flowering to maintain an attractive shape.*

☼ ◊　Z9-10 H10-8 ‡3ft (1m) ↔5ft (1.5m)

HALIMIUM 'SUSAN'

A small, spreading, evergreen shrub valued for its single or semidouble summer flowers, bright yellow with deep purple markings. The leaves are oval and gray-green. Good for rock gardens in coastal areas. Provide shelter at the foot of a warm wall where marginal. Flowers are best during long, hot summers. *H. ocymoides*, similar but more upright in habit, is also recommended.

CULTIVATION *Grow in freely draining, fairly fertile, light, sandy soil, in full sun. Provide shelter from cold winds. Trim lightly in spring, as necessary.*

☼ ◊　Z9-10 H12-9 ‡18in (45cm) ↔24in (60cm)

WITCH HAZELS (*HAMAMELIS*)

These spreading, deciduous shrubs are grown for their large clusters of usually yellow spidery flowers that appear on the branches when the shrubs are bare in winter; those of *H. vernalis* may coincide with the unfurling of the leaves. Each flower has four narrow petals and an enchanting fragrance. Most garden species also display attractive autumn foliage; the broad, bright green leaves turn red and yellow before they fall. Witch hazels bring color and scent to the garden in winter; they are good as specimen plants or grouped in a shrub border or woodland garden.

CULTIVATION *Grow in moderately fertile, moist but well-drained, acidic to neutral soil in full sun or partial shade, in an open but not exposed site. Witch hazels also tolerate deep, organic, alkaline soil. Remove wayward or crossing shoots when dormant in late winter or early spring to maintain a healthy, permanent framework.*

☼☀ ◊ Z5-9 (vernalis Z4-8) H9-5

1 ↕↔ 12ft (4m)   **2** ↕↔ 12ft (4m)

1 *Hamamelis* x *intermedia* 'Arnold Promise'   **2** *H.* x *intermedia* 'Barmstedt Gold'

3 ↕↔ 12ft (4m)

4 ↕↔ 12ft (4m)

5 ↕↔ 12ft (4m)

6 ↕↔ 12ft (4m)

7 ↕↔ 15ft (5m)

3 *H.* × *intermedia* 'Diane' **4** *H.* × *intermedia* 'Jelena'
5 *H.* × *intermedia* 'Pallida' **6** *H. mollis* **7** *H. vernalis* 'Sandra'

Hebe albicans

A neat, mound-forming shrub with tightly packed, glaucous gray-green foliage. It bears short, tight clusters of white flowers at the ends of the branches in the first half of summer. A useful evergreen hedging plant in mild coastal areas, or grow in a shrub border.

CULTIVATION *Grow in poor to moderately fertile, moist but well-drained, neutral to slightly alkaline soil in full sun or partial shade. Shelter from cold, drying winds. It needs little or no pruning.*

☼☀ ◊◊ Z9-10 H10-9   ‡24in (60cm)
          ↔36in (90cm)

Hebe cupressoides 'Boughton Dome'

This dwarf, evergreen shrub is grown for its neat shape and dense foliage that forms a pale green dome. Flowers are infrequent. The congested, slender, grayish green branches carry pale green scalelike, pale green leaves. Excellent in a rock garden; gives a topiary effect without any clipping. Thrives in coastal gardens.

CULTIVATION *Grow in moist but well-drained, poor to moderately fertile soil, in full sun or partial shade. No regular pruning is necessary.*

☼☀ ◊◊ Z8-9 H9-8   ‡12in (30cm)
          ↔24in (60cm)

HEBE × *FRANCISCANA* 'VARIEGATA'

A dense, rounded, evergreen shrub bearing colourful, oval leaves; these are mid-green with creamy white margins. Purple flowers that contrast well with the foliage are carried in dense spikes during summer and autumn. A fine, pollution-tolerant plant for a mixed border or rock garden. Where marginal, shelter at the foot of a warm wall. 'Blue Gem' is a similar plant with plain leaves.

CULTIVATION *Grow in moist but well-drained, poor to moderately fertile soil, in sun or light shade. Shelter from cold, drying winds. No pruning is necessary.*

☼ ◐ ◊◊ Z9-10 H10-9 ↕↔ 48in (120cm)

HEBE 'GREAT ORME'

An open, rounded, evergreen shrub that carries slender spikes of small, deep pink flowers that fade to white. These are borne from mid-summer to mid-autumn amid the lance-shaped, glossy dark green leaves. Good in a mixed or shrub border; shelter at the base of a warm wall where marginally hardy.

CULTIVATION *Grow in moist but well-drained, poor to moderately fertile soil, in sun or light shade. Shelter from cold winds. Pruning is unnecessary, but leggy plants can be cut back in spring.*

☼ ◐ ◊◊ Z9-10 H10-9 ↕↔ 4ft (1.2m)

HEBE MACRANTHA

This upright, spreading shrub has leathery green leaves. It bears relatively large flowers for a hebe, produced in clusters of three in early summer. A useful evergreen edging plant for seaside gardens where it is hardy.

CULTIVATION *Grow in moist but well-drained, reasonably fertile, neutral to slightly alkaline soil in full sun or partial shade. Shelter from cold, drying winds. It needs little or no pruning.*

☼ ◗ ◊◊ Z9-10 H10-9   ‡24in (60cm)
↔36in (90cm)

HEBE OCHRACEA
'JAMES STIRLING'

A compact shrub that bears its medium-sized white flowers in clusters from late spring to early summer. Like other whipcord hebes, it has small, scalelike leaves that lie flat against the stems to give the appearance of a dwarf conifer. An excellent evergreen for a rock garden, the rich ochre-yellow foliage looking very attractive in winter.

CULTIVATION *Best in moist but well-drained, neutral to slightly alkaline soil. Site in full sun or partial shade. Do not prune unless absolutely necessary.*

☼ ◗ ◊◊ Z8-10 H10-8   ‡↔24in (60cm)

HEBE PINGUIFOLIA
'PAGEI'

A low-growing, evergreen shrub
bearing purple stems with four ranks
of leathery, oval, blue-green leaves.
Abundant clusters of white flowers
appear at the tips of the shoots in
late spring and early summer. Plant
in groups as a groundcover, or in a
rock garden.

CULTIVATION *Grow in moist but well-
drained, poor to moderately fertile soil,
in sun or partial shade. Best with some
shelter from cold, drying winds. Trim to
neaten in early spring, if necessary.*

☼☀ ◊◊ Z8-10 H10-8 ↕12in (30cm)
↔36in (90cm)

HEBE RAKAIENSIS

A rounded, evergreen shrub bearing
spikes of white flowers from early to
mid-summer. The leaves are elliptic
and glossy bright green. Ideal either
as a small, spreading specimen
shrub or as a focal point in a large
rock garden.

CULTIVATION *Grow in moist but well-
drained, poor to moderately fertile soil,
in sun or partial shade. Best with some
shelter from cold, drying winds. Trim to
shape in early spring, if necessary.*

☼☀ ◊◊ Z8-10 H10-8 ↕3ft (1m) ↔4ft (1.2m)

HEDERA CANARIENSIS 'RAVENSHOLST'

This vigorous cultivar of Canary Island ivy is a self-clinging, evergreen climber useful as a groundcover or to mask a bare wall. The leaves are shallowly lobed, glossy, and dark green. It will be damaged during an unusually severe winter, but it usually grows back quickly.

CULTIVATION *Best in fertile, moist but well-drained soil that is rich in organic matter. It tolerates shade and can be pruned or trimmed at any time of year.*

☼☀ ◊◊ Z7-10 H10-7   ↕15ft (5m)

HEDERA COLCHICA

Persian ivy is a vigorous, self-clinging, evergreen climber with large, heart-shaped leaves. They are leathery in texture and dark green. This is a particularly useful climber for quickly covering an unsightly wall, as a groundcover, or for training into a large, deciduous tree.

CULTIVATION *Grow in fertile, moist but well-drained, preferably alkaline soil that is rich in organic matter. It tolerates shade and can be pruned at any time of year.*

☼☀ ◊◊ Z5-10 H10-5   ↕30ft (10m)

HEDERA COLCHICA 'DENTATA'

This Persian ivy is a very vigorous, evergreen, self-clinging climber producing large, heart-shaped, drooping, glossy green leaves. The stems and leaf stalks are flushed purple. A handsome plant for covering an unattractive wall in shade; also effective as a groundcover. 'Dentata Variegata' has mottled gray-green leaves edged with cream.

CULTIVATION *Best in moist but well-drained, fertile, ideally alkaline soil, in partial to deep shade. Prune at any time of the year to restrict size.*

☼ ☀ ◊◊ Z5-10 H10-5 ‡30ft (10m)

HEDERA COLCHICA 'SULPHUR HEART'

This colored-leaf Persian ivy is a very vigorous, self-clinging evergreen climber that can also be grown as a groundcover. The large, heart-shaped leaves are dark green suffused with creamy yellow; as they mature, the color becomes more even. Will quickly cover a wall in shade.

CULTIVATION *Grow in moist but well-drained, fertile, preferably alkaline soil. Tolerates partial shade, but leaf color is more intense in sun. Prune at any time of the year to restrict size.*

☼ ☀ ◊◊ Z5-10 H10-5 ‡15ft (5m)

ENGLISH IVIES (*HEDERA HELIX*)

Hedera helix, the English ivy, is an evergreen, woody-stemmed, self-clinging climber and the parent of an enormous selection of cultivars. Leaf forms vary from heart-shaped to deeply lobed, ranging in color from the bright gold 'Buttercup' to the deep purple 'Atropurpurea'. They make excellent groundcovers, tolerating even dry shade, and will quickly cover featureless walls; they can damage paintwork or invade gutters if not kept in check. Variegated cultivars are especially useful for enlivening dark corners and shaded walls. Small ivies make good houseplants and can be trained over topiary frames.

CULTIVATION *Best in moist but well-drained, organic, alkaline soil. Choose a position in full sun or shade; ivies with variegated leaves may lose their color in shade. Trim as necessary to keep under control.*

☼ ◑ ◊◊ Z5-10 H12-5

1 ‡25ft (8m)   2 ‡6ft (2m)   3 ‡6ft (2m)

4 ‡3ft (1m)   5 ‡3ft (1m)   6 ‡12in (30cm)

1 *H. helix* 'Atropurpurea'   2 *H. helix* 'Buttercup'   3 *H. helix* 'Glacier'
4 *H. helix* 'Goldchild'   5 *H. helix* 'Ivalace'   6 *H. helix* 'Little Diamond'

HEDERA HIBERNICA

Irish ivy is a vigorous, evergreen, self-clinging climber valued for its broadly oval, dark green leaves, which have gray-green veins and five triangular lobes. Useful for a wall or against a large tree, or as a fast-growing groundcover under trees or shrubs.

CULTIVATION *Best in moist but well-drained, fertile, ideally alkaline soil, in partial to full shade. Prune at any time of the year to restrict spread.*

☀ ◑ ● ◊◊ Z6-10 H12-6   ‡to 30ft (10m)

HELIANTHEMUM 'FIRE DRAGON'

This rock rose, also called 'Mrs Clay', is a small, spreading, evergreen shrub bearing a profusion of saucer-shaped, bright orange-red flowers. These open in succession during late spring and summer amid the oblong, gray-green leaves. Ideal for a rock garden or raised bed, or as a groundcover in groups on a sunny bank.

CULTIVATION *Grow in well-drained, slightly alkaline soil, in full sun. Trim after flowering to keep compact. Often short-lived, but easily propagated by softwood cuttings taken in late spring.*

☀ ◊ Z6-8 H8-6   ‡8–12in (20–30cm)
↔12in (30cm) or more

HELIANTHEMUM 'HENFIELD BRILLIANT'

This rock rose is a small, spreading, evergreen shrub bearing saucer-shaped, brick-red flowers in late spring and summer. The leaves are narrow and gray-green. Effective in groups on a sunny bank; also good in a rock garden or raised bed or at the front of a border.

CULTIVATION *Grow in moderately fertile, well-drained, neutral to alkaline soil, in sun. Trim after flowering to keep bushy. Often short-lived, but easily propagated by softwood cuttings in late spring.*

☼ ◊ Z6-8 H8-6   ‡8–12in (20–30cm)
↔12in (30cm) or more

HELIANTHEMUM 'RHODANTHE CARNEUM'

This long-flowering rock rose, also sold as 'Wisley Pink', is a low and spreading, evergreen shrub. Pale pink, saucer-shaped flowers with yellow-flushed centers appear from late spring to summer amid narrow, gray-green leaves. Good in a rock garden, raised bed, or mixed border.

CULTIVATION *Best in well-drained, moderately fertile, neutral to alkaline soil, in full sun. Trim after flowering to encourage further blooms.*

☼ ◊ Z6-8 H8-6   ‡to 12in (30cm)
↔to 18in (45cm) or more

HELIANTHEMUM
'WISLEY PRIMROSE'

This primrose yellow rock rose is a fast-growing, spreading, evergreen shrub. It bears a profusion of saucer-shaped flowers with golden centers over long periods in late spring and summer. The leaves are narrowly oblong and gray green. Group in a rock garden, raised bed, or sunny bank. For paler, creamy flowers, look for 'Wisley White'.

CULTIVATION *Grow in well-drained, moderately fertile, preferably neutral to alkaline soil, in full sun. Trim after flowering to encourage further blooms.*

☼ ◊ Z6-8 H8-6   ‡to 12in (30cm)
↔to 18in (45cm) or more

HELIANTHUS
'LODDON GOLD'

This double-flowered sunflower is a tall, spreading perennial with coarse, oval, mid-green leaves that are arranged along the upright stems. Grown for its large, bright yellow flowers, which open during late summer and last into early autumn. Use to extend the season of interest in herbaceous and mixed borders.

CULTIVATION *Grow in moist to well-drained, moderately fertile, organic soil. Choose a sheltered site in full sun. Flowers are best during long, hot summers. Stake flower stems.*

☼ ◊◊ Z5-9 H9-5 ‡5ft (1.5m) ↔36in (90cm)

HELIANTHUS 'MONARCH'

This semidouble sunflower is a tall, spreading perennial with sturdy, upright stems bearing oval and toothed, mid-green leaves. Large, starlike, bright golden yellow flowers with yellow-brown centers are produced from late summer to autumn. A statuesque plant for late-summer interest in a herbaceous or mixed border. 'Capenoch Star' is another recommended perennial sunflower, lemon yellow with golden centers, to 5ft (1.5m) tall.

CULTIVATION *Grow in any well-drained, moderately fertile soil. Choose a sunny, sheltered site. The stems need support.*

☼ ◊ Z5-9 H9-5   ‡6ft (2m) ↔4ft (1.2m)

HELICHRYSUM PETIOLARE

The licorice plant is a silvery, mound-forming, evergreen shrub with trailing stems. Its small leaves are densely felted and silver-gray. The inconspicuous summer flowers are often pinched off: they spoil the foliage effect. Where not hardy, grow as an annual in a hanging basket or other container; where hardy, it is useful as a groundcover.

CULTIVATION *Grow in any well-drained soil, in full sun. Pinch-prune young stems to promote bushiness. Minimum temperature 35°F (2°C).*

☼ ◊ H12-1   ‡to 20in (50cm)
↔6ft (2m) or more

HELICHRYSUM PETIOLARE 'VARIEGATUM'

This variegated licorice plant is a trailing, evergreen shrub grown for its densely felted, silver-gray and cream leaves. Small, creamy yellow flowers appear in summer but are of little ornamental interest and may be removed. Excellent in hanging baskets or other containers, where not hardy, grow as an annual or overwinter in frost-free conditions.

CULTIVATION *Grow in any well drained soil, in full sun. Trim regularly and pinch off unwanted flowers as they form. Minimum temperature 35°F (2°C).*

☼ ◊ H12-1 ‡to 20in (50cm)
↔6ft (2m) or more

HELICHRYSUM SPLENDIDUM

A compact, white-woolly, evergreen perennial bearing linear, aromatic, silver-gray foliage. Small, bright yellow flowerheads open at the tips of the upright stems from mid-summer to autumn and last into winter. Suitable for a mixed border or rock garden; the flowers can be dried for winter decoration.

CULTIVATION *Grow in well-drained, poor to moderately fertile, neutral to alkaline soil, in full sun. Remove dead or damaged growth in spring, cutting back leggy shoots into old wood.*

☼ ◊ Z9-11 H12-1 ‡↔4ft (1.2m)

HELIOTROPIUM 'PRINCESS MARINA'

A compact, evergreen shrub that is usually grown as an annual or as a conservatory plant in cold climates. Much valued for its fragrant heads of deep violet-blue flowers that appear in summer above the oblong, wrinkled, mid- to dark green, often purple-tinged leaves. Good at the front of a border, in containers, or as summer bedding.

CULTIVATION *Grow in any moist but well-drained, fertile soil or soil mix, in sun. Minimum temperature 35°F (2°C).*

☼ ◊◊ H12-1   ‡↔ to 12in (30cm)

HELLEBORUS ARGUTIFOLIUS

The large Corsican hellebore, sometimes known as *H. corsicus*, is an early-flowering, clump-forming, evergreen perennial bearing large clusters of nodding, pale green flowers. These appear in winter and early spring above the handsome dark green leaves, which are divided into three sharply toothed leaflets. Excellent for early interest in a woodland garden or mixed border.

CULTIVATION *Grow in moist, fertile, preferably neutral to alkaline soil, in full sun or partial shade. Often short-lived, but self-seeds readily.*

☼☼ ◊ Z6-9 H9-6 ‡4ft (1.2m) ↔36in (90cm)

HELLEBORUS FOETIDUS

The stinking hellebore is an upright,
evergreen perennial forming clumps
of dark green, divided leaves that
smell unpleasant when crushed. In
winter and early spring, clusters of
small, nodding, cup-shaped flowers
appear above the foliage; their green
petals are edged with red. A striking
specimen for a winter border.

CULTIVATION *Grow in moist, fertile,
neutral to alkaline soil. Choose a
position in sun or partial shade.*

☼ ◑ ◊ Z6-9 H9-6   ‡to 32in (80cm)
                 ↔18in (45cm)

HELLEBORUS NIGER

A clump-forming, usually evergreen
perennial valued for its nodding
clusters of cup-shaped white flowers
in winter and early spring. The dark
green leaves are divided into several
leaflets. Effective with snowdrops
beneath winter-flowering shrubs,
but it can be difficult to naturalize.
'Potter's Wheel' is a pretty cultivar of
this hellebore, with large flowers; for
heavier soil, look for *H.* x *nigercors*,
of which *H. niger* is a parent.

CULTIVATION *Grow in deep, fertile,
neutral to alkaline soil that is reliably
moist. Site in dappled shade with shelter
from cold, drying winds.*

☼ ◊ Z4-8 H8-1 ‡12in (30cm) ↔18in (45cm)

DAYLILIES (*HEMEROCALLIS*)

Daylilies are clump-forming, herbaceous perennials, so called because each of their showy flowers lasts for only a day; in nocturnal daylilies, the flowers open in late afternoon and last through the night. The blooms are abundant and rapidly replaced, some appearing in late spring while other cultivars flower into late summer. Flower shapes vary from circular to spider-shaped, in shades of yellow, orange, red, and purple. The leaves are straplike and deciduous or evergreen. Taller daylilies make a dramatic contribution to a border; the dwarfer types, such as 'Stella de Oro', and 'Happy Returns', are useful for small gardens or in containers.

CULTIVATION *Grow in well-drained but moist, fertile soil, in sun; Most tolerate semi-shade. Mulch in spring, and feed with a balanced fertilizer every two weeks until buds form. Divide and replant every few years, in spring or autumn.*

☼☀ ◊◊ Z3-10 H12-1

1 ↕28in (70cm) ↔ 16in (40cm)   **2** ↕36in (90cm) ↔ 18in (45cm)   **3** ↕20in (50cm) ↔ 3ft (1m)

4 ↕↔ 3ft (1m)   **5** ↕24in (60cm) ↔ 3ft (1m)   **6** ↕12in (30cm) ↔ 18in (45cm)

1 *H.* 'Corky' **2** *H.* 'Golden Chimes' **3** *H.* 'Green Flutter'
4 *H. lilioasphodelus* **5** *H.* 'Nova' **6** *H.* 'Stella de Oro'

HEPATICA NOBILIS

A small, slow-growing, anemone-
like, semi-evergreen perennial
bearing saucer-shaped, purple,
white, or pink flowers. These appear
in early spring, usually before the
foliage has emerged. The mid-green,
sometimes mottled leaves are
leathery and divided into three
lobes. Good in a shady rock garden.
H. x *media* 'Ballardii' (Z5-8 H8-5) is
a very similar plant, with reliably
deep blue flowers.

CULTIVATION *Grow in moist but well-
drained, fertile, neutral to alkaline soil,
in partial shade. Provide a mulch of
leaf mold in autumn or spring.*

☼ ◊◊ Z5-8 H8-4 ‡4in (10cm) ↔6in (15cm)

HEUCHERA MICRANTHA
VAR. *DIVERSIFOLIA*
'PALACE PURPLE'

A clump-forming perennial valued
for its glistening, dark purple-red,
almost metallic foliage, which is
topped by airy sprays of white
flowers in summer. The leaves have
five pointed lobes. Plant in groups
as a groundcover for a shady site,
but it can be slow to spread.

CULTIVATION *Grow in moist but well-
drained, fertile soil, in sun or partial
shade. Tolerates full shade where the
ground is reliably moist. Lift and divide
clumps every few years, after flowering.*

☼☼ ◊◊ Z4-8 H8-1 ‡↔ 18 (45cm)

HEUCHERA 'RED SPANGLES'

This clump-forming, evergreen perennial is valued for its sprays of small, bell-shaped, crimson-scarlet flowers. These are borne in early summer, with a repeat bloom in late summer, on dark red stems above the lobed, heart-shaped, purplish green leaves. Effective as a ground-cover when grouped together.

CULTIVATION *Grow in moist but well-drained, fertile soil, in sun or partial shade. Tolerates full shade where the ground is reliably moist. Lift and divide clumps every three years, after flowering.*

☼ ◐ ◊◊ Z3-8 H8-1　‡20in (50cm)
　　　　　　　　　　　↔10in (25cm)

HIBISCUS SYRIACUS 'OISEAU BLEU'

Also known as 'Blue Bird', this vigorous, upright, deciduous shrub bears large, mallowlike, lilac-blue flowers with red centers. These are borne from mid- to late summer amid deep green leaves. Ideal for a mixed or shrub border.

CULTIVATION *Grow in moist but well-drained, fertile, neutral to slightly alkaline soil, in full sun. Prune young plants hard in late spring to encourage branching at the base; keep pruning to a minimum once established.*

☼ ◊◊ Z5-9 H9-1　‡10ft (3m) ↔6ft (2m)

HIBISCUS SYRIACUS
'WOODBRIDGE'

A fast-growing, upright, deciduous
shrub producing large, deep rose-
pink flowers with maroon blotches
around the centers. These are borne
from late summer to mid-autumn
amid the lobed, dark green leaves.
Valuable for its late season of
interest.

CULTIVATION *Grow in moist but well-
drained, fertile, slightly alkaline soil, in
full sun. Prune young plants hard to
encourage branching; keep pruning to
a minimum once established.*

☼ ◊◊ Z5-9 H9-1　↕10ft (3m) ↔6ft (2m)

HIPPOPHAE
RHAMNOIDES

Sea buckthorn is a spiny, deciduous
shrub with attractive fruits and
foliage. Small yellow flowers in
spring are followed by orange
berries (on female plants), which
persist well into winter. The silvery
gray leaves are narrow and clawlike. Good for hedging, especially
in coastal areas.

CULTIVATION *Best in sandy, moist but
well-drained soil, in full sun. For good
fruiting, plants of both sexes must grow
together. Little pruning is required; trim
hedges in late summer, as necessary.*

☼ ◊◊ Z3-8 H8-1　↕↔ 20ft (6m)

HOHERIA GLABRATA

This deciduous, spreading tree is grown for its graceful habit and clusters of cup-shaped, fragrant white flowers, which are attractive to butterflies, in mid-summer. The broad, dark green leaves turn yellow in autumn before they fall. Best in a shrub border in a maritime climate.

CULTIVATION *Grow in moderately fertile, well-drained, neutral to alkaline soil in full sun or partial shade, sheltered from cold, drying winds. Pruning is seldom necessary, but if branches are damaged by cold, cut them back in spring.*

☼☀ ◊ Z9-10 H10-9　　↕↔22ft (7m)

HOHERIA SEXSTYLOSA

Ribbonwood is an evergreen tree or shrub with narrow, glossy, mid-green leaves with toothed margins. It is valued for its graceful shape and abundant clusters of white flowers; attractive to butterflies, they appear in late summer. The cultivar 'Stardust' is recommended.

CULTIVATION *Best in moderately fertile, well-drained, neutral to alkaline soil in full sun or partial shade, sheltered from cold, drying winds. Pruning is seldom necessary.*

☼☀ ◊ Z9-10 H10-9 ↕ 25ft (8m) ↔20ft (6m)

HOSTAS

Hostas are evergreen perennials grown principally for their dense mounds of large, overlapping, lance- to heart-shaped leaves. A wide choice of foliage color is available, from the cloudy blue-green of 'Halcyon' to the bright yellow-green 'Golden Tiara'. Many have leaves marked with yellow or white around the edges; *H.* 'Fortunei Albopicta' has bold, central splashes of creamy yellow. Upright clusters of funnel-shaped flowers, varying from white through lavender-blue to purple, are borne on tall stems in summer. Hostas are effective at the front of a mixed border, in containers, or as a groundcover under deciduous trees.

CULTIVATION *Grow in well-drained but reliably moist, fertile soil, in full sun or partial shade. Yellow-leaved hostas color best in full sun with shade at midday. Mulch in spring to conserve moisture throughout the summer.*

☼ ◑ ◐ Z4-9 H9-1

1 ↕ 20in (50cm) ↔ 3ft (1m)   **2** ↕ 22in (55cm) ↔ 3ft (1m)   **3** ↕ 22in (55cm) ↔ 3ft (1m)

4 ↕ 22in (55cm) ↔ 3ft (1m)   **5** ↕ 24in (60cm) ↔ 3ft (1m)   **6** ↕ 12in (30cm) ↔ 20in (50cm)

1 *Hosta crispula* **2** *H.* 'Fortunei Albopicta' **3** *H.* 'Fortunei Aureomarginata '
4 *H.* 'Francee' **5** *H.* 'Frances Williams' **6** *H.* 'Golden Tiara'

7 ‡3ft (1m) ↔ 30in (75cm)

8 ‡18in (45cm) ↔ 30in (75cm)

9 ‡18in (45cm) ↔ 3ft (1m)

10 ‡24in (60cm) ↔ 4ft (1.2m)

11 ‡18in (45cm) ↔ 30in (75cm)

12 ‡3ft (1m) ↔ 4ft (1.2m)

7 *Hosta* 'Honeybells' **8** *H. lancifolia* **9** *H.* 'Love Pat'
10 *H.* 'Royal Standard' **11** *H.* 'Shade Fanfare' **12** *H. sieboldiana* var. *elegans*

13 ↕30in (75cm) ↔ 4ft (1.2m)

14 ↕14–16in (35–40cm) ↔ 28in (70cm)

15 ↕3ft (1m) ↔ 18in (45cm)

16 ↕18in (45cm) ↔ 28in (70cm)

17 ↕20in (50cm) ↔ 3ft (1m)

18 ↕2in (5cm) ↔ 10in (25cm)

19 ↕30in (75cm) ↔ 3ft (1m)

13 *H.* 'Sum and Substance' **14** *H.* Tardiana Group 'Halcyon' **15** *H. undulata* var. *undulata*
16 *H.* 'Undulata Univittata' **17** *H. ventricosa* **18** *H. venusta* **19** *H.* 'Wide Brim'

HUMULUS LUPULUS 'AUREUS'

The golden hops is a twining, perennial climber grown for its attractively lobed, bright golden yellow foliage. Hanging clusters of papery, conelike, greenish yellow flowers appear in autumn. Train over a fence or trellis, or up into a small tree. The hops dry well.

CULTIVATION *Grow in moist but well drained, moderately fertile, organic soil. Tolerates partial shade, but leaf color is best in full sun. Give the twining stems support. Cut back any dead growth to ground level in early spring.*

☼☀ ◐◊ Z4-8 H8-3　　‡20ft (6m)

HYACINTHUS ORIENTALIS 'BLUE JACKET'

This navy blue hyacinth is a bulbous perennial bearing dense, upright spikes of fragrant, bell-shaped flowers with purple veins in early spring. Good for spring bedding; specially prepared bulbs can be planted in pots during autumn for an indoor display of early flowers. One of the best true-blue hyacinths. Also try the paler 'Delft Blue'.

CULTIVATION *Grow in any well-drained, moderately fertile soil or soil mix, in sun or partial shade. Protect container-grown bulbs from extreme cold.*

☼☀ ◊ Z5-9 H9-1　　‡8–12in (20–30cm)
　　　　　　　　↔3in (8cm)

HYACINTHUS ORIENTALIS 'CITY OF HAARLEM'

This primrose yellow hyacinth is a spring-flowering, bulbous perennial bearing upright spikes of fragrant, bell-shaped flowers. The lance-shaped leaves are bright green and emerge from the base of the plant. Good for spring bedding or in containers, specially prepared bulbs can be planted in autumn for early flowers indoors.

CULTIVATION *Grow in well-drained, fairly fertile soil or soil mix, in sun or partial shade. Protect container-grown plants from excessive cold.*

☼ ◐ ◊ Z5-9 H9-1　　‡8–12in (20–30cm)
　　　　　　　　　↔3in (8cm)

HYACINTHUS ORIENTALIS 'OSTARA'

This violet hyacinth is a bulbous perennial grown as spring bedding for its dense, upright spikes of bell-shaped, fragrant flowers with dark stripes. Bright green, lance-shaped leaves emerge from the base of the plant. Prepared bulbs can be planted indoors during autumn for winter flowers. Startling planted with salmon-orange 'Gipsy Queen'.

CULTIVATION *Best in well-drained, moderately fertile soil or soil mix, in sun or partial shade. Protect container-grown plants from excessive cold.*

☼ ◐ ◊ Z5-9 H9-1　　‡8–12in (20–30cm)
　　　　　　　　　↔3in (8cm)

HYACINTHUS ORIENTALIS 'PINK PEARL'

This deep pink hyacinth, bearing dense, upright spikes of fragrant, bell-shaped flowers with paler edges, is a spring-flowering, bulbous perennial. The leaves are narrow and bright green. Excellent in a mixed or herbaceous border; specially prepared bulbs can be planted in pots during autumn for an indoor display of early flowers.

CULTIVATION *Grow in any well-drained, moderately fertile soil or soil mix, in sun or partial shade. Protect container-grown bulbs from extreme cold.*

☼☀ ◊ Z5-9 H9-1   ‡8–12in (20–30cm)
↔3in (8cm)

HYDRANGEA ANOMALA SUBSP. *PETIOLARIS*

The climbing hydrangea, often sold simply as *H. petiolaris*, is a woody-stemmed, deciduous, self-clinging climber, usually grown on shady walls for its large, lacecaplike heads of creamy white, summer flowers. The mid-green leaves are oval and coarsely toothed. Often slow to establish, but it then grows quickly.

CULTIVATION *Grow in any reliably moist, fertile soil in sun or deep shade. Little pruning is required, but as the allotted space is filled, cut back overly long shoots after flowering.*

☼☀ ◊ Z4-9 H9-1   ‡50ft (15m)

HYDRANGEA ARBORESCENS 'ANNABELLE'

An upright, deciduous shrub bearing large, rounded heads of densely packed, creamy white flowers from mid-summer to early autumn. The leaves are broadly oval and pointed. Good on its own or in a shrub border; the flowerheads can be dried for winter decoration. 'Grandiflora' has even larger flowerheads.

CULTIVATION *Grow in moist but well-drained, moderately fertile, organic soil, in sun or partial shade. Keep pruning to a minimum, or cut back hard each spring to a low framework.*

☀️ ◑ ◊◊ Z4-9 H9-1 ‡5ft (1.5m) ↔ 8ft (2.5m)

HYDRANGEA ASPERA VILLOSA GROUP

A group of spreading to upright, deciduous shrubs that can become treelike with age. In late summer, they produce flattened, lacecaplike heads of small, blue-purple or rich blue flowers, surrounded by larger, lilac-white or rose-lilac flowers. The leaves are lance-shaped and dark green. Excellent in a woodland or wild garden.

CULTIVATION *Grow in moist but well-drained, moderately fertile, organic soil. Site in full sun or semi-shade. Little pruning is necessary.*

☀️ ◑ ◊◊ Z6-9 H9-5 ‡3–12ft (1–4m)

HYDRANGEA MACROPHYLLA

Cultivars of the common hydrangea, *H. macrophylla*, are rounded shrubs with oval, mid- to dark green, deciduous leaves. Their large, showy flowerheads, borne from mid- to late summer, are available in two distinct forms: lacecaps, such as 'Veitchii', have flat flowerheads, and mophead hydrangeas (Hortensias), such as 'Altona', have round flowerheads. Except in white-flowered cultivars, flower color is influenced by soil pH; acidic soils produce blue flowers, and alkaline soils give rise to pink flowers. All types of hydrangea are useful for a range of garden sites, and the flowerheads dry well for indoor arrangements.

CULTIVATION *Grow in moist but well-drained, fertile soil, in sun or partial shade with shelter from wind. Prune hard in spring to enhance flowering, cutting stems back to strong pairs of buds.*

☼ ◑ ◊◊ ♥ Z6-9 H9-2

1 ↕3ft (1m) ↔ 5ft (1.5m)   **2** ↕6ft (2m) ↔ 8ft (2.5m)   **3** ↕↔ 5ft (1.5m)

4 ↕6ft (2m) ↔ 8ft (2.5m)   **5** ↕6ft (2m) ↔ 8ft (2.5m)

1 *H. macrophylla* 'Altona' (Mophead) **2** *H. macrophylla* 'Mariesii Perfecta' (syn. *H. macrophylla* 'Blue Wave') (Lacecap) **3** *H. macrophylla* 'Lanarth White' (Lacecap) **4** *H. macrophylla* 'Générale Vicomtesse de Vibraye' (Mophead) **5** *H. macrophylla* 'Veitchii' (Lacecap)

HYDRANGEA PANICULATA

Cultivars of *H. paniculata* are fast-growing, upright, deciduous shrubs, with oval, mid- to dark green leaves. They are cultivated for their tall clusters of lacy flowers that usually appear during late summer and early autumn; some cultivars, such as 'Praecox', bloom earlier in the summer. Flowers start greenish white and turn mostly creamy white, with many forms becoming pink-tinged as they age. These versatile shrubs are suitable for many different garden uses: as specimen plants, in groups, or in containers. The flowerheads are very attractive when dried for indoor decoration.

CULTIVATION *Grow in moist but well-drained, fertile soil. Site in sun or partial shade with shelter from cold, drying winds. Pruning is not essential, but plants flower much better if pruned back annually, in early spring, to the lowest pair of healthy buds on a permanent, woody framework.*

☼☀ ◊◊ Z4–8 H8-1

2 ‡ 10–22ft (3–7m) ↔ 8ft (2.5m)

1 ‡ 10–22ft (3–7m) ↔ 10–22ft (2.5m)

3 ‡ 10–22ft (3–7m) ↔ 8ft (2.5m)

1 *H. paniculata* 'Floribunda' 2 *H. paniculata* 'Grandiflora' 3 *H. paniculata* 'Praecox'

HYDRANGEA QUERCIFOLIA

The oak-leaved hydrangea is a mound-forming, deciduous shrub bearing conical heads of white flowers that fade to pink, from mid-summer to autumn. The deeply lobed, mid-green leaves turn bronze-purple in autumn. Useful in a variety of garden situations.

CULTIVATION *Prefers well-drained but moist, moderately fertile soil, in sun or partial shade. Leaves may become yellow in shallow, alkaline soil. Keep pruning to a minimum, in spring.*

☼☀ ◐ Z5-9 H9-2 ‡6ft (2m) ↔8ft (2.5m)

HYDRANGEA SERRATA 'BLUEBIRD'

A compact, upright, long-flowering, deciduous shrub bearing flattened heads of tiny, rich blue flowers surrounded by larger, pale blue flowers from summer to autumn. The narrowly oval, pointed, mid-green leaves turn red in autumn. 'Grayswood' (Z6-9 H9-6) is a similar shrub with mauve flowers.

CULTIVATION *Grow in moist but well-drained, moderately fertile, organic soil, in sun or partial shade. Flowers may turn pink in alkaline soils. Cut back weak, thin shoots in mid-spring.*

☼☀ ◐ Z6-9 H10-8 ‡↔4ft (1.2m)

HYDRANGEA SERRATA 'ROSALBA'

An upright, compact, deciduous shrub valued for its flat flowerheads that appear from summer to autumn; these are made up of tiny pink flowers in the center, surrounded by larger white flowers that become red-marked as they age. The leaves are oval, mid-green, and pointed. Ideal as a specimen plant or in a shrub border.

CULTIVATION *Grow in well-drained but moist, moderately fertile, organic soil, in full sun or partial shade. Flowers may turn blue on acidic soils. Very little pruning is needed.*

☼☀ ◊ Z6-9 H10-8　　‡↔ 4ft (1.2m)

HYPERICUM 'HIDCOTE'

This dense, evergreen or semi-evergreen shrub produces abundant clusters of large, cupped, golden yellow flowers that open from mid-summer to early autumn. The leaves are dark green and lance-shaped. Suitable for a shrub border; for a taller but narrower shrub, to 6ft (2m) high but otherwise very similar, look for 'Rowallane' (Z7-9 H9-7).

CULTIVATION *Grow in well-drained but moist, moderately fertile soil, in sun or partial shade. Deadhead regularly, and trim annually in spring to increase the flowering potential.*

☼☀ ◊◊ Z6-9 H9-6　‡4ft (1.2m) ↔5ft (1.5m)

HYPERICUM KOUYTCHENSE

Sometimes known as *H.* 'Sungold', this species of St. John's wort is a rounded, semi-evergreen bush with arching shoots. It has dark blue-green leaves, but its biggest asset is the large clusters of golden yellow star-shaped flowers borne in profusion during summer and autumn, followed by bright bronze-red fruits. Grow in a shrub border or mixed border.

CULTIVATION *Grow in moderately fertile, moist but well-drained soil in full sun or partial shade. Prune or trim after flowering, if necessary.*

☼ ◑ ◌◑ Z6-9 H9-6 ‡3ft (1m) ↔5ft (1.5m)

IBERIS SEMPERVIRENS

A spreading, evergreen subshrub bearing dense, rounded heads of small, unevenly shaped white flowers that are often flushed with pink or lilac. These appear in late spring and early summer, covering the dark green leaves. Best in a rock garden or large wall pocket. The recommended cultivar 'Schneeflocke' can be even more floriferous.

CULTIVATION *Grow in well-drained, poor to moderately fertile, neutral to alkaline soil, in full sun. Trim lightly after flowering for neatness.*

☼ ◌ Z5-9 H9-4 ‡to 12in (30cm) ↔ to 16in (40cm)

ILEX × *ALTACLERENSIS* 'GOLDEN KING' (FEMALE)

A compact, evergreen shrub with glossy, dark green leaves edged in gold. The leaf margins may be smooth or toothed. The flowers are insignificant but develop into red berries in autumn. Tolerant of pollution and coastal exposure; a good tall windbreak or hedge where winters are not too severe.

CULTIVATION *Grow in moist but well-drained, moderately fertile soil rich in organic matter. For berries, a male holly must grow nearby. A position in full sun is ideal. Trim or prune in early spring, if necessary.*

☼ ◊◊ Z7-9 H9-7 ‡20ft (30m) ↔ 12ft (4m)

ILEX × *ALTACLERENSIS* 'LAWSONIANA' (FEMALE)

This dense and bushy holly forms a compact, evergreen tree or shrub. It bears large, usually spineless, oval, bright green leaves, which are splashed with gold and paler green in the centers. Red-brown berries, ripening to red, develop in autumn.

CULTIVATION *Grow in moist but well-drained soil, in sun for best leaf color. Grow a male holly nearby to ensure a display of berries. Free-standing plants may need some shaping when young. Remove any all-green shoots as seen.*

☼ ◊ Z7-9 H9-7 ‡20ft (6m) ↔ 15ft (5m)

ENGLISH HOLLIES (*ILEX AQUIFOLIUM*)

Ilex aquifolium, the English holly, has many different cultivars, all upright, evergreen trees or large shrubs that are usually grown on their own or as spiny hedges. They have purple stems, gray bark, and dense, glossy foliage. Most cultivars have multicolored, spiny leaves, although those of 'J.C. van Tol' are spineless and dark green. 'Ferox Argentea' has extra-spiny leaves. Male and female flowers are borne on separate plants, so female hollies, such as 'Madame Briot', must be near males, such as 'Golden Milkboy', if they are to bear a good crop of berries. Tall specimens make effective windbreaks.

CULTIVATION *Grow in moist, well-drained, fertile, organic soil. Choose a site in full sun for good leaf variegation, but tolerates partial shade. Remove any damaged wood and shape young trees in spring; hedges should be trimmed in late summer. Over-enthusiastic pruning will spoil their form.*

☀☀ ◊ Z7-9 H9-1

1 ↕ to 80ft (25m) ↔ 25ft (8m)   **2** ↕ to 20ft (6m) ↔ 8ft (2.5m)   **3** ↕ to 50ft (15m) ↔ 12ft (4m)

1 *Ilex aquifolium*   **2** 'Amber' (Female)   **3** 'Argentea Marginata' (Female)

4 ↕ to 25ft (8m) ↔ 12ft (4m)   **5** ↕ 20ft (6m) ↔ 12ft (4m)   **6** ↕ 25ft (8m) ↔ 15ft (5m)

7 ↕ 20ft (6m) ↔ 12ft (4m)   **8** ↕ 20ft (6m) ↔ 15ft (5m)   **9** ↕ 20ft (6m) ↔ 15ft (5m)

10 ↕ 20ft (6m) ↔ 4m (12ft)   **11** ↕ 20ft (6m) ↔ 12ft (4m)   **12** ↕ 30ft (10m) ↔ 12ft (4m)

4 'Ferox Argentea' (Male) **5** 'Golden Milkboy' (Male) **6** 'Handsworth New Silver' (Female)
7 'J. C. van Tol' (Female) **8** 'Madame Briot' (Female) **9** 'Pyramidalis' (Female)
10 'Pyramidalis Fructo Luteo' (Female) **11** 'Silver Milkmaid' (Female) **12** 'Silver Queen' (Male)

ILEX CRENATA 'CONVEXA' (FEMALE)

This bushy form of the Japanese holly is a dense, evergreen shrub with purple-green stems and spineless, oval to elliptic, glossy, mid- to dark green leaves. It bears an abundance of small, black berries in autumn. Lends itself for use as hedging or topiary.

CULTIVATION *Needs moist but well-drained, organic soil, in full sun or partial shade. Grow near a male holly for a good crop of berries. Cut out badly placed growth in early spring, and trim shaped plants in summer.*

☼ ◐ ◊ Z5-7 H7-4 ‡8ft (2.5m) ↔6ft (2m)

ILEX × *MESERVEAE* 'BLUE PRINCESS' (FEMALE)

This blue holly is a vigorous, dense, evergreen shrub with oval, softly spiny, very glossy, greenish blue leaves. White to pinkish white, late spring flowers are followed by a profusion of glossy red berries in autumn. The dark purplish green young stems show well when hedging plants are regularly clipped. Dislikes coastal conditions.

CULTIVATION *Grow in moist but well-drained, moderately fertile soil, in full sun or semi-shade. For berries, a male holly will need to be nearby. Prune in late summer to maintain shape.*

☼ ◐ ◊ Z5-9 H9-5 ‡↔10ft (3m)

IMPATIENS
SUPER ELFIN SERIES

These plants, widely grown as
annual bedding, have spreading
stems bearing long-lasting summer
flowers with flattened faces and
slender spurs. These bloom in a
range of pastel colors and shades of
orange, pink, red, and violet. The
oval leaves are light green. Excellent
summer bedding or container plants
for a partially shaded site.

CULTIVATION *Grow in well-drained but
moist, organic soil, in partial shade
with shelter from wind. Plant out after
all danger of frost has passed.*

☀ ◔ annual H12-1　　‡to 24in (60cm)
　　　　　　　　　　↔ to 10in (25cm (

IMPATIENS TEMPO SERIES

These plants, in either single colors
or mixed, bear a profusion of
flattened, spurred flowers that range
in color from violet and lavender-
blue to orange, pink, and red; some
have contrasting edges or bicolored
petals. Leaves are light green and
slightly toothed. Grown as annual
bedding plants, these provide long-
lasting color in containers and
summer borders.

CULTIVATION *Grow in moist but well-
drained, organic soil, in a sheltered
site. Tolerates shade. Plant out after all
danger of frost has passed.*

☀ ◔ annual H12-1　　‡to 9in (23cm)
　　　　　　　　　　↔ to 10in (25cm)

INDIGOFERA HETERANTHA

A medium-sized, spreading shrub grown for its pealike flowers and elegant foliage. The arching stems carry gray-green leaves made up of many oval to oblong leaflets. Dense, upright clusters of small, purple-pink flowers appear from early summer to autumn. Train against a warm wall where marginally hardy. *I. ambylantha* (Z7-9 H9-1) is a very similar shrub.

CULTIVATION *Grow in well-drained but moist, moderately fertile soil, in full sun. Prune in early spring, cutting back to just above ground level.*

☼ ◊ Z6-9 H9-6   ↕↔ 6–10ft (2–3m)

IPHEION UNIFLORUM 'WISLEY BLUE'

A vigorous, clump-forming, mainly spring-flowering, bulbous perennial bearing scented, star-shaped, lilac-blue flowers; each petal has a pale base and a dark midrib. Narrow, straplike, light blue-green leaves are produced in autumn. Useful in a rock garden or for underplanting herbaceous plants. 'Froyle Mill' is another recommended cultivar, its flowers more mauve in color.

CULTIVATION *Grow in moist but well-drained, moderately fertile, organic soil, in full sun. Where marginally hardy, provide a mulch in winter.*

☼ ◊ Z6-9 H9-4   ↕ 6–8in (15–20cm)

IPOMOEA
'HEAVENLY BLUE'

This summer-flowering, twining,
fast-growing form of morning glory
is grown as a climbing annual. The
large, funnel-shaped flowers, azure-
blue with pure white throats, appear
singly or in clusters of two or three.
The heart-shaped, light to mid-green
leaves have slender tips. Suitable for
a summer border, scrambling among
other plants. Seeds are highly toxic
if ingested.

CULTIVATION *Grow in well-drained,
moderately fertile soil, in sun with
shelter from cold, drying winds. Plant
out after danger of frost has passed.*

☼ ◊ annual H12-1 ‡to 10–12ft (3–4m)

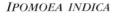

IPOMOEA INDICA

The blue dawn flower is a vigorous,
evergreen climber, perennial in frost-
free conditions. Abundant, rich
purple-blue, funnel-shaped flowers
that often fade to red are borne in
clusters of three to five from late
spring to autumn. The mid-green
leaves are heart-shaped or three-
lobed. In mild areas, grow as annuals
in a warm conservatory or summer
border. The seeds are toxic.

CULTIVATION *Grow in well-drained,
fairy fertile soil, in sun with shelter from
cold, drying winds. Plant out after all
danger of frost has passed. Minimum
temperature 45°F (7°C).*

☼ ◊ annual H12-1 ‡to 20ft (6m)

IRISES FOR MOIST TO WET SOIL

Irises that flourish in reliably moist or wet soils produce swollen, horizontal creeping stems known as rhizomes that lie just below the ground. These produce several new offsets each year, so give plants plenty or room, or divide them regularly. They have strap-shaped leaves and flower in blues, purples, white or yellow in spring and early summer. The true water irises will grow not only in damp ground but also in shallow water; these include *I. laevigata* and *I. pseudacorus*, very vigorous plants that will soon overwhelm a small pond. Where space is limited, try *I. ensata* or, in moist or even in well-drained soil around the water, plant *I. sibirica* or one of its many attractive cultivars.

CULTIVATION *Grow in deep, acidic soil enriched with well-rotted organic matter, in sun or light shade. Divide existing clumps and replant divisions in early autumn or early spring.*

☼ ◑ ◐ Z3-9 H9-1 mostly

1 ‡36in (90cm) ↔ indefinite

2 ‡36in (90cm) ↔ indefinite

3 ‡32in (80cm) ↔ indefinite

4 ‡32in (80cm) ↔ indefinite

5 ‡3–5ft (0.9–1.5m) ↔ indefinite

6 ‡3–5ft (0.9–1.5m) ↔ indefinite

1 *Iris ensata* 'Flying Tiger' **2** *I. ensata* 'Variegata' (both ensatas Z5-8 H8-4) **3** *I. laevigata* **4** *I. laevigata* 'Variegata' **5** *I. pseudacorus* **6** *I. pseudacorus* 'Variegata' (both Z5-8 H8-4)

7 ‡3ft (1m) ↔ indefinite

8 ‡8–32in (20–80cm) ↔ indefinite

9 ‡3ft (1m) ↔ indefinite

10 ‡32in (80cm) ↔ indefinite

11 ‡32in (80cm) ↔ indefinite

12 ‡3ft (1m) ↔ indefinite

13 ‡3ft (1m) ↔ indefinite

14 ‡32in (80cm) ↔ indefinite

15 ‡3ft (1m) ↔ indefinite

16 ‡32in (80cm) ↔ indefinite

17 ‡to 3ft (1m) ↔ indefinite

18 ‡to 3ft (1m) ↔ indefinite

7 *I.sibirica* 'Annemarie Troeger' **8** *I.versicolor* **9** *I. sibirica* 'Crème Chantilly' **10** *I.sibirica* 'Dreaming Yellow' **11** *I.sibirica* 'Harpswell Happiness' **12** *I.sibirica* 'Mikiko' **13** *I.sibirica* 'Oban' **14** *I.sibirica* 'Perfect Vision' **15** *I.sibirica* 'Roisin' **16** *I.sibirica* 'Smudger's Gift' **17** *I.sibirica* 'Uber den Wolken' **18** *I.sibirica* 'Zakopane'

IRIS BUCHARICA

A fast-growing, spring-flowering, bulbous perennial that carries up to six golden yellow to white flowers on each stem. The glossy, straplike leaves die back after flowering. The most commonly available form of this iris has yellow and white flowers.

CULTIVATION *Grow in rich but well-drained, neutral to slightly alkaline soil, in full sun. Water moderately when in growth; after flowering, maintain a period of dry dormancy.*

☼ ◊ Z5-9 H9-5   ↕8–16in (20–40cm)
↔ 5in (12cm)

IRIS CONFUSA

This freely spreading, rhizomatous perennial with bamboolike foliage produces a succession of up to 30 short-lived flowers on each stem during spring. They are white with yellow crests surrounded by purple or yellow spots. The leaves are arranged in fans at the base of the plant. Suitable for a sheltered, mixed or herbaceous border.

CULTIVATION *Grow in moist but well-drained, rich soil, in sun or semi-shade. Water moderately when in growth. Keep neat by removing flowered stems.*

☼☀ ◊ Z8-10 H12-8   ↕3ft (1m)
↔ indefinite

IRIS DELAVAYI

This rhizomatous, deciduous
perennial bears three-branched
flower stems in summer, each one
topped by two light to dark purple-
blue flowers. The rounded fall petals
have white and yellow flecks. The
foliage is gray-green. A handsome
perennial with its tall stems, it is
easily grown in moist soil

CULTIVATION *Grow in moist soil in full
sun or partial shade. Lift and divide
congested clumps after flowering.*

☀ ◐ ◊ Z5-8 H8-4   ‡5ft (1.5m)
                    ↔indefinite

IRIS DOUGLASIANA

A robust, rhizomatous perennial
with branched flower stems that
each bear two or three white, cream,
blue, lavender-blue, or red-purple
flowers in late spring and early
summer. The stiff, glossy, dark
green leaves are often red at the
bases. A good display plant for a
raised bed or trough.

CULTIVATION *Grow in well-drained,
neutral to slightly acidic soil. Site in full
sun for the best flowers, or light shade.
Does not transplant well, so do not lift
and divide unnecessarily.*

☀ ◐ ◊ Z7-9 H9-7   ‡6–28in (15–70cm)
                    ↔indefinite

IRIS FOETIDISSIMA 'VARIEGATA'

The stinking iris is not as unpleasant as it sounds, although the evergreen, silvery leaves, with white stripes in this cultivar, do have a nasty scent if crushed. A vigorous rhizomatous perennial, it bears yellow-tinged, dull purple flowers in early summer, followed by seed capsules that split open in autumn to display showy scarlet, yellow or, rarely, white seeds. A useful plant for dry shade.

CULTIVATION *Prefers well-drained, neutral to slightly acidic soil in shade. Divide congested clumps in autumn.*

☼☀ ◊ Z7-9 H9-7 ‡12–36in (30cm–90cm)
↔indefinite

IRIS FORRESTII

An elegant, early summer-flowering rhizomatous perennial with slender flower stems that each carry one or two scented, pale yellow flowers with brown markings. The very narrow glossy leaves are mid-green above and gray-green below. Easy to grow in an open border.

CULTIVATION *Grow in moist but well-drained, neutral to slightly acidic soil. Position in full sun or partial shade.*

☼☀ ◊◊ Z6-9 H9-6 ‡14–16in (35–40cm)
↔indefinite

IRIS GRAMINEA

A deciduous, rhizomatous perennial
bearing bright green, straplike
leaves. From late spring, rich purple-
violet flowers, with fall petals tipped
white and violet-veined, are borne
either singly or in pairs; they are
often hidden among the leaves. The
flowers have a fruity fragrance.

CULTIVATION *Grow in moist but well-
drained, neutral to slightly acidic soil.
Choose a site in full sun or semi-shade.
Does not respond well to transplanting.*

☼ ◐ ◊◊ Z6-9 H9-6 ‡8–16in (20–40cm)
↔ indefinite

IRIS 'KATHARINE HODGKIN'

This very vigorous, tiny but robust,
deciduous, bulbous perennial bears
delicately patterned, pale blue and
yellow flowers, with darker blue and
gold markings, in late winter and
early spring. The pale to mid-green
leaves grow after the flowers have
faded. Excellent in a rock garden or
at the front of a border, where it will
spread slowly to form a clump.

CULTIVATION *Grow in well-drained,
neutral to slightly alkaline soil, in an
open site in full sun.*

☼ ◊ Z5-8 H8-5 ‡5in (12cm)
↔ 2–3in (5–8cm)

BEARDED IRISES

These upright, rhizomatous perennials send up fans of sword-shaped, usually broad leaves and simple or branched stems. The flowers are produced in a wide range of colors, with well-developed, often frilly fall and standard petals, and a "beard" of white or colored hairs in the center of each fall petal. These are the most widely cultivated group of irises for garden display, usually producing several flowers per stem from spring into early summer, sometimes again later in the season. Taller irises suit a mixed border, and smaller ones may be grown in a rock garden, raised bed, or trough.

CULTIVATION *Grow in well-drained, moderately fertile, neutral to slightly acidic soil in full sun. Plant rhizomes in late summer or early autumn, thinly covered with soil. They must not be shaded by other plants. Do not mulch. Divide large or congested clumps in summer.*

☼ ◊ Z3-9 H9-1

1 ‡28in (70cm) ↔ 24in (60cm)   **2** ‡28in (70cm) ↔ 24in (60cm)

3 ‡22in (55m) ↔ 18–24in (45–60cm)   **4** ‡28in (70cm) ↔ 24in (60cm)   **5** ‡↔ 12in (30cm)

1 *Iris* 'Apricorange'   **2** *I.* 'Breakers'   **3** *I.* 'Brown Lasso'   **4** *I.* 'Early Light'   **5** *I.* 'Eyebright'

6 *I.* 'Happy Mood' 7 *I.* 'Honington' 8 *I.* 'Katie-Koo' 9 *I.* 'Maui Moonlight'
10 *I.* 'Meg's Mantle' 11 *I.* 'Miss Carla' 12 *I.* 'Nicola Jane' 13 *I.* 'Orinoco Flow'
14 *I.* 'Paradise' 15 *I.* 'Paradise Bird'

16 ↕28in (70cm) ↔ 24in (60cm)

17 ↕16–28in (40–70cm) ↔ 18–24in (45–60cm)

18 ↕28in (70cm) or more ↔ 24in (60cm)

19 ↕ to 28in (70cm) ↔ to 24in (60cm)

16 *I.* 'Phil Keen' **17** *I.* 'Pink Parchment' **18** *I.* 'Precious Heather' **19** *I.* 'Quark'

20 ‡10in (25cm) ↔ 30cm (12in)

21 ‡to 28in (70cm) ↔ to 24in (60cm)

24 ‡28in (70cm) ↔ 24in (60cm)

22 ‡to 28in (70cm) ↔ to 24in (60cm)

23 ‡to 28in (70cm) ↔ to 24in (60cm)

MORE CHOICES

'Arctic Fancy' White,
20in (50cm) tall.

'Blue-eyed Brunette'
Brown flowers with a
lilac blaze, to 36in
(90cm) tall

'Bromyard' Blue-gray
and ochre flowers, 11in
(28cm) tall.

'Stepping Out' White
with purple petal
edges, 3ft (1m) tall.

25 ‡to 28in (70cm) ↔ to 24in (60cm)

26 ‡36in (90cm) ↔ 24in (60cm)

20 *I.* 'Rain Dance' **21** *I.* 'Sherbet Lemon' **22** *I.* 'Sparkling Lemonade'
23 *I.* 'Sunny Dawn' **24** *I.* 'Sun Miracle' **25** *I.* 'Templecloud' **26** *I.* 'Vanity'

IRIS LACUSTRIS

This dwarf, deciduous, rhizomatous perennial bears small flowers in late spring. These are purple-blue to sky blue with gold crests and a white patch on each of the the fall petals; they arise from basal fans of narrow leaves. Suitable for growing in a rock garden or trough.

CULTIVATION *Grow in reliably moist, acidic soil that is rich in organic matter, in sun or partial shade. Water moderately when in growth.*

☼ ☀ ◑ ◊ Z4-8 H8-1 ‡4in (10cm) ↔ indefinite

IRIS PALLIDA 'VARIEGATA'

This semi-evergreen, rhizomatous perennial is probably the most versatile and attractive variegated iris. The straplike, bright green leaves are clearly striped with golden yellow. (For silver-striped leaves, look for 'Argentea Variegata'.) The large, scented, soft blue flowers with yellow beards are borne in clusters of two to six on branched stems in late spring and early summer. Grow in a mixed or herbaceous border.

CULTIVATION *Best in well-drained, fertile, slightly alkaline soil, in sun. Water moderately when in growth.*

☼ ◊ Z5-9 H9-4 ‡to 3ft (1m) ↔ indefinite

IRIS SETOSA

This rhizomatous perennial flowers in late spring and early summer. Each flowering stem bears several beautiful, blue or blue-purple flowers above the narrow, mid-green leaves. Easily grown in moist soil.

CULTIVATION *Grow in moist, neutral to slightly acidic soil in full sun or partial shade. Lift and divide congested clumps after flowering.*

☼ ◐ ◊ Z3-8 H8-1   ‡6–36in (15–90cm)
↔ indefinite

IRIS UNGUICULARIS

A fast-growing, evergreen, rhizomatous perennial, sometimes called *I. stylosa*, with short flower stems bearing large, fragrant blooms from late winter (sometimes even earlier) to early spring. The pale lavender to deep violet petals have contrasting veins and a band of yellow on each fall petal. The leaves are grasslike and mid-green. Ideal for the base of a sunny wall.

CULTIVATION *Grow in sharply drained, neutral to alkaline soil. Choose a warm, sheltered site in full sun. Does not like to be disturbed. Keep neat by removing dead leaves in late summer and spring.*

☼ ◊ Z7-9 H9-7   ‡12in (30cm) ↔ indefinite

IRIS VARIEGATA

This slender and robust, deciduous, rhizomatous perennial bears three to six flowers on each branched stem from mid-summer. The striking flowers are pale yellow with brown or violet veins on the fall petals; there are many color variations available. The deep green leaves are strongly ribbed.

CULTIVATION *Grow in well-drained, neutral to alkaline soil, in sun or light shade. Avoid mulching with organic matter, which may encourage rot.*

☼ ◐ ◊ Z5-9 H9-5　‡8–18in (20–45cm)
↔ indefinite

ITEA ILICIFOLIA

An evergreen shrub bearing upright at first, then spreading, arching shoots. The oval, hollylike leaves are sharply toothed. Tiny, greenish white flowers are borne in long, catkinlike clusters from mid-summer to early autumn. Needs a sheltered position in cold areas.

CULTIVATION *Grow in well-drained but moist, fertile soil, preferably against a warm wall in full sun. Protect with a winter mulch when young.*

☼ ◊ Z7-9 H9-7　‡15ft (3–5m) ↔10ft (3m)

JASMINUM MESNYI

The primrose jasmine is a half hardy, scrambling, evergreen shrub with large, usually semidouble, bright yellow flowers. These appear singly or in small clusters during spring and summer, amid the glossy, dark green leaves, which are divided into three oblong to lance-shaped leaflets. Will climb if tied to a support.

CULTIVATION *Grow in any well-drained, fertile soil, in full sun or partial shade. Cut back flowered shoots in summer to encourage strong growth from the base.*

☼ ◑ ◊ Z8-10 H12-8   ‡to 10ft (3m)
              ↔3–6ft (1–2m)

JASMINUM NUDIFLORUM

Winter jasmine is a lax, mound-forming, deciduous shrub with slender, arching stems. Small, tubular yellow flowers are borne singly on the leafless, green shoots in late winter. The dark green leaves, which develop after the flowers, are divided into three leaflets. Tie in a framework of stems against a wall, or let it sprawl unsupported.

CULTIVATION *Grow in well-drained, fertile soil. Tolerates semi-shade, but flowers best in sun. Encourage strong growth by cutting back flowered shoots.*

☼ ◑ ◊ Z6-9 H9-6   ‡↔ to 10ft (3m)

JASMINUM OFFICINALE
'ARGENTEOVARIEGATUM'

This variegated form of the common jasmine, *J. officinale*, is a vigorous, deciduous or semi-deciduous, woody climber. The gray-green, cream-edged leaves are made up of 5–9 sharply pointed leaflets. Clusters of fragrant white flowers open from summer to early autumn. If tied in initially, it will twine over supports, such as a trellis or an arch.

CULTIVATION *Grow in well-drained, fertile soil. Tolerates shade, but flowers best in full sun. Thin out crowded growth after flowering.*

☼ ☀ ◊ Z9-11 H12-9   ↕to 40ft (12m)

JASMINUM POLYANTHUM

A fast-growing, woody-stemmed, twining, evergreen climber that bears abundant clusters of small, strongly fragrant white flowers. These open from pink buds in late spring and early summer, amid the deep green, divided leaves. Allow to climb over a trellis, fence, arch, or large shrub.

CULTIVATION *Grow in well-drained, moderately fertile soil. Thin out overcrowded growth after flowering.*

☼ ◊ Z9-10 H12-9   ↕to 12ft (3m)

JUNIPERUS COMMUNIS 'COMPRESSA'

This slow-growing, spindle-shaped, dwarf form of the common juniper bears deep to blue-green, aromatic, evergreen scalelike leaves, borne in whorls of three along the stems. Small, oval or spherical fruits remain on the plant for three years, ripening from green to cloudy blue to black.

CULTIVATION *Grow in any well-drained soil, preferably in full sun or light dappled shade. No pruning is needed.*

☼ ☀ ◊ Z2-6 H6-1   ↕ to 32in (80cm)
          ↔ 18in (45cm)

JUNIPERUS X *PFITZERIANA* 'PFITZERIANA'

This spreading, dense, evergreen shrub has ascending branches of gray-green foliage that droop at the tips; it eventually forms a flat-topped, tiered bush. The flattened, scalelike leaves are borne in whorls of three. Spherical fruits are at first dark purple, becoming paler as they age. Looks nice as a specimen plant or in a large rock garden.

CULTIVATION *Grow in any well-drained soil, preferably in full sun or light dappled shade. Keep pruning to a minimum, in late autumn if necessary.*

☼ ☀ ◊ Z4-9 H9-1   ↕ 4ft (1.2m) ↔ 10ft (3m)

JUNIPERUS PROCUMBENS 'NANA'

A compact, mat-forming conifer that is excellent as a groundcover in a wide range of situations. The needlelike, aromatic, yellow-green or light green leaves are carried in groups of three. Bears berrylike, brown to black, fleshy fruits that take two or three years to ripen.

CULTIVATION *Grow in any well-drained soil, including sandy, dry, or alkaline conditions. Site in full sun or very light shade. No pruning is required.*

☼ ◐ ◊ Z5-9 H9-5 ↕6–8in (15–20cm) ↔30in (75cm)

JUNIPERUS SQUAMATA 'BLUE STAR'

This conifer is a low-growing, dense, compact, rounded bush with rust-colored, flaky bark. The silvery blue leaves are sharply pointed and grouped in whorls of three. The ripe fruits are oval and black. Useful as a groundcover or in a rock garden.

CULTIVATION *Grow in any well-drained soil, in full sun or very light shade. Very little pruning is required.*

☼ ◐ ◊ Z5-8 H8-5 ↕to 16in (40cm) ↔to 3ft (1m)

KALMIA ANGUSTIFOLIA

The sheep laurel is a tough, rabbit-proof shrub grown for its spectacular, rounded clusters of small flowers, usually pink to deep red, but occasionally white. They appear in early summer amid the dark green leaves. Useful for a shrub border or rockery; naturally mound-forming, it tolerates trimming to a neat shape if desired.

CULTIVATION *Choose a partly shaded site in moist, acidic soil, rich in organic matter. Grow in full sun only where the soil remains reliably moist. Mulch in spring with leaf mold or pine needles. Trim or prune hard after flowering.*

☼ ◐ ◊ Z7-8 H8-7 ‡24in (60cm) ↔5ft (1.5m)

KALMIA LATIFOLIA

Mountain laurel is a dense evergreen shrub producing large clusters of flowers from late spring to mid-summer. These are cup-shaped, pink or occasionally white, and open from distinctively shaped buds. The oval leaves are glossy and dark green. An excellent specimen shrub for woodland gardens, but flowers best in full sun. 'Ostbo Red' is one of many recommended cultivars.

CULTIVATION *Grow in moist, organic, acidic soil, in sun or partial shade. Mulch each spring with pine needles or leaf mold. Requires very little pruning, although deadheading is worthwhile.*

☼ ◐ ◊ Z5-9 H9-5 ‡↔ 10ft (3m)

KERRIA JAPONICA 'GOLDEN GUINEA'

This vigorous, suckering, deciduous shrub forms clumps of arching, canelike shoots that arise from ground level each year. Large, single yellow flowers are borne in mid- and late spring along the previous year's growth. ('Flore Pleno' has double flowers.) The bright green leaves are oval and sharply toothed.

CULTIVATION *Grow in well-drained, fertile soil, in full sun or partial shade. Cut flowered canes back to different levels to obtain flowers at different heights. Chop out unwanted canes and suckers to restrict spread.*

☼☀ ◊ Z4-9 H9-1 ‡6ft (2m) ↔8ft (2.5m)

KIRENGESHOMA PALMATA

A handsome, upright perennial with broad, lobed, pale green leaves. In late summer and early autumn, these are topped by loose clusters of nodding, pale yellow flowers, giving the common name of "yellow wax bells." This plant brings a gentle elegance to a shady border, pondside, or woodland garden.

CULTIVATION *Thrives in moist, acidic soil, enriched with leaf mold, in partial shade sheltered from wind. If necessary, divide clumps in spring.*

☼ ◊ Z5-8 ZH8-5 ‡24–48in (60–120cm) ↔30in (75cm)

KNIPHOFIA 'BEES' SUNSET'

This red-hot poker is a deciduous perennial grown for its elegant spikes of soft yellowish orange flowers. These appear through summer above the clumps of arching, grasslike leaves. Very attractive to bees.

CULTIVATION *Grow in deep, fertile, moist but well-drained soil, ideally sandy but enriched with organic matter. Choose a site in full sun or partial shade. Mulch young plants for their first winter, and divide mature, crowded clumps in late spring.*

☼ ◑ ◊◊ Z6-9 H9-5   ‡36in (90cm)
                      ↔24in (60cm)

KNIPHOFIA CAULESCENS

This stately evergreen perennial bears tall spikes of flowers from late summer to mid-autumn; coral-red, they fade upward as they age to pale yellow, giving them their common name of red-hot pokers. They are carried well above basal rosettes of arching, grasslike, blue-green leaves. Good for a herbaceous border; tolerant of coastal exposure.

CULTIVATION *Grow in deep, fertile, moist but well-drained soil, preferably sandy and enriched with organic matter. Position in full sun or partial shade. Mulch young plants for their first winter. Divide large clumps in late spring.*

☼ ◑ ◊◊ Z6-9 H9-4   ‡to 4ft (1.2m)
                      ↔24in (60cm)

KNIPHOFIA 'LITTLE MAID'

This clump-forming, deciduous perennial has tall heads of tubular flowers that appear from late summer to early autumn. They are pale green in bud, opening to pale buff-yellow, then fading to ivory. The leaves are narrow and grass-like. Good for late displays in a mixed or herbaceous border.

CULTIVATION *Grow in well-drained, deep, fertile, organic soil, in full sun. Keep moist when in growth. In their first winter and where marginally hardy, provide a light mulch.*

☼ ◊ Z6-9 H9-6 ‡24in (60cm) ↔18in (45cm)

KNIPHOFIA 'ROYAL STANDARD'

A clump-forming, herbaceous perennial of classic red-hot poker appearance that bears tall, conical flowerheads from mid- to late summer. The bright yellow, tubular flowers open from red buds, starting at the base and moving upward. The arching, grasslike leaves make an impressive clump.

CULTIVATION *Grow in deep, moist but well-drained, organic soil, in sun. Water freely when in growth. Provide a mulch where marginal, especially for young plants in their first winter.*

☼ ◊◊ Z6-9 H9-6 ‡3ft (1m) ↔24in (60cm)

KNIPHOFIA TRIANGULARIS

A clump-forming, deciduous perennial grown for its early to mid-autumn display of long, reddish orange, tubular flowers. These are borne in dense, spikelike heads and become slightly yellow around the mouths. The leaves are narrow, grasslike, and arching. A good choice for waterside planting.

CULTIVATION *Best in deep, moist but well-drained, organic, fertile soil, in full sun. Water freely when in growth. Mulch where marginal, especially young plants in their first winter.*

☼ ◊◊ Z6-9 H9-1 ↕24–36in (60–90cm)
↔18in (45cm)

KOLKWITZIA AMABILIS 'PINK CLOUD'

The beauty bush is a fast-growing, suckering, deciduous shrub with an arching habit. Dense clusters of bell-shaped pink flowers with yellow-flushed throats appear in abundance from late spring to early summer. The leaves are dark green and broadly oval. Excellent for a shrub border or as a specimen plant.

CULTIVATION *Grow in any well-drained, fertile soil, in full sun. Let the arching habit of young plants develop without pruning, then thin out the stems each year after flowering, to maintain vigor.*

☼ ◊ Z5-9 H9-5 ↕10ft (3m) ↔12ft (4m)

LABURNUM × *WATERERI* 'VOSSII'

This spreading, deciduous tree bears long, hanging clusters of golden yellow, pealike flowers in late spring and early summer. The dark green leaves are made up of three oval leaflets. A fine specimen tree for small gardens; it can also be trained on an arch, pergola, or tunnel frame-work. All parts are toxic if eaten.

CULTIVATION *Grow in well-drained, moderately fertile soil, in full sun. Cut back badly placed growth in winter or early spring. Remove any suckers or buds at the base of the trunk.*

☼ ◊ Z6-8 H8-6   ↕↔ 25ft (8m)

LAGURUS OVATUS

Hare's tail is an annual grass that bears fluffy, oval flowerheads in summer. These are pale green, often purple-tinged, and fade to a pale, creamy buff. The flat, narrow leaves are pale green. Effective in a border; the flowers can be cut for indoor arrangements; for drying, pick the heads before they are fully mature.

CULTIVATION *Best in light, well-drained, moderately fertile, ideally sandy soil. Choose a position in full sun.*

☼ ◊ annual H12-1 ↕20in (50cm) ↔12in (30cm)

LAMIUM MACULATUM
'WHITE NANCY'

This colorful deadnettle is a semi-evergreen perennial that spreads to form mats; this makes it effective as a groundcover between shrubs. Spikes of pure white, two-lipped flowers are produced in summer above triangular to oval, silver leaves that are edged with green.

CULTIVATION *Grow in moist but well-drained soil, in partial or deep shade. Can be invasive, so position away from other small plants, and dig up invasive roots or shoots to limit spread.*

☼◐ ◊◊ Z4-8 H8-1   ↕to 6in (15cm)
↔to 3ft (1m) or more

LAPAGERIA ROSEA

The Chilean bellflower is a long-lived, twining, evergreen climber. From summer to late autumn, it produces large, narrowly bell-shaped, waxy red flowers borne either singly or in small clusters. The leaves are oval and dark green. Where marginally hardy, give the protection of a warm, partially shaded wall. 'Nash Court' has soft pink flowers.

CULTIVATION *Grow in well-drained, moderately fertile soil, preferably in partial shade. Where marginal, shelter from wind and provide a winter mulch. Keep pruning to a minimum, removing damaged growth in spring.*

☼ ◊ Z10-11 H12-9   ↕15ft (5m)

LATHYRUS LATIFOLIUS

The everlasting or perennial pea is a tendril-climbing, herbaceous perennial with winged stems, ideal for growing through shrubs or over a bank. Clusters of pealike, pink-purple flowers appear during summer and early autumn, amid the deciduous, blue-green leaves, which are divided into two oblong leaflets. The seeds are not edible. For white flowers, choose 'Albus' or 'White Pearl'.

CULTIVATION *Grow in well-drained, fertile, organic soil, in sun or semi-shade. Cut back to ground level in spring and pinch out shoot tips to encourage bushiness. Resents disturbance.*

☼☀ ◊ Z5-9 H9-4   ‡6ft (2m) or more

LATHYRUS VERNUS

Spring vetchling is a dense, clump-forming, herbaceous perennial with upright stems. Despite its pealike appearance, it does not climb. In spring, clusters of purplish blue flowers appear above the mid- to dark green leaves, which are divided into several pointed leaflets. Suitable for a rock or woodland garden. The cultivar 'Alboroseus' has pretty bicolored flowers in pink and white.

CULTIVATION *Grow in well-drained soil, in full sun or partial shade. Tolerates poor soil but resents disturbance.*

☼☀ ◊ Z5-9 H9-4   ‡8–18in (20–45cm)
                    ↔18in (45cm)

SWEET PEAS (*LATHYRUS ODORATUS*)

The many cultivars of *Lathyrus odoratus* are annual climbers cultivated for their long display of beautiful and fragrant flowers that cut well and are available in most colors except yellow. The flowers are arranged in clusters during summer to early autumn. The seeds are not edible. Most look very effective trained on a pyramid of stakes or a trellis, or scrambling amid shrubs and perennials. Compact cultivars such as 'Patio Mixed' suit containers; some of these are self-supporting. Grow sweet peas, also, in a vegetable garden, because they attract pollinating bees and other beneficial insects.

CULTIVATION *Grow in well-drained, fertile soil; for the best flowers, add well-rotted manure the season before planting. Site in full sun or partial shade. Give a balanced fertilizer every other week when in growth. Deadhead or cut flowers regularly. Support the climbing stems.*

☼ ☀ ◊◊ annual H8–1

1 ‡6–8ft (2–2.5m)

2 ‡6–8ft (2–2.5m)

3 ‡6–8ft (2–2.5m)

4 ‡3ft (1m)

5 ‡6–8ft (2–2.5m)

6 ‡6–8ft (2–2.5m)

1 *L.* 'Aunt Jane' 2 *L.* 'Evening Glow' 3 *L.* 'Noel Sutton'
4 *L.* 'Patio Mixed' 5 *L.* 'Teresa Maureen' 6 *L.* 'White Supreme'

LAURUS NOBILIS

Bay, or bay laurel, is a conical, evergreen tree grown for its oval, aromatic, leathery, dark green leaves that are used in cooking. Clusters of small, greenish yellow flowers appear in spring, followed by black berries in autumn. Effective when trimmed into formal shapes.

CULTIVATION *Grow in well-drained but moist, fertile soil, in sun or semi-shade with shelter from cold, drying winds. Grow male and female plants together for a reliable crop of berries. Prune young plants to shape in spring; trim established plants lightly in summer.*

☼◑ ◊ Z8-10 H12-7 ‡40ft (12m) ↔30ft (10m)

LAURUS NOBILIS 'AUREA'

This golden-leaved bay is a conical tree bearing aromatic, evergreen leaves. These are oval and leathery and can be used in cooking. In spring, clusters of small, greenish yellow flowers appear, followed in autumn by black berries on female plants. Good for topiary and in containers, where it makes a much smaller plant.

CULTIVATION *Grow in well-drained but moist, fertile soil. Position in full sun or partial shade with shelter from cold winds. Prune young plants to shape in spring; once established, trim lightly in summer to encourage a dense habit.*

☼◑ ◊ Z8-10 H12-7 ‡40ft (12m) ↔30ft (10m)

LAVANDULA ANGUSTIFOLIA 'HIDCOTE'

This compact lavender with thin, silvery gray leaves and dark purple flowers is an evergreen shrub useful for edging. Dense spikes of fragrant, tubular flowers, borne at the ends of long, unbranched stalks, appear during mid- to late summer. Like all lavenders, the flowers dry best if cut before they are fully open.

CULTIVATION *Grow in well-drained, fertile soil, in sun. Cut back flower stems in autumn, and trim the foliage lightly with shears at the same time. In colder areas, leave trimming until spring. Do not cut into old wood.*

☼ ◊ Z5-8 H9-3 ‡24in (60cm) ↔30in (75cm)

LAVANDULA ANGUSTIFOLIA 'TWICKEL PURPLE'

This evergreen shrub is a close relative of 'Hidcote' (above) with a more spreading habit, paler flowers, and greener leaves. Dense spikes of fragrant purple flowers are borne in mid-summer above narrowly oblong, gray-green leaves. Good in a shrub border; as with all lavenders, the flowerheads are attractive to bees.

CULTIVATION *Grow in well-drained, fairly fertile soil, in full sun. Trim in autumn, or delay until spring in colder areas. Do not cut into old wood.*

☼ ◊ Z5-8 H9-3 ‡24in (60cm) ↔3ft (1m)

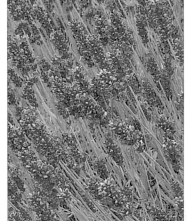

LAVANDULA × *INTER-MEDIA* **DUTCH GROUP**

A tall, robust, bushy lavender, with broad, silvery, aromatic leaves and tall, slender spikes of scented lavender-blue flowers. Suited to a sunny shrub border or large rock or scree garden; makes a good low hedge if regularly trimmed. 'Grappenhall' is very similar but is not as hardy.

CULTIVATION *Grow in well-drained, fertile soil, in sun. Cut back flower stems in autumn, and trim the foliage lightly with shears at the same time. In colder areas, leave trimming until spring. Do not cut into old wood.*

☼ ◊ Z6-8 H8-4　　　　↕↔4ft (1.2m)

LAVANDULA STOECHAS SUBSP. *PEDUNCULATA*

French lavender is a compact, evergreen shrub that blooms from late spring to summer. Dense spikes of tiny, fragrant, dark purple flowers, each spike topped by distinctive, rose-purple bracts, are carried on long stalks well above the narrow, woolly, silvery gray leaves. Effective in a sheltered shrub border or rock garden.

CULTIVATION *Grow in well-drained, fairly fertile soil, in sun. Trim back in spring or, in frost-free climates, after flowering. Avoid cutting into old wood.*

☼ ◊ Z8-9 H12-7　　　　↕↔24in (60cm)

SHRUBBY LAVATERAS (*LAVATERA*)

These upright and showy, flowering shrubs with stiff stems and sage-green leaves usually bloom from mid-summer to autumn in shades of pink and purple. Although they are short-lived, they grow quickly on any well-drained soil, including thin, dry soil, which makes them a welcome addition to any garden where quick results are desired. They also perform well in coastal areas, being able to tolerate salt-laden winds, but the shrubs will need staking if grown in a site exposed to wind.

Where marginally hardy, grow against a warm, sunny wall.

CULTIVATION *Grow in any poor to moderately fertile, well-drained to dry soil in full sun. Shelter from cold, drying winds in frost-prone areas. After cold winters, cold-damaged plants are best pruned right down to the base in spring to encourage new growth and tall, vigorous stems. In milder areas, trim to shape after flowering.*

☼ ◊ Zones vary

1 ‡↔ 6ft (2m)   **2** ‡↔ 6ft (2m)   **3** ‡↔ 6ft (2m)   **4** ‡↔ 6ft (2m)   **5** ‡↔ 6ft (2m)

1 *Lavatera* 'Barnsley' Z6-8 H8-6   **2** *L.* 'Bredon Springs' Z10-11 H12-9
3 *L.* 'Burgundy Wine' Z10-11 H12-9   **4** *L.* 'Candy Floss' Z10-11 H12-9   **5** *L.* 'Rosea' Z6-8 H8-6

ANNUAL LAVATERAS (*LAVATERA*)

These sturdy, bushy annuals are an excellent choice for planting in groups in a herbaceous border or for summer bedding, flowering continuously from mid-summer into autumn. They are softly hairy or downy plants with shallowly lobed, soft green leaves; the open funnel-shaped, pink, reddish pink, or purple blooms are complemented nicely by the foliage. Although annual lavateras are only a temporary visitor to the garden, with their cottage-garden appearance they seem to look as if they have been around for years. Excellent for a dry, sunny site and as a source of cut flowers.

CULTIVATION *Grow in light, moderately fertile, well-drained soil in full sun. Young plants need a regular supply of water until they become established; after this, the plants are fairly drought-tolerant. Watch out for aphids, which often attack young growth.*

☼ ◊ annual H12-1

1 ‡ to 24in (60cm) ↔ 18in (45cm)　　**2** ‡ to 24in (60cm) ↔ 18in (45cm)　　**3** ‡ to 24in (60cm) ↔ 18in (45cm)

4 ‡ to 30in (75cm) ↔ 18in (45cm)　　**5** ‡ to 24in (60cm) ↔ 18in (45cm)　　**6** ‡ to 30in (75cm) ↔ 18in (45cm)

1 *Lavatera* 'Beauty Formula Mixture'　**2** *L.* 'Pink Beauty'　**3** *L.* 'Salmon Beauty'
4 *L.* 'Silver Cup'　**5** *L.* 'White Beauty'　**6** *L.* 'White Cherub'

LEIOPHYLLUM BUXIFOLIUM

Sand myrtle is an upright to mat-forming, evergreen perennial grown for its glossy, dark green foliage and for its abundance of star-shaped, pinkish white flowers in late spring and early summer. The leaves tint bronze in winter. Good, free-flowering underplanting for a shrub border or woodland garden.

CULTIVATION *Grow in moist but well-drained, acidic soil rich in organic matter. Choose a site in partial or deep shade with protection from cold, drying winds. Trim after flowering; it may spread widely if left unattended.*

☼☀ ◐◌ Z6-8 H8-6 ‡12–24in (30–60cm)
↔24in (60cm) or more

LEPTOSPERMUM RUPESTRE

This low-growing, evergreen shrub with dense foliage bears star-shaped white flowers from late spring to summer. The small, aromatic leaves are glossy, elliptic, and dark green. Native to coastal areas of Tasmania, it is useful in seaside gardens provided that the climate is mild. May be sold as *L. humifusum*.

CULTIVATION *Grow in well-drained, fertile soil, in full sun or partial shade. Trim young growth in spring to promote bushiness, but do not cut into old wood.*

☼☀ ◌ Z9-10 H12-3 ‡1–5ft (0.3–1.5m)
↔3–5ft (1–1.5m)

LEPTOSPERMUM SCOPARIUM 'KIWI'

A compact shrub with arching shoots bearing an abundance of small, flat, dark crimson flowers during late spring and early summer. The small, aromatic leaves are flushed with purple when young, maturing to mid- or dark green. Suitable for a large rock garden and attractive in an alpine house display. 'Nicholsii Nanum' is similarly compact.

CULTIVATION *Grow in well-drained, moderately fertile soil, in full sun or part shade. Trim new growth in spring for bushiness; do not cut into old wood.*

☼☀ ◊ Z9-10 H10-8   ↕↔3ft (1m)

LEUCANTHEMUM × *SUPERBUM* 'WIRRAL SUPREME'

A robust, clump-forming, daisy-flowered perennial with, from early summer to early autumn, dense, double white flowerheads. These are carried singly at the end of long stems above lance-shaped, toothed, dark green leaves. Good for cut flowers. 'Aglaia' and 'T.E. Killin' are other recommended cultivars.

CULTIVATION *Grow in moist but well-drained, moderately fertile soil, in full sun or partial shade. May need staking.*

☼☀ ◊◊ Z5-8 H8-4   ↕36in (90cm)
↔30in (75cm)

LEUCOJUM AESTIVUM 'GRAVETYE GIANT'

This robust cultivar of summer snowflake is a spring-flowering, bulbous perennial with upright, strap-shaped, dark green leaves, to 16in (40cm) tall. The faintly chocolate-scented, drooping, bell-shaped white flowers with green petal tips are borne in clusters. Good planted near water, or for naturalizing in grass.

CULTIVATION *Grow in reliably moist, organic soil, preferably near water. Choose a position in partial shade*

☀ ◐ Z4-9 H9-1   ‡3ft (1m) ↔ 3in (8cm)

LEUCOJUM AUTUMNALE

A slender, late-summer-flowering, bulbous perennial bearing stems of two to four drooping, bell-shaped white flowers, tinged red at the petal bases. Narrow, upright, grasslike leaves appear at the same time as or just after the flowers. Suitable for a rock garden.

CULTIVATION *Grow in any moist but well-drained soil. Choose a position in full sun. Divide and replant bulbs once the leaves have died down.*

☀ ◖◗ Z5-9 H9-1   ‡4–6in (10–15cm)
↔ 2in (5cm)

LEWISIA COTYLEDON

This evergreen perennial produces tight clusters of open funnel-shaped, usually pinkish purple flowers; they may be white, cream, yellow, or apricot. These are borne on long stems from spring to summer. The dark green, fleshy, lance-shaped leaves are arranged in basal rosettes. Suitable for growing in wall crevices. The Sunset Group are recommended garden forms.

CULTIVATION *Grow in sharply drained, fairly fertile, organic, neutral to acidic soil. Choose a site in light shade with protection from winter moisture.*

☀ ◊ Z6-8 H8-6   ↕6–12in (15–30 cm) ↔8–16in (20–40cm)

LEWISIA TWEEDYI

An evergreen perennial with upright to arching stems that bear one to four open funnel-shaped, white to peach-pink flowers in spring and early summer. Lance-shaped, fleshy, deep green leaves flushed with purple are arranged in rosettes at the base of the plant. Good in a rock garden, or in an alpine house where not hardy.

CULTIVATION *Grow in sharply drained, orhanic, fairly fertile, neutral to acidic soil, in light shade. Protect plants in winter from excessive winter moisture.*

☀ ◊ Z4-7 H7-1 ↕8in (20cm) ↔12in (30cm)

LIGULARIA 'GREGYNOG GOLD'

A large, robust, clump-forming perennial with pyramidal spikes of daisylike, golden orange, brown-centered flowers from late summer to early autumn. These are carried on upright stems above the large, rounded, mid-green leaves. Excellent by water, it naturalizes readily in moist soils. Dark-leaved 'Desdemona', only 3ft (1m) tall, and 'The Rocket' are other recommended ligularias.

CULTIVATION *Grow in reliably moist, deep, moderately fertile soil. Position in full sun with some midday shade, and shelter from strong winds.*

☼🌢 ◑ Z4-8 H8-1　‡6ft (2m) ↔3ft (1m)

LIGUSTRUM LUCIDUM

The Chinese privet is a vigorous, conical, evergreen shrub with glossy dark green, oval leaves. Loose clusters of small white flowers are produced in late summer and early autumn, followed by oval, blue-black fruits. Good as hedging but also makes a useful, well-shaped plant for a shrub border.

CULTIVATION *Best in well-drained soil, in full sun or partial shade. Cut out any unwanted growth in winter.*

☼◑ ◊ Z8-10 H12-8　‡↔ 30ft (10m)

LIGUSTRUM LUCIDUM 'EXCELSUM SUPERBUM'

This variegated Chinese privet, with yellow-margined, bright green leaves, is a fast-growing, conical, evergreen shrub. Loose clusters of small, creamy white flowers appear in late summer and early autumn, followed by oval, blue-black fruits.

CULTIVATION *Grow in any well-drained soil, in full sun for the best leaf color. Remove unwanted growth in winter. Remove any shoots that have plain green leaves as soon as seen.*

☼ ◊ Z8-10 H12-8   ↔ 30ft (10m)

LILIUM CANDIDUM

The Madonna lily is an upright, bulbous perennial, bearing sprays of up to 20 highly fragrant, trumpet-shaped flowers on each stiff stem in mid-summer. The flowers have pure white petals with tinted yellow bases, and yellow anthers. The lance-shaped, glossy bright green leaves that appear after the flowers usually last over winter.

CULTIVATION *Grow in well-drained, neutral to alkaline soil that is rich in well-rotted organic matter. Tolerates drier soil than most lilies. Position in full sun with the base in shade.*

☼ ◊ Z6-9 H9-6   ↕ 3-6ft (1-2m)

LILIUM FORMOSANUM VAR. *PRICEI*

An elegant, clump-forming perennial bearing very fragrant, slender, trumpet-shaped flowers. These are borne singly or in clusters of up to three during summer. The flowers have curved petal tips, white insides, and strongly purple-flushed outsides. Most of the oblong, dark green leaves grow at the base of the stem. Lovely for an unheated greenhouse or conservatory.

CULTIVATION *Grow in moist, neutral to acidic, organic soil or soil mix, in sun with the base in shade. Protect from excessively hot sun.*

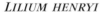

☼ ◑ Z7-9 H8-4   ↕2–5ft (0.6–1.5m)

LILIUM HENRYI

A fast-growing, clump-forming perennial that bears a profusion of slightly scented, "turkscap" flowers (with reflexed, or backward-bending petals) in late summer. These are deep orange with brown spots and red anthers, carried on purple-marked green stems above lance-shaped leaves. Excellent for a wild garden or woodland planting.

CULTIVATION *Grow in well-drained, neutral to alkaline soil with added leaf mold or well-rotted organic matter. Choose a position in partial shade.*

☼ ◊ Z3-8 H8-1   ↕3–10ft (1–3m)

LILIUM LONGIFLORUM

The Easter lily is a fast-growing perennial carrying short clusters of one to six pure white, strongly fragrant, trumpet-shaped flowers with yellow anthers. They appear during mid-summer above scattered, lance-shaped, deep green leaves. One of the smaller, less hardy lilies, it grows well in containers and under glass.

CULTIVATION *Best in well-drained soil or soil mix with added organic matter, in partial shade. Tolerates alkaline soils.*

☼ ◊ Z7-9 H9-1   ‡16–39in (40–100cm)

LILIUM MARTAGON VAR. *ALBUM*

A clump-forming, vigorous perennial bearing sprays of up to 50 small, nodding, glossy white, "turkscap" flowers with strongly curled petals. The leaves are elliptic to lance-shaped, mostly borne in dense whorls. Unlike most lilies, it has an unpleasant odor and is better sited in a border or wild garden, for which it is well suited. Looks good planted with var. *cattaniae*, with its deep maroon flowers.

CULTIVATION *Best in almost any well-drained soil, in full sun or partial shade. Water freely when in growth.*

☼☼ ◊ Z3-7 H7-1   ‡3–6 ft (1–2m)

LILIUM MONADELPHUM

This stout, clump-forming perennial, also known as *L. szovitsianum*, bears up to 30 large, fragrant, trumpet-shaped flowers on each stiff stem in early summer. The blooms are pale yellow, flushed brown-purple on the outsides and flecked purple-maroon on the insides. The scattered, bright green leaves are narrowly oval. Good for containers: it tolerates drier conditions than most lilies.

CULTIVATION *Grow in any well-drained soil, in full sun. Tolerates fairly heavy, alkaline soils.*

☼ ◊ Z5-8 H8-5   ‡3–5ft (1–1.5m)

LILIUM PINK PERFECTION GROUP

These thick-stemmed lilies bear clusters of large, scented, trumpet-shaped flowers with curled petals in mid-summer. Flower colors range from deep purplish red to purple-pink, all with bright orange anthers. The mid-green leaves are straplike. Excellent for cutting.

CULTIVATION *Grow in well-drained soil that is enriched with leaf mold or well-rotted organic matter. Choose a position in full sun with the base in shade.*

☼ ◊ Z4-8 H8-1   ‡5–6ft (1.5–2m)

LILIUM PYRENAICUM

A relatively short, bulbous lily that produces up to 12 nodding, green-yellow or yellow, purple-flecked flowers per stem, in early to mid-summer. Their petals are strongly curved back. The green stems are sometimes spotted with purple, and the lance-shaped, bright green leaves often have silver edges. Not a good lily for patio planting, since its scent is unpleasant.

CULTIVATION *Grow in well-drained, neutral to alkaline soil with added leaf mold or well-rotted organic matter. Position in full sun or partial shade.*

☼ ◑ ◊ Z4-7 H7-1 ‡12–39in (30–100cm)

LILIUM REGALE

The regal lily is a robust, bulbous perennial with very fragrant, trumpet-shaped flowers opening during mid-summer. They can be borne in clusters of up to 25 and are white, flushed with purple or purplish brown on the outsides. The narrow leaves are numerous and glossy dark green. A bold statement in a mixed border. Suitable for growing in pots.

CULTIVATION *Grow in well-drained soil enriched with organic matter. Dislikes very alkaline conditions. Position in full sun or partial shade.*

☼ ◑ ◊ Z4-7 H7-1 ‡2–6ft (0.6m–2m)

LIMNANTHES DOUGLASII

The poached egg plant is an upright to spreading annual that produces a profusion of white-edged, yellow flowers from summer to autumn. The deeply toothed, glossy, bright yellow-green leaves are carried on slender stems. Good for brightening up a rock garden or path edging. Attractive to hoverflies, which help control aphids

CULTIVATION *Grow in moist but well-drained, fertile soil, in full sun. Sow seed outdoors during spring or autumn. After flowering, it self-seeds freely.*

☼ ◊ annual H9 1　↕↔ to 6in (15cm)

LIMONIUM SINUATUM 'FOREVER GOLD'

An upright perennial bearing tightly packed clusters of bright yellow flowers from summer to early autumn. The stiff stems have narrow wings. Most of the dark green leaves are arranged in rosettes around the base of the plant. Suitable for a sunny border or in a gravel garden. The flowers dry well for indoor arrangements. Like many other statice, this is usually grown as an annual.

CULTIVATION *Grow in well-drained, preferably sandy soil, in full sun. Tolerates dry and stony conditions.*

☼ ◊ Z8-9 H12-3 ↕24in (60cm) ↔ 12in (30cm)

LINUM 'GEMMELL'S HYBRID'

A dome-forming, semi-evergreen, perennial flax bearing abundant clusters of yellow, broadly funnel-shaped flowers that open for many weeks throughout summer. The leaves are oval and blue-green. Suitable for a rock garden.

CULTIVATION *Grow in light, moderately fertile, organic soil, with protection from winter moisture. Give full sun.*

☼ ◊ Z6-9 H9-5 ‡6in (15cm) ↔to 8in (20cm)

LIRIODENDRON TULIPIFERA

The stately tulip tree has a broadly columnar habit, spreading with age. The deciduous, squarish, lobed leaves are dark green, turning butter yellow in autumn. Tulip-shaped, pale green flowers, tinged orange at the base, appear in summer and are followed by conelike fruits in autumn. An excellent specimen tree for a large garden.

CULTIVATION *Grow in moist but well-drained, moderately fertile, preferably slightly acidic soil. Choose a site in full sun or partial shade. Keep pruning of established specimens to a minimum.*

☼☼ ◊◊ Z5-9 H9-1 ‡100ft (30m) ↔50ft (15m)

LIRIOPE MUSCARI

This stout, evergreen perennial forms
dense clumps of dark green, straplike leaves. Spikes of small, violet-
purple flowers open in autumn amid
the foliage and may be followed by
black berries. Good in a woodland
border, or use as a drought-tolerant
groundcover for shady areas.

CULTIVATION *Grow in light, moist but
well-drained, moderately fertile soil.
Prefers slightly acidic conditions.
Position in partial or full shade with
shelter from wind. Tolerates drought.*

☼☀ ◊◊ Z6-10 H8-1   ‡12in (30cm)
↔18in (45cm)

LITHODORA DIFFUSA 'HEAVENLY BLUE'

A spreading, evergreen shrub,
sometimes sold as *Lithospermum*
'Heavenly Blue', that grows flat
along the ground. Deep azure blue,
funnel-shaped flowers are borne in
profusion over long periods from
late spring into summer. The leaves
are elliptic, dark green, and hairy.
Grow in an open position in a rock
garden or raised bed.

CULTIVATION *Grow in well-drained,
organic, acidic soil, in full sun. Trim
lightly after flowering.*

☼ ◊ Z6-8 H8-6   ‡6in (15cm)
↔24in (60cm) or more

LOBELIA 'CRYSTAL PALACE'

A compact, bushy perennial that is
almost always grown as an annual,
with vibrant clusters of two-lipped,
dark blue flowers during summer to
autumn. The tiny leaves are dark
green and bronzed. Useful for
edging and for spilling over the
edges of containers.

CULTIVATION *Grow in deep, fertile soil
or soil mix that is reliably moist, in full
sun or partial shade. Plant out, after
the risk of frost has passed, in spring.*

☼ ◐ ◊ annual H8-1   ‡to 4in (10cm)
↔4–6in (10–15cm)

LOBELIA 'QUEEN VICTORIA'

This short-lived, clump-forming
perennial bears almost luminous
spikes of vivid red, two-lipped
flowers from late summer to mid-
autumn. Both the leaves and stems
are deep purple-red. Effective in a
mixed border or waterside planting.
'Bee's Flame' is a very similar plant,
enjoying the same conditions. Both
are irresistible to hummingbirds.

CULTIVATION *Grow in deep, reliably
moist, fertile soil, in full sun. Short-lived
but can be easily propagated by
division in spring.*

☼ ◊ Z4-9 H9-1   ‡3ft (1m) ↔12in (30cm)

LONICERA × *ITALICA*

This vigorous, deciduous, woody-stemmed honeysuckle is a free-flowering, twining or scrambling climber. In summer and early autumn, it bears large whorls of tubular, very fragrant, soft flesh pink flowers, flushed red-purple with yellow insides; red berries follow later in the season. The leaves are oval and dark green. Train onto a wall or up into a small tree.

CULTIVATION *Grow in moist but well-drained, fertile, organic soil, in full sun or partial shade. Once established, cut back shoots by up to one-third after they have flowered.*

☼:◐: ◊◊ Z6-9 H9-6   ‡22ft (7m)

LONICERA NITIDA 'BAGGESEN'S GOLD'

A dense, evergreen shrub bearing tiny, oval, bright yellow leaves on arching stems. Inconspicuous yellow-green flowers are produced in spring, occasionally followed by small, blue-purple berries. Excellent for hedging or topiary in urban gardens, since it is pollution-tolerant.

CULTIVATION *Grow in any well drained soil, in full sun or partial shade. Trim hedges at least 3 times a year, between spring and autumn. Plants that become bare at the base will put out renewed growth if cut back hard.*

☼:◐: ◊ Z6-9 H9-6   ↔ 5ft (1.5m)

LONICERA PERICLYMENUM 'GRAHAM THOMAS'

This long-flowering form of English honeysuckle is a woody, deciduous, twining climber bearing abundant, very fragrant, tubular white flowers. These mature to yellow over a long period in summer, without the red flecking seen on *L. periclymenum* 'Belgica'. The leaves are mid-green and oval in shape.

CULTIVATION *Grow in moist but well-drained, fertile, organic soil. Thrives in full sun but prefers shade at the base. Once established, cut back shoots by up to one-third after flowering.*

☼☀ ◐◑ Z5-9 H9-4 ‡22ft (7m)

LONICERA PERICLYMENUM 'SEROTINA'

The late Dutch honeysuckle is a fast-growing, deciduous, twining climber with very fragrant, rich red-purple flowers that appear in abundance during mid- and late summer. These may be followed by red berries. The leaves are oval and mid-green. If given plenty of space, it scrambles naturally with little pruning needed.

CULTIVATION *Grow in well-drained but moist, organic, fertile soil, in sun with shade at the base. To keep trained specimens within bounds, prune shoots back by one-third after flowering.*

☼☀ ◐◑ Z5-9 H9-4 ‡22ft (7m)

LONICERA × *PURPUSII* 'WINTER BEAUTY'

This dense, semi-evergreen shrub
makes an excellent winter-flowering
hedge with an appealing scent. The
clusters of small, highly fragrant,
creamy white flowers, borne during
winter to early spring, are carried
on red-purple shoots. The leaves
are dark green, and the flowers are
occasionally followed by red berries.

CULTIVATION *Grow in any well-drained
soil, in full sun for the best flowers, or
partial shade. Prune after flowering to
remove dead wood or to restrict size.*

☼ ◐ ◊ Z7 9 H9-7 ‡6ft (2m) ↔8ft (2.5m)

LONICERA × *TELLMANNIANA*

A twining, deciduous, woody-
stemmed climber that bears clusters
of coppery-orange, tubular flowers
that open from late spring to mid-
summer. The deep green, elliptic
leaves have blue-white undersides.
Train onto a wall or fence or up into
a large shrub. Summer-flowering
L. tragophylla (Z6-9 H9-6) is one of
its parents.

CULTIVATION *Grow in moist but well-
drained, fertile, organic soil. Will
tolerate full sun, but it produces better
flowers in a more shaded position. After
flowering, trim shoots by one-third.*

☼ ◐ ◊◊ Z7-9 H9-7 ‡15ft (5m)

LOTUS BERTHELOTII

Known as parrot's beak for its hooked flowers, this trailing, evergreen subshrub bears narrowly cut silvery leaves on long stems. Striking orange-red to scarlet flowers appear in profusion throughout spring and early summer. Will not survive winter cold; it should be planted out in containers during summer and brought under cover for winter. *L. maculatus* is similar and can be used in the same way.

CULTIVATION *Grow in well-drained, moderately fertile soil or soil mix, in full sun. Cut out some older stems after flowering to encourage new growth. Minimum temperature 35°F (2°C).*

☼ ◊ H12-1　　　　‡8in (20cm) ↔indefinite

LUPINUS ARBOREUS

The tree lupine is a fast-growing, sprawling, semi-evergreen shrub grown for its spikes of fragrant, clear yellow flowers that open through the summer. The divided leaves are bright and gray-green. Native to scrub of coastal California, it is tolerant of seaside conditions.

CULTIVATION *Grow in light or sandy, well-drained, fairly fertile, slightly acidic soil in full sun. Cut off seedheads to prevent self-seeding, and trim after flowering to keep compact.*

☼ ◊ Z8-9 H9-8　　　　‡↔6ft (2m)

LYCHNIS CHALCEDONICA

Maltese cross is a clump-forming perennial that produces slightly domed, brilliant red flower-heads in early to mid-summer. These are borne on upright stems above the oval, mid-green, basal leaves. The flowers are small and cross-shaped. Good for a sunny border or wild garden, but it needs some support. It self-seeds freely.

CULTIVATION *Grow in moist but well-drained, fertile, organic soil, in full sun or light dappled shade.*

☀☀ ◊◊ Z4-8 H8-1 ‡3–4ft (1–1.2m)
↔12in (30cm)

LYSICHITON AMERICANUS

Yellow skunk cabbage is a striking, colorful perennial that flowers in early spring and is ideal for a waterside planting. Each dense spike of tiny, greenish yellow flowers is hooded by a bright yellow spathe and has an unpleasant, slightly musky scent. The large, dark green leaves, 20–48in (50–120cm) long, emerge from the base of the plant.

CULTIVATION *Grow in moist, fertile, organic soil. Position in full sun or partial shade, allowing plenty of room for the large leaves to develop.*

☀☀ ◊ Z7-9 H9-7 ‡3ft (1m) ↔4ft (1.2m)

LYSICHITON CAMTSCHATCENSIS

White skunk cabbage is a bold waterside perennial with a slightly musky scent. In early spring, dense spikes of tiny green flowers emerge, cloaked by pointed white spathes. The large, dark green leaves, up to 3ft (1m) long, grow from the base. Ideal beside a stream or a pond.

CULTIVATION *Grow in moist, waterside conditions, in fertile, organic soil. Position in full sun or partial shade, allowing room for the leaves to develop.*

☼☀ ◊ Z7-9 H9-7   ‡↔ to 3ft (1m)

LYSIMACHIA CLETHROIDES

This spreading, clump-forming, herbaceous perennial is grown for its tapering spikes of tiny, star-shaped white flowers. These droop when in bud, straightening up as the flowers open in mid- to late summer. The narrow leaves are yellow-green when young, maturing to mid-green with pale undersides. Suitable for naturalizing in a wild woodland or bog garden.

CULTIVATION *Grow in reliably moist soil that is rich in organic matter, in full sun or partial shade. May need staking.*

☼☀ ◊ Z4-9 H9-1 ‡3ft (1m) ↔24in (60cm)

LYSIMACHIA NUMMULARIA 'AUREA'

Golden creeping Jenny is a rampant, sprawling, evergreen perennial that makes an excellent groundcover plant. Its golden yellow leaves are broadly oval in shape, with heart-shaped bases. The bright yellow, cup-shaped, summer flowers further enhance the foliage color.

CULTIVATION *Grow in reliably moist soil that is enriched with well-rotted organic matter. Site in full sun or partial shade.*

☼ ◑ ◊ Z4-8 H8-1 ↕2in (5cm) ↔indefinite

LYTHRUM SALICARIA 'FEUERKERZE'

This cultivar of purple loosestrife, with more intense rose-red flowers than the species, is a clump-forming, upright perennial. The slender spikes of flowers bloom from mid-summer to early autumn above the lance-shaped, mid-green foliage. Suited to a moist border or waterside planting. Sometimes sold as 'Firecandle'. May be invasive in wetland areas.

CULTIVATION *Grow in moist, preferably fertile soil, in full sun. Remove flowered stems to prevent self-seeding.*

☼ ◊ Z4-9 H9-1 ↕3ft (1m) ↔ 18in (45cm)

MACLEAYA × *KEWENSIS* 'KELWAY'S CORAL PLUME'

A clump-forming perennial grown for its foliage and large, graceful plumes of tiny, coral-pink to deep buff flowers. These open from pink buds from early summer, appearing to float above large, olive green leaves. Grow among shrubs, or group to form a hazy screen. *M. cordata*, with paler flowers, can be used similarly.

CULTIVATION *Best in moist but well-drained, moderately fertile soil, in sun or light shade. Shelter from cold winds. May be invasive; chop away roots at the margins of the clump to confine.*

☼☀ ◊◊ Z4-9 H9-1   ‡7ft (2.2m)
                         ↔ 3ft (1m) or more

MAGNOLIA GRANDIFLORA 'EXMOUTH'

This hardy cultivar of the bull bay is a dense, evergreen tree bearing glossy dark green leaves with russet-haired undersides. *M. grandiflora* is quite distinct from other magnolias, since it blooms sporadically from late summer to autumn, producing flowers that are large, very fragrant, cup-shaped and creamy white.

CULTIVATION *Best in well-drained but moist, organic, acidic soil, in full sun or light shade. Tolerates dry, alkaline conditions. Mulch with leaf mold in spring. Keep pruning to a minimum.*

☼☀ ◊◊ Z7-9 H10-7   ‡20–60ft (6–18m)
                          ↔to 50ft (15m)

MAGNOLIA GRANDIFLORA 'GOLIATH'

This cultivar of bull bay is slightly less hardy than 'Exmouth' (see facing page, below) but has noticeably larger flowers, to 12in (30cm) across. It is a dense, conical, evergreen tree with slightly twisted, dark green leaves. The cup-shaped, very fragrant, creamy white flowers appear from late summer to autumn.

CULTIVATION *Best in well-drained but moist, organic, acidic soil, in full sun or light shade. Tolerates dry, alkaline conditions. Mulch with leaf mold in spring. Keep pruning to a minimum.*

☀◐ ◊◔ Z7-9 H10-7 ‡20–60ft (6–18m)
↔to 50ft (15m)

MAGNOLIA LILIIFLORA 'NIGRA'

A dense, summer-flowering shrub bearing goblet-shaped, deep purple-red flowers. The deciduous leaves are elliptic and dark green. Plant as a specimen or among other shrubs and trees. Unlike many magnolias, it begins to flower when quite young.

CULTIVATION *Grow in moist but well-drained, rich, acidic soil, in sun or semi-shade. Mulch in early spring. Prune young shrubs in mid-summer to encourage a good shape; once mature, very little other pruning is needed.*

☀◐ ◊◔ Z6-9 H9-1 ‡10ft (3m) ↔8ft (2.5m)

SPRING-FLOWERING MAGNOLIAS

Spring-flowering magnolias are handsome deciduous trees and shrubs valued for their elegant habit and beautiful, often fragrant blooms which emerge just before the leaves. Flowers range from the tough but delicate-looking, star-shaped blooms of *M. stellata*, to the exotic, gobletlike blooms of hybrids such as 'Ricki'. Attractive red fruits form in autumn. The architectural branch framework of the bare branches makes an interesting display for a winter garden, especially when grown as free-standing specimens. *M.* x *soulangeana* 'Rustica Rubra' can be trained against a wall.

CULTIVATION *Best in deep, moist but well-drained, organic, neutral to acidic soil. M. wilsonii tolerates alkaline conditions. Choose a position in full sun or partial shade. After formative pruning when young, restrict pruning to the removal of dead or diseased branches after flowering.*

☼ ◑ ◍◑ Zones vary H9-5

1 ↕30ft (10m) ↔ 25ft (8m) **2** ↕50ft (15m) ↔ 30ft (10m)
3 ↕↔ 30ft (10m) **4** ↕30ft (10m) ↔ 20ft (6m)

1 *M.* x *loebneri* 'Merrill' (Z5-9) **2** *M. campbellii* 'Charles Raffill' (Z7-9)
3 *M. denudata* (Z6-9) **4** *M.* 'Elizabeth' (Z6-9)

5 ‡↔ 12ft (4m)

6 ‡25ft (8m) ↔ 20ft (6m)

7 ‡30ft (10m) ↔ 15ft (5m)

8 ‡↔ 20ft (6m)

9 ‡28ft (9m) ↔ 20ft (6m)

10 ‡25ft (8m) ↔ 20ft (6m)

11 ‡10ft (3m) ↔ 12ft (4m)

5 *M.* 'Ricki' (Z6-9) **6** *M.* x *loebneri* 'Leonard Messel' (Z5-9) **7** *M. salicifolia* (Z6-9)
8 *M.* x *soulangeana* 'Rustica Rubra' (Z5-9) **9** *M.* x *kewensis* 'Wada's Memory' (Z6-9)
10 *M. wilsonii* (Z7-9) **11** *M. stellata* (Z5-9)

MAHONIA AQUIFOLIUM 'APOLLO'

Oregon grape is a low-growing evergreen shrub with dark green leaves; these are divided into several spiny leaflets and turn brownish purple in winter. Dense clusters of deep golden flowers open in spring, followed by small, blue-black fruits. Can be grown as a groundcover.

CULTIVATION *Grow in moist but well-drained, rich, fertile soil, in semi-shade; tolerates sun if the soil remains moist. Every 2 years after flowering, shear groundcover plants close to the ground.*

☼ ◐ ◊◊ Z6-9 H9-3 ‡24in (60cm) ↔4ft (1.2m)

MAHONIA JAPONICA

A dense, upright, winter-flowering, evergreen shrub bearing large, glossy dark green leaves divided into many spiny leaflets. Long, slender spikes of fragrant, soft yellow flowers are borne from late autumn into spring, followed by purple-blue fruits. Good in a shady border or woodland garden.

CULTIVATION *Grow in well-drained but moist, moderately fertile, organic soil. Prefers shade but will tolerate sun if soil remains moist. Limit pruning to removal of dead wood, after flowering.*

☼ ◐ ◊◊ Z7-8 H8-7 ‡6ft (2m) ↔10ft (3m)

MAHONIA × MEDIA 'BUCKLAND'

A vigorous, upright, evergreen shrub bearing dense and sharply spiny, dark green foliage. Small, fragrant, bright yellow flowers are produced in arching spikes from late autumn to early spring. A good vandal-resistant shrub for a boundary or front garden

CULTIVATION *Best in moist but well-drained, fairly fertile, organic soil. Thrives in semi-shade, but will become leggy in deep shade. Little pruning is needed, but overly long stems can be cut back to a framework after flowering.*

☀ ◊◊ Z8-9 H9-8 ‡15ft (5m) ↔12ft (4m)

MAHONIA × MEDIA 'CHARITY'

A fast-growing, evergreen shrub, very similar to 'Buckland' (above), but it has more upright, densely packed flower spikes. The dark green leaves are spiny, making it useful for barrier or vandalproof planting. Fragrant yellow flowers are borne from late autumn to spring.

CULTIVATION *Grow in moist but well-drained, moderately fertile, rich soil. Prefers partial shade, and will become leggy in deep shade. After flowering, bare, leggy stems can be pruned hard to promote strong growth from lower down.*

☀ ◊◊ Z8-9 H9-8 ‡15ft (5m) ↔12ft (4m)

MALUS FLORIBUNDA

The Japanese crabapple is a dense, deciduous tree with a long season of interest. Graceful, arching branches, bearing dark green foliage, flower during mid- to late spring to give a fine display of pale pink blossoms. The flowers are followed by small yellow crabapples; these often persist, providing a valuable source of winter food for garden wildlife.

CULTIVATION *Grow in moist but well-drained, moderately fertile soil, in sun or light shade. Prune to shape in the winter months when young; older specimens require little pruning.*

☼☀ ◊◊ Z4-8 H8-1 ‡↔ 30ft (10m)

MALUS 'JOHN DOWNIE'

This vigorous, deciduous tree is upright when young, becoming conical with age. Large, cup-shaped white flowers, which open from pale pink buds in late spring, are followed by egg-shaped, orange and red crab-apples. The oval leaves are bright green when young, maturing to dark green. An ideal small garden tree.

CULTIVATION *Grow in well-drained but moist, fairly fertile soil. Flowers and fruits are best in full sun, but it tolerates some shade. Remove damaged or crossing shoots when dormant to form a well-spaced crown. Avoid hard pruning of established branches.*

☼☀ ◊◊ Z5-8 H8-1 ‡30ft (10m) ↔20ft (6m)

MALUS TSCHONOSKII

This upright, deciduous tree with upswept branches produces pink-flushed white blossoms in late spring, followed in autumn by red-flushed yellow crabapples. The leaves turn from green to a vibrant gold, then red-purple in autumn. It is taller than many crabapples, but is still a beautiful specimen tree that can be accommodated in smaller gardens.

CULTIVATION *Grow in well-drained, moderately fertile soil. Best in full sun, but tolerates some shade. Forms a good shape with little or no pruning; it does not respond well to hard pruning.*

☀ ◐ ◊ Z5-8 H8-5 ‡40ft (12m) ↔22ft (7m)

MALUS × ZUMI
'GOLDEN HORNET'

A broadly pyramidal, deciduous tree bearing a profusion of large, cup-shaped, pink-flushed white flowers that open from deep pink buds in late spring. Small yellow crabapples follow and persist well into winter. The display of golden fruit is further enhanced when the dark green foliage turns yellow in autumn.

CULTIVATION *Grow in any but water-logged soil, in full sun for best flowers and fruit. To produce a well-spaced crown, remove damaged or crossing shoots on young plants when dormant. Do not prune older specimens.*

☀ ◐ ◊◊ Z5-8 H8-5 ‡30ft (10m) ↔25ft (8m)

MALVA MOSCHATA F. *ALBA*

This white to very light pink-flowered musk mallow is a bushy, upright perennial suitable for wild-flower gardens or borders. The very attractive and showy flowers are borne in clusters from early to late summer amid the slightly musk-scented, mid-green foliage.

CULTIVATION *Grow in moist but well-drained, moderately fertile soil, in full sun. Taller plants may need staking. Often short-lived, but self-seeds readily.*

☼ ◊ Z4-8 H8-1 ‡3ft (1m) ↔24in (60cm)

MATTEUCCIA STRUTHIOPTERIS

The ostrich fern forms clumps of upright or gently arching, pale green, deciduous fronds. In summer, smaller, dark brown fronds form at the center of each clump, which persist until late winter. An excellent foliage perennial for a damp, shady border and for woodland or waterside plantings.

CULTIVATION *Grow in moist but well-drained, organic, neutral to acidic soil. Chose a site in light dappled shade.*

☼ ◊◊ Z3-8 H8-1 ‡3–5ft (1–1.5m) ↔18–30in (45–75cm)

MATTHIOLA
CINDERELLA SERIES

These woody-based stocks, short-lived perennials grown as annuals, are valued for their dense spikes of sweet-scented, double flowers in a range of colors from white through pink to dark blue-purple. 'Cinderella White' and 'Cinderella Purple' are recommended single colors. An attractive addition to a summer border; the flowers cut well.

CULTIVATION *Grow in well-drained but moist, fertile, neutral to acidic soil, in a sheltered, sunny site. Plant out after the danger of frost has passed.*

☼ ◊ Z7-8 H8-1   ‡8–10in (20–25cm)
↔to 10in (25cm)

MECONOPSIS
BETONICIFOLIA

The Tibetan blue poppy is a clump-forming perennial bearing upright stems of large, saucer-shaped flowers that are clear blue or often purple-blue or white. These appear in early summer, above the oval and bluish green leaves. Naturalizes well in a woodland garden.

CULTIVATION *Best in moist but well-drained, rich, acidic soil. Site in partial shade with shelter from cold winds. May be short-lived, especially in hot or dry conditions. Divide clumps after flowering to maintain vigor.*

☼ ◊◊ Z7-8 H8-7 ‡4ft (1.2m) ↔18in (45cm)

MECONOPSIS GRANDIS

The Himalayan blue poppy is an upright, clump-forming perennial, similar to *M. betonicifolia* (see previous page, bottom), but with larger, less clustered, rich blue to purplish red flowers. These are carried above the mid- to dark green foliage in early summer. Appealing when grown in large groups in a woodland setting.

CULTIVATION *Grow in moist, leafy, acidic soil. Position in partial shade with shelter from wind. Mulch generously and water in dry spells; may fail to flower if soil becomes too dry*

☀ ◊ Z5-8 H8-5   ‡4ft (1.2m) ↔24in (60cm)

MELIANTHUS MAJOR

The honey bush is an excellent foliage shrub of upright to spreading habit. From late spring to mid-summer, spikes of blood red flowers may appear above the gray-green to bright blue-green, divided leaves. In milder climates it is ideal for a coastal garden.

CULTIVATION *Grow in moist but well-drained, fertile soil. Choose a sunny site protected from wind and excessive winter moisture. Makes an attractive pot plant if given a large enough container.*

☀ ◊ Z8-10 H12-8   ‡6–10ft (2–3m)
↔3–10ft (1–3m)

MIMULUS AURANTIACUS

This domed or sprawling, evergreen shrub bears open trumpet-shaped, yellow, orange, or dark red flowers from late summer to autumn. The rich green leaves are lance-shaped and toothed. In regions with cold winters it will be better off in a cool greenhouse.

CULTIVATION *Best in well-drained, organic soil or soil mix, in full sun. Often short-lived, but easily propagated by cuttings in mid-summer.*

⚘ ◊ Z7-10 H12-7   ↔ 3ft (1m)

MIMULUS CARDINALIS

The scarlet monkey flower is a creeping perennial with tubular, scarlet, sometimes yellow-marked flowers. They appear throughout summer amid the oval, light green leaves, on hairy stems. Good for adding color to a warm border.

CULTIVATION *Grow any well-drained, fertile, organic soil; tolerates quite dry conditions. Position in sun or light dappled shade. May be short-lived, but easily propagated by division in spring.*

☼ ◊ Z6-9 H9-6 ↕3ft (1m) ↔24in (60cm)

MOLINIA CAERULEA 'VARIEGATA'

The purple moor grass is a tufted perennial forming clumps of cream-striped, narrow, dark green leaves. Dense, purple flowering spikes are produced over a long period from spring to autumn on tall, ochre-tinted stems. A good structural plant for a border or a woodland garden.

CULTIVATION *Grow in any moist but well-drained, preferably acidic to neutral soil, in full sun or partial shade.*

☼☀ ◊ Z5-9 H9-5   ‡to 24in (60cm)
↔16in (40cm)

MONARDA 'CAMBRIDGE SCARLET'

This bee balm is a clump-forming perennial bearing shaggy heads of rich scarlet-red, tubular flowers from mid-summer to early autumn. They appear in profusion above the aromatic leaves and are very attractive to bees, hence the common name. A colorful addition to any mixed or herbaceous border.

CULTIVATION *Prefers moist but well-drained, moderately fertile, organic soil, in full sun or light dappled shade. Keep moist in summer, but protect from excessive moisture in winter.*

☼☀ ◊◊ Z4-9 H9-1 ‡3ft (1m) ↔18in (45cm)

MONARDA
'CROFTWAY PINK'

A clump-forming, herbaceous
perennial with shaggy heads of
tubular pink flowers carried above
the small, aromatic, light green
leaves from mid-summer to early
autumn. Suits mixed or herbaceous
borders; the flowers attract bees.
'Beauty of Cobham' (Z4-9 H9-1) is
similar, but with mauve outer bracts
surrounding the pink flowers.

CULTIVATION *Grow in well-drained,
fairly fertile, organic soil that is reliably
moist in summer. Site in full sun or
light shade, with protection from
excessive winter moisture.*

☀◑ ◊ Z4-8 H8-1 ‡3ft (1m) ↔18in (45cm)

MUSCARI ARMENIACUM

A vigorous, bulbous perennial that
bears dense spikes of tubular, rich
blue flowers in early spring. The
mid-green leaves are straplike and
begin to appear in autumn. Plant
massed together in borders or allow
to spread and naturalize in grass,
although it can be invasive.

CULTIVATION *Grow in moist but well-
drained, fairly fertile soil, in full sun.
Divide clumps of bulbs in summer.*

☀ ◊ Z4-8 H8-1 ‡8in (20cm) ↔2in (5cm)

MUSCARI AUCHERI

This bulbous perennial, less invasive than *M. armeniacum* (see previous page, bottom), bears dense spikes of small, bright blue spring flowers. The flower spikes, often topped with paler blue flowers, are carried above the basal clumps of strap-shaped, mid-green leaves. Suitable for a rock garden. Sometimes known as *M. tubergenianum*.

CULTIVATION *Grow in moist but well-drained, moderately fertile soil. Choose a position in full sun.*

☼ ◊ Z6-9 H9-6 ‡6in (15cm) ↔2in (5cm)

MYRTUS COMMUNIS

The common myrtle is a rounded shrub with dense, evergreen foliage. From mid-summer to early autumn, amid the small, glossy dark green, aromatic leaves, it bears great numbers of fragrant white flowers with prominent tufts of stamens. Purple-black berries appear later in the season. Can be grown as an informal hedge or a specimen shrub. Where marginally hardy, grow against a warm, sunny wall.

CULTIVATION *Best in well-drained but moist, fertile soil, in full sun. Protect from cold, drying winds. Trim in spring; tolerates close clipping.*

☼ ◊ Z8-9 H9-8 ‡↔10ft (3m)

MYRTUS COMMUNIS SUBSP. *TARENTINA*

This dense, evergreen shrub is more compact and rounded than the species (see facing page, below), with smaller leaves and pink-tinted cream flowers. These appear during mid-spring to early autumn and are followed by white berries. Grow in a border or as an informal hedge.

CULTIVATION *Grow in moist but well-drained, moderately fertile soil. Choose a site in full sun with shelter from cold, drying winds. Trim back in spring; tolerates close clipping.*

☀ ◊ Z8-9 H9-8   ↔5ft (1.5m)

NANDINA DOMESTICA

Heavenly bamboo is an upright, evergreen or semi-evergreen shrub with fine spring and autumn color. The divided leaves are red when young, maturing to green, then flushing red again in late autumn. Conical clusters of small white flowers with yellow centers appear in mid-summer, followed by long-lasting, bright red fruits.

CULTIVATION *Grow in moist but well-drained soil, in full sun. Cut back on planting, then prune in mid-spring to keep the plant neat.*

☀ ◊ Z6-9 H9-3   ↕6ft (2m) ↔5ft (1.5m)

SMALL DAFFODILS (*NARCISSUS*)

Small and miniature daffodils make good spring-flowering, bulbous perennials for both indoor and outdoor displays. They are cultivated for their elegant, mostly yellow or white flowers, of which there is great variety in shape. The blooms are carried either singly or in clusters above basal clumps of long, strap-shaped leaves on upright, leafless stems. All small daffodils are suitable for a rock garden, and they can look effective when massed together to form drifts. Because of their manageable size, these daffodils are useful for indoor displays. Some, such as *N. bulbocodium*, will naturalize in short, fine grass.

CULTIVATION *Best in well-drained, fertile soil that is moist during growth, preferably in sun. Feed with a balanced fertilizer after flowering to encourage good flowers the following year. Deadhead as flowers fade, and allow the leaves to die down naturally; do not tie them into bunches.*

☼ ◊ Z3-9 H9-1

1 ‡14in (35cm) ↔ 3in (8cm)   **2** ‡4–6in (10–15cm) ↔ 2–3in (5–8cm)   **3** ‡12in (30cm) ↔ 3in (8cm)

4 ‡6–8in (15–20cm) ↔ 2–3in (5–8cm)   **5** ‡12in (30cm) ↔ 3in (8cm)   **6** ‡12in (30cm) ↔ 3in (8cm)

1 *N.* 'Avalanche' **2** *N. bulbocodium* **3** *N.* 'Charity May'
4 *N. cyclamineus* **5** *N.* 'Dove Wings' **6** *N.* 'February Gold'

7 ↕7in (17cm) ↔ 2–3in (5–8cm)

8 ↕8in (20cm) ↔ 3in (8cm)

9 ↕8in (20cm) ↔ 3in (8cm)

10 ↕7in (17cm) ↔ 2–3in (5–8cm)

11 ↕4–6in (10–15cm) ↔ 2–3in (5–8cm)

12 ↕6in (15cm) ↔ 2–3in (5–8cm)

13 ↕4–10in (10–25cm) ↔ 2–3in (5–8cm)

7 *N.* 'Hawera' **8** *N.* 'Jack Snipe' **9** *N.* 'Jetfire' **10** *N.* 'Jumblie'
11 *N. minor* **12** *N.* 'Tête-à-tête' **13** *N. triandrus*

LARGE DAFFODILS (*NARCISSUS*)

Large daffodils are tall, bulbous perennials, easily cultivated for their showy, mostly white or yellow flowers in spring. These are borne singly or in clusters on upright, leafless stems above long, strap-shaped, mid-green foliage arising from the bulb. A great diversity of elegant flower shapes is available, those illustrated all are excellent for cutting; 'Sweetness' has blooms that last particularly well when cut. Most look very effective flowering in large groups between shrubs or in a border. Some naturalize easily in grass or under deciduous trees and shrubs in a woodland garden.

CULTIVATION *Best in well-drained, fertile soil, preferably in full sun. Keep soil reliably moist during the growing season, and feed with a balanced fertilizer after flowering to ensure good blooms the following year. Deadhead as flowers fade, and allow leaves to die down naturally.*

☼ ◊ Z3-9 H9-1

2 ‡ 16in (40cm) ↔ 5in (12cm)

1 ‡ 18in (45cm) ↔ 6in (15cm)

3 ‡ 16in (40cm) ↔ 5in (12cm)

4 ‡ 16in (40cm) ↔ 6in (15cm)

1 *N.* 'Actaea' **2** *N.* 'Empress of Ireland' **3** *N.* 'Ceylon' **4** *N.* 'Cheerfulness'

5 ↕16in (40cm) ↔ 6in (15cm)

6 ↕18in (45cm) ↔ 6in (15cm)

7 ↕14in (35cm) ↔ 6in (15cm)

8 ↕18in (45cm) ↔ 6in (15cm)

9 ↕16in (40cm) ↔ 6in (15cm)

10 ↕16in (40cm) ↔ 3in (8cm)

11 ↕18in (45cm) ↔ 6in (15cm)

12 ↕18in (45cm) ↔ 6in (15cm)

13 ↕16in (40cm) ↔ 3in (8cm)

14 ↕18in (45cm) ↔ 6in (15cm)

5 *N.* 'Ice Follies' **6** *N.* 'Kingscourt' **7** *N.* 'Merlin' **8** *N.* 'Mount Hood' **9** *N.* 'Passionale'
10 *N.* 'Suzy' **11** *N.* 'Saint Keverne' **12** *N.* 'Tahiti' **13** *N.* 'Sweetness' **14** *N.* 'Yellow Cheerfulness'

NERINE BOWDENII

This robust perennial is one of the best late-flowering bulbs. In autumn, it bears open sprays of five to ten trumpet-shaped, faintly scented, bright pink flowers with curled, wavy-edged petals. The straplike, fresh green leaves appear after the flowers, at the base of the plant. The flowers are good for cutting.

CULTIVATION *Grow in well-drained soil, in a sunny, sheltered position. Provide a deep, dry mulch in winter.*

☼ ◊ Z8–10 H12-8 ⬍18in (45cm) ↔5–6in (12–15cm)

NICOTIANA 'LIME GREEN'

This striking flowering tobacco is an upright, free-flowering, bushy annual, ideal for a summer border. It bears loose clusters of night-scented, yellow-green flowers, with long throats and flattened faces, from mid- to late summer. The leaves are mid-green and oblong. Also good near patios, where the evening scent can be appreciated. For mixed colors that include lime green, the Domino Series is recommended.

CULTIVATION *Grow in moist but well-drained, fertile soil. Choose a position in full sun or partial shade.*

☼☼ ◊ annual H12-1 ⬍24in (60cm) ↔10in (25cm)

NICOTIANA SYLVESTRIS

A vigorous, upright perennial that is grown as an annual in cold climates. Throughout summer, open clusters of long-tubed, flat-faced, sweetly scented white flowers are borne above the dark green, sticky leaves. Although plants are tall (and may need staking), try to position where their scent can be appreciated.

CULTIVATION *Grow in any well-drained, moderately fertile soil, in sun or partial shade; the flowers close in full sun. Given a dry winter mulch, it may survive a mild winter, resprouting from the base in spring.*

☼:◑ ◊ Z10-11 H12-1 ‡5ft (1.5m) ↔2ft (60cm)

NIGELLA 'MISS JEKYLL'

This tall, slender annual bears pretty, sky blue flowers during summer that are surrounded by a feathery "ruff" of bright green foliage. These are followed later in the season by attractive, inflated seed pods. The blooms last well when cut, and the seed pods can be dried for indoor flower arrangements. There is a white version, also recommended: 'Miss Jekyll Alba'.

CULTIVATION *Grow in well-drained soil, in full sun. Like all love-in-a-mists, it self-seeds freely, although seedlings may differ from the parent.*

☼ ◊ annual H12-1 ‡to 18in (45cm) ↔to 9in (23cm)

WATERLILIES (*NYMPHAEA*)

These aquatic perennials are cultivated for their showy, sometimes fragrant summer flowers and rounded, floating leaves. The shade cast by the leaves is useful in reducing growth of pond algae. Flowers are mostly white, yellow, pink, or red with yellow stamens in the centers. Spread varies greatly, so choose carefully to match the size of your water feature. Planting depths may be between 18–30in (45cm–1m), though 'Pygmaea Helvola' can grow in water no deeper than 6in (15cm).

Using aquatic planting containers makes lifting and dividing much easier.

CULTIVATION *Grow in still water in full sun. Plant in aquatic soil mix with rhizomes just below the surface, anchored with a layer of gravel. Stand young plants on bricks so that shoot tips reach the water surface; lower plants as stems lengthen. Remove yellow leaves regularly. Divide in spring. Use an aquatic fertilizer. H12-1*

☼ Z4-11 (hardy) Z10-11 (tropical)

1 ↔ 4–5ft (1.2–1.5m) hardy

2 ↔ 5–8ft (1.5–2.5m) tropical

3 ↔ 3–4ft (0.9–1.2m) hardy

4 ↔ 3–4ft (0.9–1.2m) tropical

5 ↔ 4–5ft (1.2–1.5m) hardy

6 ↔ 10–16in (25–40cm) hardy

1 *Nymphaea* 'Escarboucle' 2 *N.* 'Gladstoneana' 3 *N.* 'Gonnère'
4 *N.* 'James Brydon' 5 *N.* 'Chromatella' 6 *N. tetragona* 'Helvola'

NYSSA SINENSIS

The Chinese tupelo is a deciduous tree, conical in form, grown for its lovely foliage. The elegant leaves are bronze when young, maturing to dark green, then becoming brilliant shades of orange, red, and yellow in autumn before they fall. The flowers are inconspicuous. Ideal as a specimen tree near water.

CULTIVATION *Grow in fertile, reliably moist but well-drained, neutral to acidic soil in sun or partial shade, with shelter from cold, drying winds. Thin out crowded branches in late winter.*

☼ ◑ ◊◊ Z7-9 H9-7   ↕↔30ft (10m)

NYSSA SYLVATICA

A taller tree than *N. sinensis* (above), the black gum is similar in form, with drooping lower branches. Its dark green leaves change to a glorious display of orange, yellow, or (usually) red in autumn A brilliant tree for autumn color, with brownish gray bark that breaks up into large pieces on mature specimens. It tolerates acidic soil.

CULTIVATION *Grow in moist but well-drained, fertile, neutral to acidic soil in sun or partial shade. Shelter from cold, drying winds, and prune in late winter, if necessary.*

☼ ◑ ◊◊ Z5-9 H9-4   ↕70ft (20m)
                        ↔30ft (10m)

OENOTHERA FRUTICOSA 'FYRVERKERI'

An upright, clump-forming perennial carrying clusters of short-lived, cup-shaped, bright yellow flowers that open in succession from late spring to late summer. The lance-shaped leaves are flushed red-purple when young, contrasting beautifully with the red stems. Nice with bronze- or copper-leaved plants. *O. macrocarpa* subsp. *glauca* (Z5-8 H8-3) is quite similar, with slightly paler flowers.

CULTIVATION *Grow in sandy, well-drained, fertile soil. Choose a site in full sun.*

☼ ◊ Z4-8 H8-1   ‡12–39in (30–100cm)
↔12in (30cm)

OENOTHERA MACROCARPA

This vigorous perennial has flowers similar to *O. fruticosa* 'Fyrverkeri' (above), but its trailing habit makes this plant more suitable for border edging. The golden yellow blooms appear from late spring to early autumn amid the lance-shaped, mid-green leaves. Can also be used in a scree bed or rock garden. Also known as *O. missouriensis.*

CULTIVATION *Grow in well-drained, poor to moderately fertile soil. Position in full sun in a site that is not prone to excessive winter moisture.*

☼ ◊ Z5-8 H8-3   ‡6in (15cm) ↔20in (50cm)

OLEARIA MACRODONTA

A summer-flowering, evergreen shrub or small tree that forms an upright, broadly columnar habit. Large clusters of fragrant, daisylike white flowers with reddish brown centers are borne amid the sharply toothed, glossy dark green leaves. A good hedging plant or windbreak in coastal areas in mild climates..

CULTIVATION *Grow in well-drained, fertile soil, in full sun with shelter from cold, drying winds. Prune unwanted or cold-damaged growth in late spring.*

☼ ◊ Z9-10 H12-9 ‡20ft (6m) ↔15ft (5m)

OMPHALODES CAPPADOCICA

This clump-forming, shade-loving, evergreen perennial bears sprays of small, azure-blue, forget-me-not-like flowers with white centers. These appear in early spring above the pointed, mid-green leaves. Effective planted in groups through a woodland garden.

CULTIVATION *Grow in moist, organic, moderately fertile soil. Choose a site in partial shade.*

☼ ◊ Z6-8 H8-6 ‡to 10in (25cm) ↔to 16in (40cm)

OMPHALODES CAPPADOCICA 'CHERRY INGRAM'

This clump-forming, evergreen perennial is very similar to the species (see previous page, bottom), but with larger, deep blue flowers that have white centers. These appear in early spring, above the pointed, finely hairy, mid-green leaves. Nice in a woodland garden.

CULTIVATION *Best in reliably moist, moderately fertile, organic soil. Choose a site in partial shade.*

☼ ◊ Z6-8 H8-6   ‡to 10in (25cm)
               ↔to 16in (40cm)

ONOCLEA SENSIBILIS

The sensitive fern forms a beautifully textured mass of arching, finely divided, broadly lance-shaped, deciduous fronds. The foliage is pinkish bronze in spring, maturing to pale green. Thrives at the edge of water or in a damp, shady border.

CULTIVATION *Grow in moist, organic, preferably acidic soil. Site in partial shade, since fronds will scorch in sun.*

☼ ◊◊ Z4-9 H9-1 ‡24in (60cm) ↔indefinite

OPHIOPOGON PLANISCAPUS 'NIGRESCENS'

This evergreen, spreading perennial forms clumps of grasslike, curving, almost black leaves. It looks very unusual and effective when planted in gravel-covered soil. Spikes of small, tubular, white to lilac flowers appear in summer, followed by round, blue-black fruits in autumn.

CULTIVATION *Grow in moist but well-drained, fertile, organic, slightly acidic soil in full sun or partial shade. Top-dress with leaf mold in autumn, where practical.*

☼☀ ◔◑ Z6-10 H12-6 ‡8in (20cm) ↔12in (30cm)

ORIGANUM LAEVIGATUM

A woody-based, bushy perennial bearing open clusters of small, tubular, purplish pink flowers from late spring to autumn. The oval, dark green leaves are aromatic, powerfully so when crushed. Good in a rock garden or scree bed. The flowers are attractive to bees.

CULTIVATION *Grow in well-drained, poor to moderately fertile, preferably alkaline soil. Position in full sun. Trim back flowered stems in early spring.*

☼ ◔ Z7-10 H12-7 ‡24in (60cm) ↔18in (45cm)

ORIGANUM LAEVIGATUM 'HERRENHAUSEN'

A low-growing perennial that is hardier than the species (see previous page, bottom), with purple-flushed young leaves and denser whorls of pink flowers in summer. The mature foliage is dark green and aromatic. Attractive in a Mediterranean-style planting or rock garden.

CULTIVATION *Grow in very well-drained, poor to fairly fertile, preferably alkaline soil, in full sun. Trim back flowered stems in early spring.*

☼ ◊ Z6-10 H12-7   ↕↔ 18in (45cm)

ORIGANUM VULGARE 'AUREUM'

Golden marjoram is a colorful, bushy perennial with tiny, golden yellow leaves that age to greenish yellow. Short spikes of tiny, pretty pink flowers are occasionally produced in summer. The highly aromatic leaves can be used in cooking. Good as a groundcover on a sunny bank or in an herb garden, although it tends to spread quickly.

CULTIVATION *Grow in well-drained, poor to moderately fertile, alkaline soil. Position in full sun. Trim back after flowering to maintain a compact form.*

☼ ◊ Z5-9 H9-5   ↕↔ 12in (30cm)

OSMANTHUS X *BURKWOODII*

A dense and rounded, evergreen shrub, sometimes known as x *Osmarea burkwoodii*, carrying oval, slightly toothed, leathery, dark green leaves. Profuse clusters of small, very fragrant white flowers, with long throats and flat faces, are borne in spring. Ideal for a shrub border or as a hedge.

CULTIVATION *Grow in well-drained, fertile soil, in sun or partial shade with shelter from cold, drying winds. Prune to shape after flowering, giving hedges a trim in summer.*

:☼: ◑ ◊ Z7-9 H9-7   ‡↔ 10ft (3m)

OSMANTHUS DELAVAYI

A rounded, fragrant, evergreen shrub with arching branches bearing small, glossy dark leaves. Profuse clusters of sweetly scented, pure white flowers appear in mid- to late spring. Good for a shrub border or woodland garden, and excellent for hedging. May also be wall-trained.

CULTIVATION *Grow in well-drained, fertile soil, in full sun or partial shade with shelter from cold winds. Tolerates alkaline conditions. Prune to shape after flowering; trim hedges in summer.*

:☼: ◑ ◊ Z7-9 H9-7   ‡6–20ft (2–6m)
↔12ft (4m) or more

OSMUNDA REGALIS

The royal fern is a stately, clump-forming perennial with bright green, finely divided foliage. Distinctive, rust-colored fronds are produced at the center of each clump in summer. Excellent in a damp border or at the margins of a pond or stream. There is an attractive version of this fern with crested fronds, 'Cristata', growing slightly less tall, to 4ft (1.2m).

CULTIVATION *Grow in very moist, fertile, organic soil, in semi-shade. Tolerates full sun if soil is wet enough.*

☼ ☀ ◊◊ Z4-9 H9-1 ‡6ft (2m) ↔12ft (4m)

OSTEOSPERMUM JUCUNDUM

A neat, clump-forming, woody-based perennial bearing large, daisylike, mauve-pink flowers that are flushed bronze-purple on the undersides. The blooms open in succession from late spring until autumn. Ideal for wall crevices or at the front of a border. Also known as *O. barberae*. 'Blackthorn Seedling', with dark purple flowers, is a striking cultivar.

CULTIVATION *Best in light, well-drained, fairly fertile soil. Choose a site in full sun. Deadhead to prolong flowering.*

☼ ◊ Z9-10 H10-1 ‡4–20in (10–50cm) ↔20–39in (50–100cm)

OSTEOSPERMUM HYBRIDS

These evergreen subshrubs are grown primarily for their daisylike, bright, and cheerful flowerheads, sometimes with pinched petals or centers in contrasting colors. They are borne singly or in open clusters over a long season, which begins in late spring and ends in autumn. Numerous cultivars have been named, varying from deep magenta through to white, pink, or yellow. Osteospermums are ideal for a sunny border, although the flowers close in dull conditions. These are grown as annuals in colder areas, or in containers so that they can easily be moved into a greenhouse or conservatory during winter.

CULTIVATION *Grow in light, moderately fertile, well-drained soil in a warm, sheltered site in full sun. Overwinter in frost free conditions. Regular deadheading will encourage more flowers.*

☼ ◊ Z9-10 H10-1

1 ↕↔ 24in (60cm)   **2** ↕ 12in (30cm) ↔ 18in (45cm)   **3** ↕↔ 24in (60cm)

4 ↕↔ 18in (45cm)   **5** ↕ 14in (35cm) ↔ 18in (45cm)   **6** ↕↔ 24in (60cm)

1 *Osteospermum* 'Buttermilk'   **2** *O.* 'Hopleys'   **3** *O.* 'Pink Whirls'
4 *O.* 'Stardust'   **5** *O.* 'Weetwood'   **6** *O.* 'Whirligig'

OXALIS ADENOPHYLLA

A bulbous perennial forming clumps of pretty, gray-green leaves that are divided into many heart-shaped leaflets. In late spring, widely funnel-shaped, purple-pink flowers contrast beautifully with the foliage. Native to the Andes, it suits a well-drained rock garden, trough, or raised bed. Pink-flowered *O. enneaphylla* and blue-flowered *O.* 'Ione Hecker' (Z8-9 H9-8) are very similar, though they grow from rhizomatous roots rather than bulbs.

CULTIVATION *Grow in any moderately fertile soil with good drainage. Choose a position in full sun.*

☼ ◊ Z6-8 H8-6 ‡4in (10cm) ↔6in (15cm)

PACHYSANDRA TERMINALIS

This freely spreading, bushy, evergreen foliage perennial makes a very useful groundcover plant for a shrub border or woodland garden. The oval, glossy, dark green leaves are clustered at the tips of the stems. Spikes of small white flowers arc produced in early summer. There is a less vigorous version with white-edged leaves, 'Variegata', and a few selections, including 'Green Sheen', with glossier foliage.

CULTIVATION *Grow in any but very dry soil that is rich in organic matter, in partial or full shade.*

☀☼ ◊ Z4-8 H8-1 ‡8in (20cm) ↔indefinite

PAEONIA DELAVAYI

An upright, sparsely branched,
deciduous shrub bearing nodding,
bowl-shaped, rich dark red flowers
in early summer. The dark green
leaves are deeply cut into pointed
lobes and have blue-green undersides. A tall tree peony, good in
a shrub border.

CULTIVATION *Grow in deep, moist but
well-drained, fertile, organic soil.
Position in full sun or partial shade
with shelter from cold, drying winds.
Very occasionally cut an old, leggy stem
back to ground level in autumn, but
avoid regular or hard pruning.*

☼☀ ◊◊ Z5-8 H8-1 ‡6ft (2m) ↔4ft (1.2m)

PAEONIA LACTIFLORA
'BOWL OF BEAUTY'

A herbaceous, clump-forming
perennial bearing very large, bowl-
shaped flowers in late spring. These
have carmine-pink, red-tinted petals
arranged around a dense cluster of
creamy white stamens. The leaves
are mid-green and divided into
many leaflets. Ideal for a mixed or
herbaceous border.

CULTIVATION *Grow in deep, moist but
well-drained, fertile, organic soil,
in full sun or partial shade. Provide
support. Resents being disturbed.*

☼☀ ◊◊ Z3-8 H8-1 ‡↔3ft (1m)

PAEONIA LACTIFLORA
'DUCHESSE DE NEMOURS'

This clump-forming, free-flowering, herbaceous perennial produces large, fully double flowers that open from green-flushed buds in late spring. They are fragrant, pure white, with ruffled, yellow-based inner petals. The leaves are deep green and divided. Ideal for a mixed or herbaceous border. 'Laura Dessert' has similar, creamy pink flowers.

CULTIVATION *Grow in moist but well-drained, deep, fertile, organic soil, in full sun or semi-shade. Flowers may need support. Does not like to be disturbed once established.*

☼ ◑ ◊◊ Z3-8 H8-1 ↔ 32in (80cm)

PAEONIA LACTIFLORA
'SARAH BERNHARDT'

This herbaceous peony is similar to 'Duchesse de Nemours' (above), but with very large, rose-pink flowers. The blooms appear during late spring above the clumps of mid-green, deeply divided leaves. A lovely addition to a summer border.

CULTIVATION *Grow in moist but well-drained, deep, organic, fertile soil. Position in full sun or partial shade, and provide support for the flowering stems. Does not respond well to root disturbance.*

☼ ◑ ◊◊ Z3-8 H8-1 ↔ 3ft (1m)

PAEONIA LUTEA VAR. *LUDLOWII*

This vigorous, deciduous shrub has an upright and open form. In late spring, large, bright yellow, nodding flowers open amid the bright green foliage. The leaves are deeply divided into several pointed leaflets. Good in a shrub border or planted on its own.

CULTIVATION *Best in deep, well-drained but moist, fertile, organic soil. Site in sun or semi-shade with shelter from cold, drying winds. Avoid hard pruning, but occasionally cut old, leggy stems to ground level in autumn.*

☼ ◑ ◊◊ Z5-8 H8-1   ↕↔ 5ft (1.5m)

PAEONIA OFFICINALIS 'RUBRA PLENA'

This long-lived, clump-forming herbaceous peony makes a fine late-spring-flowering addition to any border display. The large, fully double, vivid crimson flowers, with ruffled, satiny petals, contrast well with the deep green, divided leaves. 'Rosea Plena', very similar, is also recommended.

CULTIVATION *Grow in well-drained but moist, deep, fertile, organic soil. Choose a site in full sun or partial shade. Support the flowering stems.*

☼ ◑ ◊◊ Z3-9 H8-1   ↕↔ 30in (75cm)

PAPAVER ORIENTALE
'BEAUTY OF LIVERMERE'

This tall Oriental poppy with crimson-scarlet flowers is an upright, clump-forming perennial. The flowers open during late spring and develop into large seed pods. Each petal has a bold, black mark at the base. The mid-green, divided leaves are borne on upright, bristly stems. Looks spectacular in a border.

CULTIVATION *Grow in well-drained, poor to moderately fertile soil. Choose a position in full sun.*

☼ ◊ Z4-9 H9-1   ‡3–4ft (1–1.2m)
↔36in (90cm)

PAPAVER ORIENTALE
'BLACK AND WHITE'

This Oriental poppy, white-flowered with crimson-black markings at the petal bases, is a clump-forming perennial. The flowers are borne above the mid-green foliage at the tips of white-bristly, upright stems during late spring; they are followed by distinctive seed pods. Makes a good border perennial.

CULTIVATION *Best in deep, moderately fertile soil with good drainage. Choose a position in full sun.*

☼ ◊ Z4-9 H9-1   ‡18–36in (45–90cm)
↔24–36in (60–90cm)

PAPAVER ORIENTALE
'CEDRIC MORRIS'

This Oriental poppy has very large,
soft pink flowers with black-marked
bases that are set off well against the
gray-hairy foliage. It forms upright
clumps that are well suited to
a herbaceous or mixed border.
Distinctive seed pods develop after
the flowers have faded.

CULTIVATION *Grow in deep, moderately
fertile soil with good drainage. Choose a
position in full sun.*

☼ ◊ Z4-9 H9-1 ‡18–36in (45–90cm)
↔24–36in (60–90cm)

PAPAVER RHOEAS
SHIRLEY MIXED

These field poppies are summer-
flowering annuals with single, semidouble or double, bowl-shaped
flowers in shades of yellow, orange,
pink, and red. These appear on
upright stems above the finely
divided, bright green leaves. Can be
naturalized in a wildflower meadow.

CULTIVATION *Best in well-drained, poor
to moderately fertile soil, in full sun.
Divide and replant clumps in spring.*

☼ ◊ annual H12-1 ‡3ft (1m) ↔12in (30cm)

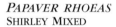

PARAHEBE CATARRACTAE

A small evergreen subshrub bearing loose clusters of white summer flowers with purple veins and red eyes. The leaves are dark green and oval, purple-tinged when young. Looks very effective tumbling over walls or rocks. Its cultivar 'Delight' is also recommended.

CULTIVATION *Grow in well-drained, poor to moderately fertile soil, in full sun. Provide shelter from cold, drying winds.*

☼ ◊ Z9-10 H10-8   ↔ 12in (30cm)

PARAHEBE PERFOLIATA

Digger's speedwell is a spreading, evergreen perennial bearing short spikes of blue, saucer-shaped flowers in late summer. The blue- or gray-green, overlapping leaves are oval and slightly leathery. Suitable for gaps in walls or a rock garden.

CULTIVATION *Grow in poor to fairly fertile soil with good drainage, in full sun. Provide shelter from cold, drying winds.*

☼ ◊ Z9-10 H12-3   ↕ 24–30in (60–75cm)
↔ 18in (45cm)

PARTHENOCISSUS HENRYANA

Chinese Virginia creeper is a woody, twining, deciduous climber with colorful foliage in autumn. The insignificant summer flowers are usually followed by blue-black berries. The conspicuously white-veined leaves, made up of three to five leaflets, turn bright red in the season. Train over a wall or a strongly built fence.

CULTIVATION *Grow in well-drained but moist, fertile soil. Tolerates sun, but leaf color is best in deep or partial shade. Young plants may need some support. Prune back unwanted growth in autumn.*

☼☀ ◊◊ Z7-8 H8-7 ↕30ft (10m)

PARTHENOCISSUS TRICUSPIDATA

Even more vigorous than Virginia creeper (*P. quinquefolia* Z3-9 H9-1), Boston ivy is a woody, deciduous climber with foliage that turns a beautiful color in autumn. The variably lobed, bright green leaves flush a brilliant red, fading to purple before they fall. Creates a strong textural effect on featureless walls.

CULTIVATION *Best in moist but well-drained, fertile, organic soil. Position in partial or full shade. Young plants may need some support before they are established. Remove any unwanted growth in autumn.*

☼☀ ◊◊ Z4-8 H8-1 ↕70ft (20m)

PASSIFLORA CAERULEA

The blue passionflower is a fast-growing, evergreen climber valued for its large, exotic flowers, crowned with prominent blue- and purple-banded filaments. These are borne from summer to autumn amid the dark green, divided leaves. Where marginally hardy, grow in the protection of a warm wall.

CULTIVATION *Best in moist but well-drained, moderately fertile soil, in a sunny, sheltered site. Remove crowded growth in spring, cutting back flowered shoots at the end of the season.*

☼ ◊◊ Z6-9 H9-6 ‡30ft (10m) or more

PASSIFLORA CAERULEA 'CONSTANCE ELLIOTT'

A fast-growing, evergreen climber, resembling the species (above), but with white flowers, borne from summer to autumn. The leaves are dark green and deeply divided into three to nine lobes. Good for a pergola where dependably hardy, but it needs the shelter of a warm wall in colder areas.

CULTIVATION *Grow in moist but well-drained, moderately fertile soil. Choose a sheltered site in full sun. Remove weak growth in spring, cutting back flowered shoots at the end of the season.*

☼ ◊◊ Z6-9 H9-6 ‡30ft (10m) or more

PASSIFLORA RACEMOSA

The red passionflower is a vigorous climber noted for its large, bright red flowers borne in hanging clusters in summer and autumn. They are followed by deep green fruits. The leathery leaves are glossy and mid-green. Very eye-catching in a greenhouse or conservatory.

CULTIVATION *Grow in a greenhouse bed or large container in soil-based potting mix. Provide full light, with shade from hot sun. Water sparingly in winter. Prune in early spring. Minimum temperature 61°F (16°C)*

☼ ◐ ◊◊ H12-7   ↕15ft (5m)

PAULOWNIA TOMENTOSA

The Empress tree is prized for its fragrant, bell- to-trumpet-shaped, pinkish lilac flowers that appear in upright spikes in late spring. The large, heart-shaped leaves are bright green. This is a fast-growing deciduous tree and is very tolerant of atmospheric pollution.

CULTIVATION *Grow in fertile, well-drained soil in full sun. Harder-than-average winter cold will destroy flower buds. Prune in late winter.*

☼ ◊ Z5-8 H8-4   ↕40ft (12m)
                              ↔30ft (10m)

SCENTED-LEAVED GERANIUMS

These geraniums, not to be confused with hardy geraniums (see pp 194–197), are tender, evergreen perennials. Many are grown specifically for their pretty, scented foliage. Their flowers, generally in pinks and mauves, are less showy and more delicate in form than those of the zonal and regal pelargoniums, bred more specifically for floral display. Leaf fragrance varies from sweet or spicy through to the citrus of *P. crispum* 'Variegatum' or the peppermint-like *P. tomentosum*. They will perfume a greenhouse or conservatory, or use as summer edging along a path or in pots on a patio, where they will be brushed against and release their scent.

CULTIVATION *Grow in well-drained, fertile, neutral to alkaline soil or soil mix. In cold areas, over-winter in frost-free conditions, cutting back topgrowth by one-third. Repot as growth resumes. Minimum temperature 35°F (2°C); may overwinter in Zones 9–11.*

☼ ◊ H12-1

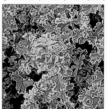

1 ‡ 20in (50cm) ↔ 10–12in (25–30cm)

2 ‡ ↔ 24in (60cm)

3 ‡ 24–36in (60–90cm) ↔ 24in (60cm)

4 ‡ to 4ft (1.2m) ↔ 12in (30cm)

5 ‡ 18in (45cm) ↔ 8–10in (20–25cm)

6 ‡ 30–36in (35–45cm) ↔ 6in (15cm)

1 *Pelargonium* 'Attar of Roses' **2** *P.* 'Bolero' **3** *P.* 'Charity'
4 *P.* 'Citriodorum' **5** *P.* 'Copthorne' **6** *P. crispum* 'Variegatum'

7 ‡24in (60cm) ↔ 12in (30cm)

8 ‡ ↔ 24in (60cm)

9 ‡12–16in (30–40cm) ↔ 8in (20cm)

10 ‡ ↔ 24in (60cm)

11 ‡12–14in (30–35cm) ↔ 6in (15cm)

12 ‡36in (90cm) ↔ 12in (30cm)

13 ‡12–14in (30–35cm) ↔ 10in (25cm)

14 ‡24in (60cm) ↔ 12in (30cm)

15 ‡12–16in (30–40cm) ↔ 12in (30cm)

16 ‡18–20in (45–50cm) ↔ 10in (25cm)

17 ‡30–36in (75–90cm) ↔ to 30in (75cm)

7 *P.* 'Gemstone' **8** *P.* 'Grace Thomas' **9** *P.* 'Lady Plymouth' **10** *P.* 'Lara Starshine'
11 *P.* 'Mabel Grey' **12** *P.* 'Nervous Mabel' **13** *P.* 'Orsett' **14** *P.* 'Peter's Luck'
15 *P.* 'Royal Oak' **16** *P.* 'Sweet Mimosa' **17** *P. tomentosum*

FLOWERING GERANIUMS

Geraniums grown for their bold flowers are tender, evergreen perennials: most cultivars are bushy, but there are also trailing types for windowboxes and hanging baskets. Flower forms vary from the tightly frilled 'Apple Blossom Rosebud' to the delicate, narrow-petaled 'Bird Dancer'; colors range from shades of orange through pink and red to rich purple, and some have colored foliage. A popular choice as bedding plants, flowering from spring into summer, although many will flower throughout the year if kept above 45°F (7°C), making them excellent for a conservatory and as houseplants.

CULTIVATION *Grow in well-drained, fertile, neutral to alkaline soil or soil mix, in sun or partial shade. Deadhead regularly to prolong flowering. In cold areas, overwinter in frost-free conditions, cutting back by one-third. Repot in late winter as new growth resumes. Minimum temperature 35°F (2°C).*

☼◐ ◊ H12-1

1 ‡10–12in (25–30cm) ↔ to 10in (25cm)

2 ‡to 12in (30cm) ↔ 10in (25cm)

3 ‡12–16in (30–40cm) ↔ 8–10in (20–25cm)

1 *Pelargonium* 'Alice Crousse' **2** *P.* 'Amethyst' **3** *P.* 'Apple Blossom Rosebud'

4 ↕ 6–8in (15–20cm) ↔ 6in (15cm) **5** ↕ 10–12in (25–30cm) ↔ 6in (15cm) **6** ↕ 18–24in (45–60cm) ↔ to 10in (25cm)

7 ↕ 4–5in (10–12cm) ↔ 3–4in (7–10cm)

8 ↕ 16–18in (40–45cm) ↔ 10in (25cm)

4 *P.* 'Bird Dancer' **5** *P.* 'Dolly Varden' **6** *P.* 'Flower of Spring'
7 *P.* 'Francis Parrett' **8** *P.* 'Happy Thought'

MORE CHOICES

'Ashfield Serenade'
Mauve with white-based
pink upper petals.

'Belinda Adams'
Miniature, with pink-
flushed white flowers.

'Ben Franklin' Rose-pink
flowers, silver leaves.

'Dame Anna Neagle'
Light pink flowers and
gold and bronze leaves.

'Madame Crousse' Pale
pink flowers, trailing.

'Vancouver Centennial'
Orange-red flowers,
bronze/brown leaves.

9 ‡ 16–18in (40–45cm) ↔ to 12in (30cm)

10 ‡ 10–12in (25–30cm) ↔ 5in (12cm)

11 ‡ to 12in (30cm) ↔ 12in (30cm)

12 ‡ 16–18in (40–45cm) ↔ 8in (20cm)

13 ‡ to 24in (60cm) ↔ to 10in (25cm)

14 ‡ to 24in (60cm) ↔ 10in (25cm)

15 ‡ 8in (20cm) ↔ 7in (18cm)

9 *Pelargonium* 'Irene'   **10** *P.* 'Mr Henry Cox'   **11** *P.* Multibloom Series
12 *P.* 'Paton's Unique'   **13** *P.* 'The Boar'   **14** *P.* 'Voodoo'   **15** *P.* Video Series

REGAL GERANIUMS

These bushy, half-hardy perennials and shrubs have gloriously showy, blowsy flowers, earning them the sobriquet "the queen of geraniums." Their main flowering period is from spring to early summer, with blooms carried in clusters in reds, pinks, purples, orange, white, and reddish black; colors are combined in some cultivars. Often grown as container plants in cold-winter areas both for indoor and outdoor display, although they may also be used in summer bedding designs.

CULTIVATION *Best in good-quality, moist but well-drained potting mix in full light with shade from strong sun. Water moderately during growth, feeding every two weeks with a liquid fertilizer. Water sparingly if overwintering in a frost-free greenhouse. Cut back by one-third and repot in late winter. Outdoors, grow in fertile, neutral to alkaline, well-drained soil in full sun. Deadhead regularly. Minimum temperature 45°F (7°C).*

☀ ◐◐ H5-1

1 ↕ 18in (45cm) ↔ to 10in (25cm)

2 ↕ 18in (45cm) ↔ to 10in (25cm)   **3** ↕ 18in (45cm) ↔ to 10in (25cm)

MORE CHOICES

'Chew Magna' Pink petals with a red blaze.

'Leslie Judd' Salmon-pink and wine-red.

'Lord Bute' Dark reddish black flowers.

'Spellbound' Pink with wine-red petal markings.

4 ↕ 12–16in (30–40cm) ↔ to 8in (20cm)   **5** ↕ 12–16in (30–40cm) ↔ to 8in (20cm)

1 *Pelargonium* 'Ann Hoystead' **2** *P.* 'Bredon'
3 *P.* 'Carisbrooke' **4** *P.* 'Lavender Grand Slam' **5** *P.* 'Sefton'

PENSTEMONS

Penstemons are elegant, semi-evergreen perennials valued for their spires of tubular, foxglovelike flowers, in white and shades of pink, red, and purple, held above lance-shaped leaves. Smaller penstemons, such as *P. newberryi*, are at home in a rock garden or as edging plants, while larger cultivars make reliable border perennials that flower throughout summer and into autumn. 'Andenken an Friedrich Hahn' and 'Schoenholzeri' are among the hardiest cultivars, although most types benefit from a dry winter mulch where marginally hardy. Penstemons tend to be short-lived and are best replaced after a few seasons.

CULTIVATION *Grow border plants in well-drained, organic soil, and dwarf cultivars in sharply drained, gritty, poor to moderately fertile soil. Choose a site in full sun or partial shade. Deadhead regularly to prolong the flowering season.*

☼☀ ◊ Zones vary H10-7

1 ↕4ft (1.2m) ↔ 18in (45cm) **2** ↕↔ 18–24in (45–60cm) **3** ↕30in (75cm) ↔ 24in (60cm)

1 *P.* 'Alice Hindley' (Z7-10) **2** *P.* 'Apple Blossom' (Z4-10)
3 *P.* 'Andenken an Friedrich Hahn' (syn. *P.* 'Garnet') (Z7-10)

4 ‡36in (90cm) ↔ 30in (75cm)

5 ‡18–24in (45–60cm) ↔ 12in (30cm)

6 ‡10in (25cm) ↔ 12in (30cm)

7 ‡36in (90cm) ↔ 24in (60cm)

8 ‡24in (60cm) ↔ 18in (45cm)

4 *P.* 'Chester Scarlet' (Z6-9) **5** *P.* 'Evelyn' (Z7-10) **6** *P. newberryi* (Z5-7) **7** *P.* 'Schoenholzeri' (syn. *P.* 'Firebird', *P.* 'Ruby') (Z7-10) **8** *P.* 'White Bedder' (syn. *P.* 'Snowstorm') (Z6-9)

PERILLA FRUTESCENS VAR. *CRISPA*

An upright, bushy annual grown for its frilly, pointed, deep purple to broze, almost iridescent foliage. Spikes of tiny white flowers appear in summer. The dark foliage makes a contrasting background to the bright flowers of summer bedding plants. Abundantly self-seeds

CULTIVATION *Grow in moist but well-drained, fertile soil. Position in sun or partial shade. Plant in spring after all danger of frost has passed.*

☀️◑ ◊◊ annual H12-1　‡to 3ft (1m)
　　　　　　　　　　　↔to 12in (30cm)

PEROVSKIA 'BLUE SPIRE'

This upright, deciduous subshrub, grown for its foliage and flowers, suits a mixed or herbaceous border. Branching, airy spikes of tubular, violet-blue flowers are borne in profusion during late summer and early autumn, above the silvery gray, divided leaves. Tolerates coastal conditions.

CULTIVATION *Best in poor to moderately fertile soil that is well-drained. Tolerates alkaline soil. For vigorous, bushy growth, prune back hard each spring to a low framework. Position in full sun.*

☀️ ◊ Z6-9 H9-4　‡4ft (1.2m) ↔3ft (1m)

PERSICARIA AFFINIS
'SUPERBA'

A vigorous, evergreen perennial, formerly in the genus *Polygonum*, that forms mats of lance-shaped, deep green leaves that turn rich brown in autumn. Dense spikes of long-lasting, pale pink flowers, aging to dark pink, are borne from mid-summer to mid-autumn. Plant in groups at the front of a border or use as a groundcover. 'Darjeeling Red' is similar and equally good.

CULTIVATION *Grow in any moist soil, in full sun or partial shade. Dig out invasive roots in spring or autumn.*

☼ ◐ ◊ Z3-8 H8-1   ↕ to 10in (25cm)
↔ 24in (60cm)

PERSICARIA BISTORTA
'SUPERBA'

A fast-growing, semi-evergreen perennial, formerly in the genus *Polygonum*, that makes a good groundcover. Dense, cylindrical, soft pink flowerheads are produced over long periods from early summer to mid-autumn, above the clumps of mid-green foliage.

CULTIVATION *Best in any well-drained, reliably moist soil, in full sun or partial shade. Tolerates dry soil.*

☼ ◐ ◊◊ Z4-8 H8-1   ↕ 30in (75cm)
↔ 36in (90cm)

PERSICARIA VACCINIIFOLIA

This creeping, evergreen perennial, formerly in the genus *Polygonum*, bears glossy mid-green leaves that flush red in autumn. In late summer and autumn, spikes of deep pink flowers appear on branching, red-tinted stems. Suits a rock garden by water, or at the front of a border. Good as a groundcover.

CULTIVATION *Grow in any moist soil, in full sun or semi-shade. Control spread by digging up invasive roots in spring or autumn.*

☼☀ ◑ Z7-9 H9-7   ‡8in (20cm) ↔20in (50cm) or more

PETUNIA
CARPET SERIES

These very compact, spreading petunias are usually grown as annuals for their abundant, trumpet-shaped flowers. These open over a long period from late spring to early autumn, in shades of pink through strong reds and oranges to yellow and white. The leaves are oval and dark green. Ideal as dense, colorful summer bedding, particularly in poor soil.

CULTIVATION *Grow in well-drained soil, in a sunny, sheltered site. Deadhead to prolong flowering. Plant out only once all danger of frost has passed.*

☼◊ annual H12-3 ‡6in (15cm) ↔to 3ft (1m)

PETUNIA
MIRAGE SERIES

These dense, spreading annuals
are very similar to the Carpet
Series (facing page, below), but
the trumpet-shaped flowers come
in shades of not only red and pink
but also blues and purples. These
are borne from late spring until early
autumn above the dark green, oval
leaves. Particularly useful as a
bedding plant on poor soils.

CULTIVATION *Grow in any light, well-
drained soil, in full sun with shelter
from wind. Deadhead to prolong
flowering. Plant out after the danger
of frost has passed.*

☀ ◊ annual H12-3 ‡12in (30cm) ↔3ft (1m)

PHALARIS ARUNDINACEA
'PICTA'

Gardeners' garters is an evergreen,
clump-forming perennial grass with
narrow, white-striped leaves. Tall
plumes of pale green flowers, fading
to buff as they mature, are borne on
upright stems during early to mid-
summer. Good as a groundcover,
but it can be very invasive.

CULTIVATION *Grow in any soil, in full
sun or partial shade. Cut down all but
the new young shoots in early summer
to encourage fresh growth. To control
spread, lift and divide regularly.*

☀☀ ◊ Z4-9 H9-1 ‡3ft (1m) ↔indefinite

PHILADELPHUS 'BEAUCLERK'

A slightly arching, deciduous shrub valued for its clusters of fragrant, large white flowers with slightly pink-flushed centers. These are borne in early and mid-summer, amid the broadly oval, dark green leaves. Grow in a shrub border, on its own, or as a screen.

CULTIVATION *Grow in any well-drained, moderately fertile soil. Tolerates shallow, alkaline soil and light shade, but flowers are best in full sun. Cut back 1 in 4 stems to the ground after flowering to stimulate strong growth.*

☼ ◊ Z5-8 H8-1   ↕↔ 8ft (2.5m)

PHILADELPHUS 'BELLE ETOILE'

This arching, deciduous shrub is similar to, but more compact than 'Beauclerk' (above). An abundance of very fragrant, large white flowers with bright yellow centers appears during late spring to early summer. The leaves are tapered and dark green. Good in a mixed border.

CULTIVATION *Grow in any moderately fertile soil with good drainage. Flowers are best in full sun, but tolerates partial shade. After flowering, cut 1 in 4 stems back to the ground to stimulate strong new growth.*

☼ ◊ Z5-8 H8-1 ↕4ft (1.2m) ↔8ft (2.5m)

PHILADELPHUS CORONARIUS 'VARIEGATUS'

This upright, deciduous shrub has attractive, mid-green leaves that are heavily marked with white around the edges. Short clusters of very fragrant white flowers open in early summer. Use to brighten up the back of a mixed border or woodland garden, or on its own.

CULTIVATION *Grow in any fairly fertile soil with good drainage, in sun or semi-shade. For the best foliage, grow in light shade and prune in late spring. For the best flowers, grow in sun, cutting some stems to the ground after flowering.*

☼ ◐ ◊ Z5-8 H8-3 ‡8ft (2.5m) ↔6ft (2m)

PHILADELPHUS 'MANTEAU D'HERMINE'

This deciduous shrub is low and spreading in habit, with long-lasting, double, very fragrant, creamy white flowers. These appear from early to mid-summer amid the pale to mid green, elliptic leaves. Good in a mixed border.

CULTIVATION *Grow in any well-drained, fairly fertile soil. Tolerates partial shade, but flowers are best in full sun. Cut back 1 in 4 stems to the ground after flowering, for strong new growth.*

☼ ◐ ◊ Z5-8 H8-3 ‡3ft (1m) ↔5ft (1.5m)

PHLOMIS FRUTICOSA

Jerusalem sage is a mound-forming, spreading, evergreen shrub, carrying sagelike and aromatic, gray-green leaves with woolly undersides. Short spikes of hooded, dark golden yellow flowers appear from early to mid-summer. Effective when massed in a border.

CULTIVATION *Best in light, well-drained, poor to fairly fertile soil, in sun. Prune out any weak or leggy stems in spring.*

☼ ◊ Z8-9 H9-8   ‡3ft (1m) ↔5ft (1.5m)

PHLOMIS RUSSELIANA

An upright, evergreen border perennial, sometimes known as either *P. samia* or *P. viscosa*, bearing pointed, hairy, mid-green leaves. Spherical clusters of hooded, pale yellow flowers appear along the stems from late spring to autumn.

CULTIVATION *Grow in any well-drained, moderately fertile soil, in full sun or light shade. May self-seed.*

☼☀ ◊ Z4-9 H9-1 ‡3ft (1m) ↔30in (75cm)

PHLOX DIVARICATA 'CHATTAHOOCHEE'

A short-lived, semi-evergreen border perennial bearing many flat-faced, long-throated, lavender-blue flowers with red eyes. These are produced over a long period from summer to early autumn amid the lance-shaped leaves that are carried on purple-tinted stems.

CULTIVATION *Grow in moist but well-drained, organic, fertile soil. Chose a site in partial shade.*

☀: △△ Z4-8 H8-1 ‡6in (15cm) ↔12in (30cm)

PHLOX DOUGLASII 'BOOTHMAN'S VARIETY'

A low and creeping, evergreen perennial that forms mounds of narrow, dark green leaves. Dark-eyed, violet-pink flowers with long throats and flat faces appear in late spring or early summer. Good in a rock garden or wall or as edging in raised beds.

CULTIVATION *Grow in well-drained, fertile soil, in full sun. In areas with low rainfall, position in dappled shade.*

☀☀ △ Z5-7 H7-3 ‡8in (20cm) ↔12in (30cm)

PHLOX DOUGLASII 'CRACKERJACK'

This low-growing perennial is covered in reddish magenta flowers in late spring or early summer. The evergreen foliage is dense and dark green. An attractive, compact plant, ideal for a rock garden, in a dry wall, as edging, or as a groundcover.

CULTIVATION *Grow in well-drained, fertile soil in full sun or, in areas with low rainfall, in dappled shade.*

☼ ◊ Z5-7 H7-5   ‡to 5in (12cm)
                            ↔to 8in (20cm)

PHLOX DOUGLASII 'RED ADMIRAL'

A low-growing, spreading, evergreen perennial that looks good trailing over rocks or spilling over the edge of a border. The mounds of dark green foliage are carpeted with deep crimson, flat-faced flowers during late spring and early summer.

CULTIVATION *Grow in well-drained, fertile soil, in full sun. In areas with low rainfall, position in partial shade.*

☼ ◊ Z5-7 H7-3‡8in (20cm) ↔12in (30cm)

PHLOX DRUMMONDII CULTIVARS

The Greek name *Phlox* means "a flame," referring to the very bright colors of the blooms. *P. drummondii*, the annual phlox, is the parent of many named cultivars used primarily for bold summer bedding. They are upright to spreading, bushy annuals that bear bunched clusters of hairy purple, pink, red, lavender-blue, or white flowers in late spring. The flowers are often paler at the centers, with contrasting marks at the bases of the petal lobes. The stem-clasping leaves are mid-green. Useful in rock gardens, herbaceous borders, flower beds, or in containers; if raised in a greenhouse, they may come into bloom earlier.

CULTIVATION *Grow in reliably moist but well-drained, sandy soil in full sun. Enrich the soil with plenty of organic matter before planting and feed once a week with a dilute liquid fertilizer. Slugs and snails are attracted to young plants.*

☼ ◊◊ annual H12-1

1 ↕4–18in (10–45cm) ↔ 10in (25cm) **2** ↕4–18in (10–45cm) ↔ 10in (25cm) **3** ↕4–18in (10–45cm) ↔ 10in (25cm)

4 ↕4–18in (10–45cm) ↔ 10in (25cm) **5** ↕4–18in (10–45cm) ↔ 10in (25cm) **6** ↕4–18in (10–45cm) ↔ 10in (25cm)

1 *Phlox drummondii* 'Beauty Mauve' **2** 'Beauty Pink' **3** 'Brilliancy Mixed'
4 'Brilliant' **5** 'Buttons Salmon with Eye' **6** 'Phlox of Sheep'

PHLOX 'KELLY'S EYE'

A vigorous, evergreen, mound-forming perennial producing a colorful display of long-throated, flat-faced, pale pink flowers with red-purple centers in late spring and early summer. The leaves are dark green and narrow. Suitable for a rock garden or wall crevices.

CULTIVATION *Grow in fertile soil that has good drainage, in full sun. In low-rainfall areas, site in partial shade.*

☼ ◊ Z4-8 H8-1   ↕↔8in (20cm)

PHLOX MACULATA 'ALPHA'

A cultivar of meadow phlox with tall, fat clusters of lilac-pink flowers that appear above the foliage in the first half of summer. It is an upright herbaceous perennial with wiry stems. Ideal in a moist border and a good source of fragrant cut flowers.

CULTIVATION *Grow in fertile, moist soil in full sun or partial shade. Remove spent flowers to prolong flowering, and cut back to the ground in autumn. May need staking.*

☼ ◊ Z5-8 H8-4   ↕to 36in (90cm)
                  ↔18in (45cm)

PHLOX PANICULATA CULTIVARS

Cultivars of the so-called garden phlox, *P. paniculata*, are herbaceous plants bearing dome-shaped or conical clusters of flowers above lance-shaped, toothed, mid-green leaves. Appearing throughout summer and into autumn, the flat-faced, long-throated, delicately fragranced flowers are white, pink, red, purple or blue, often with contrasting centers; they are long-lasting when cut. Larger flowers can be encouraged by removing the weakest shoots in spring when the plant is still quite young.

All types are well suited to a herbaceous border; most cultivars need staking, but others, such as 'Fujiyama', have particularly sturdy stems.

CULTIVATION *Grow in any reliably moist, fertile soil. Choose a position in full sun or partial shade. Feed with a balanced liquid fertilizer in spring and deadhead regularly to prolong flowering. After flowering, cut back all foliage to ground level.*

☼ ◑ ◊ Z4-8 H8-1

1 ‡4ft (1.2m) ↔ 24in (60cm) **2** ‡36in (90cm) ↔ 18in (45cm) **3** ‡4ft (1.2m) ↔ 24in (60cm)

4 ‡3½ft (1.1m) ↔ to 3ft (1m) **5** ‡3ft (1m) ↔ 18in (45cm) **6** ‡4ft (1.2m) ↔ 24–39in (60–100cm)

1 *Phlox paniculata* 'Brigadier' **2** 'Eventide' **3** 'Fujiyama'
4 'Le Mahdi' **5** 'Mother of Pearl' **6** 'Windsor'

PHORMIUM COOKIANUM SUBSP. *HOOKERI* 'CREAM DELIGHT'

This mountain flax forms a clump of broad, arching leaves, to 5ft (1.5m) long, each with broad vertical bands of creamy yellow. Tall, upright clusters of tubular, yellow-green flowers appear in summer. An unusual plant, often used as a focal point. Good in a large container, and tolerant of coastal exposure.

CULTIVATION *Grow in fertile, moist but well-drained soil in full sun. Where marginal, provide a deep, dry winter mulch. Divide crowded clumps in spring.*

☀ ◊◊ Z9-10 H10-3 ‡6ft (2m) ↔10ft (3m)

PHORMIUM COOKIANUM SUBSP. *HOOKERI* 'TRICOLOR'

This striking perennial, very useful as a focal point in a border, forms arching clumps of broad, light green leaves, to 5ft (1.5m) long; they are boldly margined with creamy yellow and red stripes. Tall spikes of tubular, yellow-green flowers are borne in summer. Where not hardy, grow in a container during the summer, and overwinter under glass.

CULTIVATION *Grow in moist but well-drained soil, in sun. Provide a deep, dry winter mulch where marginal.*

☀ ◊◊ Z9-10 H10-3 ‡2-6ft (0.6-2m) ↔1-10ft (0.3-3m)

PHORMIUM 'SUNDOWNER'

A clump-forming, evergreen
perennial valued for its form and
brilliant coloring. It has broad,
bronze-green leaves, to 5ft (1.5m)
long, with creamy rose-pink
margins. In summer, tall, upright
clusters of tubular, yellow-green
flowers are borne, followed by
decorative seedheads that persist
through winter. A good choice for
coastal gardens.

CULTIVATION

☼ ◊◊ Z9-10 H10-3   ‡↔to 6ft (2m)

PHORMIUM TENAX

The New Zealand flax is an
evergreen perennial that forms
clumps of very long, tough leaves,
to 10ft (3m) in length in ideal
conditions. They are dark green
above and blue-green beneath.
Dusky red flowers appear in
summer on very tall, thick, and
upright spikes. One of the largest
phormiums – a striking plant with
decorative seedheads in winter.

CULTIVATION *Best in deep, reliably
moist but well-drained soil in a warm,
sheltered site in full sun. Mulch deeply
for winter and divide overcrowded
clumps in spring.*

☼ ◊◊ Z9-10 H10-3   ‡12ft (4m) ↔6ft (2m)

PHORMIUM TENAX
PURPUREUM GROUP

An evergreen perennial that forms clumps of long, stiff, sword-shaped, deep copper to purple-red leaves. Large spikes of dark red, tubular flowers on blue-purple stems appear in summer. Ideal for coastal gardens. Can be container-grown, or choose the similar but much smaller 'Nanum Purpureum'.

CULTIVATION *Grow in deep, fertile, organic soil that is reliably moist. Position in full sun with shelter from cold winds. Where marginal, provide a deep, dry mulch in winter.*

☼ ◊ Z9-10 H10-3 ‡8ft (2.5m) ↔3ft (1m)

PHORMIUM
'YELLOW WAVE'

An evergreen perennial forming clumps of broad, arching, yellow-green leaves with mid-green vertical stripes; they take on chartreuse tones in autumn. Spikes of tubular red flowers emerge from the center of each leaf clump in summer. Especially good for seaside gardens, it will add a point of interest to any border, especially in winter when it remains bold and attractive.

CULTIVATION *Best in fertile, moist but well-drained soil in full sun. Provide a deep, dry mulch for winter where marginal. Divide clumps in spring.*

☼ ◊◊ Z9-10 H10-3 ‡10ft (3m) ↔6ft (2m)

PHOTINIA × FRASERI
'RED ROBIN'

An upright, compact, evergreen
shrub often grown as a formal or
semi-formal hedge for its bright red
young foliage, the effect of which is
prolonged by clipping. The mature
leaves are leathery, lance-shaped,
and dark green. Clusters of small
white flowers appear in mid-spring.
'Robusta' is another recommended
cultivar.

CULTIVATION *Grow in moist but well-
drained, fertile soil, in full sun or semi-
shade. Clip hedges 2 or 3 times a year
to perpetuate the colorful foliage.*

☼ ◑ ◊◊ Z8-9 H9-8   ↕↔ 15ft (5m)

PHOTINIA VILLOSA

A spreading, shrubby tree grown for
its foliage, flowers, and fruits. Flat
clusters of small white flowers
appear in late spring and develop
into attractive red fruits. The dark
green leaves are bronze when
young, turning orange and red in
autumn before they fall. Attractive
all year round, and tolerant of
permanently damp soil.

CULTIVATION *Grow in fertile, moist but
well-drained, neutral to acidic soil in
full sun or partial shade. Remove any
congested, damaged, or diseased
growth in late winter.*

☼ ◑ ◊◊ Z4-9 H9-1   ↕↔ 15ft (5m)

PHYGELIUS AEQUALIS
'YELLOW TRUMPET'

An upright, evergreen shrub forming loose spikes of hanging, tubular, pale cream-yellow flowers during summer. The leaves are oval and pale green. Good in a herbaceous or mixed border; where margnally hardy, provide protection against a warm, sunny wall.

CULTIVATION *Best in moist but well-drained soil, in sun. Provide shelter from wind and cut cold-damaged stems back to the base in spring. Deadhead to prolong flowering. Dig up unwanted shoots to contain spread.*

☼ ◊◊ Z7-9 H9-7   ↨↔ 3ft (1m)

PHYGELIUS CAPENSIS

The Cape figwort is an evergreen shrub valued for its summer display of upright spikes of orange flowers. The foliage is dark green, and the plant may be mistaken for a novel-colored fuchsia. Grow near the back of a herbaceous border, against a warm, sunny wall for protection. Hummingbirds are attracted to this.

CULTIVATION *Grow in fertile, moist but well-drained soil in full sun with shelter from cold, drying winds. Remove spent flower clusters to encourage more blooms, and provide a dry winter mulch where marginally hardy. Cut back to the ground in spring.*

☼ ◊◊ Z8-9 H9-8 ↕4ft (1.2m) ↔5ft (1.5m)

PHYGELIUS × *RECTUS*
'AFRICAN QUEEN'

An upright, evergreen border shrub
that bears long spikes of hanging,
tubular, pale red flowers with
orange to yellow mouths. These
appear in summer above the oval,
dark green leaves. Best against a
warm wall where marginally hardy.

CULTIVATION *Grow in moist but well-
drained, fertile soil, in sun with shelter
from cold, drying winds. Cut cold-
damaged stems back to the base in
spring. Deadhead to prolong flowering.*

☼ ◊◊ Z8-9 H9-8 ‡3ft (1m) ↔4ft (1.2m)

PHYGELIUS × *RECTUS*
'DEVIL'S TEARS'

An upright, evergreen shrub with
dark green foliage. In summer, it
carries spikes of hanging, red-pink
flowers with yellow throats. A
reasonably compact shrub with
abundant flowers, ideal for a
herbaceous or mixed border.

CULTIVATION *Best in moist but well
drained, reasonably fertile soil in full
sun. Remove spent flower clusters to
encourage further blooming, and cut
the plant back to ground level in spring,
if damaged over winter; otherwise, trim
to shape.*

☼ ◊◊ Z8-9 H9-8 ‡↔5ft (1.5m)

PHYGELIUS × RECTUS 'SALMON LEAP'

This upright shrub is very similar to 'Devil's Tears' (see previous page), but with orange flowers that turn slightly back toward the stems. They appear in large sprays above the dark green foliage. Good in a mixed or herbaceous border.

CULTIVATION *Grow in moist but well-drained, fertile soil in full sun. Remove spent flower clusters to encourage more blooms. Cut the plant back to ground level in spring if damaged by winter weather; otherwise, trim to shape.*

☼ ◐◊ Z8-9 H9-8
‡4ft (1.2m)
↔5ft (1.5m)

PHYLLOSTACHYS NIGRA

Black bamboo is an arching, clump-forming, evergreen shrub. The gentle, lance-shaped, dark green leaves are produced on slender green canes that turn black in their second or third year. Use as a screen or as a large feature plant.

CULTIVATION *Grow in moist but well-drained soil, in sun or partial shade with shelter from cold winds. Mulch over winter. Cut out damaged and overcrowded canes in spring or early summer. Confine spread by burying a barrier around the roots.*

☼◐ ◐◊ Z7-10 H12-7
‡10–15ft (3–5m)
↔6–10ft (2–3m)

PHYLLOSTACHYS NIGRA VAR. *HENONIS*

This clump-forming, evergreen bamboo is similar to the black bamboo in habit (see facing page, below), but it has bright green canes that mature to yellow-green in the second or third year. The lance-shaped, dark green leaves are downy and rough when young.

CULTIVATION *Grow in well-drained but moist soil, in sun or semi-shade. Shelter from cold winds and mulch over winter. Thin crowded clumps in late spring. Bury a barrier around the roots to confine spread.*

☀️◐ ◊◊ Z7-10 H12-7 ‡10–15ft (3–5m) ↔6–10ft (2–3m)

PHYSOCARPUS OPULIFOLIUS 'DART'S GOLD'

A rounded and thicket-forming, deciduous shrub valued for its three-lobed leaves, which are a spectacular golden yellow when young. Dense clusters of small, white or pale pink flowers appear in spring. Lightens up a shrub border.

CULTIVATION *Best in moist but well-drained, acidic soil, but tolerates most conditions except shallow, alkaline soil. Site in sun or partial shade. Cut old stems back to the base after flowering; dig out spreading shoots to confine spread.*

☀️◐ ◊◊ Z3-7 H7-1 ‡6ft (2m) ↔8ft (2.5m)

PHYSOSTEGIA VIRGINIANA 'VIVID'

An upright, densely clump-forming border perennial bearing spikes of bright purple-pink, hooded flowers from mid-summer to early autumn above the narrow, mid-green leaves. The flowers are good for cutting and will remain in a new position if they are moved on the stalks; because of this, it is known as the obedient plant. Looks good mixed with the white cultivar, 'Summer Snow'.

CULTIVATION *Grow in reliably moist, fertile organic soil. Position in full sun or partial shade.*

☼ ◐ ◊ Z4-8 H8-1 ‡12–24in (30–60cm)
↔12in (30cm)

PICEA GLAUCA VAR. *ALBERTIANA* 'CONICA'

A conical, slow-growing, evergreen conifer with dense, blue-green foliage. The short, slender needles are borne on buff-white to ash-gray stems. Oval cones appear during summer, green at first, then maturing to brown. Makes an excellent neat specimen tree for a small garden.

CULTIVATION *Grow in deep, moist but well-drained, preferably neutral to acidic soil, in full sun. Prune in winter if necessary, but keep to a minimum.*

☼ ◊◊ Z3-7 H6-1 ‡6–20ft (2–6m)
↔3–8ft (1–2.5m)

PICEA MARIANA 'NANA'

This dwarf, low-growing form of
black spruce is a mound-forming
conifer with scaly, gray-brown bark.
The evergreen, bluish gray needles
are short, soft, and slender. Useful in
a rock garden or conifer bed or as
an edging plant.

CULTIVATION *Best in deep, moist but
well-drained, fertile, organic soil, in
partial shade. Completely remove any
shoots that show vigorous upright
growth as soon as they are seen.*

☼ ◊ Z3-7 H6-1   ↕↔ 20in (50cm)

PICEA PUNGENS 'KOSTER'

This conical evergreen conifer,
with attractive horizontal branches,
becomes more columnar with age,
and the young growth is clothed in
silvery blue foliage. The long, sharp-
pointed needles turn greener as they
mature. Cylindrical green cones are
borne during the summer, aging to
pale brown. Good in large gardens
as a prominent specimen tree.
'Hoopsii' is very similar indeed,
with blue-white foliage.

CULTIVATION *Grow in well-drained,
fertile, neutral to acidic soil, in full sun.
Prune in late autumn or winter if
necessary, but keep to a minimum.*

☼ ◊ Z3-8 H8-1   ‡50ft (15m) ↔15ft (5m)

PIERIS 'FOREST FLAME'

An upright, evergreen shrub valued
for its slender, glossy, lance-shaped
leaves that are bright red when
young; they mature through pink
and creamy white to dark green.
Upright clusters of white flowers
enhance the effect in early to mid-
spring. Ideal for a shrub border or a
peaty, acidic soil; it will not thrive in
alkaline soil.

CULTIVATION *Grow in moist but well-
drained, fertile, organic, acidic soil, in
full sun or partial shade. Shelter from
cold, drying winds. It can be trimmed
lightly after flowering.*

☼ ◑ ◊◊ Z6-9 H9-6 ‡12ft (4m) ↔6ft (2m)

PIERIS FORMOSA VAR. *FORRESTII* 'WAKEHURST'

This upright, evergreen, acidic-soil-
loving shrub has brilliant red young
foliage that matures to dark green.
The large, slightly drooping clusters
of small, fragrant white flowers from
mid-spring are also attractive. Grow
in a woodland garden or shrub
border. 'Jermyns' is very similar, with
darker red young leaves.

CULTIVATION *Best in well-drained but
moist, fertile, organic, acidic soil. Site
in full sun or partial shade with shelter
from cold winds. It can be trimmed
lightly after flowering.*

☼ ◑ ◊◊ Z7-9 H9-7 ‡15ft (5m) ↔12ft (4m)

PIERIS JAPONICA 'BLUSH'

A rounded, evergreen shrub that bears small, pink-flushed white flowers in late winter and early spring. These are carried in long, drooping clusters amid the glossy dark green foliage. A good early-flowering border shrub.

CULTIVATION *Grow in well-drained but moist, fertile, organic, acidic soil. Site in full sun or partial shade. Trim lightly after flowering, removing any dead, damaged or diseased shoots.*

☼ ◐ ◊◊ Z6-8 H8-6 ‡12ft (4m) ↔10ft (3m)

PILEOSTEGIA VIBURNOIDES

A slow-growing, woody, evergreen climber that is dusted with feathery clusters of tiny, creamy white flowers in late summer and autumn. The glossy dark green, leathery leaves look very attractive against a large tree trunk or shady wall.

CULTIVATION *Grow in well-drained, fertile soil, in full sun or shade. Shorten stems after flowering as the plant begins to outgrow the allotted space.*

☼ ◐ ◊ Z7-10 H12-7 ‡20ft (6m)

PINUS MUGO 'MOPS'

This dwarf pine is an almost spherical conifer with scaly, gray bark and thick, upright branches. The shoots are covered with long, well-spaced, dark to bright green needles. The dark brown, oval cones take a few years to ripen. Effective in a large rock garden or, where space allows, planted in groups.

CULTIVATION *Grow in any well-drained soil, in full sun. Very little pruning is required since growth is slow.*

☼ ◊ Z3-7 H7-1 ‡to 3ft (1m) ↔to 6ft (2m)

PITTOSPORUM TENUIFOLIUM

A columnar, evergreen shrub, much valued for its glossy green leaves with wavy edges. Fast growing at first, it then broadens out into a tree. Tiny, honey-scented, purple-black, bell-shaped flowers open from late spring. Makes a good hedge. There is a gold-leaved version, 'Warnham Gold'.

CULTIVATION *Grow in well-drained but moist, fertile soil, in full sun or partial shade. Provide shelter from cold winds. Trim to shape in spring; avoid pruning after mid-summer.*

☼☀ ◊◊ Z9-10 H12-9 ‡12–30ft (4–10m) ↔6–15ft (2–5m)

PITTOSPORUM TENUIFOLIUM 'TOM THUMB'

A compact, rounded, evergreen foliage shrub that would suit a mixed border designed for year-round interest. The glossy bronze-purple leaves are elliptic and wavy-edged. Tiny, honey-scented, purple flowers are borne in late spring and early summer. Shelter against a warm wall where marginally hardy.

CULTIVATION *Grow in well-drained but moist, fertile soil, in full sun for best color. Provide shelter from cold winds. Trim to shape in spring; established plants need little pruning.*

☼ ◑ ◊◊ Z9-10 H12-9 ‡3ft (1m) ↔24in (60cm)

PITTOSPORUM TOBIRA

Japanese mock orange is a rounded, evergreen shrub or small tree with leathery, dark green, oval leaves. Clusters of sweet-scented, creamy white flowers are borne in late spring and early summer, followed by yellow-brown seed capsules. A fine specimen plant that can be pot-grown and overwintered under glass. 'Variegatum' has smaller leaves edged in white.

CULTIVATION *Best in moist but well-drained, fertile soil or soil mix, in full sun or partial shade. Prune back to restrict growth in winter or early spring.*

☼ ◑ ◊◊ Z9-10 H12-9 ‡6-30ft (2-10m) ↔5-10ft (1.5-3m)

PLATYCODON GRANDIFLORUS

The balloon flower is a clump-forming perennial producing clusters of large purple to violet-blue flowers that open from balloon-shaped buds in late summer, above bluish green, oval leaves. For a rock garden or herbaceous border. 'Apoyama', with deep-colored flowers, and 'Mariesii' are recommended cultivars.

CULTIVATION *Best in deep, well-drained, fertile soil that does not dry out, in full sun or partial shade. Flower stems may need staking. Established plants dislike root disturbance.*

☼ ◑ ◊ Z4-9 H9-1   ↕to 24in (60cm)
↔12in (30cm)

PLEIOBLASTUS AURICOMUS

This upright bamboo is an evergreen shrub grown for its brilliant green, yellow-striped foliage. The bristly-edged, lance-shaped leaves are carried on purple-green canes. Effective in an open glade in a woodland garden. Good in sun, backed by trees or tall shrubs.

CULTIVATION *Grow in moist but well-drained, fertile, organic soil, in full sun for best leaf color. Provide shelter from cold, drying winds. Thin over-crowded clumps in late spring or early summer. Confine spread by burying a barrier around the roots.*

☼ ◊◑ Z7-11 H12-7   ↕↔ to 5ft (1.5m)

PLEIOBLASTUS VARIEGATUS

This upright, evergreen bamboo is much shorter than *P. auricomis* (see facing page, below), with cream- and green-striped foliage. The lance-shaped leaves, borne on hollow, pale green canes, are covered in fine white hairs. Suits a sunny border backed by shrubs, and where it has space to spread; it will swamp less vigorous neighbors unless confined.

CULTIVATION *Grow in moist but well-drained, fertile, organic soil, in sun with shelter from cold winds. Thin out clumps in late spring. Bury a barrier around the roots to confine spread.*

☼ ◊◊ Z7-11 H12-7 ‡30in (75cm) ↔4ft (1.2m)

PLUMBAGO AURICULATA

Cape leadwort is a scrambling, semi-evergreen, frost-tender shrub often trained as a climber. It bears dense trusses of long-throated, sky blue flowers from summer to late autumn, amid the oval leaves. In colder climates, plants overwintered under glass can be moved outside in summer. Often sold as *P. capensis*.

CULTIVATION *Grow in well-drained, fertile soil or soil mix, in full sun or light shade. Pinch out the tips of young plants to promote bushiness, and tie climbing stems to a support. Cut back to a permanent framework in early spring.*

☼☀ ◊ Z9-10 H12-1 ‡10-20ft (3-6m) ↔3-10ft (1-3m)

POLEMONIUM 'LAMBROOK MAUVE'

This clump-forming perennial, a garden variety of Jacob's ladder, forms rounded mounds of neat, divided, mid-green leaves. An abundance of funnel-shaped, sky blue flowers cover the foliage from late spring to early summer. Good in any border or in a wild garden.

CULTIVATION *Grow in well-drained but moist, moderately fertile soil, in full sun or partial shade. Deadhead regularly.*

☼☀ ◊◊ Z4-8 H8-1 ↕↔ 18in (45cm)

POLYGONATUM x *HYBRIDUM*

Solomon's seal is a perennial for a shady border, bearing hanging clusters of tubular, small white flowers with green mouths, along slightly arching stems. These appear in late spring among elliptic, bright green leaves. Round blue-black fruits develop after the flowers. For a woodland garden. *P.* x *odoratum* 'Flore Pleno' is a very similar but smaller plant.

CULTIVATION *Grow in moist but well-drained, fertile organic soil. Position in partial or full shade.*

☼☀ ◊◊ Z6-9 H9-6 ↕to 5ft (1.5m) ↔12in (30cm)

POLYSTICHUM ACULEATUM

The prickly shield fern is an elegant, evergreen perennial producing a shuttlecock of finely divided, dark green fronds. An excellent foliage plant for shady areas in a rock garden or well-drained border.

CULTIVATION *Grow in fertile soil that has good drainage, in partial or deep shade. Choose a site sheltered from excessive winter moisture. Remove the previous year's dead fronds before the new growth unfurls in spring.*

 ☼ ◐ ● ◊ Z3-6 H6-1 ↕24in (60cm) ↔3ft (1m)

POLYSTICHUM SETIFERUM

The soft shield fern is a tall, evergreen perennial, with finely divided, dark green fronds that are soft to the touch. The foliage forms splayed, shuttlecock like clumps. Suits a shady border or rock garden. 'Divisilobum Densum' is a handsome cultivar with densely feathery fronds; 'Pulcherrimum Bevis' has tall, sweeping fronds.

CULTIVATION *Grow in well-drained, fertile soil, in partial or deep shade. Choose a site that is protected from excessive winter moisture. Remove any dead or damaged fronds in spring.*

☼ ◐ ● ◊ Z6-9 H9-6 ↕4ft (1.2m) ↔3ft (1m)

POTENTILLA FRUTICOSA

Cultivars of *P. fruticosa* are compact and rounded, deciduous shrubs that produce an abundance of flowers over a long period from late spring to mid-autumn. The leaves are dark green and composed of several oblong leaflets. Flowers are saucer-shaped and wild-roselike, sometimes borne singly, but often in clusters of three. Most cultivars are yellow-flowered, but blooms may also be white, as with 'Abbotswood', or flushed with pink, as in 'Daydawn'. These are undemanding shrubs that make invaluable additions to mixed or shrub borders; they can also be grown as attractive low hedges.

CULTIVATION *Grow in well-drained, poor to moderately fertile soil. Best in full sun, but many tolerate partial shade. Trim lightly after flowering, cutting older wood to the base and removing weak, twiggy growth. Old shrubs sometimes respond well to renovation, but may be better replaced.*

☼ ◊ Z3-7 H7-1

1 ‡30in (75cm) ↔ 4ft (1.2m)

2 ‡3ft (1m) ↔ 5ft (1.5m)

3 ‡3ft (1m) ↔ 4ft (1.2m)

4 ‡3ft (1m) ↔ 5ft (1.5m)

1 *P. fruticosa* 'Abbotswood' **2** *P. fruticosa* 'Elizabeth'
3 *P. fruticosa* 'Daydawn' **4** *P. fruticosa* 'Primrose Beauty'

POTENTILLA
'GIBSON'S SCARLET'

A dense, clump-forming herbaceous
perennial grown for its very bright
scarlet flowers, borne in succession
throughout summer. The soft green
leaves are divided into five leaflets.
Good for a rock garden or for a
bold summer color in a mixed or
herbaceous border. 'William
Rollisson' is a similar plant, with
more orange-red, semidouble
flowers.

CULTIVATION *Grow in well-drained,
poor to moderately fertile soil. Choose
a position in full sun.*

☼ ◊ Z5-8 H8-5 ‡18in (45cm) ↔24in (60cm)

POTENTILLA
MEGALANTHA

A compact, clump-forming perennial
bearing a profusion of upright, cup-
shaped, rich yellow flowers during
mid- to late summer. The slightly
hairy, mid-green leaves are divided
into three coarsely scalloped leaflets.
Good for the front of a border.

CULTIVATION *Grow in poor to fairly
fertile soil that has good drainage.
Choose a position in full sun.*

☼ ◊ Z5-8 H8-5 ‡6–12in (15–30cm)
↔6in (15cm)

POTENTILLA NEPALENSIS 'MISS WILMOTT'

A summer-flowering perennial that forms clumps of mid-green, divided leaves on wiry, red-tinged stems. The small pink flowers, with cherry red centers, are borne in loose clusters. Good for the front of a border or in cottage-style plantings.

CULTIVATION *Grow in any well-drained, poor to moderately fertile soil. Position in full sun or light dappled shade.*

☼ ◐ ◊ Z5-8 H8-5 ‡12–18in (30–45cm)
↔24in (60cm)

PRIMULA DENTICULATA

The drumstick primrose is a robust, clump-forming perennial bearing spherical clusters of small purple flowers with yellow centers. They are carried on thick, upright stalks from spring to summer, above the basal rosettes of oblong to spoon-shaped, mid-green leaves. Thrives in damp, but not waterlogged, soil; ideal for a waterside planting.

CULTIVATION *Best in moist, organic, neutral to acidic or peaty soil. Choose a site in partial shade, but tolerates full sun where soil is reliably damp.*

☼ ◐ ◖ Z2-8 H8-1 ‡↔18in (45cm)

PRIMULA ELATIOR

The oxlip is a semi-evergreen perennial wildflower that can vary in appearance. Clusters of tubular yellow flowers emerge from the basal rosettes of scalloped, mid-green leaves on stiff, upright stems in spring and summer. Plant in groups to naturalize in a moist meadow.

CULTIVATION *Grow in moderately fertile, deep, moist but well-drained soil. Site in partial shade, but full sun is tolerated as long as the soil remains moist at all times.*

☼ ☀ ◊◊ Z4-8 H8-1 ‡↔12in (30cm)

PRIMULA FLACCIDA

A rosette-forming, deciduous perennial for an open woodland garden or alpine house. In summer, tall flowering stems bear conical clusters of funnel-shaped and downward-pointing, floury, lavender-blue flowers, carried above the pale to mid-green leaves.

CULTIVATION *Grow in deep or partial shade in peaty, gritty, moist but sharply drained, acidic soil. Protect from excessive winter moisture.*

☼ ☀ ◊◊ Z4-8 H8-1 ‡20in (50cm)
↔12in (30cm)

PRIMULA FLORINDAE

The giant cowslip is a deciduous, summer-flowering perennial that grows naturally by pools and streams. It forms clumps of oval, toothed, mid-green leaves that are arranged in rosettes at the base of the plant. Drooping clusters of up to 40 funnel-shaped, sweetly scented yellow flowers are borne well above the foliage on upright stems. Good in a bog garden or waterside setting.

CULTIVATION *Grow in deep, reliably moist, organic soil, in partial shade. Tolerates full sun if soil remains moist.*

☼☀ ◊ Z3-8 H8-1 ‡4ft (1.2m) ↔ 3ft (1m)

PRIMULA FRONDOSA

This deciduous border perennial, with its rosettes of spoon-shaped, mid-green leaves, carries yellow-eyed, pink to purple flowers in late spring or early summer. They are carried in loose clusters of up to 30 at the top of upright stems, and each has a pale yellow eye at its center.

CULTIVATION *Best in deep, moist, neutral to acidic loam or peaty soil enriched with organic matter. Site ideally in partial shade, but it tolerates full sun if the soil is reliably moist.*

☼☀ ◊ Z4-8 H8-1 ‡6in (15cm) ↔ 10in (25cm)

PRIMULA
GOLD-LACED GROUP

A group of semi-evergreen primroses grown for their showy spring flowers in the border or in containers. Clusters of golden-eyed, very dark mahogany-red or black flowers, with a thin gold margin around each petal, are carried atop upright flowering stems above the sometimes reddish foliage.

CULTIVATION *Grow in moist, deep, neutral to acidic loam or peaty soil that is rich in organic matter. Choose a site in partial shade, or in full sun if the soil is reliably moist.*

☼☀ ◐ Z5-8 H8-4 ↕↔12in (30cm)

PRIMULA 'GUINEVERE'

A fast-growing, evergreen, clump-forming perennial, sometimes called 'Garryarde Guinevere', that bears clusters of pale purplish pink flowers. They have yellow centers, flat faces, and long throats and are carried above the deep bronze, oval leaves in spring. Suits damp, shady places.

CULTIVATION *Grow in moist, neutral to acidic soil that is well-drained, in partial shade. Tolerates full sun, but only if the soil remains always damp.*

☼☀ ◐ Z4-8 H8-1 ↕5in (12cm) ↔10in (25cm)

POLYANTHUS PRIMROSES (*PRIMULA*)

Garden polyanthus are rosette-forming, evergreen perennials with a complex parentage, which probably includes *P. veris* (see p.419) and *P. elatior* (see p.413). The plants form sturdy, basal rosettes of oval, heavily veined leaves, overshadowed by the colorful clusters of flat-faced flowers from late winter to early spring. A splendid array of primary and pastel colors is available, mostly red, blue-violet, orange, yellow, white, or pink, with yellow centers. Groups such the Crescendo and

Rainbow series are among the most easily grown bedding and container plants, brightening up gardens, patios, and windowsills in winter.

CULTIVATION *Grow in moderately fertile, moist but well-drained, organic soil or soil-based mix in a cool site in full sun or partial shade. Sow seed in summer, and plant out in autumn in well-prepared soil. Divide large clumps in autumn.*

☀ ☼ ◊◊ Z4-8 H8-1

2 ‡6in (15cm) ↔ 12in (30cm)

1 ‡6in (15cm) ↔ 12in (30cm)

3 ‡6in (15cm) ↔ 12in (30cm)

4 ‡6in (15cm) ↔ 12in (30cm)

1 *Primula* 'Crescendo Bright Red' **2** *P.* 'Crescendo Pink and Rose Shades'
3 *P.* 'Rainbow Blue Shades' **4** *P.* 'Rainbow Cream Shades'

PRIMULA KEWENSIS

A primrose for a windowsill, greenhouse, or conservatory, this is an evergreen perennial that forms rosettes of noticeably toothed, slightly floury, mid-green leaves. It gives an early spring display of fragrant yellow flowers in whorls along upright flowering stems.

CULTIVATION *In a container, grow in soil-based potting mix with added grit or peat. As a houseplant, choose a site with bright filtered light.*

☼◑ ◊◊ Z9-10 H10-9 ‡to 18in (45cm)
↔8in (20cm)

PRIMULA OBCONICA
'LIBRE MAGENTA'

In cold climates, the many obconicas make colorful display plants for a cool greenhouse. This one has branched heads of magenta flowers that darken with age, on dark, hairy stems emerging from among coarse, mid-green leaves. Also makes a good house- or cool conservatory plant; min. temp. 36°F (2°C).

CULTIVATION *In a container, grow in soil-based potting mix with added grit or peat. Choose a spot with bright filtered light. Water freely when in growth and feed weekly with a half-strength liquid fertilizer.*

☼◑ ◊ Z10 H6-1 ‡↔ 12in (30cm)

CANDELABRA PRIMROSES (*PRIMULA*)

Candelabra primroses are robust, herbaceous perennials, so called because their flowers are borne in tiered clusters that rise above the basal rosettes of broadly oval leaves in late spring or summer. Depending on the species, the foliage may be semi-evergreen, evergreen, or deciduous. The flowers have flat faces and long throats; as with most cultivated primroses, there is a wide choice of colors, from the brilliant red 'Inverewe' to the golden yellow *P. prolifera*.

Some flowers change color as they mature; those of *P. bulleyana* fade from crimson to orange. All look most effective when grouped together in a bog garden or waterside setting.

CULTIVATION *Grow in deep, moist, neutral to acidic, organic soil. Site in partial shade, although full sun is tolerated if the soil remains moist at all times. Divide and replant clumps in early spring.*

☀ ◑ ◊ Z5-8 H8-1

1 ‡↔ 24in (60cm)

2 ‡↔ 24in (60cm)

3 ‡30in (75cm) ↔ 24in (60cm)

4 ‡ to 3ft (1m) ↔ 24in (60cm)

5 ‡ to 3ft (1m) ↔ 24in (60cm)

1 *P. bulleyana* **2** *P. prolifera* (syn. *P. belodoxa*) **3** *P.* 'Inverewe'
4 *P. pulverulenta* **5** *P. pulverulenta* Bartley Hybrids

PRIMULA ROSEA

A deciduous perennial that bears rounded clusters of glowing pink, long-throated flowers on upright stalks in spring. Clumps of oval, toothed, mid-green leaves emerge after the flowers; these are tinted red-bronze when young. Good for a bog garden or waterside planting.

CULTIVATION *Grow in deep, reliably moist, neutral to acidic, organic soil. Prefers partial shade, but tolerates full sun if the soil is moist at all times.*

☼ ◑ Z3-8 H8-1   ↕↔ 8in (20cm)

PRIMULA VERIS

The cowslip is a semi-evergreen, spring-flowering perennial with a variable appearance. Thick flower stems carry dense clusters of small, funnel-shaped, sweetly scented, nodding yellow flowers above the clumps of lance-shaped, crinkled leaves. Lovely naturalized in damp grassy areas

CULTIVATION *Best in deep, moist but well-drained, fertile, organic soil in semi-shade or full sun, if soil remains reliably damp.*

☼☼ ◑ Z3-8 H8-1   ↕↔ 10in (25cm)

PRIMULA 'WANDA'

A very vigorous, semi-evergreen perennial that bears clusters of flat-faced, claret red flowers with yellow centers over a long period in spring. The oval, toothed, purplish green leaves are arranged in clumps at the base of the plant. Good in a waterside setting.

CULTIVATION *Best in deep, moist but well-drained, fertile, organic soil. Prefers partial shade but tolerates full sun if soil remains damp.*

☼ ◑ ◊◊ Z3-8 H8-1 ‡4–6in (10–15cm)
↔12–16in (30–40cm)

PRUNELLA GRANDIFLORA 'LOVELINESS'

This vigorous, spreading perennial bears dense, upright spikes of light purple, tubular flowers in summer. The lance-shaped, deep-green leaves are arranged in clumps at ground level. Versatile groundcover when planted in groups; the flowers are attractive to beneficial insects.

CULTIVATION *Grow in any soil, in sun or partial shade. May swamp smaller plants, so allow room to expand. Divide clumps in spring or autumn to maintain vigour. Deadhead to prevent self-seeding.*

☼ ◑ ◊◊ Z5-8 H8-5 ‡6in (15cm)
↔to 3ft (1m) or more

PRUNUS × *CISTENA*

An upright, slow-growing, deciduous
shrub valued in particular for its
foliage, which is red when young,
maturing to red-purple. Bowl-
shaped, pinkish white flowers open
from mid- to late spring, sometimes
followed by small, cherrylike,
purple-black fruits. Good as a
windbreak hedge.

CULTIVATION *Grow in any but water-
logged soil, in full sun. Prune back
overcrowded shoots after flowering.
To grow as a hedge, prune the shoot
tips of young plants then trim in mid-
summer to encourage branching.*

☼ ◊◊ Z4-8 H8-1   ‡↔ 5ft (1.5()

PRUNUS GLANDULOSA
'ALBA PLENA'

This small cherry is a neat, rounded,
deciduous shrub producing dense
clusters of pure white, bowl-shaped,
double flowers during late spring.
The narrowly oval leaves are pale to
mid-green. Brings beautiful spring
blossoms to a mixed or shrub
border. The cultivar 'Sinensis' Z5-8
H8-4) has double pink flowers.

CULTIVATION *Grow in any moist but
well-drained, moderately fertile soil, in
sun. Can be pruned to a low framework
each year after flowering to enhance
the flowering performance.*

☼ ◊◊ Z5-8 H8-3   ‡↔ 5ft (1.5m)

PRUNUS 'KIKU-SHIDARE-ZAKURA'

Also known as 'Cheal's Weeping', this small deciduous cherry tree is grown for its weeping branches and clear pink blossoms. Dense clusters of large, double flowers are borne in mid- to late spring, with or before the lance-shaped, mid-green leaves, which are flushed bronze when young. Excellent in a small garden.

CULTIVATION *Best in any moist but well-drained, moderately fertile soil, in full sun. Tolerates alkalinity. After flowering, prune out only dead, diseased or damaged wood; remove any shoots growing from the trunk as they appear.*

☼ ◊◊ Z6-8 H8-6   ‡↔ 10ft (3m)

PRUNUS LAUROCERASUS 'OTTO LUYKEN'

This compact cherry laurel is an evergreen shrub with dense, glossy, dark green foliage. Abundant spikes of white flowers are borne in mid- to late spring and often again in autumn, followed by conical red fruits that ripen to black. Plant in groups as a low hedge or to cover bare ground.

CULTIVATION *Grow in any moist but well-drained, moderately fertile soil, in full sun. Prune in late spring or early summer to restrict size.*

☼ ◊◊ Z6-9 H9-6   ‡3ft (1m) ↔5ft (1.5m)

PRUNUS LUSITANICA
SUBSP. *AZORICA*

This Portugal laurel is a slow-growing, evergreen shrub bearing slender spikes of small, fragrant white flowers in early summer. The oval, glossy, dark green leaves have red stalks. Purple berries appear later in the season. Attractive year-round as a dense screen or hedge.

CULTIVATION *Grow in any moist but well-drained, fairly fertile soil, in sun with shelter from cold, drying winds. In late spring, prune to restrict size, or to remove old or overcrowded shoots.*

☼ ◊◊ Z7-9 H9-7   ↔ to 70ft (20m)

PRUNUS SERRULA

A rounded, deciduous tree that is valued for its striking, glossy, copper-brown to mahogany-red bark that peels with age. Small, bowl-shaped white flowers in spring are followed by cherrylike fruits in autumn. The leaves are lance-shaped and dark green, turning yellow in autumn. Best used as a specimen tree.

CULTIVATION *Best in moist but well-drained, moderately fertile soil, in full sun. Remove dead or damaged wood after flowering, and remove any shoots growing from the trunk as they appear.*

☼ ◊◊ Z6-8 H8-6   ↔ 30ft (10m)

FLOWERING CHERRIES (*PRUNUS*)

Ornamental cherries are cultivated primarily for their white, pink, or red flowers that create a mass of bloom, usually on bare branches, from late winter to late spring; cultivars of *P. x subhirtella* flower from late autumn. Most popular cultivars not only bear dense clusters of showy, double flowers but have other ornamental characteristics to extend their interest beyond the flowering season: *P. sargentii*, for example, has brilliant autumn foliage color, some have shiny, colored bark.

All of these features make flowering cherries superb specimen trees for small as well as large gardens.

CULTIVATION *Grow in any moist but well-drained, fairly fertile soil, in sun. Keep all pruning to an absolute minimum; restrict formative pruning to shape to young plants only. Remove any damaged or diseased growth in mid-summer, and keep trunks clear of sprouting shoots.*

☼ ◑◗ Zones vary H8-4

1 ↕70ft (20m) ↔ 30ft (10m) **2** ↕↔40ft (12m) **3** ↕30ft (10m) ↔ 25ft (8m)

4 ↕30ft (10m) ↔ 25ft (8m) **5** ↕50ft (15m) ↔ 30ft (10m) **6** ↕30ft (10m) ↔ 25ft (8m)

1 *P. avium* (Z4-8) **2** *P. avium* 'Plena' (Z4-8) **3** *P.* 'Kanzan' (Z6-8)
4 *P.* 'Okame' (Z5-8) **5** *P. padus* 'Colorata' (Z4-8) **6** *P.* 'Pandora' (Z6-8)

8 ‡↔ 25ft (8m)

9 ‡ to 70ft (20m) ↔ 50ft (15m)

7 ‡ 50ft (15m) ↔ 30ft (10m)

10 ‡ 25ft (8m) ↔ 30ft (10m)

11 ‡ 15ft (5m) ↔ 25ft (8m)

13 ‡ 30ft (10m) ↔ 20ft (6m)

14 ‡ 25ft (8m) ↔ 30ft (10m)

12 ‡↔ 25ft (8m)

15 ‡ 25ft (8m) ↔ 30ft (10m)

16 ‡ to 50ft (15m) ↔ 30ft (10m)

7 *P. padus* 'Watereri' (Z4-8) **8** *P.* 'Pink Perfection' (Z5-8) **9** *P. sargentii* (Z5-9)
10 *P.* 'Shirofugen' (Z6-8) **11** *P.* 'Shôgetsu' (Z6-8) **12** *P.* x *subhirtella* 'Autumnalis Rosea' (Z6-8)
13 *P.* 'Spire' (Z6-8) **14** *P.* 'Taihaku' (Z6-8) **15** *P.* 'Ukon' (Z6-8) **16** *P.* x *yedoensis* (Z6-8)

PSEUDOPANAX LESSONII 'GOLD SPLASH'

This evergreen, upright to spreading shrub or tree bears yellow-splashed, deep green foliage. In summer, less conspicuous clusters of yellow-green flowers are carried amid toothed leaves that are divided into teardrop-shaped leaflets. Purple-black fruits appear later in the season. Where not hardy, grow in a container as a foliage plant for a conservatory.

CULTIVATION *Best in well-drained, fertile soil or soil mix, in sun or partial shade. Prune to restrict spread in early spring. Minimum temperature 35°F (2°C).*

☼ ◐ ◊ H12-7   ‡10–20ft (3–6m)
↔6–12ft (2–4m)

PULMONARIA 'LEWIS PALMER'

This lungwort, sometimes called *P.* 'Highdown', is a deciduous perennial that forms clumps of upright, flowering stems. These are topped by open clusters of pink then blue, funnel-shaped flowers in early spring. The coarse, softly hairy leaves, dark green with white spots, are arranged along the stems. Grow in a wild or woodland garden.

CULTIVATION *Best in moist but not waterlogged, fertile, organic soil, in deep or light shade. Divide and replant clumps after flowering every few years.*

☼ ● ◊ Z5-8 H8-5   ‡↔18in (45cm)

PULMONARIA
'MARGERY FISH'

This lungwort is a clump-forming, deciduous perennial with attractive foliage and spring flowers. The leaves, silvered above with spotted edges and midribs, are often at their best in summer, after the coral to red-violet flowers have died away. For woodland, among shrubs, in a wild garden, or at the front of a border.

CULTIVATION *Grow in organic, fertile, moist but not wet soil, in full or partial shade. Remove old leaves after flowering and divide large clumps at the same time, or in autumn.*

☼☀ ◐ Z6-8 H8-4   ↕7–11in (18–28cm)
↔24in (60cm)

PULMONARIA OFFICINALIS
'SISSINGHURST WHITE'

A neat, clump-forming, evergreen perennial valued for its pure white spring flowers and white spotted foliage. The elliptic, hairy, mid- to dark green leaves are carried on upright stems below funnel-shaped flowers that open from pale pink buds in early spring. Plant in groups as a groundcover in a shady position.

CULTIVATION *Grow in moist but not waterlogged, organic soil. Best in deep or light shade, but tolerates full sun. Divide and replant clumps every 2 or 3 years, after flowering.*

☼☀ ◐ Z6-8 H8-6   ↕to 12in (30cm)
↔18in (45cm)

PULMONARIA RUBRA

This lovely clump-forming, evergreen perennial is a good groundcover plant for a shady position. It has attractive, bright green foliage and brings early color with its funnel-shaped, bright brick- to salmon-colored flowers from late winter to mid-spring. They are attractive to bees and other beneficial insects.

CULTIVATION *Grow in organic, fertile, moist but not waterlogged soil, in full or partial shade. Remove old leaves after flowering. Divide large or crowded clumps after flowering or in autumn.*

☼☀ ◐ Z5-8 H8-4   ‡to 16in (40c)
   ↔36in (90cm)

PULMONARIA SACCHARATA ARGENTEA GROUP

This group of evergreen perennials has almost completely silver leaves. A striking color contrast occurs from late winter to early spring, when funnel-shaped red flowers appear; these age to a dark violet. They make good clumps at the front of a shady mixed border.

CULTIVATION *Best in fertile, moist but not waterlogged, organic soil sited in full or partial shade. After flowering, remove old leaves and divide congested clumps.*

☼☀ ◐ Z4-8 H8-1 ‡12in (30cm) ↔24in (60cm)

PULSATILLA HALLERI

This silky-textured herbaceous perennial, ideal for a rock garden, is densely covered in long, silver hairs. It bears upright, bell-shaped, pale violet-purple flowers in late spring above finely divided, light green leaves. The first flowers often open before the new spring leaves have fully unfurled.

CULTIVATION *Grow in fertile, very well-drained gritty soil in full sun. May resent disturbance, so leave established plants undisturbed.*

☼ ◊ Z5-7 H7-5 ↕8in (20cm) ↔6in (15cm)

PULSATILLA VULGARIS

The pasque flower is a compact perennial forming tufts of finely divided, light green foliage. Its bell-shaped, nodding, silky-hairy flowers are carried above the leaves in spring, they are deep to pale purple or occasionally white, with golden centers. Good in a rock garden, scree bed, or trough, or between paving.

CULTIVATION *Best in fertile soil with very good drainage. Site in full sun and away from excessive winter moisture. Do not disturb once planted.*

☼ ◊ Z5-7 H7-5 ↕4–8in (10–20cm) ↔8in (20cm)

PULSATILLA VULGARIS 'ALBA'

This clump-forming perennial, a white form of the pasque flower, bears nodding, bell-shaped, silky-hairy white flowers with bold yellow centers in spring. These are carried above the finely divided, light green foliage, which is hairy when young. Very pretty in a rock garden or scree bed.

CULTIVATION *Best in fertile soil with very good drainage. Position in full sun with protection from excessive winter moisture. Resents disturbance.*

☼ ◊ Z5-7 H7-5   ↕↔8in (20cm)

PYRACANTHA 'ORANGE GLOW'

An upright to spreading, spiny, evergreen shrub bearing profuse clusters of tiny white flowers in late spring. Orange-red to dark orange berries follow in autumn and persist well into winter. The leaves are oval and glossy, dark green. Excellent as a vandal-resistant barrier hedge, which may also attract nesting birds.

CULTIVATION *Grow in well-drained, fertile soil, in full sun to deep shade. Shelter from cold, drying winds. Prune in mid-spring, and trim new leafy growth again in summer to expose the berries.*

☼ ◊ Z7-9 H9-7   ↕↔ 10ft (3m)

PYRACANTHA 'WATERERI'

A vigorous, upright, spiny shrub that forms a dense screen of evergreen foliage, ornamented by its abundance of white spring flowers and bright red berries in autumn. The leaves are elliptic and dark green. Good as a barrier hedge or in a shrub border; can also be trained against a shady wall. Attractive to birds. For yellow berries, look for 'Soleil d'Or' or *P. rogersiana* 'Flava' both Z7-9 H9-7.

CULTIVATION *Grow in well-drained, fertile soil, in sun or shade with shelter from cold winds. Cut back unwanted growth in mid-spring, and trim leafy growth in summer to expose the berries.*

☼ ◐ ◊ Z7-9 H9 7   ↔ 8ft (2.5m)

PYRUS CALLERYANA 'CHANTICLEER'

This very thorny ornamental pear has a narrowly conical shape and makes a good specimen tree for a small garden. Attractive sprays of small white flowers in mid-spring are followed by spherical brown fruits in autumn. The oval, finely scalloped leaves are glossy, dark green and deciduous; they turn red before they fall. Tolerates urban pollution.

CULTIVATION *Grow in any well-drained, fertile soil, in full sun. Prune in winter to maintain a well-spaced crown.*

☼ ◊ Z5-8 H8-5   ↕ 50ft (15m) ↔ 20ft (6m)

PYRUS SALICIFOLIA 'PENDULA'

This weeping pear is a deciduous tree with silvery gray, willowlike leaves that are downy when young. Dense clusters of small, creamy white flowers appear during spring, followed by pear-shaped green fruits in autumn. A fine, pollution-tolerant tree for an urban garden.

CULTIVATION *Grow in fertile soil with good drainage, in sun. Prune young trees in winter to create a well-spaced, balanced framework of branches.*

☼ ◊ Z5-9 H9-5 ↕25ft (8m) ↔20ft (6m)

RAMONDA MYCONI

A tiny, neat, evergreen perennial with basal rosettes of dark green, slightly crinkled, broadly oval leaves. In late spring and early summer,, deep violet-blue flowers are borne above the foliage on short stems. Pink-and white-flowered variants also occur. Grow in a rock garden or on a dry wall. *R. nathaliae* (7.6-7 H7-6) is similar, with paler leaves.

CULTIVATION *Plant in moist but well-drained, moderately fertile, organic soil, in partial shade. Set plants at an angle to avoid water pooling in the rosettes and causing rot. Leaves wither if too dry, but recover with watering.*

☼ ◊◊ Z5-7 H7-5 ↕4in (10cm) ↔8in (20cm)

RANUNCULUS ACONITIFOLIUS 'FLORE PLENO'

White bachelor's buttons is a clump-forming, herbaceous perennial bearing small, almost spherical, fully double white flowers that last for a long time during late spring and early summer. The toothed leaves are deeply lobed and glossy dark green. Good for a woodland garden.

CULTIVATION *Grow in moist but well-drained, organic soil. Site in deep or partial shade.*

☀️◐ ◊◊ Z5-9 H9-5   ‡24in (60cm)
↔18in (45cm)

RANUNCULUS CALANDRINIOIDES

This clump-forming perennial produces clusters of up to three cup-shaped, white or pink-flushed flowers from late winter to early spring. The lance-shaped, blue-green leaves emerge from the base in spring and die down in summer. Grow in a rock garden, scree bed, or alpine house.

CULTIVATION *Best in gritty, sharply drained, organic soil in sun. Water sparingly when dormant in summer.*

☀️ ◊ Z7-8 H8-7   ‡8in (20cm) ↔6in (15cm)

RANUNCULUS GRAMINEUS

This clump-forming buttercup is a perennial that is equally at home in a herbaceous border or rock garden. Cup-shaped, lemon yellow flowers are carried above the grasslike, finely hairy leaves in late spring and early summer.

CULTIVATION *Grow in moist but well-drained, fertile soil. Choose a position in full sun or partial shade.*

☼ ◐ ◊◊ Z6-8 H8-6   ‡to 12in (30cm)
                                       ↔to 6in (15cm)

RHAMNUS ALATERNUS 'ARGENTEOVARIEGATA'

This Italian buckthorn is a fast-growing, upright to spreading, evergreen shrub bearing oval, leathery, gray-green leaves with creamy white margins. Clusters of tiny, yellow-green flowers are borne in spring, followed by spherical red fruits that ripen to black.

CULTIVATION *Grow in any well-drained soil, in full sun. Prune out unwanted growth in early spring; remove any shoots with all-green leaves as seen.*

☼ ◊ Z7-9 H9-7   ‡15ft (5m) ↔12ft (4m)

RHODANTHEMUM HOSMARIENSE

A spreading subshrub valued for its profusion of daisylike flowerheads with white petals and yellow eyes. These are borne from early spring to autumn, covering the silver, softly hairy, finely divided leaves. Grow at the base of a warm wall or in a rock garden. In an alpine house, it will flower year-round if deadheaded.

CULTIVATION *Grow in very well-drained soil in a sunny position. Deadhead regularly to prolong flowering.*

☼ ◊ Z9–10 H12-7 ↕4–12in (10–30cm)
↔12in (30cm)

RHODOCHITON ATROSANGUINEUS

This is an evergreen, slender-stemmed climber, also known as *R. volubilis*, that can be grown as an annual in colder climates. Hanging, tubular, black to purple flowers with red-purple, bell-shaped "skirts" are borne during summer and autumn amid the heart-shaped, rich green leaves. Support larger plants with wiring or a trellis.

CULTIVATION *Grow in moist but well-drained, fertile, organic soil, in full sun; the roots must be in shade. Pinch out shoot tips to promote a bushy habit; Minimum temperature 37°F (3°C)..*

☼ ◊◊ H12-9 ↕10ft (3m)

EVERGREEN AZALEAS (*RHODODENDRON*)

Azaleas can be distinguished from true rhododendrons by their smaller dark green leaves and more tubular flowers. They also tend to make smaller, more spreading, twiggy shrubs. Botanically, rhododendrons have at least ten stamens per flower, and azaleas just five. Evergreen azaleas make beautiful, spring-flowering shrubs, blooming in almost every color, and good for a variety of uses: dwarf or compact types are excellent in containers on shaded patios, and larger varieties will brighten up areas in permanent light shade. They do well in sun provided that the soil is not allowed to dry out.

CULTIVATION *Ideal in moist but well-drained, organic, acidic soil in part-day shade. Shallow planting is essential. Little formative pruning is necessary. If older plants become congested, thin in early summer. Maintain a mulch of leaf mold, but do not cultivate around the root area.*

☼ ◐ ◊ Zones vary H9-5 as a group

1 ↕↔ 4ft (1.2m) **2** ↕↔ 3½ft (1.3m) **3** ↕↔ 24in (60cm)

4 ↕↔ 24in (60cm) **5** ↕↔ 24in (60cm) **6** ↕↔ 24in (60cm)

1 *Rhododendron* 'Azuma-kagami' (Z7-9) **2** *R.* 'Beethoven' (Z6-9) **3** *R.* 'Hatsugiri' (Z7-9)
4 *R.* 'Hinode-giri' (Z6-9) **5** *R.* 'Hinomayo' (Z7-9) **6** *R.* 'Irohayama' (Z7-9)

7 ‡↔ 5ft (1.5m)

8 ‡↔ 5ft (1.5m)

9 ‡↔ 4ft (1.2m)

MORE CHOICES

'Addy Wery' Vermilion-red flowers.

'Elsie Lee' Light reddish mauve flowers.

'Greeting' Red-orange.

'Gumpo' Pinkish white.

'Hexe' Crimson.

'Hino-crimson' Brilliant red flowers.

'Kure-no-yuki' White, also called 'Snowflake'.

'Louise Dowdle' Vivid red-purple flowers.

'Vida Brown' Rose-red.

'Wombat' Pink flowers.

10 ‡↔ 24–36in (60–90cm)

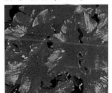

11 ‡↔ 4ft (1.2m)

12 ‡↔ 4ft (1.2m)

7 *R.* 'John Cairns' (Z6-9) **8** *R.* 'Kirin' (Z6-9) **9** *R.* 'Palestrina' (Z6-9)
10 *R.* 'Rosebud' (Z6-9) **11** *R.* 'Vuyk's Scarlet' (Z6-8) **12** *R.* 'Vuyk's Rosyred' (Z6-8)

DECIDUOUS AZALEAS (*RHODODENDRON*)

A group of very hardy flowering shrubs, the only rhododendrons whose dark green leaves are deciduous, often coloring brilliantly before they fall. Deciduous azaleas are perhaps the most beautiful types of rhododendron, with large clusters of sometimes fragrant, white to yellow, orange, pink, or red flowers in spring and early summer. There is quite a variety in size, shape, and growth habit, but they suit most garden uses well, especially in light shade. *R. luteum* thrives in sun where the soil is reliably moist. Grow them in containers if your soil is unsuitable.

CULTIVATION *Grow in moist but well-drained, acidic soil enriched with plenty of organic matter, ideally in partial shade. Shallow planting is essential; maintain a thick mulch of leaf mold, which will nourish the plant. Little or no pruning is necessary. Do not cultivate around the base of the plant; this will damage the roots.*

☼ ◑ ◊ Zones vary H10-5 as a group

1 ‡↔ 8ft (2.5m) **2** ‡↔ 10ft (3m) **3** ‡↔ 7ft (2.2m)

4 ‡↔ 5–8ft (1.5–2.5m) **5** ‡↔ 5ft (1.5m)

1 *Rhododendron albrechtii* (Z6-8) **2** *R. austrinum* (Z6-10)
3 *R.* 'Cecile' (Z5-8) **4** *R.* 'Corneille' (Z5-8) **5** *R.* 'Homebush' (Z5-8)

6 ↕↔ 6ft (2m)

MORE CHOICES

'Coccineum Speciosum'
Orange-red flowers.
'Daviesii' White.
'Gibraltar' Crimson buds
opening to orange with a
yellow flash.
R. kaempferi Semi-
evergreen; red flowers.
'Klondyke' Red buds
opening to orange gold
'Satan' Bright red.
'Silver Slipper' White
flushed pink with an
orange flare
'Spek's Brilliant' Bright
orange-scarlet.

7 ↕↔ 12ft (4m)

8 ↕↔ 5–8ft (1.5–2.5m)

9 ↕↔ 6ft (2m)

10 ↕↔ 8ft (2.5m)

11 ↕↔ 6ft (2m)

6 *R.* 'Irene Koster' (Z7-9) **7** *R. luteum* (Z6-9) **8** *R.* 'Narcissiflorum' (Z5-8)
9 *R.* 'Persil' (Z5-8) **10** *R.* 'Spek's Orange' (Z5-8) **11** *R.* 'Strawberry Ice' (Z5-8)

LARGE RHODODENDRONS

Large, woodland-type rhododendrons, which can reach treelike proportions, are grown primarily for their bright, sometimes fragrant, mostly spring flowers which are available in a wide spectrum of shapes and colors. They are ideal for adding color to shaded areas or woodland gardens. Most leaves are oval and dark green, although the attractive young foliage of *R. bureaui* is light brown. Some cultivars, like 'Cynthia' or 'Purple Splendour', are tolerant of direct sun (in reliably moist soil), making them more versatile than others; they make glorious, spring-flowering screens or hedges for a large garden.

CULTIVATION *Grow in moist but well-drained, organic, acidic soil. Most prefer dappled shade in sheltered woodland. Shallow planting is essential. Little formative pruning is necessary, although most can be renovated after flowering to leave a balanced framework of old wood.*

☼ ◐ ◊◊ Zones vary H9-5 as a group

1 ‡↔ 10ft (3m)

2 ‡↔ 10ft (3m)

3 ‡↔ 11ft (3.5m)

1 *R.* 'Blue Peter' (Z6-9) **2** *R. bureaui* (Z6-9) **3** *R.* 'Crest' (Z7-9)

1 ↕↔ 20ft (6m)

5 ↕ to 40ft (12m) ↔ 15ft (5m)

6 ↕↔ 12ft (4m)

7 ↕↔ 10ft (3m)

8 ↕↔ 12ft (4m)

9 ↕↔ 10ft (3m)

10 ↕↔ 10ft (3m)

11 ↕↔ 10ft (3m)

4 *R.* 'Cynthia' (Z6-9) **5** *R. falconeri* (Z8-9) **6** *R.* 'Fastuosum Flore Pleno' (Z5-8) **7** *R.* 'Furnivall's Daughter' (Z7-9) **8** *R.* 'Loderi King George' (Z7-9) **9** *R.* 'Purple Splendour' (Z6-9) **10** *R.* 'Sappho' (Z6-9) **11** *R.* 'Susan' (Z6-9)

MEDIUM-SIZED RHODODENDRONS

These evergreen rhododendrons, between 5–10ft (1.5 3m) tall, are much-valued for their attractive, often scented blooms; the flowers are carried amid dark green foliage throughout spring. 'Yellow Hammer' will often produce an early show of flowers in autumn, and the foliage of 'Winsome' is unusual for its bronze tints when young. A vast number of different medium-sized rhododendrons are available, all suitable for shrub borders or grouped together in mass plantings. Some sun-tolerant varieties, especially low-growing forms like 'May Day', are suitable for informal hedging.

CULTIVATION *Grow in moist but well-drained, organic, acidic soil. Most prefer light dappled shade. Shallow planting is essential. 'Fragrantissimum' requires extra care in colder areas; provide a thick winter mulch and avoid siting in a frost pocket. Trim after flowering, if necessary.*

☼ ◑ ◊◊ Zones vary H9-7 as a group

1 ‡↔ 6ft (2m)

2 ‡↔ 1.5m (5ft)

1 *R.* 'Fabia' (Z8-9) **2** *R.* 'Golden Torch' (Z7-9)

3 ‡↔ 6ft (2m) **4** ‡↔ 5ft (1.5m) **5** ‡↔ 5ft (1.5m) **6** ‡↔ 6ft (2m) **7** ‡↔ 6ft (2m) **8** ‡↔ 5ft (1.5m)

3 *R.* 'Fragrantissimum' (Z9-10) **4** *R.* 'Hydon Dawn' (Z7-9) **5** *R.* 'May Day' (Z7-9)
6 *R.* 'Titian Beauty' (Z7-9) **7** *R.* 'Yellow Hammer' (Z7-9) **8** *R.* 'Winsome' (Z7-9)

DWARF RHODODENDRONS

Dwarf rhododendrons are low-growing, evergreen shrubs with mid- to dark green, lance-shaped leaves. They flower throughout spring in a wide variety of showy colors and flower forms. If soil conditions are too alkaline for growing rhododendrons in the open garden, these compact shrubs are ideal in containers on shaded patios; 'Ptarmigan' is is particularly suited to this kind of planting since it is able to tolerate periods without water. Dwarf rhododendrons are also effective in rock gardens. In areas with cold winters, the earliest spring flowers may be vulnerable to frost.

CULTIVATION *Grow in moist but well-drained, leafy, acidic, organic soil. Site in sun or partial shade, but avoid the deep shade directly beneath a tree canopy. Best planted in spring or autumn; shallow planting is essential. No pruning is necessary.*

☼ ☼ ◑ ◊◊ Zones vary H9-6 as a group

1 ↨↔ 3½ft (1.1m)   **2** ↨↔ 4ft (1.2m)   **3** ↨↔ 24in (60cm)   **4** ↨↔ 18–36in (45–90cm)

1 *R.* 'Cilpinense' (Z8-9) **2** *R.* 'Doc' (Z5-9) **3** *R.* 'Dora Amateis' (Z6-9) **4** *R.* 'Ptarmigan' (Z7-9)

RHUS TYPHINA 'DISSECTA'

Rhus typhina, staghorn sumac (also seen as *R. hirta*), is an upright, deciduous shrub with velvety red shoots that resemble antlers. This form has long leaves, divided into many finely cut leaflets, which turn a brilliant orange-red in autumn. Upright clusters of less significant, yellow-green flowers are produced in summer, followed by velvety clusters of deep crimson-red fruits.

CULTIVATION *Grow in moist but well-drained, fairly fertile soil, in full sun to obtain best autumn color. Remove any suckering shoots arising from the ground around the base of the plant.*

☼ ◊◊ Z3-8 H8-1   ‡6ft (2m) ↔10ft (3m)

RIBES SANGUINEUM 'BROCKLEBANKII'

This slow-growing flowering currant is an upright, deciduous shrub with rounded, aromatic, yellow leaves, bright when young and fading in summer. The tubular, pale pink flowers, borne in hanging clusters in spring, are followed by small, blue-black fruits. 'Tydeman's White' is a very similar shrub, sometimes a little taller, with pure white flowers.

CULTIVATION *Grow in well-drained, fairly fertile soil. Site in sun, with shade during the hottest part of the day. Prune out some older stems after flowering. Cut back overgrown specimens in winter.*

☼◐ ◊ Z6-8 H8-6   ↔4ft (1.2m)

RIBES SANGUINEUM 'PULBOROUGH SCARLET'

This vigorous flowering currant, larger than 'Brocklebankii', (see previous page, bottom) is an upright, deciduous shrub, bearing hanging clusters of tubular, dark red flowers with white centers in spring. The aromatic, dark green leaves are rounded with toothed lobes. Small, berrylike, blue-black fruits develop during the summer.

CULTIVATION *Grow in well-drained, moderately fertile soil, in full sun. Cut out some older stems after flowering; overgrown specimens can be pruned hard in winter or early spring.*

☼ ◊◊ Z6-9 H9-1 ‡6ft (2m) ↔ 8ft (2.5m)

ROBINIA HISPIDA

The bristly locust is an upright and arching, deciduous shrub with spiny shoots, useful for shrub borders on poor, dry soils. Deep rose-pink, pea-like flowers appear in hanging spikes during late spring and early summer; these are followed by brown seed pods. The large, dark green leaves are divided into many oval leaflets.

CULTIVATION *Grow in any but water-logged soil, in sun. Provide shelter from wind to avoid damage to the brittle branches. No pruning is necessary.*

☼ ◊ Z6-10 H8-5 ‡8ft (2.5m) ↔ 10ft (3m)

ROBINIA PSEUDOACACIA
'FRISIA'

The black locust, *R. pseudoacacia*, is
a fast-growing, broadly columnar,
deciduous tree, in this cultivar
bearing gentle, yellow-green foliage
that is golden yellow when young,
turning orange-yellow in autumn.
Usually sparse, hanging clusters of
fragrant, pealike, small white flowers
appear in early summer. The stems
are normally spiny.

CULTIVATION *Grow in moist but well-
drained, fertile soil in full sun. When
young, maintain a single trunk by
removing competing stems as soon as
possible. Do not prune once established.*

☼ ◊◊ Z4-9 H9-1 ‡50ft (15m) ↔25ft (8m)

RODGERSIA PINNATA
'SUPERBA'

A clump-forming perennial that
bears upright clusters of star-shaped,
bright pink flowers. These are borne
in mid to late summer above bold,
heavily veined, dark green foliage.
The divided leaves, up to 36in
(90cm) long, are purplish bronze
when young. Good near water, in a
bog garden, or for naturalizing at a
woodland margin. For creamy white
flowers, look for *R. podophylla*.

CULTIVATION *Best in moist, organic soil,
in full sun or semi-shade. Provide
shelter from cold, drying winds. Will
not tolerate drought.*

☼◑ ◊ Z5-8 H8-5 ‡4ft (1.2m) ↔30in (75cm)

HYBRID TEA ROSES (*ROSA*)

These deciduous shrubs are often grown in formal bedding displays, laid out with neat paths and edging. They are distinguished from other roses in that they carry their large flowers either singly or in clusters of two or three. The first blooms appear in early summer, and repeat flushes continue well into autumn. In a formal bed, group five or six of the same cultivar together, and interplant with some standard roses to add some variation in height. These roses also combine well with herbaceous perennials and other shrubs in mixed borders.

CULTIVATION *Grow in moist but well-drained, fertile soil in full sun. Cut spent flower stems back to the first leaf for repeat blooms. Prune main stems to about 10in (25cm) above ground level in early spring, and remove any dead or diseased wood as necessary at the base.*

☼ ◊◊ Z5-9 H9-1

1 ‡↔ 24in (60cm)

2 ‡ to 6ft (2m) ↔ 32in (80cm)

3 ‡3½ft (1.1m) ↔ 30in (75cm)

4 ‡3½ft (1.1m) ↔ 30in (75cm)

5 ‡30in (75cm) ↔ 24in (60cm)

1 *Rosa* ABBEYFIELD ROSE 'Cocbrose' **2** *R.* ALEXANDER 'Harlex'
3 *R.* BLESSINGS **4** *R.* ELINA 'Dicjana' **5** *R.* FREEDOM 'Dicjem'

6 ‡22in (55cm) ↔ 24in (60cm)

7 ‡32in (80cm) ↔ 26in (65cm)

8 ‡30in (75cm) ↔ 28in (70cm)

9 ‡30in (75cm) ↔ 24in (60cm)

10 ‡3ft (1m) ↔ 30in (75cm)

11 ‡4ft (1.2m) ↔ 3ft (1m)

12 ‡3ft (1m) ↔ 24in (60cm)

13 ‡3ft (1m) ↔ 30in (75cm)

14 ‡32in (80cm) ↔ 24in (60cm)

15 ‡3½ft (1.1m) ↔ 24in (60cm)

16 ‡3ft (1m) ↔ 30in (75cm)

6 *R.* 'Indian Summer' **7** *R.* 'Ingrid Bergman' **8** *R.* JUST JOEY **9** *R.* LOVELY LADY 'Dicjubell' **10** *R.* PAUL SHIRVILLE 'Harqueterwife' **11** *R.* PEACE 'Madame A. Meilland' **12** *R.* REMEMBER ME 'Cocdestin' **13** *R.* ROYAL WILLIAM 'Korzaun' **14** *R.* SAVOY HOTEL 'Harvintage' **15** *R.* SILVER JUBILEE **16** *R.* 'Troika'

FLORIBUNDA ROSES (*ROSA*)

These very free-flowering roses come in a very wide range of flower colors. They are set apart from hybrid tea roses by their large, many-flowered clusters of relatively small blooms. Nearly all are fragrant, some being much more so than others. They lend themselves well to informal or cottage garden designs, mixing well with herbaceous perennials as well as other shrubs. Remember to consider the color of the flowers when choosing all neighboring plants, since blooms will continue to appear from late spring to well into autumn.

CULTIVATION *Best in moist but well-drained, fairly fertile soil in full sun. Deadhead for repeat blooms. Prune main stems to about 12in (30cm) above ground level in early spring, and remove any dead or diseased wood as necessary.*

☼ ◊◊ Z5-9 H9-1

1 ‡20in (50cm) ↔ 24in (60cm)

2 ‡3ft (1m) ↔ 30in (75cm)

3 ‡30in (75cm) ↔ 24in (60cm)

4 ‡3ft (1m) ↔ 24in (60cm)

5 ‡4ft (1.2m) ↔ 3ft (1m)

6 ‡32in (80cm) ↔ 30in (75cm)

1 *Rosa* AMBER QUEEN 'Harroony'   **2** *R.* ANISLEY DICKSON 'Dickimono'   **3** *R.* ANNA LIVIA 'Kormetter'   **4** *R.* 'Arthur Bell'   **5** *R.* CHINATOWN   **6** *R.* CITY OF LONDON 'Harukfore'

7 ↕30in (75cm) ↔ 24in (60cm)

8 ↕3ft (1m) ↔ 30in (75cm)

9 ↕32in (80cm) ↔ 26in (65cm)

10 ↕↔ 30in (75cm)

11 ↕32in (80cm) ↔ 24in (60cm)

12 ↕4ft (1.2m) ↔ 3ft (1m)

13 ↕28in (70cm) ↔ 24in (60cm)

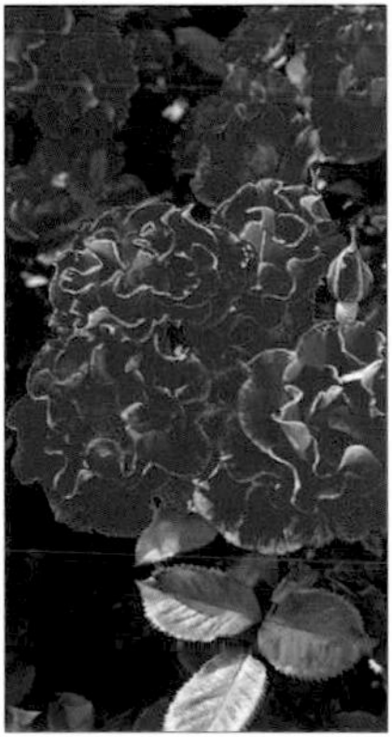

14 ↕30in (75cm) ↔ 24in (60cm)

15 ↕ to 8ft (2.2m) ↔ 3ft (1m)

7 *R.* ESCAPADE 'Harpade' **8** *R.* 'Fragrant Delight' **9** *R.* ICEBERG 'Korbin' **10** *R.* MANY HAPPY RETURNS 'Harwanted' **11** *R.* MARGARET MERRIL 'Harkuly' **12** *R.* MOUNTBATTEN 'Harmantelle' **13** *R.* SEXY REXY 'Macrexy' **14** *R.* TANGO 'Macfirwal' **15** *R.* 'The Queen Elizabeth'

CLIMBING ROSES (*ROSA*)

Climbing roses are often vigorous plants that will reach varying heights depending on the cultivar. All types have stiff, arching stems, usually with dense, glossy leaves divided into small leaflets. The frequently scented flowers are borne in summer, some in one exuberant flush, others having a lesser repeat flowering. They can be trained against walls or fences as decorative features in their own right, planted as a complement to other climbers, such as clematis, or allowed to scramble up into other wall-trained shrubs or even old trees. They are invaluable for disguising unsightly garden buildings or as a backdrop to a summer border.

CULTIVATION *Best in moist but well-drained, fairly fertile soil, in sun. Deadhead unless hips are wanted. As plants mature, prune back to within the allowed area after flowering. Occasionally cut an old main stem back to the base to renew growth. Do not prune in the first two years.*

☼ ◊◊ mostly 5-9 H9-1

2 ‡3m (10ft) ↔ 2.5m (8ft)

3 ‡↔2.2m (7ft)

4 ‡to 30ft (10m) ↔ 20ft (6m)

5 ‡to 15ft (5m) ↔ 12ft (4m)

1 ‡↔to 20ft (6m)

1 *Rosa banksiae* 'Lutea' (Z8-9) 2 *R*. COMPASSION 3 *R*. DUBLIN BAY 'Macdub'
4 *R. filipes* 'Kiftsgate' (Z7-9) 5 *R*. 'Gloire de Dijon' (Z6-9)

6 ‡ to 10ft (3m) ↔ 6ft (2m)

7 ‡ 10ft (3m) ↔ 7ft (2.2m)

8 ‡ ↔ 8ft (2.5m)

9 ‡ 15ft (5m) ↔ 10ft (3m)

10 ‡ 10ft (3m) ↔ 8ft (2.5m)

11 ‡ to 20ft (6m) ↔ 12ft (4m)

12 ‡ to 10ft (3m) ↔ 6ft (2m)

6 *R.* GOLDEN SHOWERS **7** *R.* HANDEL 'Macha' **8** *R.* 'Maigold' **9** *R.* 'Madame Alfred Carrière'
10 *R.* 'New Dawn' **11** *R.* 'Madame Grégoire Staechelin' **12** *R.* 'Zéphirine Drouhin' (Z6-9)

RAMBLING ROSES (*ROSA*)

Rambling roses are very similar to climbers (see page 380) but have more lax, flexible stems. These are easier to train onto complex structures such as arches, tunnels, and pergolas, or ropes and chains suspended between rigid uprights, provided they are solidly built; most ramblers are vigorous. Unlike climbers, they can succumb to mildew if trained flat against walls. Ramblers have divided, glossy green leaves, borne on thorny or prickly stems. Flowers are often scented, arranged singly or in clusters, and are borne during summer. Some bloom only once, others having a lesser repeat flowering later on.

CULTIVATION *Best in moist but well-drained, fertile soil, in full sun. Train stems of young plants on to a support, to establish a permanent framework; prune back to this each year after flowering has finished, and remove any damaged wood as necessary.*

☼ ◊◊ Z5-9 H9-1

1 ↕ to 15ft (5m) ↔ 10ft (3m)　　　**2** ↕ to 5m (15ft) ↔ 4m (12ft)

1 *Rosa* 'Albéric Barbier'　**2** *R.* 'Albertine'

3 ↕ to 30ft (10m) ↔ 20ft (6m)

4 ↕ to 15ft (5m) ↔ to 12ft (4m)

5 ↕↔ 20ft (6m)

6 ↕ to 20ft (6m) ↔ 12ft (4m)

7 ↕↔ to 12ft (4m)

8 ↕↔ 12ft (4m)

3 *R.* 'Bobbie James' **4** *R.* 'Félicité Perpétue' **5** *R.* 'Rambling Rector'
6 *R.* 'Seagull' **7** *R.* 'Sanders' White Rambler' **8** *R.* 'Veilchenblau'

PATIO AND MINIATURE ROSES (*ROSA*)

These small or miniature shrub roses, bred especially for their compact habit and small flower size, greatly extend the range of garden situations in which roses can be grown. They produce flowers in a wide range of colors, blooming over long periods from summer to autumn amid deciduous, glossy, green leaves. With the exception of 'Ballerina', which can grow to a height of about 5ft (1.5m), most are under 3ft (1m) tall, making them invaluable for confined, sunny spaces.

Planted in large containers or raised beds, they are also excellent for decorating patios

CULTIVATION *Grow in well-drained but moist, moderately fertile soil that is rich in well-rotted organic matter. Choose an open, sunny site. Remove all but the strongest shoots in late winter, then reduce these by about one-third of their height. Cut out any dead or damaged wood as necessary.*

☼ ◊◊ Z5-9 H9-1

1 ‡ 18in (45cm) ↔ 16in (40cm) **2** ‡ to 5ft (1.5m) ↔ 4ft (1.2m) **3** ‡ 30in (75cm) ↔ 24in (60cm)

4 ‡ 18in (45cm) ↔ 12in (30cm) **5** ‡ 20in (50cm) ↔ 16in (40cm) **6** ‡ 30in (75cm) ↔ 30in (60cm)

1 *Rosa* ANNA FORD 'Harpiccolo' **2** *R.* 'Ballerina' **3** *R.* 'Cecile Brunner'
4 *R.* CIDER CUP 'Dicladida' **5** *R.* GENTLE TOUCH 'Diclulu' **6** *R.* 'Mevrouw Nathalie Nypels'

7 ↕ 4ft (1.2m) ↔ 3ft (1m)

8 ↕ 16in (40cm) ↔ 24in (60cm)

9 ↕ 10in (25cm) ↔ 12in (30cm)

10 ↕ 16in (40cm) ↔ 14in (35cm)

11 ↕ ↔ 14in (35cm)

12 ↕ ↔ 24–30in (60–90cm)

13 ↕ ↔ 3–5ft (1–1.5m)

7 *R.* 'Perle d'Or' **8** *R.* QUEEN MOTHER 'Korquemu' **9** *R.* 'Stacey Sue'
10 *R.* SWEET DREAM 'Fryminicot' **11** *R.* SWEET MAGIC 'Dicmagic'
12 *R.* 'The Fairy' **13** *R.* 'Yesterday'

GROUNDCOVER ROSES (*ROSA*)

Groundcover roses are low-growing, spreading, deciduous shrubs, ideal for the front of a border, in both formal and informal situations. They produce beautiful, fragrant flowers over long periods from summer into autumn, amid divided, glossy green leaves, on thorny or prickly, sometimes trailing stems. Only those of really dense habit, such as SWANY 'Meiburenac', will provide weed-smothering cover, and even these are effective only if the ground is weed-free to begin with. Most give their best cascading over a low wall or when used to clothe a steep bank that is otherwise difficult to plant.

CULTIVATION *Best in moist but well-drained, reasonably fertile, organic soil, in full sun. Prune shoots back after flowering each year to well within the intended area of spread, removing any dead or damaged wood. Annual pruning will enhance flowering performance.*

☼ ◊◊ Z5-9 H9-1

1 ‡34in (85cm) ↔ 3½ft (1.1m)

2 ‡18in (45cm) ↔ 4ft (1.2m)

3 ‡30in (75cm) ↔ 4ft (1.2m)

4 ‡3ft (1m) ↔ 4ft (1.2m)

1 *Rosa* BONICA 'Meidomonac' 2 *R.* 'Nozomi'
3 *R.* RED BLANKET 'Intercell' 4 *R.* ROSY CUSHION 'Interall'

5 ‡6in (15cm) ↔ 18in (45cm)

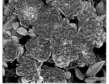

6 ‡20in (50cm) ↔ 5ft (1.5m)

7 ‡32in (80cm) ↔ 4ft (1.2m)

9 ‡30in (75cm) ↔ 4ft (1.2m)

8 ‡to 30in (75cm) ↔ 5½ft (1.7m)

5 *R.* SNOW CARPET 'Maccarpe' 6 *R.* SUMA 'Harsuma'
7 *R.* SURREY 'Korlanum' 8 *R.* SWANY 'Meiburenac' 9 *R.* TALL STORY 'Dickooky'

OLD GARDEN ROSES (*ROSA*)

The history of old garden roses extends back to Roman times, demonstrating their lasting appeal in garden design. They are deciduous shrubs, composed of a very large number of cultivars categorized into many groups, such as the gallica, damask, and moss roses. Because almost all old garden roses flower in a single flush in early summer, they should be mixed with other flowering plants to maintain a lasting display. Try underplanting non-climbing types with spring bulbs, and climbing cultivars can be interwoven with a late-flowering clematis.

CULTIVATION *Best in moist but well-drained, fertile soil in full sun. Little pruning is necessary; occasionally remove an old stem at the base to alleviate congested growth and to promote new shoots. Trim to shape in spring as necessary. Unless hips are wanted, remove spent flowers as they fade.*

☼ ◊◊ Z4-9 H9-1

1 ‡7ft (2.2m) ↔ 5ft (1.5m) **2** ‡4ft (1.2m) ↔ 3ft (1m) **3** ‡3ft (1m) ↔ 4ft (1.2m)

4 ‡5ft (1.5m) ↔ 4ft (1.2m) **5** ‡5ft (1.5m) ↔ 4ft (1.2m) **6** ‡5ft (1.5m) ↔ 4ft (1.2m)

1 *Rosa* 'Alba Maxima' **2** *R.* 'Belle de Crècy' **3** *R.* 'Cardinal de Richelieu' **4** *R.* 'Céleste'
5 *R.* x *centifolia* 'Cristata' (*syn.* 'Chapeau de Napoléon') **6** *R.* x *centifolia* 'Muscosa'

7 ↕ ↔ 4ft (1.2m) or more

8 ↕ ↔ to 6ft (2m)

9 ↕ ↔ 4ft (1.2m)

10 ↕ 5ft (1.5m) ↔ 4ft (1.2m)

11 ↕ 4½ft (1.3m) ↔ 4ft (1.2m)

12 ↕ 5ft (1.5m) ↔ 4ft (1.2m)

13 ↕ to 6ft (2m) ↔ 4ft (1.2m)

14 ↕ 5ft (1.5m) ↔ 4ft (1.2m)

15 ↕ 5ft (1.5m) ↔ 4ft (1.2m)

16 ↕ 5ft (1.5m) ↔ 4ft (1.2m)

17 ↕ ↔ 4ft (1.2m)

18 ↕ ↔ 3ft (1m)

7 *R.* 'Charles de Mills' **8** *R.* 'De Rescht' **9** *R.* 'Duc de Guiche' **10** *R.* 'Fantin-Latour' **11** *R.* 'Félicité Parmentier' **12** *R.* 'Ferdinand Pichard' **13** *R.* 'Henri Martin' **14** *R.* 'Ispahan' **15** *R.* 'Königin von Dänemark' **16** *R.* 'Madame Hardy' **17** *R.* 'Président de Sèze' **18** *R.* 'Tuscany Superb'

MODERN SHRUB ROSES (*ROSA*)

These roses are slightly larger and more spreading than most others, combining the stature of old garden roses with some of the benefits of modern types. Their general good health and vigor makes them easy to grow, and they repeat-flower over a long period, making ideal summer-flowering, deciduous shrubs for the back of a low-maintenance shrub border in a large garden. Like other roses, there is a wide choice in flower shape and color, and several have a superb fragrance.

Flowering begins in early summer, with repeat flushes well into autumn.

CULTIVATION *Grow in well-drained but moist, moderately fertile, organic soil. Choose an open, sunny site. To keep them at a manageable size, prune every year in early spring. It is often better to let them grow naturally, however; their form is easily spoiled by severe or careless pruning.*

☼ ◊◊ Z5-9 (mostly) H9-1

1 ↕5ft (1.5m) ↔3½ft (1.1m)   **2** ↕↔4ft (1.2m)   **3** ↕↔ to 11ft (3.5m)

4 ↕6ft (2m) ↔5ft (1.5m)   **5** ↕↔5ft (1.5m)   **6** ↕5ft (1.5m) ↔4ft (1.2m)

1 *Rosa* 'Blanche Double de Coubert'   **2** *R.* 'Buff Beauty'   **3** *R.* 'Cerise Bouquet' (Z3-9)
4 *R.* CONSTANCE SPRY   **5** *R.* 'Cornelia'   **6** *R.* 'Felicia'

7 ‡6ft (2m) ↔ 3ft (1m)

8 ‡5ft (1.5m) ↔ 3ft (1m)

9 ‡4ft (1.2m) ↔ 5ft (1.5m)

10 ‡5ft (1.5m) ↔ 4ft (1.2m)

11 ‡↔ 7ft (2.2m)

12 ‡↔ /ft (2.2m)

13 ‡↔ 3½ft (1.1m)

14 ‡ 7ft (2.2m) ↔ 6ft (2m)

15 ‡6ft (2m) ↔ 3ft (1m)

16 ‡↔ 3½ft (1.1m)

17 ‡6ft (2m) ↔ 4ft (1.2m)

7 *R.* 'Fred Loads' **8** *R.* GERTRUDE JEKYLL 'Ausbord' **9** *R.* GRAHAM THOMAS 'Ausmas'
10 *R.* 'Jacqueline du Pré' **11** *R.* 'Marguerite Hilling' **12** *R.* 'Nevada' **13** *R.* 'Penelope'
14 *R.* 'Roseraie de l'Häy' (Z4-9) **15** *R.* 'Sally Holmes' **16** *R.* 'The Lady' **17** *R.* WESTERLAND 'Korwest'

ROSES FOR WILD AREAS (*ROSA*)

The best types of rose for wild gardens are the species or wild roses; many naturalize easily. Either shrubs or climbers, most have a natural-looking, scrambling or arching growth habit with single, five-petaled, often fragrant flowers that appear in early summer on the previous year's growth. Although the main flowering season is fleeting, in many the flowers develop into beautiful rosehips, just as attractive as the flowers. Hips vary in color from orange to red or black and often persist into winter, providing valuable food for hungry wildlife.

CULTIVATION *Best in moist but well-drained, reasonably fertile, organic soil. In a wild garden, little pruning is needed; to control hedges, trim after flowering each year, removing any dead or damaged wood. The flowers are borne on the previous summer's stems, so do not remove too many older branches.*

☼ ◊◊ Zones vary H9-1

1 ↕7ft (2.2m) ↔ 8ft (2.5m)

2 ↕32in (80cm) ↔ 3ft (1m)

3 ↕3ft (1m) ↔ 4ft (1.2m)

4 ↕32in (80cm) ↔ 3ft (1m)

5 ↕6ft (2m) ↔ 5ft (1.5m)

1 *R.* 'Complicata' (Z4-9) 2 *R.* 'Fru Dagmar Hastrup' (Z2-9) 3 *R. gallica* var. *officinalis* (Z3-9)
4 *R. gallica* var. *officinalis* 'Versicolor' (Z3-9) 5 *R. glauca* (Z2-8)

6 ↕ 3½ft (1.1m) ↔ 4½ft (1.3m)

7 ↕ 5–8ft (1.5–2.5m) ↔ 4–6ft (1.2–2m)

8 ↕ to 10ft (3m) ↔ 6ft (2m)

9 ↕ 4ft (1.2m) ↔ 3ft (1m)

10 ↕ 6ft (2m) ↔ 3ft (1m)

11 ↕ ↔ 3–8ft (1–2.5m)

12 ↕ 6ft (2m) ↔ 3ft (1m)

13 ↕ 8ft (2.5m) ↔ 3ft (1m)

6 *R.* 'Golden Wings' (Z4-9) **7** *R. mulliganii* (Z5-9) **8** *R. nutkana* 'Plena' (Z3-9)
9 *R.* x *odorata* 'Mutabilis' (Z7-9) **10** *R. primula* (Z5-9) **11** *R. rugosa* 'Rubra' (Z2-9)
12 *R. xanthina* 'Canary Bird' (Z5-9) **13** *R. xanthina* var. *hugonis* (Z5-9)

ROSMARINUS OFFICINALIS 'MISS JESSOP'S UPRIGHT'

This vigorous, upright rosemary is an evergreen shrub with aromatic foliage that can be used in cooking. From mid-spring to early summer, whorls of small, purple-blue to white flowers are produced amid the narrow, dark green, white-felted leaves, often with a repeat show in autumn. A good hedging plant for a kitchen garden. For white flowers, try 'Sissinghurst White'.

CULTIVATION *Grow in well-drained, poor to moderately fertile soil. After flowering, trim any shoots that spoil the symmetry.*

☼ ◊ Z8-10 H10-8   ‡↔ 6ft (2m)

ROSMARINUS OFFICINALIS PROSTRATUS GROUP

These low-growing types of rosemary are aromatic, evergreen shrubs ideal for a rock garden or the top of a dry wall. Whorls of small, two-lipped, purple-blue to white flowers are produced in late spring, and often again in autumn. The dark green leaves have white-felted undersides and can be cut in sprigs for culinary use. Plant in a sheltered position where marginally hardy.

CULTIVATION *Grow in well-drained, poor to moderately fertile soil, in full sun. Trim or lightly cut back shoots that spoil the symmetry, after flowering.*

☼ ◊ Z8-10 H10-8 ‡6in (15cm) ↔5ft (1.5m)

RUBUS 'BENENDEN'

This flowering raspberry is an
ornamental, deciduous shrub with
spreading, arching, thornless
branches and peeling bark. It is
valued for its abundance of large,
saucer-shaped, roselike flowers with
glistening, pure white petals in late
spring and early summer. The lobed
leaves are dark green. Suitable for a
shrub border.

CULTIVATION *Grow in any rich, fertile
soil, in full sun or partial shade. After
flowering, occasionally remove some old
stems to the base to relieve overcrowding
and to promote new growth.*

☼:◒: ◊ Z5-9 H9-5　　↕↔ 10ft (3m)

RUBUS THIBETANUS

The ghost bramble is an upright,
summer-flowering, deciduous shrub
named for its conspicuously white-
coated, prickly stems in winter. The
small, saucer-shaped, red-purple
flowers are carried amid fernlike,
white-hairy, dark green leaves,
followed by spherical black fruits,
also with a whitish coating.
R. cockburnianus (Z5-9 H9-5) is also
valued for its white winter stems.

CULTIVATION *Grow in any fertile soil,
in sun or partial shade. Each spring,
cut all flowered stems back to the
ground, leaving the previous season's
new, unflowered shoots unpruned.*

☼:◒: ◊ Z7-9 H9-7　　↕↔ 8ft (2.5m)

RUDBECKIA FULGIDA VAR. *SULLIVANTII* 'GOLDSTURM'

This black-eyed Susan is a clump-forming perennial valued for its strongly upright form and large, daisylike, golden yellow flowerheads with cone-shaped, blackish brown centers. These appear above the substantial clumps of lance-shaped, mid-green leaves during late summer and autumn. It is a bold addition to a late summer border, and the cut flowers last reasonably well in water.

CULTIVATION *Grow in any moist but well-drained soil that does not dry out, in full sun or light shade.*

☼ ◑ ◊◊ Z4–9 H9–1   ‡ to 24in (60cm)
↔18in (45cm)

RUDBECKIA 'GOLDQUELLE'

A tall but compact perennial that bears large, fully double, bright lemon yellow flowers from mid-summer to mid-autumn. These are carried above loose clumps of deeply divided, mid-green leaves. The flowers are good for cutting.

CULTIVATION *Grow in any moist but well-drained soil, in full sun or light dappled shade.*

☼ ◑ ◊◊ Z3–9 H9–1   ‡ to 36in (90cm)
↔18in (45cm)

SALIX BABYLONICA VAR. *PEKINENSIS* 'TORTUOSA'

The dragon's claw willow is a fast-growing, upright, deciduous tree with curiously twisted shoots that are striking in winter. In spring, yellow-green catkins appear with the contorted, bright green leaves with gray-green undersides. Plant away from drains, since roots are invasive and water-seeking. Also sold as *S. matsudana* 'Tortuosa'.

CULTIVATION *Grow in any but very dry or shallow, alkaline soil. Choose a sunny site. Thin occasionally in late winter to stimulate new growth, which best exhibits the twisted growth pattern.*

☼ ◑ Z6-9 H9-6 ‡50ft (15m) ↔25ft (8m)

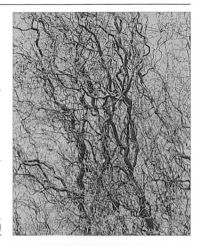

SALIX 'BOYDII'

This tiny, very slow-growing, upright, deciduous shrub with gnarled branches is suitable for planting in a rock garden or trough. The small, almost rounded leaves are rough-textured, prominently veined, and grayish green. Catkins are only produced occasionally, in early spring.

CULTIVATION *Grow in any deep, moist but well-drained soil, in full sun; willows dislike shallow, alkaline soil. When necessary, prune in late winter to maintain a healthy framework.*

☼ ◐◑ Z4-7 H7-1 ‡12in (30cm) ↔8in (20cm)

SALIX CAPREA 'KILMARNOCK'

The Kilmarnock willow is a small, weeping, deciduous tree ideal for a small garden. It forms a dense, umbrella-like crown of yellow-brown shoots studded with silvery catkins in mid- and late spring, before the foliage appears. The broad, toothed leaves are dark green on top and gray-green beneath.

CULTIVATION *Grow in any deep, moist but well-drained soil, in full sun. Prune annually in late winter to prevent the crown from becoming congested. Remove shoots on the clear trunk.*

☼ ◐ ◊◊ Z6-8 H8-6   ↕6ft (2m) ↔6ft (2m)

SALIX HASTATA 'WEHRHAHNII'

This small, slow-growing, upright, deciduous shrub, with dark purple-brown stems and contrasting silvery gray, early spring catkins, makes a beautiful specimen for winter color displays. The leaves are oval and bright green.

CULTIVATION *Grow in any moist soil, in sun; does not tolerate shallow, alkaline soils. Prune in spring to maintain a balance between young stems, which usually have the best winter color, and older wood with catkins.*

☼ ◊ Z5-8 H8-5   ↕↔3ft (1m)

SALIX LANATA

The woolly willow is a rounded, slow-growing, deciduous shrub with thick shoots that have an attractive white-woolly texture when young. Large, upright, golden to gray-yellow catkins emerge on older wood in late spring among the dark green, broadly oval, silvery-gray-woolly leaves.

CULTIVATION *Grow in moist but well-drained soil, in sun. Tolerates semi-shade, but dislikes shallow, alkaline soil. Prune occasionally in late winter or early spring to maintain a balance between old and young stems.*

☼☼ ◊◊ Z3-5 H5-1 ‡3ft (1m) ↔5ft (1.5m)

SALPIGLOSSIS
CASINO SERIES

These upright and compact, weather-resistant annuals, ideal for summer bedding, freely produce a contrasting display of funnel-shaped flowers throughout summer and autumn. Colors range from blue and purple to red, yellow, or orange, heavily veined in deeper tints. The lance-shaped, mid-green leaves have wavy margins.

CULTIVATION *Grow in moist but well-drained, fertile soil, in sun. Stems need support. Deadhead regularly. Plant out only after any risk of frost has passed.*

☼ ◊ annual H6-1 ‡to 24in (60cm) ↔to 12in (30cm)

SALVIA ARGENTEA

This short-lived perennial forms large clumps of soft, felty gray leaves around the base of the plant. Spikes of hooded, two-lipped, white or pinkish white flowers are borne in mid- and late summer, on strong, upright stems. Removing the spike before it blooms may prolong the life of the plant.

CULTIVATION *Grow in light, very well-drained to gravelly soil. Use a cloche or glass panel to protect from excessive winter moisture.*

☼ ◊ Z5-8 H8-5 ‡36in (90cm) ↔24in (60cm)

SALVIA CACALIIFOLIA

Usually grown as an annual in cool climates, this upright and hairy, herbaceous perennial bears spikes of deep blue flowers in early summer, held above mid-green foliage. A distinctive sage with a brilliant flower color, for bedding, filling gaps in borders, or containers.

CULTIVATION *Grow in light, moderately fertile, moist but well-drained soil enriched with organic matter. Choose a site in full sun to light dappled shade.*

☼☀ ◊◊ Z9-10 H9-1 ‡36in (90cm) ↔12in (30cm)

SALVIA COCCINEA
'PSEUDOCOCCINEA'

A bushy, short-lived perennial often grown as an annual in colder climates, with toothed, dark green, hairy leaves and loose, slender spikes of soft cherry red flowers from summer to autumn. An exotic-looking addition to a summer display, and good in containers.

CULTIVATION *Grow in light, moderately fertile well-drained soil, rich in organic matter Site in full sun.*

☼ ◊ Z11 H12-1 ‡24in (60cm) ↔12in (30cm)

SALVIA DISCOLOR

This upright, herbaceous perennial, which is normally treated as a summer annual in colder climates, is valued for both its flowers and foliage. Its green leaves have a densely white-woolly surface, forming an unusual display in themselves until the long spikes of deep purplish black flowers extend above them in late summer and early autumn.

CULTIVATION *Thrives in light, moderately fertile, moist but well-drained, organic soil. A position in full sun or light shade is best.*

☼ ☀ ◊◊ Z9-10 H10-1 ‡18in (45cm) ↔12in (30cm)

SALVIA FULGENS

An upright, evergreen, summer-flowering subshrub bearing spikes of tubular, two-lipped red flowers. The oval, toothed or notched leaves are rich green above and densely white-woolly beneath. Provides brilliant color for bedding or containers.

CULTIVATION *Grow in light, moist but well-drained, moderately fertile, organic soil in full sun or semi-shade.*

☼ ◑ ◊ Z9-10 H12-3 ‡6in (15cm) ↔8in (20cm)

SALVIA GUARANITICA 'BLUE ENIGMA'

A subshrubby perennial that grows well as a summer annual for bedding displays in cool climates. It is admired for its deep blue flowers, more fragrant than those of the species, that tower above the mid-green foliage from the end of summer until late autumn.

CULTIVATION *Grow in light, moderately fertile, moist but well-drained soil enriched with organic matter. Choose a site in full sun to light dappled shade.*

☼ ◑ ◊◊ Z8-10 H10-1 ‡5ft (1.5m) ↔36in (90cm)

SALVIA LEUCANTHA

The Mexican bush sage is a small evergreen shrub. The leaves are mid-green, white-downy beneath, and long spikes of white flowers with purple to lavender-blue calyces appear in autumn. Also beautiful year-round in a greenhouse bed or large container.

CULTIVATION *Grow in moist but well-drained, fertile soil in sun or partial shade. Under glass, grow in well-drained potting soil mix in full light with shade from hot sun, and water moderately while in flower.*

☼ ◑ ◊◊ Z10–11 H10–1 ↕3ft (1m) or more
↔16–36in (40–90cm)

SALVIA MICROPHYLLA 'PINK BLUSH'

An unusual flower color for this shrubby perennial, with mid-green leaves and tall, slender spires of intense fuchsia-pink flowers. 'Kew Red' and 'Newby Hall' are also recommended, both with red flowers.

CULTIVATION *Grow in light, moist but well-drained, moderately fertile soil that is rich in organic matter, in full sun. Plants damaged by cold may be trimmed, but do not cut into old wood.*

☼ ◊ Z9–10 H10–1 ↕3ft (90cm) ↔2ft (60cm)

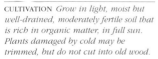

SALVIA OFFICINALIS 'ICTERINA'

A very attractive, yellow and green variegated form of culinary sage that has a mound-forming, subshrubby habit and aromatic, evergreen, velvety leaves. Less significant spikes of small, lilac-blue flowers appear in early summer. Ideal for an herb or kitchen garden. 'Kew Gold' (Z5-8 H8-5) is a very similar plant, although its leaves are often completely yellow.

CULTIVATION *Grow in moist but well-drained, fairly fertile, organic soil. Site in full sun or partial shade.*

☼ ◊ Z7-8 H8-5 ‡32in (80cm) ↔3ft (1m)

SALVIA OFFICINALIS PURPURASCENS GROUP

Purple culinary sage is an upright, evergreen subshrub suitable for a sunny border. Its red-purple, aromatic young leaves and spikes of lilac-blue flowers produce an attractive combination, the latter appearing during the first half of summer. A useful plant to add color to an herb garden.

CULTIVATION *Grow in light, moderately fertile, organic, moist but well-drained soil in full sun or light shade. Trim to shape each year after flowering.*

☼ ☀ ◊◊ Z7-8 H8-1 ‡to 32in (80cm) ↔3ft (1m)

SALVIA OFFICINALIS 'TRICOLOR'

This variegated sage is an upright, evergreen perennial with gray-green woolly, aromatic leaves with cream and pink to beet purple marking. In early to mid-summer, it produces spikes of lilac-blue flowers, attractive to butterflies.

CULTIVATION *Grow in moist but well-drained, reasonably fertile soil enriched with organic matter, in full sun or light dappled shade. Trim back ungainly growth each year after flowering.*

☼ ◑ ◊◊ Z7-8 H8-1　　　↕ ↔ 3ft (1m)

SALVIA PATENS 'CAMBRIDGE BLUE'

This lovely cultivar of *S. patens* is an upright perennial with tall, loose spikes of pale blue flowers. It is a striking addition to a herbaceous or mixed border or to bedding and patio containers. The flowers are borne during mid-summer to mid-autumn above the oval, hairy, mid-green leaves. Where marginally hardy, provide shelter at the base of a warm wall.

CULTIVATION *Grow in well-drained soil, in full sun. Overwinter young plants in frost-free conditions.*

☼ ◊ Z8-9 H9-1　　↕ 18–24in (45–60cm)
　　　　　　　　　↔ 18in (45cm)

SALVIA PRATENSIS
HAEMATODES GROUP

A short-lived perennial, sometimes
sold as *S. haematodes*, forming basal
clumps of large, dark green leaves.
In early and mid-summer, spreading
spikes of massed blue-violet flowers
with paler throats emerge from the
center of the clump. Provides
color for bedding, filling gaps in
beds and borders, or containers.
'Indigo' is another attractive
recommended cultivar.

CULTIVATION *Grow in moist but well-
drained, moderately fertile, organic soil.
Site in full sun or light shade.*

☼ ◊ Z3-9 H9-1 ‡36in (90cm) ↔12in (30cm)

SALVIA SPLENDENS
'SCARLET KING'

This compact, bushy perennial, with
dense spikes of long-tubed, scarlet
flowers, is usually grown as an
annual in cold climates. The flowers
are borne from summer to autumn
above dark green toothed leaves.
Its long-lasting, brilliant flowers are
an invaluable addition to any
bedding or container display.

CULTIVATION *Grow in moist but well-
drained, moderately fertile, organic soil.
Choose a site in full sun.*

☼ ◊ annual H12-1 ‡to 10in (25cm)
↔9–14in (23–35cm)

SALVIA × *SYLVESTRIS* 'MAINACHT'

A neat, clump-forming, pleasantly aromatic perennial bearing tall, dense, upright spikes of indigo-blue flowers during early and mid-summer. The narrow, softly hairy, mid-green leaves are scalloped at the edges. Provides strong contrast for silver-leaved plants in a herbaceous border. 'Blauhugel' and 'Tänzerin' are other recommended cultivars.

CULTIVATION *Grow in well-drained, fertile soil, in sun. Tolerates drought. Cut back after the first flush of flowers to encourage a later set of blooms.*

☼ ◊ Z5-9 H9-1 ‡28in (70cm) ↔18in 45cm)

SALVIA ULIGINOSA

The bog sage is a graceful, upright perennial bearing spikes of clear blue flowers from late summer to mid-autumn. These are carried above lance-shaped, toothed, mid-green leaves, on branched stems. Good for moist borders; where not hardy, it can be container-grown in a cool conservatory.

CULTIVATION *Needs moist but well-drained, fertile soil or soil mix. Choose a sunny, sheltered position. Taller plants will need support.*

☼ ◊ Z8-10 H12-8 ‡6ft (2m) ↔36in (90cm)

SAMBUCUS NIGRA 'GUINCHO PURPLE'

This popular cultivar of the common elder is an upright shrub with dark green, divided leaves; these turn black-purple then red in autumn. In early summer, musk-scented, pink-tinged white flowers are borne in large, flattened clusters, followed by small black fruits. Elders are ideal in new gardens, because they establish themselves in a short space of time.

CULTIVATION *Grow in any fertile soil, in sun or partial shade. For the best foliage effect, either cut all stems to the ground in winter or prune out old stems and reduce length of young shoots by half.*

☼ ◑ ◊ Z6-8 H8-6   ↕↔ 20ft (6m)

SANTOLINA CHAMAECYPARISSUS

Lavender cotton is a rounded, evergreen shrub grown for its foliage. The slender, white-woolly stems are densely covered with narrow, gray-white, finely cut leaves. The small yellow flowerheads in summer can be removed to enhance the foliage effect. Suitable for a mixed border or as low, informal hedging. For a dwarf version, look for var. *nana*.

CULTIVATION *Grow in well drained, poor to moderately fertile soil, in full sun. Remove old flowerheads, and trim long shoots in autumn. Cut old, straggly plants back hard each spring.*

☼ ◊ Z6-9 H9-4   ↕ 20in (50cm) ↔ 3ft (1m)

SANTOLINA ROSMARINIFOLIA 'PRIMROSE GEM'

A dense, rounded, evergreen shrub, similar to *S. chamaecyparissus* (see facing page, below), but with bright green leaves and paler flowers. These are borne at the tips of slender stems in mid-summer, above the finely cut aromatic leaves. Useful for filling gaps in a sunny border.

CULTIVATION *Grow in well drained, poor to moderately fertile soil, in full sun. In autumn, remove old flower-heads and prune long shoots. Cut old, straggly plants back hard each spring.*

☼ ◊ Z6-9 H9-6 ‡24in (60cm) ↔3ft (1m)

SAPONARIA OCYMOIDES

Tumbling Ted is a sprawling, mat-forming perennial that carries a profusion of tiny pink flowers in summer. The hairy, bright green leaves are small and oval. Excellent as part of a dry bank, scree, or rock garden, although it may swamp smaller plants. 'Rubra Compacta' is a neater version of this plant, with dark red flowers.

CULTIVATION *Grow in gritty, sharply drained soil, in full sun. Cut back hard after flowering to keep compact.*

☼ ◊ Z3-9 H9-1 ‡3in (8cm) ↔18in (45cm) or more

SAPONARIA × *OLIVANA*

A cushion-forming, summer-flowering perennial that produces abundant clusters of small, pale pink flowers around the edge of a mound of small and narrow, mid-green leaves. Good for rock gardens, scree slopes, and dry banks.

CULTIVATION *Grow in sharply drained soil, in a sunny site. Topdress the soil around the plant with grit or gravel.*

☼ ◊ Z6-8 H8-1 ‡2in (5cm) ↔6in (15cm)

SARCOCOCCA CONFUSA

Christmas box is a dense, evergreen shrub, giving an unparalleled winter fragrance. Clusters of small white flowers appear in mid-winter, followed by small, glossy black fruits. The tiny, oval leaves are glossy and dark green. Excellent as a low hedge near a door or entrance. Tolerates atmospheric pollution, dry shade, and neglect.

CULTIVATION *Grow in moist but well-drained, fertile, organic soil. Site in deep or semi-shade with protection from wind. Remove dead and damaged growth each year in spring.*

☼◑ ◊ Z6-9 H9-6 ‡6ft (2m) ↔3ft (1m)

SARCOCOCCA HOOKERIANA VAR. *DIGYNA*

This perfumed, evergreen shrub is very similar to *S. confusa* (see facing page, below), but with a more compact and spreading habit. The tiny, fragrant white flowers, which are followed by small, black or blue-black fruits, have pink anthers; they are borne amid glossy leaves, more slender and pointed than those of *S. hookeriana*, in winter. The flowers are good for cutting.

CULTIVATION *Grow in moist but well-drained, fertile, organic soil, in shade. Dig up spreading roots in spring to confine to its allotted space.*

 ☼ ☼ ◑ 7.6-9 H9-6 ‡5ft (1.5m) ↔6ft (2m)

SARRACENIA FLAVA

Yellow pitcher plant is a carnivorous perennial bearing nodding yellow flowers in spring. Some leaves are modified into large, upright, nectar-secreting, insect-catching pitchers. These are yellow-green and red-marked, with round mouths and hooded tops. Where not hardy, grow in a cool greenhouse or conservatory.

CULTIVATION *Grow in wet, rich, acidic soil or soil mix, in sun. Irrigate freely with lime-free water, but keep slightly drier in winter.*

☼ ◑◑ Z7-10 H12-7 ‡20–39in (50–100cm) ↔to 3ft (1m)

SAXIFRAGA 'JENKINSIAE'

This neat and slow-growing, evergreen perennial forms very dense cushions of gray-green foliage. It produces an abundance of solitary, cup-shaped, pale pink flowers with dark centers in early spring, on short, slender red stems. Good for rock gardens or troughs.

CULTIVATION *Best in moist but sharply drained, moderately fertile, neutral to alkaline soil, in full sun. Provide shade from the hottest summer sun.*

☼ ◊ Z6-7 H7-6 ‡2in (5cm) ↔8in (20cm)

SAXIFRAGA 'SOUTHSIDE SEEDLING'

A mat-forming, evergreen perennial that is suitable for a rock garden. Open sprays of small, cup-shaped white flowers, spotted heavily with red, are borne in late spring and early summer. The oblong to spoon-shaped, pale green leaves form large rosettes close to the soil level.

CULTIVATION *Grow in very sharply drained, moderately fertile, alkaline soil. Choose a position in full sun.*

☼ ◊ Z4-6 H6-1 ‡12in (30cm) ↔8in (20cm)

SCABIOSA CAUCASICA 'CLIVE GREAVES'

This delicate, perennial scabious, with solitary, lavender-blue flower-heads, is ideal for a cottage garden. The blooms have pincushion-like centers and are borne above the clumps of gray-green leaves during mid- to late summer. The flowerheads cut well for indoor arrangements

CULTIVATION *Grow in well-drained, moderately fertile, neutral to slightly alkaline soil, in full sun. Deadhead to prolong flowering.*

☼ ◊ Z4-9 H9-1   ↕↔ 24in (60cm)

SCABIOSA CAUCASICA 'MISS WILLMOTT'

A clump-forming perennial that is very similar to 'Clive Greaves' (above), but with white flowerheads. These are borne in mid- to late summer and are good for cutting. The lance-shaped leaves are gray-green and arranged around the base of the plant. Appropriate for a cottage garden.

CULTIVATION *Grow in well-drained, moderately fertile, neutral to slightly alkaline soil, in full sun. Deadhead to prolong flowering.*

☼ ◊ Z4-9 H9-1 ↕36in (90cm) ↔24in (60cm)

SCHIZOSTYLIS COCCINEA 'MAJOR'

A vigorous, robust, clump-forming perennial bearing gladiolus-like spikes of large red flowers. These appear in late summer on stiff and upright stems above the narrow, almost floppy, mid-green leaves. Good in sheltered spots, for a border front, or above water level in a waterside planting. 'Jennifer' is very similar, with pink flowers.

CULTIVATION *Grow in moist but well-drained, fertile soil, with a site in full sun. Plants rapidly become congested but are easily lifted and divided every few years in spring.*

☼ ◑ Z7-9 H9-7 ‡24in (60cm) ↔12in (30cm)

SCHIZOSTYLIS COCCINEA 'SUNRISE'

This clump-forming, vigorous perennial has the same general appearance, demands, and usage as 'Major' (above), but with upright spikes of salmon-pink flowers that open in autumn. The long leaves are sword-shaped and ribbed. When cut, the flowers last well in water.

CULTIVATION *Best in moist but well-drained, fertile soil, in sun. Naturally forms congested clumps, but these are easily lifted and divided in spring.*

☼ ◑ Z7-9 H9-7 ‡24in (60cm) ↔12in (30cm)

SCILLA BIFOLIA

A small, bulbous perennial bearing early-spring flowers, this naturalizes well under trees and shrubs or in grass. The slightly one-sided spikes of several star-shaped, blue to purple-blue flowers are carried above the clumps of narrow, basal leaves.

CULTIVATION *Grow in well-drained, moderately fertile, organic soil, in full sun or partial shade.*

☼ ◊ Z3-8 H8-1 ‡6in (15cm) ↔2in (5cm)

SCILLA MISCHTSCHENKOANA 'TUBERGENIANA'

This dwarf, bulbous perennial has slightly earlier flowers than *S. bifolia* (above) that are silvery blue with darker stripes. They are grouped together in elongating spikes, appearing at the same time as the semi-upright, narrow, mid-green leaves. Naturalizes in open grass. Also known as *S. tubergeniana*.

CULTIVATION *Grow in well-drained, moderately fertile soil that is rich in well-rotted organic matter, in full sun.*

☼ ◊ Z6-9 H9-6 ‡6in (15cm) ↔2in (5cm)

SEDUM KAMTSCHATICUM 'VARIEGATUM'

This clump-forming, semi-evergreen perennial has eye-catching, fleshy leaves, mid-green with pink tints and cream margins. During late summer, these contrast nicely with flat-topped clusters of small, star-shaped, yellow flowers that age to crimson later in the season. Suitable for rock gardens and borders.

CULTIVATION *Grow in well-drained, gritty, fertile soil. Choose a site in full sun, but will tolerate light shade.*

☼ ◊ Z4-9 H9-5 ‡4in (10cm) ↔10in (25cm)

SEDUM 'RUBY GLOW'

This low-growing perennial is an ideal choice for softening the front of a mixed border. It bears masses of small, star-shaped, ruby red flowers from mid-summer to early autumn above clumps of fleshy, green-purple leaves. The nectar-rich flowers attract bees, butterflies, and other beneficial insects

CULTIVATION *Grow in well-drained, fertile soil that has adequate moisture in summer. Position in full sun.*

☼ ◊ Z5-9 H9-5 ‡10in (25cm) ↔18in (45cm)

SEDUM SPATHULIFOLIUM 'CAPE BLANCO'

A vigorous, evergreen perennial that forms a mat of silvery green foliage, often tinted bronze-purple, with a heavy bloom of white powder over the innermost leaves. Small clusters of star-shaped, bright yellow flowers are borne just above the leaves in summer. A very attractive addition to a trough or raised bed.

CULTIVATION *Grow in well-drained, moderately fertile, gritty soil. Position in full sun, but tolerates light shade.*

☼ ◊ Z5-9 H9-5 ‡4in (10cm) ↔24in (60cm)

SEDUM SPATHULIFOLIUM 'PURPUREUM'

This fast-growing, summer-flowering perennial forms tight, evergreen mats of purple-leaved rosettes; the central leaves are covered with a thick, silvery bloom. Flat clusters of small, star-shaped, bright yellow flowers appear throughout summer. Suitable for a rock garden or the front of a sunny, well-drained border.

CULTIVATION *Grow in gritty, moderately fertile soil with good drainage, in sun or partial shade. Trim occasionally to prevent encroachment on other plants.*

☼☀ ◊ Z5-9 H9-5 ‡4in (10cm) ↔24in (60cm)

SEDUM SPECTABILE 'BRILLIANT'

This cultivar of *S. spectabile*, the ice plant, is a clump-forming, deciduous perennial with brilliant pink flowerheads, excellent for the front of a border. The small, star-shaped flowers, packed into dense, flat clusters on fleshy stems, appear in late summer above the succulent, gray-green leaves. The flowerheads are attractive to bees and butterflies and dry well on or off the plant.

CULTIVATION *Grow in well-drained, fertile soil with adequate moisture during summer, in full sun.*

☀ ◊ Z4-9 H9-1   ↔ 18in (45cm)

SEDUM SPURIUM 'SCHORBUSER BLUT'

This vigorous, evergreen perennial forms mats of succulent, mid-green leaves that become purple-tinted when mature. Rounded clusters of star-shaped, deep pink flowers are borne during late summer. Suitable for a rock garden.

CULTIVATION *Grow in well-drained, moderately fertile, neutral to slightly alkaline soil, in full sun. Tolerates light shade. To improve flowering, divide the clumps or mats every 3 or 4 years.*

☀☀ ◊ Z4-9 H9-1 ↕4in (10cm) ↔24in (60cm)

SEDUM TELEPHIUM
SUBSP. *MAXIMUM* 'ATROPURPUREUM'

This clump-forming, deciduous perennial is valued for its very dark purple foliage that contrasts well with other plants. During summer and early autumn, attractive pink flowers with orange-red centers are clustered above the oval, slightly scalloped leaves.

CULTIVATION *Grow in well drained, moderately fertile, neutral to slightly alkaline soil, in full sun. Divide clumps every 3 or 4 years to improve flowering.*

☼ ◊ Z4-9 H9-1   ‡18–24in (45–60cm)
↔12in (30cm)

SELAGINELLA KRAUSSIANA

Trailing spikemoss is a mat-forming, evergreen perennial with a mosslike appearance. The trailing stems are clothed in tiny, scalelike, bright green leaves. An excellent foliage plant that can easily be grown in a conservatory in coldclimates. Also recommended are 'Variegata', with cream-splashed leaves, and 'Brownii', which forms neat mounds, 6in (15cm) across.

CULTIVATION *Grow in moist, peaty soil, in semi-shade. Keep just moist in winter. Needs a humid atmosphere under glass. Minimum temperature 35°F (2°C).*

☼ ◊ H12-9   ‡1in (2.5cm) ↔indefinite

SEMPERVIVUM ARACHNOIDEUM

The cobweb houseleek is a mat-forming, evergreen succulent, so named because the foliage is webbed with white hairs. The small, fleshy, mid-green to red leaves are arranged in tight rosettes. In summer, flat clusters of star-shaped, reddish pink flowers appear on leafy stems. Suitable for growing in a scree bed, wall crevice, or trough.

CULTIVATION *Grow in gritty, sharply drained, poor to moderately fertile soil. Choose a position in full sun.*

☼ ◊ Z5-8 H8-5 ‡3in (8cm) ↔12in (30cm)

SEMPERVIVUM CILIOSUM

A mat-forming, evergreen succulent carrying very hairy, dense rosettes of incurved, lance-shaped, gray-green leaves. It bears flat, compact heads of star-shaped, greenish yellow flowers throughout summer. The rosettes of leaves die after flowering but are rapidly replaced. Best in an alpine house in areas prone to very wet winters.

CULTIVATION *Grow in gritty, sharply drained, poor to moderately fertile soil, in sun. Tolerates drought conditions, but dislikes excessive winter moisture or climates that are warm and humid.*

☼ ◊ Z7-10 H12-7 ‡3in (8cm) ↔12in (30cm)

SEMPERVIVUM TECTORUM

The common hen and chicks is a vigorous, mat-forming, evergreen succulent with large, open rosettes of thick, oval, bristle-tipped, blue-green leaves, often suffused red-purple. In summer, dense clusters of star-shaped, red-purple flowers appear on upright, hairy stems. Very attractive growing on old roof tiles or among terracotta fragments.

CULTIVATION *Grow in gritty, sharply drained, poor to moderately fertile soil. Choose a site in full sun.*

☼ ◊ Z4-8 H8-1 ‡6in (15cm) ↔20in (50cm)

SENECIO CINERARIA 'SILVER DUST'

This mound-forming, moderately fast-growing, evergreen shrub is usually grown as an annual for its attractive, lacy foliage. The almost white leaves are deeply cut and densely hairy. Plants kept into the second season bear loose heads of coarse, daisylike, mustard-yellow flowerheads in mid-summer; many gardeners prefer to remove them. Ideal for creating massed foliage effects in summer bedding.

CULTIVATION *Grow in well-drained, fertile soil, in sun. Nip out flower buds if desired, or deadhead regularly.*

☼ ◊ Z7-10 H12-8 ‡↔ 12in (30cm)

SILENE SCHAFTA

A clump-forming, spreading, semi-evergreen perennial with floppy stems bearing small, bright green leaves. Profuse sprays of long-tubed, deep magenta flowers with notched petals are borne from late summer to autumn. Suitable for a raised bed or rock garden.

CULTIVATION *Grow in well-drained, neutral to slightly alkaline soil, in full sun or light dappled shade.*

☀️◐ ◊ Z5-7 H7-4 ↕↔12in (30cm)

SKIMMIA × *CONFUSA* 'KEW GREEN' (MALE)

A compact, dome-shaped, evergreen shrub carrying aromatic, pointed, mid-green leaves. Conical spikes of fragrant, creamy white flowers open in spring. There are no berries, but it will pollinate female skimmias if they are planted nearby. Good in a shrub border or woodland garden.

CULTIVATION *Grow in moist but well-drained, moderately fertile, organic soil. Tolerates full sun to deep shade, atmospheric pollution, and neglect. Requires little or no pruning.*

☀️◐ ◊ Z6-9 H9-6 ↕1½–10ft (0.5–3m)
↔5ft (1.5m)

SKIMMIA JAPONICA
'RUBELLA' (MALE)

This tough, dome-shaped, evergreen shrub bears dark red flower buds in autumn and winter, opening in spring as fragrant heads of white flowers. The oval leaves have red rims. No berries are produced, but it will pollinate female skimmias nearby. (Where space permits only one plant, 'Robert Fortune' produces both flowers and berries.) Tolerates pollution and coastal conditions.

CULTIVATION *Grow in moist, fertile, neutral to slightly acidic soil, in partial or full shade. Cut back any shoots that spoil the shape.*

:☼: ◊ Z7-9 H9-7   ‡↔ to 20ft (6m)

SMILACINA RACEMOSA

False spikenard is a clump-forming perennial bearing dense, feathery spikes of creamy white, often green-tinged flowers in mid- to late spring. These are occasionally followed by red berries. The lance-shaped, pale green, luxuriant leaves turn yellow in autumn. A beautiful specimen for a woodland garden or shady border.

CULTIVATION *Grow in moist, neutral to acidic, fertile, organic soil in light or deep shade.*

:☼: ◊ Z4-9 H9-1   ‡ to 36in (90cm)
                     ↔24in (60cm)

SOLANUM CRISPUM 'GLASNEVIN'

This long-flowering Chilean potato tree is a fast-growing, scrambling, woody-stemmed, evergreen climber. Fragrant, deep purple-blue flowers, borne in clusters at the tips of the stems during summer and autumn, are followed by small, yellow-white fruits. The leaves are oval and dark green. Grow on a warm, sunny wall where marginally hardy.

CULTIVATION *Grow in any moist but well-drained, moderately fertile soil, in full sun or semi-shade. Cut back weak and badly placed growth in spring. Tie to a support as growth proceeds.*

☼☀ ◊◊ Z9-10 H12-1   ↕20ft (6m)

SOLANUM JASMINOIDES 'ALBUM'

This white-flowered potato vine is a scrambling, woody-stemmed, semi-evergreen climber. It produces broad clusters of fragrant, star-shaped, milk-white flowers, with prominent, lemon-yellow anthers, from summer into autumn. They are followed by black fruits. The leaves are mid- to dark green and oval.

CULTIVATION *Grow in any moist but well-drained, fertile soil, in full sun or semi-shade. Thin out shoots in spring. The climbing stems need support.*

☼☀ ◊◊ Z8-10 H12-1   ↕20ft (6m)

SOLIDAGO 'GOLDENMOSA'

This compact, vigorous goldenrod
is a bushy perennial topped with
bright golden yellow flowerheads in
late summer and early autumn. The
leaves are wrinkled and mid-green.
Valuable in a wild garden or for late
summer color; the flowers are good
for cutting. Note: goldenrods do not
cause hayfever. Other plants
blooming at the same time, notably
ragweeds, are the culprits.

CULTIVATION *Grow in well-drained,
poor to moderately fertile, preferably
sandy soil, in full sun. Remove flowered
stems to prevent self-seeding.*

☼ ◊ Z5-9 H9-5 ‡30in (75cm) ↔18in (45cm)

SOLLYA HETEROPHYLLA

The bluebell creeper is a twining,
evergreen climber that must be
grown in a cool greenhouse in cold
climates. Clusters of nodding, bell-
shaped blue flowers, followed by
blue berries, are borne over a long
period from early summer to
autumn. The leaves are lance-shaped
and deep green. Train over an arch
or pergola, or into a host shrub.

CULTIVATION *Grow in moist but well-
drained, moderately fertile, organic soil
or soil mix, in a sunny, sheltered site.
Water sparingly during winter.
Minimum temperature 35°F (2°C).*

☼ ◊◊ H12-1 ‡5–6ft (1.5–2m)

SORBUS ARIA 'LUTESCENS'

This compact whitebeam is a broadly columnar, deciduous tree, bearing oval and toothed, silvery gray foliage that turns russet and gold in autumn. Clusters of white flowers appear in late spring, followed by brown-speckled, dark red berries. It makes a beautiful specimen tree, tolerating a wide range of conditions. 'Majestica' is similar but taller, with larger leaves.

CULTIVATION *Grow in moist but well-drained, fertile soil, in sun. Tolerates heavy clay soils, semi-shade, urban pollution, and exposed conditions. Remove any dead wood in summer.*

☀☼ ◊◊ Z6-8 H8-6 ‡30ft (10m) ↔25ft (8m)

SORBUS HUPEHENSIS VAR. *OBTUSA*

This variety of the Hubei mountain ash is an open and spreading tree that gives a fine display of autumn color. Broad clusters of white flowers in late spring are followed by round white berries; these ripen to dark pink later in the season. The blue-green leaves, divided into many leaflets, turn scarlet before they fall.

CULTIVATION *Grow in any moist but well-drained soil, preferably in full sun, but tolerates light shade. Remove any dead or diseased wood in summer.*

☀☼ ◊◊ Z6-8 H8-6 ‡↔ 25ft (8m)

SORBUS 'JOSEPH ROCK'

This broadly columnar, upright, deciduous tree has bright green leaves that are divided into many sharply toothed leaflets. These color attractively to orange, red, and purple in autumn. In late spring, white flowers appear in broad clusters, followed by round, pale yellow berries that ripen to orange-yellow.

CULTIVATION *Grow in moist but well-drained, fertile soil, in sun. Very prone to fireblight, the main sign of which is blackened leaves; affected growth must be pruned back in summer to at least 24in (60cm) below the diseased area.*

☼ ◊◊ Z7-8 H8-7 ‡30ft (10m) ↔22ft (7m)

SORBUS REDUCTA

A deciduous shrub that forms a low thicket of upright branches. Much-valued for its ornamental, dark green foliage that turns a rich red in autumn. Small, open clusters of white flowers appear in late spring, followed by white, crimson-flushed berries. Tolerates pollution.

CULTIVATION *Grow in well-drained, moderately fertile soil, in an open, sunny site. To thin congested plants, remove shoots that arise from the base while they are still young and soft.*

☼ ◊ Z5-8 H8-4 ‡5ft (1.5m) ↔6ft (2m)

SORBUS VILMORINII

A spreading shrub or small tree with elegant, arching branches bearing dark green leaves divided into many leaflets. The deciduous foliage gives a lovely display in autumn, turning orange- or bronze-red. Clusters of white flowers appear in late spring and early summer, followed later in the season by dark red berries that age to pink then white.

CULTIVATION *Grow in well-drained, moderately fertile, organic soil, in full sun or dappled shade. Remove any dead or diseased wood in summer.*

☀ ◑ ◊ Z6-8 H8-6   ↕↔ 15ft (5m)

SPARTIUM JUNCEUM

Spanish broom is an upright shrub with slender, dark green shoots which are almost leafless. A profusion of fragrant, pealike, rich golden yellow flowers appear at the end of the stems from early summer to early autumn. These are followed by flattened, dark brown seed pods. Particularly useful on poor soils.

CULTIVATION *Grow in any but water-logged soil, in a warm, sunny site. When young, cut back main stems by half each spring to promote a bushy habit. Once established, trim every few years, but do not cut into old wood.*

☀ ◊◊ Z8-10 H12-8 ↕6in (15cm) ↔8in (20cm)

SPIRAEA JAPONICA
'ANTHONY WATERER'

A compact, deciduous shrub that
makes a good informal flowering
hedge. The lance-shaped, dark
green leaves, usually margined with
creamy white, are red when young.
Dense heads of tiny pink flowers are
borne amid the foliage in mid- to
late summer.

CULTIVATION *Grow in any well-drained,
fairly fertile soil that does not dry out,
in full sun. On planting, cut back stems
to leave a framework 6in (15cm) high;
prune back close to this every year in
spring. Deadhead after flowering.*

☼ ◊ Z4-9 H9-1   ↕↔ to 5ft (1.5m)

SPIRAEA JAPONICA
'GOLDFLAME'

This compact, deciduous, flowering
shrub bears pretty, bright yellow
leaves that are bronze-red when
young. Dense, flattened heads of
tiny, dark pink flowers appear at the
tips of slightly arching stems during
mid- and late summer. Ideal for a
rock garden. 'Nana' is even smaller,
to 18in (45cm) tall.

CULTIVATION *Grow in well-drained soil
that does not dry out completely, in full
sun. On planting, cut back stems to a
framework 6in (15cm) high; prune
back close to this each year in spring.
Deadhead after flowering.*

☼ ◊ Z4-9 H9-1   ↕↔ 30in (75cm)

SPIRAEA NIPPONICA 'SNOWMOUND'

This fast-growing and spreading, deciduous shrub has arching, reddish green stems. The dense clusters of small white flowers in mid-summer make an invaluable contribution to any shrub border. The rounded leaves are bright green when young, darkening as they age.

CULTIVATION *Grow in any moderately fertile soil that does not dry out too much during the growing season, in full sun. Cut back flowered stems in autumn, and remove any weak growth.*

☼ ◊ Z4-8 H8-1 ↕↔ 4ft (1.2m)

SPIRAEA × *VANHOUTTEI*

Bridal wreath is a fast-growing, deciduous shrub, more compact in habit than *S. nipponica* 'Snowmound' (above), but with similar mounds of white flowers during early summer. The diamond-shaped leaves are dark green above with blue-green under-sides. Grow as an informal hedge or in a mixed border.

CULTIVATION *Grow in any well-drained, fertile soil that does not dry out, in sun. In autumn, cut back flowered stems, removing any weak or damaged growth.*

☼ ◊ Z4-8 H8-1 ↕6ft (2m) ↔5ft (1.5m)

STACHYURUS PRAECOX

This spreading, deciduous shrub
bears oval, mid-green leaves on
arching, red-purple shoots. Hanging
spikes of tiny, bell-shaped, pale
yellow-green flowers appear on the
bare stems in late winter and early
spring. Suitable for a shrub border,
and lovely in a woodland garden.

CULTIVATION *Grow in moist but well-
drained, organic, fertile, neutral to
acidic soil. Prefers partial shade but
tolerates full sun if soil is kept reliably
moist. Regular pruning is unnecessary.*

☼ ◑ ◌◑ Z7-9 H9-7 ‡3–12ft (1–4m)
↔10ft (3m)

STIPA GIGANTEA

Golden oats is a fluffy, evergreen,
perennial grass forming dense tufts
of narrow, mid-green leaves. In
summer, these are topped by silvery
to purplish green flowerheads that
turn gold when mature and persist
well into winter. Makes an imposing
feature at the back of a border.

CULTIVATION *Grow in well-drained,
fertile soil, in full sun. Remove dead
leaves and flowerheads in early spring.*

☼ ◌ Z8-10 H12-8 ‡8ft (2.5m) ↔4ft (1.2m)

STYRAX JAPONICUS

Japanese snowbell is a gracefully spreading, deciduous tree bearing hanging clusters of fragrant, bell-shaped, dainty white flowers that are often tinged with pink. These appear during mid- to late spring amid oval, rich green leaves that turn yellow or red in autumn. Ideal for a woodland garden.

CULTIVATION *Grow in moist but well-drained, neutral to acidic soil, in full sun with shelter from cold, drying winds. Tolerates dappled shade. Allow to develop naturally without pruning.*

☼☀ ◊◊ Z6-8 H8-6 ‡30ft (10m) ↔25ft (8m)

STYRAX OBASSIA

The fragrant snowbell is a broadly columnar, deciduous tree bearing beautifully rounded, dark green leaves that turn yellow in autumn. Fragrant, bell-shaped white flowers are produced in long, spreading clusters in mid- and late spring.

CULTIVATION *Grow in moist but well-drained, fertile, organic, neutral to acid soil, in full sun or partial shade. Shelter from cold, drying winds. Dislikes pruning; leave to develop naturally.*

☼☀ ◊◊ Z6-8 H8-6 ‡40ft (12m) ↔22ft (7m)

SYRINGA 505

SYMPHYTUM ×
UPLANDICUM
'VARIEGATUM'

This upright, clump-forming, bristly
perennial has large, lance-shaped,
mid-green leaves with broad cream
margins. Drooping clusters of pink-
blue buds open to blue-purple
flowers from late spring to late
summer. Best in a wild garden or
shady border. Less invasive than
green-leaved types.

CULTIVATION *Grow in any moist soil, in*
sun or partial shade. For the best foliage
effect, remove flowering stems before
they bloom. Liable to form plain green
leaves if grown in poor or infertile soil.

☼ ◑ ◊ Z3-9 H9-1 ‡36in (90cm) ↔24in (60cm)

SYRINGA MEYERI
'PALIBIN'

This compact, slow-growing,
deciduous shrub with a rounded
shape is much valued for its
abundant clusters of fragrant,
lavender-pink flowers in spring.
The leaves are dark green and oval.
Makes a bold contribution to any
shrub border.
Sometimes seen as *S. palibiniana*.

CULTIVATION *Grow in deep, moist but*
well-drained, fertile, preferably alkaline
soil, in full sun. Deadhead for the first
few years until established. Prune out
weak and damaged growth in winter.

☼ ◊◊ Z4-7 H7-1 ‡6ft (2m) ↔5ft (1.5m)

SYRINGA PUBESCENS
SUBSP. *MICROPHYLLA*
'SUPERBA'

This upright to spreading, conical, deciduous shrub bears spikes of fragrant, rose-pink flowers at the tips of slender branches. First appearing in spring, they continue to open at irregular intervals until autumn. The oval, mid-green leaves are red-green when young. Makes a good screen or informal hedge. 'Miss Kim' is a smaller, more compact cultivar.

CULTIVATION *Grow in moist but well-drained, fertile, organic, neutral to alkaline soil, in full sun. Prune out any weak or damaged growth in winter.*

☼ ◐◊ Z5-8 H8-4   ‡↔to 20ft (6m)

SYRINGA VULGARIS
'CHARLES JOLY'

This dark-purple-flowered form of common lilac is a spreading shrub or small tree. Very fragrant, double flowers appear during spring in dense, conical clusters. The deciduous leaves are heart-shaped to oval and dark green. Use as a backdrop in a shrub or mixed border.

CULTIVATION *Grow in moist but well-drained, fertile, organic, neutral to alkaline soil, in full sun. Young shrubs require minimal pruning; old, lanky stems can be cut back hard in winter.*

☼ ◐◊ Z4-8 H8-1   ‡↔22ft (7m)

SYRINGA VULGARIS 'KATHERINE HAVEMEYER'

A spreading lilac, forming a large shrub or small tree, producing dense clusters of very fragrant, double, lavender-blue flowers. These open from purple buds in spring. The deciduous, mid-green leaves are heart shaped. 'Madame Antoine Buchner' is a very similar recommended lilac with slightly pinker flowers.

CULTIVATION *Grow in moist but well-drained, fertile, neutral to alkaline, organic soil in sun. Mulch regularly. Little pruning is necessary, but it tolerates hard pruning to renovate it.*

☼ ◊◊ Z4 8 H8-1   ↔ 22ft (7m)

SYRINGA VULGARIS 'MADAME LEMOINE'

This lilac is very similar in form to 'Katherine Havemeyer' (above) but has compact spikes of large, very fragrant, double white flowers. These are borne in late spring and early summer amid the deciduous, heart-shaped to oval, mid-green leaves. 'Vestale' is another recommended white lilac, with single flowers.

CULTIVATION *Grow in deep, moist but well-drained, fertile, neutral to alkaline, organic soil, in sun. Do not prune young plants, but older shrubs can be cut back hard in winter to renovate.*

☼ ◊◊ Z4-8 H8-1   ↔ 22ft (7m)

TAMARIX TETRANDRA

This large, arching shrub, with feathery foliage on purple-brown shoots, bears plumes of light pink flowers in mid- to late spring. The leaves are reduced to tiny, needle-like scales. Particularly useful on light, sandy soils; in mild coastal gardens, it makes a good windbreak or hedge. For a similar shrub that flowers in late summer, look for *T. ramossissima* 'Rubra' (Z5-9 H9-4).

CULTIVATION *Grow in well-drained soil in full sun. Cut back young plants by almost half after planting. Prune each year after flowering, or the shrub may become top-heavy and unstable.*

☼ ◊ Z5-9 H9-5 ↕↔ 10ft (3m)

TANACETUM COCCINEUM 'BRENDA'

A bushy, herbaceous perennial, grown for its daisylike, magenta-pink, yellow-centerd flowerheads in early summer borne on upright stems above aromatic, finely divided, gray-green foliage. The cut flowers last well in water. 'James Kelway' is very similar, while 'Eileen May Robinson' has pale pink flowers.

CULTIVATION *Grow in well-drained, fertile, neutral to slightly acidic soil, in an open, sunny site. Cut back after the first flush of flowers to encourage a second flowering later in the season.*

☼ ◊ Z5-9 H9-4 ↕28–32in (70–80cm) ↔18in (45cm)

TAXUS BACCATA

English yew is a slow-growing, broadly conical, evergreen conifer. The needlelike, dark green leaves are arranged in two ranks along the shoots. Male plants bear yellow cones in spring, and female plants produce cup-shaped, fleshy, bright red fruits in autumn. Excellent as a dense hedge and as a backdrop to colorful plants. All parts are toxic.

CULTIVATION *Grow in any well-drained, fertile soil, in sun to deep shade. Tolerates alkaline or acidic soils. Plant both sexes togethe, for berries. Trim or cut back to renovate in summer or early autumn.*

☼ ◐ ◊ Z7-8 H8-5 ‡70ft (20m) ↔30ft (10m)

TAXUS BACCATA 'DOVASTONII AUREA' (FEMALE)

This slow-growing, evergreen conifer has wide-spreading, horizontally tiered branches that weep at the tips. It is smaller than the English yew (above) and has yellow-margined to golden yellow foliage. Fleshy, bright red fruits appear in autumn. All parts of this plant are poisonous if eaten.

CULTIVATION *Grow in any well-drained, fertile soil, in sun or deep shade. Tolerates alkaline or acidic conditions. Plant close to male yews for a reliable display of autumn berries. Trim or cut back to renovate in summer or early autumn.*

☼ ◐ ◊ Z7-8 H8-5 ‡15ft (5m) ↔6ft (2m)

TAXUS BACCATA
'FASTIGIATA' (FEMALE)

Irish yew is a dense, strongly upright, evergreen conifer that becomes columnar with age. The dark green leaves are not two-ranked like other yews but stand out all around the shoots. All are female, bearing fleshy, berrylike, bright red fruits in late summer. All parts are toxic if eaten.

CULTIVATION *Grow in any reliably moist soil but tolerates most conditions including very dry, alkaline soils, in full sun or deep shade. Plant with male yews for a reliable crop of berries. Trim or cut back to renovate, in summer or early autumn, if necessary.*

☼ ◐ ◊◊ Z7-8 H8-5 ‡30ft (10m) ↔12ft (4m)

THALICTRUM DELAVAYI
'HEWITT'S DOUBLE'

An upright, clump-forming perennial, more floriferous than *T. delavayi*, that produces upright sprays of long-lasting, pomponlike, rich mauve flowers from mid-summer to early autumn. Finely divided, mid-green leaves are carried on slender stems shaded dark purple. An excellent foil in a herbaceous border to plants with bolder leaves and flowers.

CULTIVATION *Grow in moist but well-drained, organic soil, in sun or light shade. Divide clumps and replant every few years to maintain vigor.*

☼ ◐ ◊◊ Z5-9 H9-4 ‡4ft (1.2m) ↔24in (60cm)

THALICTRUM FLAVUM SUBSP. *GLAUCUM*

This subspecies of yellow meadow rue is a summer-flowering, clump-forming perennial that bears large, upright heads of fragrant, sulfur-yellow flowers. These appear above mid-green, divided leaves. Good at the margins of a woodland.

CULTIVATION *Best in moist, organic soil in partial shade. Tolerates sun and dry soil. Flower stems may need staking.*

☼-◐ ◊◊ Z6-9 H9-6 ‡3ft (1m) ↔24in (60cm)

THUJA OCCIDENTALIS 'HOLMSTRUP'

This shrublike form of eastern arborvitae is a slow-growing conifer with a conical shape. The dense, mid-green leaves are apple-scented and arranged in vertical sprays. Small oval cones appear amid the foliage. Plant alone as a specimen tree or use as a hedge.

CULTIVATION *Grow in deep, moist but well-drained soil in full sun. Shelter from cold, drying winds. Trim as necessary in spring and late summer.*

☼ ◊◊ Z2-7 H7-1 ‡to 12ft (4m) ↔10–15ft (3–5m)

THUJA OCCIDENTALIS 'RHEINGOLD'

This bushy, spreading, slow-growing conifer is valued for its golden yellow foliage that is pink-tinted when young and turns bronze in winter. Small, oval cones are carried amid the billowing sprays of apple-scented, scalelike leaves. Good as a specimen tree.

CULTIVATION *Grow in deep, moist but well-drained soil, in a sheltered, sunny site. Trim in spring and late summer, but be careful not to spoil the form.*

☼ ◊◊ Z2-7 H7-1   ↕3–6ft (1–2m)
↔10–15ft (3–5m)

THUJA ORIENTALIS 'AUREA NANA'

This dwarf Oriental arborvitae is an oval-shaped conifer with fibrous, red-brown bark. The yellow-green foliage, which fades to bronze over winter, is arranged in flat, vertical sprays. Flask-shaped cones are borne amid the foliage. Good in a rock garden.

CULTIVATION *Grow in deep, moist but well-drained soil, in sun with shelter from cold, drying winds. Trim in spring and again in late summer as necessary.*

☼ ◊◊ Z6-9 H9-6   ↕↔ to 24in (60cm)

THUJA PLICATA 'STONEHAM GOLD'

This slow-growing, dwarf form of western red cedar is a conical conifer with fissured, red-brown bark and flattened, irregularly arranged sprays of bright gold, aromatic foliage; the tiny, scalelike leaves are very dark green within the bush. The cones are small and elliptic. Ideal for a rock garden.

CULTIVATION *Grow in deep, moist but well-drained soil, in full sun with shelter from cold, drying winds. Trim in spring and again in late summer.*

☼ ◊◊ Z6-8 H8-6   ↕↔ to 6ft (2m)

THUNBERGIA GRANDIFLORA

The blue trumpet vine is a vigorous, woody-stemmed, evergreen climber that can be grown as an annual in cold climates. Lavender- to violet-blue, sometimes white, trumpet-shaped flowers with yellow throats appear in hanging clusters during summer. The oval to heart-shaped, dark green leaves are softly hairy.

CULTIVATION *Grow in moist but well-drained, fertile soil or soil mix, in sun. Provide shade during the hottest part of the day. Give the climbing stems support. Minimum temperature 50°F (10°C).*

☼ ◊◊ H12-10   ↕15–30ft (5–10m)

THUNBERGIA MYSORENSIS

This spring-flowering, fast-growing, woody-stemmed climber bears hanging spikes of large yellow flowers with brownish red to purple tubes. The narrow, evergreen leaves are dark green with prominent veins. Must be grown in a warm conservatory or heated greenhouse in climates with cold winters.

CULTIVATION *Grow in moist but well-drained, fertile, organic soil or soil mix with shade from midday sun. Give the climbing stems support. Minimum temperature 59°F (15°C).*

☼ ◐◐ H12-10   ‡to 20ft (6m)

THYMUS × CITRIODORUS 'BERTRAM ANDERSON'

A low-growing, rounded, evergreen shrub carrying small, narrow, gray-green leaves strongly suffused with yellow. They are aromatic and can be used in cooking. Heads of pale lavender-pink flowers are borne above the foliage in summer. Lovely in an herb garden. Sometimes sold as 'Anderson's Gold'.

CULTIVATION *Best in well-drained, neutral to alkaline soil, in full sun. Trim after flowering, and remove sprigs for cooking as they are needed.*

☼ ◊ Z6-9 H9-6   ‡to 12in (30cm)
                       ↔to 10in (25cm)

THYMUS × *CITRIODORUS* 'SILVER QUEEN'

This rounded, evergreen shrub is similar to 'Bertram Anderson' (see facing page, below), but with silver-white foliage. Masses of oblong, lavender-pink flowerheads are borne throughout summer. Plant in an herb garden; the aromatic leaves can be used in cooking.

CULTIVATION *Grow in well-drained, neutral to alkaline soil, in full sun. Trim after flowering, and remove sprigs for cooking as needed.*

☀ ◊ Z6-9 H9-6   ↕to 12in (30cm) ↔to 10in (25cm)

THYMUS SERPYLLUM VAR. *COCCINEUS*

A mat-forming, evergreen subshrub with finely hairy, trailing stems bearing tiny, aromatic, mid-green leaves. Crimson-pink flowers are borne in congested whorls during summer. Suitable for planting in paving crevices, where the foliage will release its fragrance when stepped on. May also be seen as *T. praecox* 'Coccineus'.

CULTIVATION *Grow in well-drained, neutral to alkaline, gritty soil. Choose a position in full sun. Trim lightly after flowering to keep the plant neat.*

☀ ◊ Z4-9 H9-1 ↕10in (25cm) ↔18in (45cm)

TIARELLA CORDIFOLIA

This vigorous, summer-flowering, evergreen perennial is commonly known as foam flower and gets its name from the tiny, star-shaped, creamy white flowers. These are borne in a profusion of upright sprays above lobed, pale green leaves that turn bronze-red in autumn. Ideal as a groundcover in a woodland garden, as is the similar *T. wherryi* (Z5-9 H9-4).

CULTIVATION *Best in cool, moist, organic soil in deep or light shade. Tolerates a wide range of soil types.*

☀◑ ◑ Z3-7 H7-1 ‡4–12in (10–30cm)
↔to 12in (30cm)

TOLMIEA MENZIESII
'TAFF'S GOLD'

A spreading, clump-forming, semi-evergreen perennial carrying ivy-like, long-stalked, pale lime green leaves mottled with cream and pale yellow. An abundance of tiny, nodding, slightly scented, green and chocolate brown flowers appear in slender, upright spikes during late spring and early summer. Plant in groups to cover the ground in a woodland garden.

CULTIVATION *Grow in moist but well-drained, organic soil, in partial or deep shade. Sun will scorch the leaves.*

☀◑ ◑◑ Z6-9 H9-6 ‡12–24in (30–60cm)
↔3ft (1m)

TRACHELOSPERMUM JASMINOIDES

Star jasmine is an evergreen, woody-stemmed climber with attractive, oval, glossy, dark green leaves. The very fragrant flowers, creamy white aging to yellow, have five twisted petal lobes. They are borne during mid- to late summer, followed by long seed pods. Where marginally hardy, grow in the shelter of a warm wall with a deep mulch. The variegated-leaved form, 'Variegatum', (H10-1) is also recommended.

CULTIVATION *Grow in any well-drained, moderately fertile soil, in full sun or partial shade. Tie in young growth.*

☀️◑ ◊ Z9-10 H12-9　‡28ft (9m)

TRADESCANTIA X *ANDERSONIANA* 'J.C.WEGUELIN'

This tufted, clump-forming perennial bears large, pale blue flowers with three wide-open, triangular petals. These appear from early summer to early autumn in paired clusters at the tips of branching stems. The slightly fleshy, mid-green leaves are long, pointed, and arching. Effective in a mixed or herbaceous border.

CULTIVATION *Grow in moist, fertile soil, in sun or partial shade. Deadhead to encourage repeat flowering.*

☀️◑ ◊ Z5-9 H9-5 ‡24in (60cm) ↔18in (45cm)

TRADESCANTIA X *ANDERSONIANA* 'OSPREY'

This clump-forming perennial bears clusters of large white flowers on the tips of the upright stems from early summer to early autumn. Each flower has three triangular petals surrounded by two leaflike bracts. The mid-green leaves are narrow and often purple-tinted. A long-flowering plant for a mixed or herbaceous border. Lovely mixed with dark blue-flowered 'Isis'.

CULTIVATION *Grow in moist but well-drained, fertile soil in sun or partial shade. Deadhead to prevent self-seeding.*

☼☀ ◊◊ Z5-9 H9-4   ↕24in (60cm)
      ↔18in (45cm)

TRICYRTIS FORMOSANA

An upright, herbaceous perennial grown for its white, purple-spotted, star-shaped flowers on zig-zagging, softly hairy stems. These appear in early autumn above lance-shaped, dark green leaves that clasp the stems. An unusual plant for a shady border or open woodland garden.

CULTIVATION *Grow in moist. organic soil. Choose a sheltered site in deep or partial shade. Provide a deep winter mulch where there is unlikely to be deep snow cover.*

☼☀ ◊ Z6-9 H9-6   ↕to 32in (80cm)
      ↔18in (45cm)

TRILLIUM GRANDIFLORUM

Wake robin is a vigorous, clump-forming perennial grown for its large, three-petaled, pure white flowers that often fade to pink. These are carried during spring and summer on slender stems above a whorl of three large, dark green, almost circular leaves. Effective in the company of hostas. The cultivar 'Flore Pleno' has double flowers.

CULTIVATION *Grow in moist but well-drained, leafy, neutral to acidic soil, in deep or light shade. Provide an annual mulch of leaf mold in autumn.*

☀☀ ◊◊ Z5-8 H8-4   ↕16in (40cm)
↔12in (30cm)

TRILLIUM LUTEUM

An upright, clump-forming perennial valued for its sweet-scented, gold- or bronze-green flowers in spring. These are produced above a whorl of oval, pointed, mid-green leaves that are heavily marked with paler green. Attractive in a moist, shady border.

CULTIVATION *Grow in moist but well-drained, organic, preferably acidic to neutral soil, in deep or partial shade. Mulch with leaf mold each autumn.*

☀☀ ◊◊ Z5-8 H8-5   ↕to 16in (40cm)
↔to 12in (30cm)

TROLLIUS × CULTORUM 'ORANGE PRINCESS'

This globeflower is a robust, clump-forming perennial with orange-gold flowers. These are held above the mid-green foliage in late spring. The leaves are deeply cut with five rounded lobes. Good for bright color beside a pond or stream or in a damp border. For bright yellow flowers, choose the otherwise similar 'Goldquelle'.

CULTIVATION *Best in heavy, moist, fertile soil, in full sun or partial shade. Cut stems back hard after the first flush of flowers to encourage further blooms.*

☼ ◐ ◊ Z5-8 H8-4   ↕to 36in (90cm)
↔18in (45cm)

TROPAEOLUM MAJUS 'HERMINE GRASHOFF'

This double-flowered nasturtium is a strong-growing, often scrambling, annual climber. Long-spurred, bright red flowers appear during summer and autumn above the light green, wavy-margined leaves. Excellent for hanging baskets and other containers.

CULTIVATION *Grow in moist but well-drained, fairly poor soil, in full sun. The climbing stems need support. Minimum temperature 35°F (2°C).*

☼ ◊ H12-1   ↕3–10ft (1–3m)
↔5–15ft (1.5–5m)

TROPAEOLUM SPECIOSUM

The flame nasturtium is a slender, herbaceous climber that produces long-spurred, bright vermilion flowers throughout summer and autumn. These are followed by small, bright blue fruits. The mid-green leaves are divided into several leaflets. Effective growing through dark-leaved hedging plants that contrast with its flowers.

CULTIVATION *Grow in moist, organic, neutral to acidic soil in full sun or partial shade. Provide shade at the roots, and support the climbing stems.*

☼☀ ◊◊ Z8-10 H12-1   ‡to 10ft (3m)

TSUGA CANADENSIS 'JEDDELOH'

This dwarf form of Canada hemlock is a small, vase-shaped conifer with deeply furrowed, purplish gray bark. The bright green foliage is made up of needlelike leaves that are arranged in two ranks along the stems. An excellent small specimen tree for shady places; also popular for bonsai training.

CULTIVATION *Grow in moist but well-drained, organic soil, in full sun or partial shade. Trim during summer.*

☼☀ ◊◊ Z4-8 H8-1 ‡5ft (1.5m) ↔6ft (2m)

TULIPA CLUSIANA VAR. *CHRYSANTHA*

This yellow-flowered lady tulip is a bulbous perennial that flowers in early- to mid-spring. The bowl- to star-shaped flowers, tinged red or brownish purple on the outsides, are produced in clusters of up to three per stem above the linear, gray-green leaves. Suitable for a raised bed or rock garden.

CULTIVATION *Grow in well-drained, fertile soil, in full sun with shelter from strong winds. Deadhead and remove any fallen petals after flowering.*

☼ ◊ Z4–7 H8–1   ‡12in (30cm)

TULIPA LINIFOLIA

This slender, variable, bulbous perennial bears bowl-shaped red flowers in early and mid-spring. These are carried above the linear, gray-green leaves with wavy red margins. The petals have yellow margins and black-purple marks at the base. Good for a rock garden.

CULTIVATION *Grow in sharply drained, fertile soil, in full sun with shelter from strong winds. Deadhead and remove any fallen petals after flowering.*

☼ ◊ Z4–7 H8–1   ‡8in (20cm)

TULIPA LINIFOLIA
BATALINII GROUP

Slender, bulbous perennials, often
sold as *T. batalinii*, bearing solitary,
bowl-shaped, pale yellow flowers
with dark yellow or bronze marks
on the insides. These appear from
early to mid-spring above linear,
gray-green leaves with wavy red
margins. Use in spring bedding; the
flowers are good for cutting.

CULTIVATION *Grow in sharply drained,
fertile soil, in full sun with shelter from
strong winds. Deadhead and remove
any fallen petals after flowering.*

☼ ◊ Z4-7 H8-1 ‡14in (35cm)

TULIPA TURKESTANICA

This bulbous perennial produces up
to 12 star-shaped white flowers per
stem in early and mid-spring. They
are flushed with greenish gray on
the outsides and have yellow or
orange centers. The linear, gray-
green leaves are arranged beneath
the flowers. Grow in a rock garden
or sunny border, away from paths or
seating areas, because the flowers
have an unpleasant scent.

CULTIVATION *Grow in well-drained,
fertile soil, in full sun with shelter from
strong winds. Deadhead and remove
any fallen petals after flowering.*

☼ ◊ Z4-7 H8-1 ‡12in (30cm)

TULIPA CULTIVARS

These cultivated varieties of tulip are spring-flowering, bulbous perennials with a much wider range of flower color than any other spring bulbs, from the buttercup yellow 'Hamilton' through to the violet-purple 'Blue Heron' and the multicolored, red, white, and blue 'Union Jack'. This diversity makes them invaluable for bringing variety into the garden, either massed together in large containers or beds, or planted in a mixed border. Flower shape is also varied; as well as the familiar cup-shaped blooms, as in 'Dreamland', there are also conical, goblet-, and star-shaped forms. All are good for cutting.

CULTIVATION *Grow in well-drained, fertile soil, in sun with shelter from strong winds and excessive moisture. Remove spent flowers. Plant the bulbs in autumn.*

☼ ◊ Z4-7 H8-1

1 ↕ 6in (15cm) **2** ↕ 24in (60cm) **3** ↕ 20in (50cm)

4 ↕ 16in (40cm) **5** ↕ 20in (50cm) **6** ↕ 12in (30cm)

1 *T.* 'Ancilla' **2** *T.* 'Blue Heron' **3** *T.* 'China Pink'
4 *T.* 'Don Quichotte' **5** *T.* 'Hamilton' **6** *T.* 'Oriental Splendour'

7 ‡24in (60cm)

8 ‡12in (30cm)

9 ‡14in (35cm)

10 ‡24in (60cm)

11 ‡8in (20cm)

12 ‡16in (40cm)

13 ‡24in (60cm)

14 ‡20in (50cm)

7 *T.* 'Dreamland' 8 *T.* 'Keizerskroon' 9 *T.* 'Prinses Irene' 10 *T.* 'Queen of Sheba'
11 *T.* 'Red Riding Hood' 12 *T.* 'Spring Green' 13 *T.* 'Union Jack' 14 *T.* 'West Point'

UVULARIA GRANDIFLORA

Large merrybells is a slow-spreading, clump-forming perennial bearing solitary or paired, narrowly bell-shaped, sometimes green-tinted yellow flowers. They hang gracefully from slender, upright stems during mid- to late spring above the downward-pointing, lance-shaped, mid-green leaves. Excellent for a shady border or woodland garden.

CULTIVATION *Grow in moist but well-drained, fertile, organic soil in deep or partial shade.*

☼☀ ◊◊ Z3-7 H7-1   ‡to 30in (75cm)
↔12in (30cm)

VACCINIUM CORYMBOSUM

The highbush blueberry is a dense, deciduous, acidic-soil-loving shrub with slightly arching shoots. The oval leaves are mid-green, turning yellow or red in autumn. Hanging clusters of small, often pink-tinged white flowers appear in late spring and early summer, followed by sweet, edible, blue-black berries. Nicely suited to an open woodland garden or special acidic-soil bed.

CULTIVATION *Grow in moist but well-drained, peaty or sandy, acidic soil, in sun or light shade. Trim in winter.*

☼☀ ◊◊ Z3-7 H7-1   ‡↔5ft (1.5m)

VACCINIUM GLAUCOALBUM

A mound-forming, dense, evergreen shrub bearing elliptic, leathery, dark green leaves with bright bluish white undersides. Very small, pink-tinged white flowers appear in hanging clusters during late spring and early summer, followed by edible, white-bloomed, blue-black berries. Good in an open woodland garden.

CULTIVATION *Grow in open, moist but well-drained, peaty or sandy, acidic soil, in sun or part shade. Trim in spring.*

☼☀ ◊◊ Z3 7 H12-9 ‡20–40in (50–120cm)
↔3ft (1m)

VACCINIUM VITIS-IDAEA KORALLE GROUP

These heavy-fruiting cowberries are creeping, evergreen shrubs with oval, glossy dark green leaves, shallowly notched at the tips. In late spring and early summer, small, bell-shaped, white to deep pink flowers appear in dense, nodding clusters. These are followed by a profusion of round, bright red berries that are edible but taste acidic. Makes a good groundcover for an open woodland garden.

CULTIVATION *Best in peaty or sandy, moist but well-drained, acidic soil, in full sun or part shade. Trim in spring.*

☼☀ ◊◊ Z2-6 H6-2 ‡10in (25cm) ↔indefinite

VELTHEIMIA BRACTEATA

A bulbous perennial with basal rosettes of thick, waxy, straplike, glossy, dark green leaves, from which upright flowering stems grow in spring, to be topped by a dense cluster of tubular, pink-purple flowers with yellow spots. An unusual house or conservatory plant where winter protection is needed.

CULTIVATION *Plant bulbs in autumn with the neck just above soil level, in soil-based potting mix with added sharp sand. Site in full sun, reducing watering as the leaves fade. Keep the soil just moist during dormancy. Minimum temperature 35–41°F (2–5°C).*

☼ ◊ H12-10 ‡18in (45cm) ↔12in (30cm)

VERATRUM NIGRUM

An imposing, rhizomatous perennial that produces a tall and upright, branching spike of many reddish brown to black flowers from the center of a basal rosette of pleated, mid-green leaves. The small, star-shaped flowers that open in late summer have an unpleasant scent, so choose a moist, shady site not too close to paths or patios

CULTIVATION *Grow in deep, fertile, moist but well-drained soil with added organic matter. If in full sun, make sure the soil remains moist. Shelter from cold, drying winds. Divide congested clumps in autumn or early spring.*

☼☼ ◊◊ Z6-9 H9-5 ‡48in (120cm) ↔24in (60cm)

VERBASCUM BOMBYCIFERUM

This mullein is a very tall perennial that forms basal rosettes of densely packed leaves covered in silky silver hairs. Short-lived, it dies back in summer after the magnificent display of its tall, upright flower spike that is covered in silver hairs and sulfur-yellow flowers. For a large border, or it may naturalize by self-seeding in a wild garden.

CULTIVATION *Grow in alkaline, poor, well-drained soil in full sun. Support may be needed in fertile soil because of the resultant more vigorous growth. Divide plants in spring, if necessary.*

☼ ◊ Z4-8 H8-1 ‡8ft (1.8m) ↔24in (60cm)

VERBASCUM 'COTSWOLD BEAUTY'

A tall, evergreen, short-lived perennial that makes a bold addition to any large border. It bears upright spikes of saucer-shaped, peachy pink flowers, with darker centers, over a long period from early to late summer. These spikes tower over the wrinkled, gray-green foliage, most of which is clumped near the base of the plant. It may naturalize in a wild or lightly wooded garden.

CULTIVATION *Best in well-drained, poor, alkaline soil in full sun. In fertile soil, it grows taller and will need support. Divide in spring, if necessary.*

☼ ◊ Z5-9 H9-4 ‡4ft (1.2m) ↔18in (45cm)

VERBASCUM 'GAINSBOROUGH'

This short-lived, semi-evergreen perennial is valued for its spires of saucer-shaped, soft yellow flowers, borne throughout summer. Most of the oval and gray-green leaves are arranged in rosettes around the base of the stems. A very beautiful, long-flowering plant for a herbaceous or mixed border.

CULTIVATION *Grow in well-drained, fertile soil, in an open, sunny site. Often short-lived, but it is easily propagated by root cuttings taken in winter.*

☼ ◊ Z5-9 H9-3 ‡4ft (1.2m) ↔12in (30cm)

VERBASCUM DUMULOSUM

This evergreen subshrub forms small, spreading domes of densely felted, gray or gray-green leaves on white-downy stems. In late spring and early summer, clusters of small, saucer-shaped yellow flowers with red-purple eyes appear amid the foliage. Where marginal, grow in crevices of a warm, sunny wall.

CULTIVATION *Best in gritty, sharply drained, moderately fertile, preferably alkaline soil, in full sun. Shelter from excessive winter moisture.*

☼ ◊ Z6-9 H9-4 ‡to 10in (25cm)
↔to 16in (40cm)

VERBASCUM 'HELEN JOHNSON'

This evergreen perennial produces
spikes of saucer-shaped flowers in
an unusual light pink-brown during
early to late summer. The oval,
wrinkled, finely downy, gray-green
leaves are arranged in rosettes
around the base of the stems.
Naturalizes well in a wild garden.

CULTIVATION *Grow in well-drained,
poor, alkaline soil, in full sun. Flower
stems will need staking in fertile soil,
where it grows larger.*

☼ ◊ Z6 9 H9-5   ‡36in (90cm)
                     ↔12in (30cm) or more

VERBASCUM 'LETITIA'

This dense, rounded, evergreen
subshrub produces a continuous
abundance of small, clear yellow
flowers with reddish purple centers
throughout summer. The lance-
shaped, irregularly toothed, gray-
green leaves are carried beneath the
clustered flowers. Suitable for a
raised bed or rock garden. Where
marginally hardy, grow in crevices
of a protected drystone wall.

CULTIVATION *Best in sharply drained,
fairly fertile, alkaline soil, in sun. Avoid
sites with excessive winter moisture.*

☼ ◊ Z5-9 H9-5   ‡to 10in (25cm)
                     ↔to 12in (30cm)

VERBENA 'SISSINGHURST'

A mat-forming perennial bearing rounded heads of small, brilliant magenta-pink flowers that appear from late spring to autumn – most prolifically in summer. The dark green leaves are cut and toothed. Excellent for edging a path or growing in a container. In cold areas, overwinter under glass.

CULTIVATION *Grow in moist but well-drained, moderately fertile soil or soil mix. Choose a site in full sun.*

☀ ◊ Z7-11 H12-1   ‡to 8in (20cm)
↔to 3ft (1m)

VERONICA GENTIANOIDES

This early-summer-flowering, mat-forming perennial bears shallowly cup-shaped, pale blue or white flowers. These are carried in upright spikes that arise from rosettes of glossy, broadly lance-shaped, dark green leaves at the base of the plant. Excellent for the edge of a border.

CULTIVATION *Grow in moist but well-drained, moderately fertile soil, in full sun or light shade.*

☀☼ ◊ Z4-7 H7-1   ‡↔ 18in (45cm)

VERONICA PROSTRATA

The prostrate speedwell is a dense, mat-forming perennial. In early summer, it produces upright spikes of saucer-shaped, pale to deep blue flowers at the tips of sprawling stems. The small, bright to mid-green leaves are narrow and toothed. Grow in a rock garden. The cultivar 'Spode Blue' is also recommended.

CULTIVATION *Best in moist but well-drained, poor to moderately fertile soil. Choose a position in full sun.*

☀ ◊ Z5-8 H8-4   ‡to 6in (15cm)
↔to 16in (40cm)

VERONICA SPICATA
SUBSP. *INCANA*

The silver speedwell is an entirely silver-hairy, mat-forming perennial with upright flowering stems. These are tall spikes of star-shaped, purple-blue flowers, borne from early to late summer. The narrow leaves are silver-hairy and toothed. Ideal for a rock garden. The cultivar 'Wendy', with bright blue flowers, is also recommended.

CULTIVATION *Grow in well-drained, poor to moderately fertile soil, in full sun. Avoid excessive winter moisture.*

☀ ◊ Z3-8 H8-1   ‡↔ 12in (30cm)

VIBURNUM X *BODNANTENSE* 'DAWN'

A strongly upright, deciduous shrub carrying toothed, dark green leaves, bronze when young. From late autumn to spring, when branches are bare, small, tubular, heavily scented, dark pink flowers that age to white are borne in clustered heads, followed by small, blue-black fruits. 'Charles Lamont' is another lovely cultivar of this shrub, as is 'Deben', with almost white flowers.

CULTIVATION *Grow in any deep, moist but well-drained, fertile soil, in full sun. On old crowded plants, cut the oldest stems back to the base after flowering.*

☀ ◊◊ Z7-8 H8-7   ‡10ft (3m) ↔6ft (2m)

VIBURNUM X *CARLCEPHALUM*

This vigorous, rounded, deciduous shrub has broadly heart-shaped, irregularly toothed, dark green leaves that turn red in autumn. Rounded heads of small, fragrant white flowers appear amid the foliage during late spring. Suits a shrub border or a woodland garden.

CULTIVATION *Grow in deep, moisture-retentive, fertile soil. Tolerates sun or semi-shade. Little pruning is necesary.*

☀☀ ◊ Z6-8 H8-6   ‡↔ 10ft (3m)

VIBURNUM DAVIDII

A compact, evergreen shrub that forms a dome of dark green foliage consisting of oval leaves with three distinct veins. In late spring, tiny, tubular white flowers appear in flattened heads; female plants bear tiny but decorative, oval, metallic blue fruits, later in the season. Looks good planted in groups.

CULTIVATION *Best in deep, moist but well-drained, fertile soil, in sun or semi-shade. Grow male and female shrubs together for reliable fruiting. Keep neat, if desired, by cutting wayward stems back to strong shoots, or to the base of the plant, in spring.*

☼☀ ◊◊ Z8-9 H9-8 ‡↔ 3–5ft (1–1.5m)

VIBURNUM FARRERI

This strongly upright, deciduous shrub has oval, toothed, dark green leaves which are bronze when young and turn red-purple in autumn. During mild periods in winter and early spring, small, fragrant, white or pink-tinged flowers are borne in dense clusters on the bare stems. These are occasionally followed by tiny, bright red fruits.

CULTIVATION *Grow in any reliably moist but well-drained, fertile soil, in full sun or partial shade. Thin out old shoots after flowering.*

☼☀ ◊◊ Z6-8 H8-6 ‡10ft (3m) ↔8ft (2.5m)

VIBURNUM OPULUS 'XANTHOCARPUM'

A vigorous, deciduous shrub bearing maplelike, lobed, mid-green leaves that turn yellow in autumn. Flat heads of showy white flowers are produced in late spring and early summer, followed by large bunches of spherical, bright yellow berries. 'Notcutt's Variety' and 'Compactum' are recommended red-berried cultivars, the latter much smaller, to only 5ft (1.5m) tall.

CULTIVATION *Grow in any moist but well-drained soil in sun or semi-shade. Cut out older stems after flowering to relieve overcrowding.*

☼◑ ◊◊ Z4–8 H8–1 ‡15ft (5m) ↔12ft (4m)

VIBURNUM PLICATUM 'MARIESII'

A spreading, deciduous shrub bearing distinctly tiered branches. These are clothed in heart-shaped, toothed, dark green leaves that turn red-purple in autumn. In late spring, saucer-shaped white flowers appear in spherical, lacecaplike heads. Few berries are produced; for a heavily fruiting cultivar, look for 'Rowallane'.

CULTIVATION *Grow in any well-drained, fairly fertile soil, in sun or semi-shade. Requires little pruning other than to remove damaged wood after flowering; be careful not to spoil the form.*

☼◑ ◊ Z4–8 H8–1 ‡10ft (3m) ↔12ft (4m)

VIBURNUM TINUS 'EVE PRICE'

This very compact, evergreen shrub has dense, dark green foliage. Over a long period from late winter to spring, pink flower buds open to tiny, star-shaped white flowers carried in flattened heads; they are followed by small, dark blue-black fruits. Can be grown as an informal hedge.

CULTIVATION *Grow in any moist but well-drained, moderately fertile soil, in sun or partial shade. Train or clip after flowering to maintain desired shape.*

 ☼☀ ◐◑ Z8-10 H12-8   ↔ 10ft (3m)

VINCA MAJOR 'VARIEGATA'

This variegated form of the greater periwinkle, also known as 'Elegantissima', is an evergreen subshrub with long, slender shoots bearing oval, dark green leaves that have creamy white margins. Dark violet flowers are produced over a long period from mid-spring to autumn. Useful as a groundcover for a shady bank, but it may become invasive.

CULTIVATION *Grow in any moist but well-drained soil. Tolerates deep shade but flowers best with part-day sun.*

☼☀ ◐◑ Z7-11 H12-7   ↕18in (45cm) ↔ indefinite

VINCA MINOR 'ATROPURPUREA'

This dark-flowered lesser periwinkle is a mat-forming, groundcover shrub with long trailing shoots. Dark plum-purple flowers are produced over a long period from mid-spring to autumn, amid the oval, dark green leaves. For light blue flowers, choose 'Gertrude Jekyll'.

CULTIVATION *Grow in any but very dry soil, in full sun for best flowering, but tolerates partial shade. Restrict growth by cutting back hard in early spring.*

☼ ◑ ◊◊ Z4–9 H9–1 ↕4–8in (10–20cm)
↔indefinite

VIOLA CORNUTA

The horned violet is a spreading, evergreen perennial that produces an abundance of slightly scented, spurred, violet to lilac-blue flowers; the petals are widely separated, with white markings on the lower ones. The flowers are borne amid the mid-green, oval leaves from spring to summer. Suitable for a rock garden. The Alba Group has white flowers.

CULTIVATION *Grow in moist but well-drained, poor to moderately fertile soil, in sun or partial shade. Cut back after flowering to keep compact.*

☼ ◑ ◊◊ Z7–9 H9–1 ↕to 6in (15cm)
↔to 16in (40cm)

VIOLA 'JACKANAPES'

A robust, clump-forming, evergreen
perennial bearing spreading stems
with oval and toothed, bright green
leaves. Spurred, golden yellow
flowers with purple streaks appear
in late spring and summer; the
upper petals are deep brownish
purple. Good for containers or
summer bedding.

CULTIVATION *Grow in moist but well-
drained, fairly fertile soil, in full sun or
semi-shade. Often short-lived but is
easily grown from seed sown in spring.*

☼☀ ◊◊ Z4-8 H8-1   ‡to 5in (12cm)
↔to 12in (30cm)

VIOLA 'NELLIE BRITTON'

This clump-forming, evergreen
perennial with spreading stems
produces an abundance of spurred,
pinkish mauve flowers over a long
period in summer. The oval, mid-
green leaves are toothed and glossy.
Suitable for the front of a border.

CULTIVATION *Best in well-drained but
moist, moderately fertile soil, in full sun
or partial shade. Deadhead frequently
to prolong flowering.*

☼☀ ◊◊ Z5-7 H7-1   ‡to 6in (15cm)
↔to 12in (30cm)

VITIS COIGNETIAE

The crimson glory vine is a fast-growing, deciduous climber with large, heart-shaped, shallowly lobed, dark green leaves that turn bright red in autumn. Small, blue-black grapes appear in autumn. Train against a wall or over a trellis.

CULTIVATION *Grow in well-drained, neutral to alkaline soil, in sun or semi-shade. Autumn color is best on poorer soils. Pinch out the growing tips after planting and allow the strongest shoots to form a permanent framework. Prune back to this each year in mid-winter.*

☀☀ ◊ Z5-9 H9-1 ↕50ft (15m)

VITIS VINIFERA 'PURPUREA'

This purple-leaved grape is a woody, deciduous climber bearing rounded, lobed, toothed leaves; these are white-hairy when young, turning plum-purple, then dark purple, before they fall. Tiny, pale green summer flowers are followed by small purple grapes in autumn. Grow over a sturdy fence or pergola, or through a large shrub or tree.

CULTIVATION *Grow in well-drained, slightly alkaline soil, in sun or semi-shade. Autumn color is best on poorer soils. Prune back to an established framework each year in mid-winter.*

☀☀ ◊ Z6-9 H9-6 ↕22ft (7m)

WEIGELA FLORIDA 'FOLIIS PURPUREIS'

A compact, deciduous shrub with arching shoots that produces clusters of funnel-shaped, dark pink flowers with pale insides in late spring and early summer. The bronze-green foliage is made up of oval, tapered leaves. Pollution-tolerant, so it is ideal for urban gardens.

CULTIVATION *Best in well-drained, fertile, organic soil in full sun. Prune out some older branches at ground level each year after flowering.*

☼ ◊ Z5-8 H8-1   ‡3ft (1m) ↔5ft (1.5m)

WEIGELA FLORIDA 'VARIEGATA'

A dense, deciduous shrub that produces abundant clusters of funnel-shaped, dark pink flowers with pale insides. These are borne in late spring and early summer amid attractive, gray-green leaves with white margins. Suitable for a mixed border or open woodland. Tolerates urban pollution. 'Praecox Variegata' (Z5-8 H8-4) is another attractive variegated weigela.

CULTIVATION *Grow in any well-drained, fertile, organic soil in full sun. Prune out some of the oldest branches each year after flowering.*

☼ ◊ Z5-8 H8-1   ‡6–8ft (2–2.5m)

WISTERIA FLORIBUNDA 'ALBA'

This white-flowered Japanese wisteria is a fast-growing, woody climber with bright green, divided leaves. The fragrant, pealike flowers appear during spring in very long, drooping spikes; beanlike, velvety green seed pods usually follow. Train against a wall, up into a tree, or over a sturdy framework.

CULTIVATION *Grow in moist but well-drained, fertile soil, in sun or partial shade. Prune back new growth in summer and in late winter to control spread and promote flowering.*

☼ ◐ ◊◊ Z5-9 H9-1 ‡28ft (9m) or more

WISTERIA FLORIBUNDA 'MULTIJUGA'

This lilac-blue-flowered Japanese wisteria is a vigorous, woody-stemmed climber. Long, hanging flower clusters open during spring, usually followed by beanlike, velvety green seed pods. Each mid-green leaf is composed of many oval leaflets. Train against a wall or up into a tree.

CULTIVATION *Grow in moist but well-drained, fertile soil, in full sun or partial shade. Trim in mid-winter, and again 2 months after flowering.*

☼ ◐ ◊◊ Z5-9 H9-1 ‡28ft (9m) or more

WISTERIA SINENSIS

Chinese wisteria is a vigorous,
deciduous climber that produces
long, hanging spikes of fragrant,
pealike, lilac-blue or white flowers.
These appear amid the bright green,
divided leaves in late spring and
early summer, usually followed by
beanlike, velvety green seed pods.
'Alba' is a white-flowered form.

CULTIVATION *Grow in moist but well-
drained, fertile soil. Provide a sheltered
site in sun or partial shade. Cut back
long shoots to 2 or 3 buds, in late winter.*

 ☼ ◑ ◊◊ Z5-8 H8-4 ‡28ft (9m) or more

YUCCA FILAMENTOSA 'BRIGHT EDGE'

An almost stemless, clump-forming
shrub with basal rosettes of rigid,
lance-shaped, dark green leaves, to
30in (75cm) long, with broad yellow
margins. Tall spikes, to 6ft (2m) or
more, of nodding, bell-shaped white
flowers, tinged with green or cream,
are borne in summer. A striking,
architectural specimen for a border
or courtyard. The leaves of
'Variegata' are edged white.

CULTIVATION *Grow in any well-drained
soil, in full sun. Remove old flowers
at the end of the season. Where
marginally hardy, mulch over winter.*

☼ ◊ Z5-10 H10-1 ‡30in (75cm) ↔5ft (1.5m)

YUCCA FLACCIDA 'IVORY'

An almost stemless, evergreen shrub that forms a dense, basal clump of swordlike leaves. Tall spikes, to 5ft (1.5m) or more, of nodding, bell-shaped white flowers are borne in mid- and late summer. The lance-shaped, dark blue-green leaves, fringed with curly or straight threads, are arranged in basal rosettes. Thrives in coastal gardens and on sandy soils.

CULTIVATION *Grow in any well-drained soil but needs a hot, dry position in full sun to flower well. Where marginally hardy, mulch over winter.*

☀ ◊ Z5-9 H9-1   ↕↔5ft (1.5m)

ZANTEDESCHIA AETHIOPICA

This relatively small-flowered calla lily is a clump-forming perennial. Almost upright, cream-yellow flowers are borne in succession from late spring to mid-summer, followed by long, arrow-shaped leaves, evergreen in mild areas. May be used as a waterside plant in shallow water.

CULTIVATION *Best in moist but well-drained, fertile, organic soil. Choose a site in full sun or partial shade. Mulch deeply for winter where marginally hardy.*

☀◑ ◊◐ Z8-10 H7-1   ↕36in (90cm)
                      ↔24in (60cm)

ZANTEDESCHIA AETHIOPICA 'GREEN GODDESS'

This green-flowered calla lily is a clump-forming, robust perennial that is evergreen in mild climates. Upright and white-centered flowers appear from late spring to mid-summer above the dull green, arrow-shaped leaves. Good in shallow water.

CULTIVATION *Grow in moist, organic, fertile soil. Choose a site in full sun or partial shade. Mulch deeply over winter where marginally hardy.*

☼ ◑ ◐ ◇ Z8-10 H7-1 ↕36in (90cm) ↔24in (60cm)

ZAUSCHNERIA CALIFORNICA 'DUBLIN'

This deciduous California fuchsia, sometimes called 'Glasnevin', is a clump-forming perennial bearing a profusion of tubular, bright red flowers during late summer and early autumn. The gray green leaves are lance-shaped and hairy. Provides spectacular, late-season color for a drystone wall or border. Where marginally hardy, grow at the base of a warm wall.

CULTIVATION *Best in well-drained, moderately fertile soil, in full sun. Provide shelter from cold, drying winds.*

☼ ◇ Z8-10 H12-8 ↕to 10in (25cm)
↔to 12in (30cm)

THE PLANTING GUIDE

CONTAINER PLANTS FOR SPRING

A pot of evergreens and bright spring flowers and bulbs brings cheer to a front door or patio on a chilly early spring day. Tailor the soil to suit the plants: camellias and rhododendrons can be grown in acidic soil mix, for example. Keep containers in a sheltered place for early flowers, water in the winter if necessary (not frozen soil), and fertilize as growth begins in spring.

AGAPANTHUS CAMPANULATUS 'ALBOVITTATUS'
Perennial Z9-11 H12-8 Soft blue flowers in large heads above white-striped leaves.
↕ 3ft (90cm) ↔ 18in (45cm)

AJUGA REPTANS 'CATLIN'S GIANT'
Perennial Z3-8 H8-2 Clumps of green leaves and spikes of blue flowers.
↕ 8in (20cm) ↔ 24–36in (60–90cm)

BERGENIA 'BALLAWLEY'
Perennial   page 88

CAMELLIA JAPONICA CULTIVARS
Evergreen shrubs   pages 100–101

CAMELLIA × *WILLIAMSII* 'DONATION'
Evergreen shrub   page 104

CHAENOMELES SPECIOSA 'GEISHA GIRL'
Shrub Z5-9 H9-4 Soft apricot, semidouble flowers in abundance.
↕ 3ft (1m) ↔ 4ft (1.2m)

CHAMAECYPARIS LAWSONIANA 'MINIMA GLAUCA'
Evergreen shrub Z5-9 H9-4 A small neat conifer with blue-green leaves.
↕ 24in (60cm)

CHIONODOXA FORBESII 'PINK GIANT'
Bulb Z3-9 H9-1 Star-shaped, white-centered pink flowers.
↕ 4–8in (10–20cm) ↔ 1¼in (3cm)

CHIONODOXA SARDENSIS
Bulb Z3-9 H9-1 Bright blue, starry flowers in early spring.
↕ 4–8in (10–20cm) ↔ 1¼in (3cm)

CROCUS CHRYSANTHUS 'LADYKILLER'
Bulb Z3-8 H8-1 White, scented flowers with purple stripes on buds.
↕ 3in (7cm) ↔ 2in (5cm)

ERICA CARNEA 'MYRETOUN RUBY'
Evergreen shrub Z5-7 H7-5 Spreading habit, with pink flowers that deepen as they age.
↕ 6in (15cm) ↔ 18in (45cm)

HEDERA HELIX 'KOLIBRI'
Evergreen shrub Z5-11 H12-5 Trailing stems; leaves variegated white and green.
↕ 18in (45cm)

HYACINTHUS ORIENTALIS 'CITY OF HAARLEM'
Bulb   page 263

HYACINTHUS ORIENTALIS 'GIPSY QUEEN'
Bulb Z5-9 H9-5 Orange-pink, scented flowers.
↕ 10in (25cm)

HYACINTHUS ORIENTALIS 'HOLLYHOCK'
Bulb Z5-9 H9-5 Double red flowers.
↕ 8in (20cm)

HYACINTHUS ORIENTALIS 'VIOLET PEARL'
Bulb Z5-9 H9-5 Spikes of scented, amethyst violet flowers with paler petal edges.
↕ 10in (25cm)

ILEX × *ALTACLERENSIS* 'GOLDEN KING'
Evergreen shrub   page 271

MYOSOTIS 'BLUE BALL'
Biennial Z5-9 H9-5 Compact plant with azure blue flowers.
↕ 6in (15cm) ↔ 8in (20cm)

NARCISSUS 'CEYLON'
Bulb   page **348**

NARCISSUS 'CHEERFULNESS'
Bulb   page **348**

NARCISSUS SMALL DAFFODILS
Bulbs   pages **346–347**

PIERIS 'FOREST FLAME'
Evergreen shrub   page **402**

PIERIS FORMOSA VAR. *FORRESTII* 'WAKEHURST'
Evergreen shrub   page **402**

PIERIS JAPONICA 'PURITY'
Evergreen shrub Z6-8 H8-6 Compact, with white flowers and pale young growth.
↕ ↔ 3ft (1m)

PRIMULA GOLD-LACED GROUP
Perennial   page **415**

PRIMULA 'GUINEVERE'
Perennial   page **415**

RHODODENDRON CILPINENSE GROUP
Evergreen shrub   page **444**

RHODODENDRON 'CURLEW'
Evergreen shrub Z7-9 H9-7 Small clusters of bright yellow flowers.
↕ ↔ 24in (60cm)

RHODODENDRON 'DOC'
Evergreen shrub   page **444**

RHODODENDRON 'HOMEBUSH'
Shrub   page **438**

RHODODENDRON 'MOTHER'S DAY'
Evergreen shrub Z7-9 H9-7 Bright red-flowered evergreen azalea.
↕ ↔ 5ft (1.5m)

RHODODENDRON 'PTARMIGAN'
Evergreen shrub

RHODODENDRON 'SUSAN'
Evergreen shrub   page **441**

TULIPA 'APRICOT BEAUTY'
Bulb Z3-8 H8-1 Pastel, salmon-pink flowers of great beauty.
↕ 14in (35cm)

TULIPA 'CAPE COD'
Bulb Z3-8 H8-1 Yellow flowers striped with red above prettily marked leaves.
↕ 8in (20cm)

TULIPA 'CARNAVAL DE NICE'
Bulb Z3-8 H8-1 Red and white-striped blooms like double peonies.
↕ 16in (40cm)

TULIPA CLUSIANA VAR. *CHRYSANTHA*
Bulb   page **522**

TULIPA CULTIVARS
Bulbs   pages **524–525**

TULIPA PRAESTANS 'UNICUM'
Bulb Z3-8 H8-1 Cream-edged leaves and one to four scarlet flowers per stem.
↕ 12in (30cm)

TULIPA 'TORONTO'
Bulb Z3-8H 8-1 Multiflowered tulips with three to five flowers of deep coral-pink.
↕ 10in (25cm)

VIOLA UNIVERSAL SERIES
Biennial Z7-11 H7-1 Wide range of colors with flowers throughout spring.
↕ 6in (15cm) ↔ to 12in (30cm)

VIOLA 'VELOUR BLUE'
Biennial Z7-11 H7-1 Compact plants with masses of small light blue flowers.
↕ 6in (15cm) ↔ 8in (20cm)

CONTAINER PLANTS FOR SUMMER

Containers can bring color to areas that have no soil; they can be filled with permanent plants, or used to add extra color when filled with annuals and tender perennials. In a large pot, combine the two with a shrub augmented by lower, temporary plants. There is a huge choice, but every container will need regular water and fertilizer if it is to look its best.

ABUTILON 'CANARY BIRD'
Shrub Z9-10 H12-1 Bushy plant with pendulous yellow flowers.
↕↔ to 10ft (3m)

ABUTILON MEGAPOTAMICUM
Shrub   page 30

AGAPANTHUS CAMPANULATUS
SUBSP. *PATENS*
Perennial   page 47

ARGYRANTHEMUM 'VANCOUVER'
Perennial   page 67

CLEMATIS 'DOCTOR RUPPEL'
Climber   page 129

CROCOSMIA 'LUCIFER'
Perennial   page 152

CUPHEA IGNEA
Perennial   page 155

DIASCIA BARBERAE
'BLACKTHORN APRICOT'
Perennial   page 174

DIASCIA VIGILIS
Perennial Z7-9 H9-7 The creeping stems carry loose spikes of pink flowers with yellow centers.
↕ 12in (30cm) ↔ 24in (60cm)

FUCHSIA 'ANNABEL'
Shrub   page 213

FUCHSIA 'CELIA SMEDLEY'
Shrub   page 214

FUCHSIA 'DISPLAY'
Shrub Z8-10 H10-1 Upright plant with carmine and pink flowers.
↕ 24–30in (60–75cm) ↔ 18–24in (45–60cm)

FUCHSIA 'NELLIE NUTTALL'
Shrub   page 215

FUCHSIA 'SNOWCAP'
Shrub   page 215

FUCHSIA 'SWINGTIME'
Shrub   page 215

FUCHSIA 'THALIA'
Shrub   page 215

FUCHSIA 'WINSTON CHURCHILL'
Shrub Z8-10 H12-1 Pink and lavender, double flowers.
↕↔ 18–30in (45–75cm)

GAZANIAS
Perennials   page 222

HOSTA 'FRANCEE'
Perennial   page 259

HYDRANGEA MACROPHYLLA
'AYESHA'
Shrub Z6-9 H9-3 Unusual because the blooms are cupped, resembling *Syringa* (lilac) flowers.
↕ 5ft (1.5m) ↔ 6ft (2m)

LILIUM FORMOSANUM VAR. *PRICEI*
Perennial   page 315

LILIUM LONGIFLORUM
Perennial   page 316

LILIUM MONADELPHUM
Perennial   page 317

LOTUS MACULATUS
Perennial Z11, H12-1 Narrow, silvery leaves contrast with orange, clawlike flowers on trailing shoots.
↕ 8in (20cm) ↔ indefinite

NICOTIANA LANGSDORFII
Annual Z11 H12-1 Spikes of small, green, tubular flowers with flaring trumpets.
↕ to 5ft (1.5m) ↔ to 14in (35cm)

OSTEOSPERMUM CULTIVARS
Perennials

PELARGONIUM 'ATTAR OF ROSES'
Perennial

PELARGONIUMS, FLOWERING
Perennials

PENSTEMON 'ANDENKEN AN FRIEDRICH HAHN'
Perennial

PENSTEMON 'HEWELL PINK BEDDER'
Perennial Z7-10 H10-7 A free-flowering, bushy plant with tubular, pink flowers.
↕ 18in (45cm) ↔ 12in (30cm)

PETUNIA 'LAVENDER STORM'
Annual Z8-11 H12-3 Compact, ground-covering plants with large blooms.
↕ 12in (30cm) ↔ 16in (40cm)

PETUNIA 'MILLION BELLS BLUE'
Annual Z9-11 H12-1 Masses of small flowers on bushy, compact plants.
↕ 10in (25cm)

PETUNIA 'PRISM SUNSHINE'
Annual Z9-11 H12-1 A reliable, large-flowered yellow petunia.
↕ 15in (38cm)

PLUMBAGO AURICULATA
Scrambling shrub

ROSA 'ANNA FORD'
Patio rose

ROSA 'GENTLE TOUCH'
Patio rose

ROSA 'QUEEN MOTHER'
Patio rose

ROSA 'SWEET MAGIC'
Patio rose

ROSA 'THE FAIRY'
Patio rose

SALVIA PATENS 'CAMBRIDGE BLUE'
Perennial

SCAEVOLA AEMULA 'BLUE WONDER'
Perennial Z11 H12-1 Blue, fan-shaped flowers on a sprawling, vigorous bush.
↕ 6in (15cm) ↔ 5ft (1.5m)

TROPAEOLUM MAJUS 'HERMINE GRASHOFF'
Climber

VERBENA 'LAWRENCE JOHNSTON'
Perennial Z7-11 H12-1 Bright green foliage with intense, fiery red flowers.
↕ 18in (45cm) ↔ 24in (60cm)

VERBENA 'SISSINGHURST'
Annual Z7-11 H12-1 Spreading plant with fine leaves and magenta-pink flowers.
↕ to 8in (20cm) ↔ to 3ft (1m)

CONTAINER PLANTS FOR AUTUMN

Autumn is a season of great change as the leaves of deciduous plants become brilliant before they fall. Most annuals have finished their display, but some plants, especially fuchsias, asters, salvias, dwarf chrysanthemums, and dahlias, continue to provide splashes of colorful flowers. Evergreens form a strong and solid background to all garden displays.

ARGYRANTHEMUM 'JAMAICA PRIMROSE'
Perennial page 67

CABBAGE 'NORTHERN LIGHTS'
Biennial Z11-12 H8-1 Frilled ornamental cabbage in shades of white, pink, and red.
‡↔ 12in (30cm)

CANNA 'LUCIFER'
Perennial Z8-11 H12-1 Dwarf, with green leaves and red, yellow-edged flowers.
‡ 24in (60cm) ↔ 20in (50cm)

CHAMAECYPARIS LAWSONIANA 'ELLWOOD'S GOLD'
Conifer page 117

CLEMATIS 'MADAME JULIA CORREVON'
Climber page 133

ESCALLONIA LAEVIS 'GOLD BRIAN'
Evergreen shrub Z8-9 H9-8 Pink flowers held against bright yellow leaves.
‡↔ 3ft (1m)

GAULTHERIA MUCRONATA 'CRIMSONIA'
Evergreen shrub Z8-9 H9-8 Acidic-soil-loving, fine-leaved shrub with showy, deep pink berries.
‡↔ 4ft (1.2m)

HIBISCUS SYRIACUS 'WOODBRIDGE'
Shrub page 257

HYPERICUM × MOSERIANUM 'TRICOLOR'
Shrub Z6-9 H9-6 Variegated narrow leaves, flushed pink, and yellow flowers.
‡ 12in (30cm) ↔ 24in (60cm)

JUNIPERUS COMMUNIS 'COMPRESSA'
Conifer page 293

MYRTUS COMMUNIS
Evergreen shrub page 344

NANDINA DOMESTICA 'FIREPOWER'
Shrub Z6-9 H9-3 Compact plant with red autumn color and berries.
‡ 18in (45cm) ↔ 24in (60cm)

OSMANTHUS HETEROPHYLLUS 'VARIEGATUS'
Evergreen shrub Z7-9 H9-7 Hollylike cream-edged leaves and fragrant, white flowers in autumn.
‡↔ 15ft (5m)

RUDBECKIA HIRTA 'TOTO'
Annual Z3-7 H7-1 Orange flowers with black centers on very compact plants.
‡↔ 8in (20cm)

THUJA ORIENTALIS 'AUREA NANA'
Conifer page 512

VIBURNUM TINUS 'VARIEGATUM'
Evergreen shrub Z8-10 H10-8 The leaves are broadly margined with creamy yellow.
‡↔ 10ft (3m)

CONTAINER PLANTS FOR WINTER

Few plants flower during cold winter months; use those that do in containers by doors and windows, where they can be seen from the comfort of the home. Many evergreens, especially variegated ones, look cheery when other plants are bare. Plant shrubs out in the garden after a few years in pots. To give a little protection against freezing, wrap pots with bubble plastic.

AUCUBA JAPONICA 'CROTONIFOLIA'
Evergreen shrub   page **78**

CYCLAMEN COUM
Bulb 5-9 H9-4 Deep green heart-shaped leaves and pink flowers.
↕2–3in (5–8cm) ↔ 4in (10cm)

ERICA CARNEA 'SPRINGWOOD WHITE'
Evergreen shrub   page **187**

ERICA × DARLEYENSIS 'ARTHUR JOHNSON'
Evergreen shrub Z7-9 H8-7 The upright stems have deep green leaves and bear pink flowers in winter.
↕30in (75cm) ↔ 42in (60cm)

EUONYMUS FORTUNEI 'HARLEQUIN'
Evergreen shrub Z5-9 H9-4 Compact shrub, young leaves heavily splashed with white.
↕↔ 16in (40cm)

FATSIA JAPONICA 'VARIEGATA'
Evergreen shrub Z8-10 H10-8 Large, lobed leaves, edged with white; creamy white flowers on mature plants
↕↔ 8ft (2m)

FESTUCA GLAUCA 'BLAUFUCHS'
Ornamental grass   page **207**

GAULTHERIA MUCRONATA 'MULBERRY WINE'
Evergreen shrub   page **220**

HEDERA HELIX 'EVA'
Evergreen climber Z5-10 H10-1 Small gray-green leaves edged white.
↕4ft (1.2m)

ILEX AQUIFOLIUM 'FEROX ARGENTEA'
Evergreen shrub   page **273**

LAMIUM MACULATUM 'BEACON SILVER'
Perennial Z4-8 H8-1 Bright silver-gray foliage and magenta-pink flowers.
↕8in (20cm) ↔ 3ft (1m)

LAURUS NOBILIS
Evergreen shrub or small tree page **304**

LIRIOPE MUSCARI 'JOHN BURCH'
Perennial Z6-11 H8-1 Grassy plant with gold-striped leaves and violet flowers.
↕12in (30cm) ↔ 18in (45cm)

SKIMMIA JAPONICA 'RUBELLA'
Evergreen shrub   page **495**

VIBURNUM DAVIDII
Evergreen shrub   page **535**

VIOLA 'FLORAL DANCE'
Biennial Z4-8 H8-1 Winter pansies in mixed colors.
↕6in (15cm) ↔ to 12in (30cm)

VIOLA 'MELLO 21'
Biennial Z4-8 H8-1 Pansy mixture of 21 colors.
↕6in (15cm) ↔ to 12in (30cm)

YUCCA GLORIOSA 'VARIEGATA'
Evergreen shrub Z5-11 H12-1 Erect shrub with sharp, pointed leaves edged with yellow.
↕↔ 6ft (2m)

CONTAINERS IN SUNNY SITES

A sunny position where pots can be placed allows the cultivation of a huge range of plants. Apart from most bedding, many tender plants that must spend cold winters under cover should thrive in a sheltered sunny position and bring a touch of the exotic. Specimen plants are best grown in their own containers; simply group them together to create masterful associations.

ALOE VARIEGATA
Succulent page **53**

BRACHYSCOME 'STRAWBERRY MIST'
Perennial Z11 H12-1 Low, spreading plant with feathery foliage and pink daisylike flowers. Sometimes sold as *Brachycome*.
‡ 10in (25cm) ↔ 18in (45cm)

CORDYLINE AUSTRALIS 'ALBERTII'
Evergreen shrub page **137**

CORREA BACKHOUSEANA
Evergreen shrub page **140**

ERICA ERIGENA 'IRISH DUSK'
Evergreen shrub Z6-8 H8-6 Deep pink flowers are produced from autumn to spring on plants with grayish green leaves.
‡ 24in (60cm) ↔ 18in (45cm)

FELICIA AMELLOIDES 'SANTA ANITA'
Subshrub page **206**

FUCHSIA 'MADAME CORNÉLLISSEN'
Shrub Z11 H12-1 Upright, with masses of red and white single flowers.
‡ ↔ 24in (60cm)

GAZANIA 'DAYBREAK RED STRIPE'
Perennial Z8-10 H10-1 Raise from seed for showy yellow blooms striped with red.
‡ to 8in (20cm) ↔ to 10in (25cm)

GERANIUM 'ANN FOLKARD'
Perennial page **226**

GERANIUM CINEREUM VAR. *SUBCAULESCENS*
Perennial page **227**

GERANIUM PALMATUM
Perennial Z7-9 H9-1 Bold clumps of foliage with large mauve flowers in summer.
‡ ↔ to 4ft (1.2m)

HEBE ALBICANS
Evergreen shrub page **240**

HEBE 'MRS WINDER'
Evergreen shrub Z9-10 H10-8 Dark foliage, flushed purple, and violet flowers in late summer.
‡ 3ft (1m) ↔ 4ft (1.2m)

HOSTA 'KROSSA REGAL'
Perennial Z3-8 H8-1 A magnificent cultivar with upright gray leaves and tall spikes of lilac flowers.
‡ 28in (70cm) ↔ 30in (75cm)

IMPATIENS SUPER ELFIN SERIES
Annuals page **275**

IPOMOEA 'HEAVENLY BLUE'
Annual climber page **277**

JASMINUM MESNYI
Climber page **291**

LATHYRUS ODORATUS 'PATIO MIXED'
Annual climber page **303**

LEPTOSPERMUM SCOPARIUM 'RED DAMASK'
Evergreen shrub Z9-11 H12-9 Tiny leaves and double, deep pink flowers.
‡ ↔ 10ft (3m)

LOBELIA ERINUS 'KATHLEEN MALLARD'
Annual H9-1 Neat, double-flowered blue lobelia.
‡ 4in (10cm) ↔ 12in (30cm)

MIMULUS AURANTIACUS
Evergreen shrub page **341**

MYRTUS COMMUNIS SUBSP.
TARENTINA
Evergreen shrub page **345**

OSTEOSPERMUM 'SILVER SPARKLER'
Perennial Z10-11 H6-1 White daisylike
flowers and bright, variegated leaves.
↕↔ 18in (45cm)

PASSIFLORA 'AMETHYST'
Climber H7-1 Fast-growing frost-tender
climber that produces beautiful lavender
flowers all summer.
↕ 12ft (4m)

PELARGONIUM 'CLORINDA'
Perennial Z11 H12-1 Rough, scented
foliage and quite large, bright pink flowers.
↕ 18–20in (45–50cm) ↔ 8–10in (20–25cm)

PELARGONIUM 'DEACON MOONLIGHT'
Perennial Z11 H12-1 Pale lilac double
flowers above neat foliage on compact
plants.
↕ 8in (20cm) ↔ 10in (25cm)

PELARGONIUM 'DOLLY VARDEN'
Perennial page **375**

PELARGONIUM 'VISTA DEEP ROSE'
Perennial Z11 H12-1 Single color in this
seed-raised F2 series.
↕↔ 12in (30cm)

PENSTEMON 'APPLE BLOSSOM'
Perennial page **378**

PENSTEMON 'OSPREY'
Perennial Z5-9 H9-1 Spikes of white
flowers edged with pink.
↕↔ 18in (45cm)

PETUNIA 'DUO PEPPERMINT'
Annual Z8-11 H12-1 Double, pink flowers,
quite weather-resistant in wet summers.
↕ 8in (20cm) ↔ 12in (30cm)

PHORMIUM 'SUNDOWNER'
Perennial page **393**

REHMANNIA GLUTINOSA
Perennial Z9-10 H10-8 Slightly sticky leaves
on tall stems that carry dusky pink,
foxglovelike flowers.
↕ 6–12in (15–30cm) ↔ to 12in (30cm)

RHODOCHITON ATROSANGUINEUS
Evergreen climber page **435**

SEMPERVIVUM ARACHNOIDEUM
Succulent page **492**

SOLENOPSIS AXILLARIS
Perennial Z11 H12-1 Dome shaped,
feathery, with delicate but showy star-
shaped, blue flowers.
↕↔ 12in (30cm)

THYMUS × *CITRIODORUS*
'AUREUS'
Evergreen shrub Z6-9 H9-4 Low-growing
bush, scented of lemon, with gold leaves
and pink flowers.
↕ 12in (30cm) ↔ to 10in (25cm)

TROPAEOLUM MAJUS
'MARGARET LONG'
Perennial Z11 H12-1 Compact, trailing
plant with double soft orange flowers.
↕↔ 12in (30cm)

TWEEDIA CAERULEA
Perennial Z11 H12-1 A straggly twining
plant with gray leaves and starry sky blue
flowers.
↕ 24–36in (60cm–1m)

CONTAINERS IN SHADE

A shady site can be a difficult place to grow plants – the soil is often dry – but a wide range of interesting plants can be grown in containers. Remember that rain may not reach plants under trees;

regular watering is needed all year, plus fertilizing in summer. Add bulbs for spring color and flowering plants in summer. Combine plants for form and texture as well as color.

ACER PALMATUM VAR. *DISSECTUM*
'CRIMSON QUEEN'
Shrub Z5-8 H8-2 Arching shoots with finely toothed purple leaves.
‡ 10ft (3m) ↔ 12ft (4m)

AGERATUM 'SOUTHERN CROSS'
Annual H12-1 Neat, bushy plants with white and blue fluffy flowers.
‡↔ 10in (25cm)

AJUGA REPTANS 'RAINBOW'
Perennial Z3-9 H9-1 Mats of bronze leaves spotted with pink and yellow; blue flowers.
‡ 6in (15cm) ↔ 18in (45cm)

BEGONIA NONSTOP SERIES
Perennials H7-1 Compact plants with double flowers in many colors.
‡↔ 12in (30cm)

CAMELLIA JAPONICA 'LAVINIA MAGGI'
Evergreen shrub   page 101

DRYOPTERIS ERYTHROSORA
Fern Z6-9 H9-6 Colorful fern with copper-red young fronds.
‡ 24in (60cm) ↔ 15in (38cm)

DRYOPTERIS WALLICHIANA
Fern   page 180

X *FATSHEDERA LIZEI* 'ANNEMIEKE'
Evergreen shrub Z8-11 H12-1 Procumbent stems and leaves with bright gold centers. Sometimes sold as 'Lemon and Lime'.
‡ 4–6ft (1.2–2m) or more ↔ 10ft (3m)

FATSIA JAPONICA
Evergreen shrub   page 206

FUCHSIA 'DOLLAR PRINCESS'
Shrub H12-7 A robust plant with small, red and purple, double flowers.
‡ 12–18in (30–45cm) ↔ 18–24in (45–60cm)

HEDERA HELIX 'IVALACE'
Evergreen climber   page 246

HEDERA HELIX 'MANDA'S CRESTED'
Evergreen climber Z5-11 H12-1 Uneven, curled and twisted, fingered leaves.
‡ 4ft (1.2m)

HOSTA 'ROYAL STANDARD'
Perennial   page 260

ILEX CRENATA 'CONVEXA'
Evergreen shrub   page 274

IMPATIENS 'BLACKBERRY ICE'
Annual Z11 H12-1 Double purple flowers and white-variegated foliage.
‡ to 28in (70cm)

IMPATIENS SUPER ELFIN SERIES
Annuals   page 275

IPHEION UNIFLORUM 'WISLEY BLUE'
Bulbous perennial   page 276

PIERIS JAPONICA 'LITTLE HEATH'
Evergreen shrub Z6-9 H9-5 Compact, acidic-soil-loving, with white-edged leaves flushed pink in spring.
‡↔ 24in (60cm)

RHODODENDRON 'VUYK'S SCARLET'
Evergreen shrub   page 437

VIOLA 'IMPERIAL ANTIQUE SHADES'
Biennial Z9-11 H7-1 Large flowers in pink, cream, and parchment colors.
‡ 6in (15cm) ↔ 8in (25cm)

FOLIAGE FOR HANGING BASKETS

Although flowering plants are the most popular choice for hanging baskets, they can often be enhanced with attractive foliage plants. Silver-leaved plants are the most widely grown foil for flowers, but there are trailing plants that have gold, green, and red foliage, and it is not difficult to plant a beautiful basket using solely plants chosen for their colorful and contrasting leaves.

AJUGA REPTANS 'BURGUNDY GLOW'
Perennial   page 49

ASPARAGUS DENSIFLORUS 'MYERSII'
Perennial   page 70

BEGONIAS, FOLIAGE
Perennials   pages 80–81

CHLOROPHYTUM COMOSUM
'VITTATUM'
Perennial Z10-11 H12-1 Variegated narrow leaves; arching stems bearing plantlets.
‡ 6–8in (15–20cm) ↔ 6–12in (15–30cm)

GLECHOMA HEDERACEA 'VARIEGATA'
Perennial Z5-9 H9 1 Long, pendent stems with gray green leaves edged with white.
↔ trailing to 6ft (2m)

HEDERA HELIX 'GOLDCHILD'
Evergreen climber   page 246

HELICHRYSUM PETIOLARE
Evergreen shrub   page 250

HELICHRYSUM PETIOLARE
'LIMELIGHT'
Shrub Z10-11 H12-1 Arching stems with felted pale green leaves, yellow in sun.
‡ 3ft (1m) ↔ indefinite

HELICHRYSUM PETIOLARE
'VARIEGATUM'
Evergreen shrub   page 251

LAMIUM MACULATUM 'AUREUM'
Perennial Z4-8 H8-1 Creeping, with bright yellow leaves marked white, and pink flowers.
‡ 8in (20cm) ↔ 3ft (1m)

LOTUS BERTHELOTII
Subshrub   page 326

LYSIMACHIA CONGESTIFLORA
'OUTBACK SUNSET'
Perennial Z6-9 H9-5 Semi-trailing, with green, cream, and bronze leaves and clusters of yellow flowers.
‡ 6in (15cm) ↔ 12in (30cm)

LYSIMACHIA NUMMULARIA 'AUREA'
Perennial   page 329

PELARGONIUM 'SWANLAND LACE'
Perennial Z11 H12-6 Trailing plant with pink flowers and leaves veined with yellow.
‡ ↔ 12in (30cm)

PLECTRANTHUS FORSTERI
'MARGINATUS'
Perennial H12-1 Scented foliage, edged with white. New growth arches strongly.
‡ 10in (25cm) ↔ 3ft (1m)

SAXIFRAGA STOLONIFERA
'TRICOLOR'
Perennial Z6-9 H9-5 Round leaves edged white and flushed pink; plantlets form on long runners.
‡ ↔ to 12in (30cm)

SELAGINELLA KRAUSSIANA
Perennial   page 491

TROPAEOLUM ALASKA SERIES
Annuals Z11 H12-1 Easily raised, bushy nasturtiums with white-splashed leaves.
‡ to 12in (30cm) ↔ to 18in (45cm)

Flowers for Hanging Baskets

Most gardens, and houses or apartments without gardens, can be brightened by a few hanging baskets. They are easy to plant, and there are lots of cheerful plants to choose from, all with a long flowering season and a low or trailing habit. Baskets require regular watering and fertilizing to grow and flower well all summer. Automatic irrigation systems take the worry out of vacation watering.

ABUTILON MEGAPOTAMICUM
Shrub page 30

ACALYPHA REPTANS
Perennial Z10-11 H12-1 Spreading plant with short red-hot cats'-tail flowers.
‡ 6in (15cm) ↔ 24in (60cm)

ANAGALLIS MONELLII
Perennial Z7-8 H8-7 Spreading plant with small leaves and bright, intense, deep blue flowers.
‡ 4–8in (10–20cm) ↔ 16in (40cm)

ANTIRRHINUM 'CANDELABRA LEMON BLUSH'
Perennial Z7-9 H9-1 Bushy habit with trailing flower stems carrying pale yellow flowers, flushed with pink.
‡↔ 15in (38cm)

BEGONIA FUCHSIOIDES
Perennial Z11 H12-1 Arching stems set with tiny, glossy leaves bear pendent pink or red flowers.
‡ 30in (75cm) ↔ 18in (45cm)

BEGONIA 'ILLUMINATION ORANGE'
Perennial page 82

BEGONIA 'IRENE NUSS'
Perennial page 83

BEGONIA SUTHERLANDII
Perennial page 83

BIDENS FERULIFOLIA
Perennial page 90

CONVOLVULUS SABATIUS
Perennial page 136

DIASCIA 'LILAC BELLE'
Perennial Z7-9 H9-7 Loose spikes of mauve-pink flowers.
‡ 8in (20cm) ↔ 12in (30cm)

FUCHSIA 'GOLDEN MARINKA'
Shrub page 216

FUCHSIA 'JACK SHAHAN'
Shrub page 216

FUCHSIA 'LA CAMPANELLA'
Shrub page 216

FUCHSIA 'LENA'
Shrub page 216

IMPATIENS TEMPO SERIES
Annuals page 275

LOBELIA 'COLOUR CASCADE'
Annual H9-1 Trailing stems with flowers in shades of blue, pink, and white.
‡ 6in (15cm) ↔ 18in (45cm)

LOBELIA RICHARDSONII
Perennial Z4-9 H9-1 Bushy but rather sparse, trailing stems with small leaves and blue flowers.
‡ 6in (15cm) ↔ 12in (30cm)

MIMULUS AURANTIACUS
Evergreen shrub page 341

PAROCHETUS COMMUNIS
Perennial Z8-10 H10-8 A fast-growing trailer with cloverlike leaves and pale blue, pealike flowers.
‡ 4in (10cm) ↔ 12in (30cm)

PELARGONIUM 'AMETHYST'
Perennial page 374

PELARGONIUM 'LILA MINI CASCADE'
Perennial Z11 H12-1 Single, pink flowers on a compact but vigorous plant.
‡ 18–20in (45–50cm) ↔ 6–8in (15–20cm)

PELARGONIUM 'MADAME CROUSSE'
Perennial Z11 H12-1 Trailing plant with semidouble pink flowers.
‡ 20–24in (50–60cm) ↔ 6–8in (15–20cm)

PELARGONIUM 'OLDBURY CASCADE'
Perennial Z11 H12-1 Rich red flowers on a compact plant with cream-variegated leaves.
‡ 18in (45cm) ↔ 12in (30cm)

PELARGONIUM 'ROULETTA'
Perennial Z11 H12-1 Double white flowers, heavily margined with red.
‡ 20–24in (50–60cm) ↔ 6–8in (15–20cm)

PELARGONIUM 'THE BOAR'
Perennial page 376

PELARGONIUM 'VILLE DE PARIS'
Perennial Z11 H12-1 Single, pink flowers produced in profusion on a pendulous plant.
‡ 24in (60cm) ↔ 18in (45cm)

PELARGONIUM 'YALE'
Perennial Z11 H12-1 The trailing stems carry clusters of semidouble bright red flowers.
‡ 8–10in (20–25cm) ↔ 6–8in (15–20cm)

PETUNIA DADDY SERIES
Annuals Z9-11 H12-1 Large flowers, heavily veined with darker shades.
‡ to 14in (35cm) ↔ 12–36in (30–90cm)

PETUNIA 'MARCO POLO ADVENTURER'
Annual Z9-11 H12-1 Large, double flowers of bright rose pink on trailing plants.
‡ ↔ 15in (38cm)

PETUNIA 'SURFINIA PASTEL PINK'
Annual Z8-11 H12-1 Large flowers of mid-pink on a strong plant that trails well.
‡ 9–16in (23–40cm) ↔ 12–36in (30–90cm)

SUTERA CORDATA 'KNYSNA HILLS'
Perennial Z11 H12-1 Bushy plant with massed heads of tiny, pale pink flowers.
‡ 8in (20cm) ↔ 24in (60cm)

SUTERA CORDATA 'SNOWFLAKE'
Perennial Z11 H12-1 Spreading, small-leafed plant with tiny, five-petaled white flowers for months.
‡ 4in (10cm) ↔ 24in (60c[)

VERBENA 'IMAGINATION'
Perennial Z10-11 H12-1 Seed-raised, loosely-branched plants with small, deep violet flowers.
‡ ↔ 15in (30cm)

VERBENA 'TAPIEN PINK'
Perennial Z10-11 H12-1 Trailing stems with clusters of small pink flowers.
‡ ↔ 15in (38cm)

VIOLA 'SUNBEAM'
Biennial Z4-8 H8-1 Semi-trailing plant with small yellow flowers.
‡ ↔ 12in (30cm)

SPRING-FLOWERING BULBS

The first signs that winter is giving way to spring are usually the flowers of spring bulbs. From tiny winter aconites that open as the leaves push through the soil to majestic crown imperials,

there are bulbs for every situation. Most are tolerant of a wide range of soils, and many can be grown in the shade of trees. Grown in pots, they can be brought into the home to be enjoyed.

ALLIUM CRISTOPHII
page **51**

ANEMONE BLANDA 'WHITE SPLENDOUR'
page **58**

CAMASSIA CUISICKII
Z3-11 H12-1 Sheaves of narrow leaves and tall racemes of blue starlike blooms.
‡ 24–32in (60–80cm) ↔ 4in (10cm)

CHIONODOXA LUCILIAE
page **120**

CHIONODOXA SARDENSIS
Z4-8 H8-1 Deep blue starry flowers on slender stems.
‡ 4–8in (10–20cm) ↔ 1¼in (3cm)

CORYDALIS FLEXUOSA
Z6-8 H8-6 Clumps of delicate foliage and nodding bright blue flowers.
‡ 6–12in (15–30cm) ↔ 8in (20cm)

CORYDALIS SOLIDA 'GEORGE BAKER'
page **142**

CROCUS ANGUSTIFOLIUS
Z3-8 H8-1 Clusters of orange-yellow flowers in spring.
‡ ↔ 2in (5cm)

CROCUS CHRYSANTHUS 'BLUE PEARL'
Z3-8 H8-1 Lilac-blue flowers with white and yellow centers.
‡ 3in (8cm) ↔ 1½in (4cm)

CROCUS CHRYSANTHUS 'E. A. BOWLES'
page **153**

CROCUS SIEBERI 'HUBERT EDELSTEIN'
page **153**

CROCUS SIEBERI 'TRICOLOR'
page **153**

CROCUS TOMMASINIANUS
Z3-8 H8-1 An early-flowering crocus with slender, silvery lilac flowers.
‡ 3–4in (8–10cm) ↔ 1in (2.5cm)

ERANTHIS HYEMALIS
page **185**

ERYTHRONIUM CALIFORNICUM 'WHITE BEAUTY'
Z3-9 H9-1 The recurved white flowers are heldabove mottled leaves.
‡ 6–14in (15–35cm) ↔ 4in (10cm)

ERYTHRONIUM 'PAGODA'
page **194**

FRITILLARIA ACMOPETALA
page **210**

FRITILLARIA IMPERIALIS 'AUREOMARGINATA'
Z5-9 H9-1 Tall stems carrying heads of orange flowers, with yellow-margined leaves.
‡ 5ft (1.5m) ↔ 10–12in (25–30cm)

FRITILLARIA PALLIDIFLORA
page **211**

GALANTHUS NIVALIS
Z3-9 H9-1 The common but easily grown snowdrop, best planted while in leaf.
‡ ↔ 4in (10cm)

HERMODACTYLUS TUBEROSUS
Z7-9 H9-7 Straggly leaves almost hide the velvety green and black irislike flowers.
‡8–16in (20–40cm) ↔ 2in (5cm)

HYACINTHUS ORIENTALIS
'BLUE JACKET'
page **262**

HYACINTHUS ORIENTALIS
'ANNA MARIE'
Z5-9 H9-5 Spikes of scented, pale pink flowers.
‡8in (20cm) ↔ 3in (8cm)

IPHEION UNIFLORUM 'FROYLE MILL'
Z6-9 H9-5 Clump-forming plant with onion-scented leaves and violet, star-shaped flowers.
‡6–8in (15–20cm)

IRIS BUCHARICA
page **280**

IRIS RETICULATA 'CANTAB'
Z5-8 H8-4 Pale blue flowers with deeper falls. Long leaves develop after flowering.
‡4–6in (10–15cm)

MUSCARI LATIFOLIUM
Z4-8 H8-1 Broad leaves and bicolored spikes of flowers in pale and dark blue.
‡8in (20cm) ↔ 2in (5cm)

NARCISSUS 'ACTAEA'
page **348**

NARCISSUS BULBOCODIUM
page **346**

NARCISSUS 'FEBRUARY GOLD'
page **346**

NARCISSUS 'HAWERA'
page **347**

NARCISSUS 'ICE FOLLIES'
page **349**

NARCISSUS 'LITTLE WITCH'
Z3-9 H9-1 Golden yellow flowers with reflexed petals.
‡9in (22cm)

NARCISSUS MINOR
page **347**

NARCISSUS 'PASSIONALE'
page **349**

NARCISSUS TRIANDRUS
page **347**

SCILLA BIFOLIA
page **487**

SCILLA MISCHTSCHENKOANA
'TUBERGENIANA'
page **487**

SCILLA SIBERICA
Z5-8 H8-1 Bell-shaped flowers of cobalt blue above bright green leaves.
‡4–8in (10–20cm) ↔ 2in (5cm)

TULIPA 'APELDOORN'S ELITE'
Z3-9 H9-1 Rich yellow flowers feathered with red to give a subtle effect.
‡24in (60cm)

TULIPA 'BALLADE'
Z3-9 H9-1 Elegant flowers of rich pink with white petal edges and tips.
‡20in (60cm)

TULIPA 'CHINA PINK'
page **524**

TULIPA 'MAUREEN'
Z3-9 H9-1 Oval flowers of ivory-white.
‡20in (50cm)

TULIPA 'MRS JOHN T. SCHEEPERS'
Z3-9 H9-1 Large flowers of pale yellow.
‡24in (60cm)

TULIPA 'RED SURPRISE'
Z3-9 H9-1 Bright red, starry flowers.
‡8in (20cm)

SUMMER-FLOWERING BULBS

Summer-flowering bulbs bring sparkle to gardens with their bright colors and exotic shapes. Unfortunately, many are not hardy in frost-prone climates, but they are not expensive, and most can be lifted in autumn and kept in a frost-free shed. Dahlias and gladioli are familiar to everyone, but modern lilies are easy to grow, too, and tigridias and hedychiums are even more exotic.

ALLIUM GIGANTEUM
page 51

ALLIUM HOLLANDICUM 'PURPLE SENSATION'
page 51

ALLIUM KARATAVIENSE
page 52

BLETILLA STRIATA
Z5-8 H8-2 Terrestrial orchid: a leafy plant with spikes of 1–6 small, pink flowers.
↕ ↔ 12–24in (30–60cm)

CRINUM × *POWELLII*
Z7-11 H12-8 Huge bulbs produce large leaves and long pink trumpet flowers.
↕ 5ft (1.5m) ↔ 12in (30cm)

CROCOSMIA 'EMILY McKENZIE'
Z6-9 H9-6 Sword-shaped leaves and bright orange flowers marked with bronze.
↕ 24in (60cm) ↔ 3in (8cm)

DAHLIA 'BISHOP OF LLANDAFF'
page 162

DAHLIA 'GLORIE VAN HEEMSTEDE'
Z8-11 H12-1 Medium-sized bright yellow flowers shaped like waterlilies.
↕ 4½ft (1.3m) ↔ 2ft (60cm)

DAHLIA 'JESCOT JULIE'
Z8-11 H12-1 Long-petaled flowers of orange and red.
↕ 36in (1m) ↔ 18in (45cm)

DAHLIA 'PEARL OF HEEMSTEDE'
Z8-11 H12-1 This waterlily dahlia has flowers of silvery pink.
↕ 3ft (1m) ↔ 18in (45cm)

DRACUNCULUS VULGARIS
Z8-10 H10-8 Spotted stems support interesting leaves and huge, purple, unpleasantly scented flowers.
↕ to 5ft (1.5m) ↔ 24in (60cm)

EREMURUS 'CLEOPATRA'
Z6-9 H9-6 Rosettes of straplike leaves and tall spikes of small soft orange flowers.
↕ 5ft (1.5m) ↔ 24in (60cm)

EUCOMIS BICOLOR
Z8-10 H10-1 Rosettes of broad leaves below spikes of starry, cream, purple-edged blooms.
↕ 12–24in (30–60cm) ↔ 8in (20cm)

GLADIOLUS CALLIANTHUS
page 231

GLADIOLUS COMMUNIS SUBSP. *BYZANTINUS*
page 232

GLADIOLUS 'GREEN WOODPECKER'
Z8-10 H12-1 Greenish yellow flowers with red markings.
↕ 5ft (1.5m) ↔ 5in (12cm)

HEDYCHIUM COCCINEUM
Z8-10 H10-8 An exotic-looking plant with spikes of tubular, scented, orange, pink, or cream flowers.
↕ 10ft (3m) ↔ 3ft (1m)

HEDYCHIUM GARDNERIANUM
Perennial Z9-10 H10-9 Large heads of spidery, showy, sweetly scented cream flowers.
↕ 6–7ft (2–2.2m)

HEDYCHIUM 'TARA'
Z8-10 H10-8 A selection of *H. coccineum* with deeper-colored flowers.
↕ 10ft (3m) ↔ 3ft (1m)

IXIA VIRIDIFLORA
Z10-11 H12-1 Unusual pale turquoise-green flowers on tall, wiry stems.
↕ 12–24in (30–60cm)

LEUCOJUM AESTIVUM 'GRAVETYE GIANT'
page **311**

LILIUM 'BLACK DRAGON'
Z4-8 H8-1 Tall stems carry pure white, scented flowers that are deep maroon in bud.
↕ 5ft (1.5m)

LILIUM 'EVEREST'
Z4-8 H8-1 Large white flowers, heavily scented, with dark spots, on tall stems.
↕ 5ft (1.5m)

LILIUM HENRYI
page **315**

LILIUM 'KAREN NORTH'
Z4-8 H8-1 Elegant flowers with reflexed petals of orange-pink with deeper spots.
↕ 3–4½ft (1–1.3m)

LILIUM MARTAGON VAR. *ALBUM*
page **316**

LILIUM PYRENAICUM
page **318**

LILIUM REGALE
page **318**

NECTAROSCORDUM SICULUM
Z6-10 H10-1 Plants smell strongly of garlic and produce loose umbels of pendulous cream flowers marked dark red.
↕ to 4ft (1.2m) ↔ 4in (10cm)

RHODOHYPOXIS BAURII 'TETRA RED'
Z9-10 H10-9 Forms clumps or mats of bright, squat, starry flowers.
↕ ↔ 4in (10cm)

TIGRIDIA PAVONIA
H9-1 Broad, spotted flowers in shades of red, yellow, and white, each lasting one day.
↕ 5ft (1.5m) ↔ 4in (10cm)

TROPAEOLUM POLYPHYLLUM
Z8-10 H10-8 Trailing stems with finely divided gray leaves, and bright yellow flowers.
↕ 2–3in (5–8cm) ↔ to 3ft (1m)

ZANTEDESCHIA AETHIOPICA 'GREEN GODDESS'
page **545**

AUTUMN-FLOWERING BULBS

Bulbs and corms can provide color and interest when most plants are dying down. Most require full sun and well-drained soil if their flowers are to benefit from the last fine days of the year. Many do not fit easily with bulb production cycles and do not flower well until they are established in the garden, so they may need some effort to find in catalogs and nurseries.

ALLIUM CALLIMISCHON
Z5-9 H9-5 Slender stems with white or pale pink flowers for dry soils.
‡ 4–14in (8–35cm) ↔ 2in (5cm)

X *AMARYGIA PARKERI*
Z9-10 H10-9 This hybrid produces large pink trumpet flowers in mild gardens.
‡ 3ft (1m) ↔ 12in (30cm)

AMARYLLIS BELLADONNA
Z7-10 H10-7 The dark stems support beautiful pink trumpets.
‡ 24in (60cm) ↔ 4in (10cm)

COLCHICUM SPECIOSUM 'ALBUM'
page **135**

COLCHICUM 'WATERLILY'
Z4-9 H9-1 Beautiful white goblets appear without leaves.
‡ 7in (18cm) ↔ 4in (10cm)

CRINUM X *POWELLII* 'ALBUM'
page **151**

CROCUS BANATICUS
page **154**

CROCUS BORYI
Z4-8 H8-1 Each corm produces up to four pale lilac and cream flowers.
‡ 3in (8cm) ↔ 2in (5cm)

CROCUS GOULIMYI
page **154**

CROCUS KOTSCHYANUS
page **154**

CROCUS MEDIUS
page **154**

CROCUS OCHROLEUCUS
page **154**

CROCUS PULCHELLUS
page **154**

CROCUS SPECIOSUS
Z3-8 H8-1 Violet-blue, scented flowers with orange stigmas.
‡ 6in (15cm)

CYCLAMEN HEDERIFOLIUM
page **158**

LEUCOJUM AUTUMNALE
page **311**

MERENDERA MONTANA
Z6-9 H9-6 Starry lilac flowers; needs well-drained soil.
‡ ↔ 2in (5cm)

NERINE BOWDENII
page **350**

STERNBERGIA LUTEA
Z7-9 H9-7 Deep green leaves and bright yellow crocuslike flowers.
‡ 6in (15cm) ↔ 3in (8cm)

TROPAEOLUM TUBEROSUM 'KEN ASLET'
Z8-10 H10-8 Clambering stems with small leaves and yellow, hooded flowers.
‡ 6–12ft (2–4m)

ZEPHYRANTHES CANDIDA
Z9-10 H10-9 Clumps of narrow leaves and white, crocus-like flowers over many weeks.
‡ 4–8in (10–20cm) ↔ 3in (8cm)

SPRING BEDDING

When the last bedding plants of the season die down, it is time to replace them with young plants that will survive the winter then flower in spring. Most of these are biennials, such as Canterbury bells, sweet Williams, and wallflowers. Add winter-flowering pansies for early color, especially in containers. Plant spring bulbs among the bedding plants for extra interest.

BELLIS PERENNIS 'POMPONETTE'
page 84

CAMPANULA MEDIUM 'CALYCANTHEMA'
Biennial Z5-8 H8-4 Cup-and-saucer Canterbury bells in pink, blue, and white.
‡ to 30in (75cm)

DIANTHUS BARBATUS 'AURICULA-EYED MIXED'
Biennial Z3-9 H9-1 Traditional sweet Williams with flowers zoned in white, pink, and maroon.
‡ to 24in (60cm)

ERYSIMUM CHEIRI 'CLOTH OF GOLD'
Biennial Z3-7 H7-1 Bright yellow, scented flowers.
‡ 18in (45cm)

ERYSIMUM CHEIRI 'FIREKING IMPROVED'
Biennial Z3-7 H7-1 Orange-red flowers.
‡ 18in (45cm)

ERYSIMUM CHEIRI 'PRINCE PRIMROSE YELLOW'
Dwarf type with large flowers.
‡ 12in (30cm)

HYACINTHUS ORIENTALIS 'FONDANT'
Bulb Z5-9 H9-5 Flowers of pure pink.
‡ 10in (25cm)

HYACINTHUS ORIENTALIS 'OSTARA'
page 263

HYACINTHUS ORIENTALIS 'PINK PEARL'
page 264

HYACINTHUS ORIENTALIS 'VIOLET PEARL'
Bulb Z5-9 H9-5 Amethyst-colored flowers.
‡ 10in (25cm)

MYOSOTIS 'SPRING SYMPHONY BLUE'
Biennial Z5-9 H9-5 The blue flowers associate well with most spring bulbs.
‡ 6in (15cm)

POLYANTHUS PRIMROSES
page 416

TULIPA 'HALCRO'
Bulb Z3-8 H8-1 Large flowers of deep salmon-red.
‡ 28in (70cm)

TULIPA 'ORANJE NASSAU'
Bulb Z3-8 H8-1 Fiery flowers in shades of red and scarlet.
‡ 12in (30cm)

TULIPA 'SPRING GREEN'   **page 525**

VIOLA 'FELIX'
Biennial Z7-11 H7-1 Yellow and purple, "whiskered" flowers on tufted plants.
‡ 6in (15cm)

VIOLA 'RIPPLING WATERS'
Biennial Z7-11 H7-1 Large flowers of dark purple edged with white in spring.
‡ 6in (15cm)

VIOLA ULTIMA SERIES
Biennial Z7-11 H7-1 Wide range of colors on plants that flower through mild spells.
‡ 6in (15cm)

SUMMER BEDDING

Although bedding out on the grand scale will probably never be as popular as it was in Victorian times, most gardeners find room for plants that grow and flower quickly once planted out. Although most are not tolerant of frost, some are annuals and others are tender perennials. Most also have a long flowering period and, even if only for one season, are excellent value.

AGERATUM HOUSTONIANUM 'PACIFIC'
Annual H12-1 Compact plants with dense heads of purple-blue flowers.
‡8in (20cm)

ANTIRRHINUM SONNET SERIES
Annuals   page 62

BEGONIA 'PIN UP'
Perennial   page 83

BEGONIA OLYMPIA SERIES
Perennials H12-1 Compact, large-flowered bedding begonias.
‡↔8in (20cm)

DAHLIA 'COLTNESS GEM'
Perennial Z8-11 H12-1 Reliable, single-flowered dahlias in clear, bright colours.
‡↔18in (45cm)

DIASCIA RIGESCENS
Perennial   page 174

HELIOTROPIUM 'PRINCESS MARINA'
Perennial   page 252

IMPATIENS DECO SERIES
Annuals Z11 H12-1 Large, bright flowers on plants with dark green leaves.
‡↔ to 8in (20cm)

LOBELIA 'COMPLIMENT SCARLET'
Perennial Z4-8 H8-1 Bold plant with green foliage and large scarlet flowers on tall spikes.
‡30in (75cm) ↔12in (30cm)

LOBELIA 'CRYSTAL PALACE'
Annual   page 322

LOBELIA ERINUS 'MRS CLIBRAN'
Annual H9-1 A compact plant with white-eyed, bright blue flowers.
‡4–6in (10–15cm)

NICOTIANA 'LIME GREEN'
Annual   page 350

NICOTIANA X *SANDERAE* 'DOMINO SALMON PINK'
Annual H12-1 Upward-facing flowers of salmon-pink on compact plants.
‡12–18in (30–45cm)

NICOTIANA SYLVESTRIS
Perennial   page 351

NIGELLA 'MISS JEKYLL'
Annual   page 351

PELARGONIUM MULTIBLOOM SERIES
Perennials   page 376

PELARGONIUM VIDEO SERIES
Perennials   page 376

PENSTEMON 'BEECH PARK'
Perennial Z7-10 H10-7 Large pink and white trumpets throughout summer. Sometimes sold as 'Barbara Barker'.
‡30in (75cm) ↔18in (45cm)

PENSTEMON 'BURGUNDY'
Perennial Z7-10 H10-7 Deep, wine red flowers above dark green leaves.
‡36in (90cm) ↔18in (45cm)

PENSTEMON 'MAURICE GIBBS'
Perennial Z7-10 H10-7 Large-leaved plants bear spikes of cerise flowers with white throats.
‡30in (75cm) ↔18in (45cm)

PENSTEMON 'MYDDELTON GEM'
Perennial Z7-10 H10-7 Long-flowering plant with pale green leaves and deep pink, tubular flowers.
‡30in (75cm) ↔ 18in (45cm)

PETUNIA CARPET SERIES
Annuals   page 382

PETUNIA 'MIRAGE REFLECTIONS'
Annual Z8-11 H12-1 Weather-resistant multiflora petunias in pastel colors with darker veins.
‡12in (30cm) ↔ 24in (60cm)

PHLOX DRUMMONDII 'TAPESTRY'
Annual H12-1 Wide range of pastel colors and bicolors on bushy plants.
‡20in (50cm) ↔ 15in (38cm)

POLEMONIUM 'LAMBROOK MAUVE'
Perennial   page 408

PORTULACA GRANDIFLORA
SUNDIAL SERIES
Annuals Z12-1 Sun-loving plants with brilliant flowers, with petals like satin
‡4in (10cm) ↔ 6in (15cm)

RUDBECKIA HIRTA 'RUSTIC DWARFS'
Annual Z3-7 H7-1 Mixture of autumn shades on large, dark-eyed flowers.
‡to 24in (60cm)

SALPIGLOSSIS CASINO SERIES
Annuals   page 471

SALVIA COCCINEA 'LADY IN RED'
Annual Z11 H12-1 Bushy plants bear slender spikes of small but showy red flowers all summer.
‡16in (40cm)

SALVIA FARINACEA 'VICTORIA'
Annual Z8-10 H10-1 The small, deep blue flowers are crowded on spikes held well above the leaves.
‡to 24in (60cm) ↔ to 12in (30cm)

SALVIA FULGENS
Subshrub   page 474

SALVIA PRATENSIS HAEMATODES
GROUP
Perennial   page 478

SALVIA SPLENDENS 'SCARLET KING'
Perennial   page 478

SALVIA SPLENDENS SIZZLER SERIES
Annuals Z11·H12-1
Early-flowering plants with blooms in colors from red to lavender and white.
‡10–12in (25–30cm)

TAGETES 'DISCO ORANGE'
Annual H12-1 Weather-resistant, single flowers.
‡8–10in (20–25cm)

TAGETES 'SAFARI SCARLET'
Annual H12-1 Large, bright double flowers.
‡8–10in (20–25cm)

TAGETES 'ZENITH RED'
Annual H12-1 Marigold with double red flowers.
‡12in (30cm)

VERBENA × *HYBRIDA*
'PEACHES AND CREAM'
Annual Z11 H12-1 Seed-raised spreading plants with peach-colored flowers that fade to cream.
‡12in (30cm) ↔ 18in (45cm)

VERBENA × *HYBRIDA* 'SILVER ANNE'
Perennial Z11 H12-1 Sweetly scented pink flowers that fade almost to white, above divided foliage.
‡12in (30cm) ↔ 24in (60cm)

VARIEGATED HERBACEOUS PLANTS

Variegation may be restricted to a narrow rim around the edge of a leaf, or it may be more spectacular. Regular patterning with white, cream, or gold may help define the shape of large leaves, but random streaks and splashes can make some plants look unhealthy. Remember that plants may revert back to their plain form: always remove any shoots with plain green leaves.

AQUILEGIA VULGARIS VERVAENEANA
GROUP
Perennial Z3-8 H8-1 Leaves are marbled and splashed with yellow and green, below white, pink, or blue flowers.
‡36in (90cm) ↔ 18in (45cm)

ARABIS PROCURRENS 'VARIEGATA'
Perennial   page 63

ARMORACIA RUSTICANA 'VARIEGATA'
Perennial Z4-8 H8-1 Deep-rooted plants with large leaves heavily splashed with white, especially in spring.
‡3ft (1m) ↔ 18in (45cm)

ASTRANTIA 'SUNNINGDALE
VARIEGATED'
Perennial   page 77

BRUNNERA MACROPHYLLA
'HADSPEN CREAM'
Perennial   page 92

COREOPSIS 'CALYPSO'
Perennial Z4-9 H9-1 Narrow leaves edged with gold; yellow flowers with a red zone.
‡ ↔ 15in (38cm)

GAURA LINDHEIMERI
'CORRIE'S GOLD'
Perennial Z6-9 H9-6 White flowers on delicate stems; small gold-edged leaves.
‡to 5ft (1.5m) ↔ 36in (90cm)

HEMEROCALLIS FULVA
'KWANZO VARIEGATA'
Perennial Z3-10 H10-1 Arching leaves with bright white stripes, and occasional double orange flowers.
‡30in (75cm)

HOSTA 'FORTUNEI ALBOPICTA'
Perennial   page 259

HOSTA 'GOLDEN TIARA'
Perennial   page 259

HOSTA 'GREAT EXPECTATIONS'
Perennial Z4-9 H9-1 Glaucous green, puckered leaves with broad yellow centers, and grayish white flowers.
‡22in (55cm) ↔ 34in (85cm)

HOSTA 'SHADE FANFARE'
Perennial   page 260

HOSTA SIEBOLDII VAR. *ELEGANS*
Perennial   page 260

HOSTA TARDIANA GROUP 'HALCYON'
Perennial   page 261

HOSTA UNDULATA VAR.
UNIVITTATA
Perennial   page 261

HOSTA VENUSTA
Perennial   page 261

HOSTA 'WIDE BRIM'
Perennial   page 261

HOUTTUYNIA CORDATA
'CHAMELEON'
Perennial Z6-11 H12-6 Vivid leaves in shades of cream, green and red, and small, white flowers.
‡to 6–12in (15–30cm) or more ↔ indefinite

IRIS LAEVIGATA 'VARIEGATA'
Perennial   page 278

IRIS PALLIDA 'VARIEGATA'
Perennial   page 288

LYSIMACHIA PUNCTATA 'ALEXANDER'
Perennial Z4-8 H8-3 Creeping plant with
spires of yellow flowers, and white-edged
foliage tinged pink in spring.
‡3ft (1m) ↔ 2ft (60cm)

MIMULUS LUTEUS 'VARIEGATUS'
Perennial Z7-9 H9-7 Creeping plant with
yellow flowers and pale green leaves
edged with white.
‡12in (30cm) ↔ 18in (45cm)

MOLINIA CAERULEA 'VARIEGATA'
Ornamental grass   page 342

PERSICARIA VIRGINIANA 'PAINTER'S
PALETTE'
Perennial Z5-9 H9-5 Bright foliage splashed
with white and marked with red and
brown, on red stems. Variegation comes
true from seed.
‡16–48in (40–120cm) ↔ 24–56in (60–140cm)

PHALARIS ARUNDINACEA 'PICTA'
Ornamental grass   page 383

PHLOX PANICULATA 'PINK POSIE'
Perennial Z4-8 H8-1 Compact, strong-
growing phlox with white-edged leaves
and pink flowers.
‡30in (75cm) ↔ 24in (60cm)

PHORMIUM COOKIANUM SUBSP.
HOOKERI 'TRICOLOR'
Evergreen perennial   page 392

PHYSOSTEGIA VIRGINIANA
'VARIEGATA'
Perennial Z4-8 H8-1 Upright plant with
grayish leaves edged with white, and deep
pink flowers.
‡30in (75cm) ↔ 24in (60cm)

PLEIOBLASTUS AURICOMUS
Bamboo   page 406

PULMONARIA RUBRA 'DAVID WARD'
Perennial Z6-8 H8-6 Coral-red flowers in
spring, and large leaves broadly margined
with white.
‡to 16in (40cm) ↔ 36in (90cm)

SAXIFRAGA STOLONIFERA
'TRICOLOR'
Evergreen perennial Z6-9 H9-5 A slightly
tender plant with round leaves edged with
white and pink.
‡↔ 12in (30cm)

SISYRINCHIUM STRIATUM
'AUNT MAY'
Perennial Z7-8 H8-7 Upright fans of
narrow, gray leaves edged with cream, and
spikes of cream flowers.
‡↔ to 20in (50cm)

SYMPHYTUM × *UPLANDICUM*
'VARIEGATUM'
Perennial   page 505

VERONICA GENTIANOIDES
'VARIEGATA'
Perennial Z4-7 H7-1 Mats of deep green
leaves margined with white, and spikes of
small, pale blue flowers.
‡18in (45cm)

VINCA MAJOR 'VARIEGATA'
Perennial   page 537

VARIEGATED TREES AND SHRUBS

While flowers usually have a short season, foliage provides color for at least half the year – and all year if evergreen. Variegated shrubs increase that interest with their bright coloring,

and some have flowers that complement the foliage. Many variegated evergreens are useful to brighten shady areas and are good in pots and containers; they are also popular with flower arrangers.

ACER CAMPESTRE 'CARNIVAL'
Tree Z6-8 H8-4
Pink-splashed leaves.
‡ 25ft (8m) ↔ 15ft (5m)

ACER NEGUNDO 'FLAMINGO'
Tree   page **33**

ACER PALMATUM 'BUTTERFLY'
Shrub or small tree   page **34**

ACER PLATANOIDES
'DRUMMONDII'
Tree   page **37**

ACER PSEUDOPLATANUS
'LEOPOLDII'
Tree Z4-7 H7-1 The leaves are pink at first in spring, then speckled with yellow.
‡ ↔ 30ft (10m)

ARALIA ELATA 'VARIEGATA'
Tree   page **64**

BERBERIS THUNBERGII
'ROSE GLOW'
Shrub   page **86**

BUDDLEJA DAVIDII
'HARLEQUIN'
Shrub Z6-9 H9-3 Striking leaves edged with white, and purple flowers.
‡ ↔ 8ft (2.5m)

BUDDLEJA DAVIDII 'SANTANA'
Shrub Z6-9 H9-3 Mottled foliage in shades of green and yellow, and purple flowers.
‡ ↔ 8ft (2.5m)

BUXUS SEMPERVIRENS
'ELEGANTISSIMA'
Evergreen shrub   page **95**

CAMELLIA × *WILLIAMSII*
'GOLDEN SPANGLES'
Evergreen shrub Z8-10 H10-7 Bright pink flowers and gold-splashed leaves.
‡ ↔ 8ft (2.5m)

CEANOTHUS 'PERSHORE ZANZIBAR'
Evergreen shrub Z9-10 H10-8 Fast-growing, with fluffy blue flowers in late spring, and lemon yellow and bright green foliage.
‡ ↔ 8ft (2.5m)

CORNUS ALBA 'ELEGANTISSIMA'
Shrub Z2-8 H8-1 Dark red stems with gray-green leaves, edged with white, that turn pink in autumn.
‡ ↔ 10ft (3m)

CORNUS ALBA 'SPAETHII'
Shrub   page **138**

CORNUS ALTERNIFOLIA
'ARGENTEA'
Shrub Z4-8 H8-1 Tiers of horizontal branches, clothed with small leaves that are edged
in white.
‡ 10ft (3m) ↔ 8ft (2.5m)

CORNUS MAS 'VARIEGATA'
Shrub Z5-8 H8-5 After producing yellow flowers in spring, the plant is bright with white-edged leaves.
‡ 8ft (2.5m) ↔ 6ft (2m)

FUCHSIA MAGELLANICA VAR.
GRACILIS 'VARIEGATA'
Shrub Z6-9 H9-6 The leaves are colored in
smoky pinks and grays, with small, red
and purple flowers.
$\updownarrow$ to 10ft (3m) ↔ 6–10ft (2–3m)

FUCHSIA MAGELLANICA VAR.
MOLINAE 'SHARPITOR'
Shrub Z6-9 H9-6 Plant with pretty, white-
edged leaves and pale pink flowers
$\updownarrow$ to 10ft (3m) ↔ 6–10ft (2–3m)

HIBISCUS SYRIACUS 'MEEHANII'
Shrub Z5-9 H9-5 Sun-loving. Purple-blue
flowers; leaves with broad white edges.
$\updownarrow$ 10ft (3m) ↔ 6ft (2m)

HYDRANGEA MACROPHYLLA
'TRICOLOR'
Shrub Z6-9 H9-3 Gray-green leaves marked
with white, and pale pink flowers.
$\updownarrow$ 5ft (1.5m) ↔ 4ft (1.2m)

OSMANTHUS HETEROPHYLLUS
'VARIEGATUS'
Evergreen shrub Z7-9 H9-7 Hollylike leaves
with broad yellow margins, and fragrant,
tiny flowers in autumn.
$\updownarrow$ ↔ 8ft (2.5m)

PHILADELPHUS 'INNOCENCE'
Shrub Z5-8 H8-5 Arching shrub with
creamy yellow leaves and semidouble
white flowers.
$\updownarrow$ 10ft (3m) ↔ 6ft (2m)

PIERIS 'FLAMING SILVER'
Evergreen shrub Z6-8 H8-6 Acidic-soil-
loving plant with narrow foliage, edged
white, that is pink in spring.
$\updownarrow$ ↔ 8ft (2.5m)

PITTOSPORUM TENUIFOLIUM
'IRENE PATERSON'
Evergreen shrub Z9-10 H10-9 Slow-
growing shrub with white-speckled leaves.
$\updownarrow$ 4ft (1.2m) ↔ 2ft (60cm)

RHODODENDRON
'PRESIDENT ROOSEVELT'
Evergreen shrub Z7-9 H9-7 Weakly
branching, acidic-soil-loving shrub with
gold-splashed leaves and red flowers.
$\updownarrow$ ↔ 6ft (2m)

SAMBUCUS NIGRA 'PULVERULENTA'
Shrub Z4-9 H9-1 Bright, slow-growing
shrub for part-shade with young leaves
heavily splashed with white.
$\updownarrow$ ↔ 6ft (2m)

GOLD-LEAVED PLANTS

Gold-leaved plants bring a splash of sunshine to the garden. In contrast to plants with variegated leaves, most fully gold-leaved plants are rather prone to scorch in full sun so are best in light shade. But avoid dark shade, or the leaves may become lime green. Some plants are gold for only a part of their growth; their young, gold tips fade to green, but this contrast is still pleasing.

ACER CAPPADOCICUM 'AUREUM'
Tree Z6-8 H8-6 The leaves unfurl yellow in spring, turn green in summer, then turn gold in autumn.
‡ 50ft (15m) ↔ 30ft (10m)

ACER SHIRASAWANUM 'AUREUM'
Tree Z5-7 H7-4 The bright yellow leaves turn red in autumn.
‡↔ 20ft (6m)

BEGONIA 'TIGER PAWS'
Perennial page 81

CALLUNA VULGARIS 'BEOLEY GOLD'
Evergreen shrub page 98

CAREX ELATA 'AUREA'
Ornamental grass page 109

CAREX OSHIMENSIS 'EVERGOLD'
Ornamental grass page 109

CHAMAECYPARIS LAWSONIANA 'MINIMA AUREA'
Conifer Z5-9 H9-5 Small evergreen, conical shrub with lime green and gold foliage.
‡ 3ft (1m)

CHAMAECYPARIS LAWSONIANA 'STARDUST'
Conifer Z5-9 H9-5 Yellow, fernlike foliage.
‡ 50ft (15m) ↔ 25ft (8m)

CHAMAECYPARIS OBTUSA 'CRIPPSII'
Conifer Z4-8 H8-1 A slow-growing tree with gold foliage.
‡ 50ft (15m) ↔ 25ft (8m)

CHOISYA TERNATA 'SUNDANCE'
Evergreen shrub page 121

CORNUS ALBA 'AUREA'
Shrub Z2-8 H8-1 Beautiful soft gold foliage that is prone to sunscorch on dry soils.
‡↔ 3ft (1m)

CORTADERIA SELLOANA 'AUREOLINEATA'
Ornamental grass page 141

ERICA ARBOREA 'ALBERT'S GOLD'
Evergreen shrub Z9-10 H10-9 Attractive, upright habit, with gold foliage but few flowers.
‡ 6ft (2m) ↔ 32in (80cm)

ERICA CARNEA 'FOXHOLLOW'
Evergreen shrub page 187

ERICA CARNEA 'WESTWOOD YELLOW'
Evergreen shrub Z5-7 H7-5 Upright habit, with yellow foliage, and pale pink flowers in winter.
‡ 8in (20cm) ↔ 12in (30cm)

ERICA × *STUARTII* 'IRISH LEMON'
Evergreen shrub page 189

FAGUS SYLVATICA 'DAWYCK GOLD'
Tree Z5-7 H7-5 An upright, narrow, compact tree with bright yellow leaves.
‡ 60ft (18m) ↔ 22ft (7m)

FRAXINUS EXCELSIOR 'JASPIDEA'
Tree Z5-8 H8-5 The winter shoots are yellow, as are the leaves in spring and autumn.
‡ 100ft (30m) ↔ 70ft (20m)

FUCHSIA 'GENII'
Shrub page 212

GLEDITSIA TRIACANTHOS 'SUNBURST'
Tree

HAKONECHLOA MACRA 'AUREOLA'
Ornamental grass

HEDERA HELIX 'BUTTERCUP'
Evergreen climber

HOSTA 'SUM AND SUBSTANCE'
Perennial

HUMULUS LUPULUS 'AUREUS'
Climbing perennial

ILEX CRENATA 'GOLDEN GEM'
Evergreen shrub Z5 7 H7 3 Compact, small-leaved shrub with bright gold leaves and sparse, black berries.
‡3ft (1m) ↔ 4–5ft (1.2–1.5m)

IRIS PSEUDACORUS 'VARIEGATUS'
Perennial

LAURUS NOBILIS 'AUREA'
Evergreen shrub

LONICERA NITIDA
'BAGGESEN'S GOLD'
Evergreen shrub

ORIGANUM VULGARE 'AUREUM'
Perennial herb

PELARGONIUM CRISPUM
'VARIEGATUM'
Perennial

PHILADELPHUS CORONARIUS
'AUREUS'
Deciduous shrub Z5-8 H8-5 Gold young leaves turning green-yellow in summer, white fragrant flowers in early summer.
‡8ft (2.5m) ↔ 5ft (1.5m)

PHORMIUM 'YELLOW WAVE'
Perennial

PHYSOCARPUS OPULIFOLIUS
'DART'S GOLD'
Shrub

RIBES SANGUINEUM
'BROCKLEBANKII'
Shrub

ROBINIA PSEUDOACACIA 'FRISIA'
Tree

SALVIA OFFICINALIS 'KEW GOLD'
Evergreen subshrub Z7-8 H8-7 Aromatic golden leaves sometimes flecked with green; mauve flower spikes in summer.
‡8–12in (20–30cm) ↔ 12in (30cm)

SAMBUCUS RACEMOSA
'SUTHERLAND GOLD'
Shrub Z3-7 H7-1 Finely divided foliage of bright yellow that is best when plants are regularly pruned.
‡↔ 6ft (2m)

SPIRAEA JAPONICA 'GOLDFLAME'
Shrub

DARK AND PURPLE FOLIAGE

The primary value of dark foliage in the garden is as a foil to other plants, though many are very beautiful in their own right. An adjacent purple-leaved plant makes gold, variegated, and silver plants look even more brilliant and is the perfect foil for white, pink, yellow, and orange flowers. Most purple-leaved plants develop their best color in full sun, looking dull and greenish in shade.

ACER PLATANOIDES 'CRIMSON KING'
Tree   page 36

AEONIUM 'ZWARTKOP'
Succulent shrub   page 45

AJUGA REPTANS 'ATROPURPUREA'
Perennial   page 48

BERBERIS THUNBERGII
F. *ATROPURPUREA*
Shrub Z4-8 H8-1 The deep purple foliage turns bright red in autumn before it falls, revealing the spiny stems.
‡6ft (2m) ↔ 8ft (2.5m)

BERBERIS THUNBERGII 'RED CHIEF'
Shrub Z4-8 H8-1 Deep, reddish purple foliage on an upright shrub.
‡5ft (1.5m) ↔ 24in (60cm)

CERCIS CANADENSIS
'FOREST PANSY'
Tree Z6-9 H9-6 Pink flowers on bare twigs in early spring are followed by beautiful purple foliage.
‡↔ 30ft (10m)

CIMICIFUGA SIMPLEX 'BRUNETTE'
Perennial Z4-8 H8-1 Coarsely divided purple foliage, and dark stems with white fluffy flowers in autumn.
‡3–4ft (1–1.2m) ↔ 24in (60cm)

CLEMATIS MONTANA VAR. *RUBENS*
'TETRAROSE'
Climber   page 128

CORYLUS MAXIMA 'PURPUREA'
Shrub   page 143

COTINUS COGGYGRIA
'ROYAL PURPLE'
Shrub   page 144

COTINUS 'GRACE'
Shrub   page 145

CRYPTOTAENIA JAPONICA
F. *ATROPURPUREA*
Biennial Z5-8 H8-4 Three-lobed leaves on upright stems, wholly colored with purple, and tiny flowers.
‡↔ 24in (60cm)

ERICA CARNEA 'VIVELLII'
Evergreen shrub   page 187

EUPHORBIA DULCIS 'CHAMELEON'
Perennial Z4-9 H9-1 Purple foliage on bushy plants with lime green bracts.
‡↔ 12in (30cm)

FAGUS SYLVATICA
'DAWYCK PURPLE'
Tree Z5-7 H7-5 This columnar tree has deep purple leaves.
‡70ft (20m) ↔ 15ft (5m)

FAGUS SYLVATICA
'PURPUREA PENDULA'
Tree Z5-7 H7-5 The deep purple leaves hang from pendent branches on this small, domed tree.
‡↔ 10ft (3m)

GERANIUM SESSILIFLORUM SUBSP.
NOVAE-ZELANDIAE 'NIGRICANS'
Perennial Z8-9 H9-8 Small, mat-forming plant with dull, bronze-purple foliage and small white flowers.
‡3in (8cm) ↔ 6in (15cm)

HEBE 'MRS. WINDER'
Evergreen shrub Z9-10 H10-8 A compact shrub with dark leaves that are purple when young, and violet-blue flowers.
‡ 3ft (1m) ↔ 4ft (1.2m)

HEDERA HELIX 'ATROPURPUREA'
Evergreen climber page 246

HEUCHERA MICRANTHA VAR.
DIVERSIFOLIA 'PALACE PURPLE'
Perennial page 255

OPHIOPOGON PLANISCAPUS
'NIGRESCENS'
Perennial page 357

PENSTEMON DIGITALIS
'HUSKER RED'
Perennial Z2-8 H8-1 Semi-evergreen perennial with red and purple foliage and pale pink flowers.
‡ 20–30in (50–75cm) ↔ 12in (30cm)

PHYSOCARPUS OPULIFOLIUS
'DIABLO'
Shrub Z3-7 H7-1 Deep purple, almost brown leaves, and clusters of small pink flowers.
‡ 6ft (2m) ↔ 3ft (1m)

RHEUM PALMATUM
'ATROSANGUINEUM'
Perennial Z5-9 H9-4 Scarlet buds open to reveal large, architectural leaves that fade to deep green.
‡ 6ft (2m)

ROSA GLAUCA
Species rose page 464

SALVIA OFFICINALIS
PURPURASCENS GROUP
Evergreen shrub page 476

SAMBUCUS NIGRA
'GUINCHO PURPLE'
Shrub page 480

SEDUM TELEPHIUM SUBSP.
MAXIMUM 'ATROPURPUREUM'
Perennial page 491

TRADESCANTIA PALLIDA
'PURPUREA'
Perennial Z11 H12-1 This sprawling plant has bright purple leaves and small pink flowers.
‡ 8in (20cm) ↔ 16in (40cm)

VIBURNUM SARGENTII 'ONONDAGA'
Shrub Z4-7 H7-1 Upright-growing shrub with purple leaves that turn red in autumn, and pale pink flowers.
‡ 6ft (2m)

VIOLA RIVINIANA 'PURPUREA'
Perennial Z5-8 H8-4 Low-growing plant with small purple leaves and flowers. Seeds profusely.
‡ 4–8in (10–20cm) ↔ 8–16cm (20–40cm)

VITIS VINIFERA 'PURPUREA'
Climber page 540

WEIGELA FLORIDA
'FOLIIS PURPUREIS'
Shrub page 541

SILVER FOLIAGE

Most plants that have silver leaves have adapted to hot, sunny climates, and these are plants for full sun in the garden. They are also adapted to low rainfall in many cases, so they can form the basis of a drought garden or gravel garden. Their color makes them ideal to associate with pink and white flowers, and with purple foliage. In addition, many have fragrant leaves.

ACACIA BAILEYANA
Shrub Z10-11 H12-10 The foliage is less fine than *A. dealbata* but steely gray; the flowers are bright yellow.
‡ 15–25ft (5–8m) ↔ 10–20ft (3–6m)

ACCA SELLOWIANA
Evergreen shrub Z8-10 H10-8 Green leaves with silver reverses, flowers with fleshy, red and white edible petals.
‡ 6ft (2m) ↔ 8ft (2.5m)

ACHILLEA TOMENTOSA
Perennial page 41

ANAPHALIS TRIPLINERVIS
Perennial Z3-8 H8-4 Clump-forming plant with silver-gray leaves and white flowers in late summer.
‡ 32–36in (80–90cm) ↔ 18–24in (45–60cm)

ANAPHALIS TRIPLINERVIS 'SOMMERSCHNEE'
Perennial page 56

ANTENNARIA MICROPHYLLA
Perennial page 61

ANTHEMIS PUNCTATA SUBSP. *CUPANIANA*
Perennial page 61

ARTEMISIA ABSINTHIUM 'LAMBROOK SILVER'
Perennial page 69

ARTEMISIA ALBA 'CANESCENS'
Perennial Z4-8 H8-1 Very finely divided gray leaves that form a feathery mass.
‡ 18in (45cm) ↔ 12in (30cm)

ARTEMISIA LUDOVICIANA 'SILVER QUEEN'
Perennial page 69

ARTEMISIA PONTICA
Evergreen perennial Z4-8 H8-1 A creeping perennial that has masses of upright stems with feathery leaves that form a mounded clump.
‡ 16–32in (40–80cm) ↔ indefinite

ATRIPLEX HALIMUS
Shrub Z7-9 H9-7 Slightly tender, but wind-tolerant, fast-growing plant with small, shiny, silver leaves.
‡ 6ft (2m) ↔ 8ft (2.5m)

BRACHYGLOTTIS 'SUNSHINE'
Evergreen shrub page 91

CEDRUS ATLANTICA F. *GLAUCA*
Conifer Z6-9 H9-6 The blue Atlas cedar in time becomes a large, magnificent specimen tree with blue-gray foliage.
‡ 130ft (40m) ↔ 30ft (10m)

CONVOLVULUS CNEORUM
Evergreen shrub page 136

CYTISUS BATTANDIERI
Shrub page 159

DIANTHUS 'BECKY ROBINSON'
Perennial page 172

DIANTHUS 'HAYTOR WHITE'
Perennial page 172

ECHEVERIA AGAVOIDES
Succulent page 181

ELAEAGNUS 'QUICKSILVER'
Evergreen shrub page 183

ERICA TETRALIX 'ALBA MOLLIS'
Evergreen shrub

EUCALYPTUS GUNNII
Evergreen tree

HALIMIUM 'SUSAN'
Evergreen shrub

HEBE PIMELEOIDES 'QUICKSILVER'
Evergreen shrub Z9-10 H10-8 Ground-hugging shrub with tiny silver leaves and pale lilac flowers.
‡ 12in (30cm) ↔ 24in (60cm)

HEBE PINGUIFOLIA 'PAGEI'
Evergreen shrub

HEBE 'RED EDGE'
Evergreen shrub Z9-10 H10-8 Spreading, low shrub with red-edged gray leaves.
‡ 18in (45cm) ↔ 24in (60cm)

HELIANTHEMUM 'WISLEY PRIMROSE'
Evergreen shrub

HELICHRYSUM SPLENDIDUM
Perennial

HELICTOTRICHON SEMPERVIRENS
Ornamental grass Z4-9 H9-1 A tufted perennial forming a mound of gray-blue leaves, with taller flower stems in summer.
‡ 4½ft (1.4m) ↔ 2ft (60cm)

LAVANDULA × *INTERMEDIA* DUTCH GROUP
Shrub

PULMONARIA 'MARGERY FISH'
Perennial

PYRUS SALICIFOLIA 'PENDULA'
Tree

ROMNEYA COULTERI
Perennial Z7-8 H8-7 Vigorous, suckering plant with coarsely toothed silver leaves and white, yellow-centered flowers.
‡ 6ft (2m) ↔ indefinite

SALIX 'BOYDII'
Shrub

SALIX LANATA
Shrub

SALVIA ARGENTEA
Perennial

SALVIA DISCOLOR
Perennial

SANTOLINA CHAMAECYPARISSUS
Evergreen shrub

SEDUM SPATHULIFOLIUM 'CAPE BLANCO'
Perennial

SENECIO CINERARIA 'SILVER DUST'
Evergreen shrub

SENECIO CINERARIA 'WHITE DIAMOND'
Evergreen shrub Z8-10 H10-1 The almost white leaves resemble oak leaves in shape.
‡ 12–16in (30–40cm) ↔ 12in (30cm)

SENECIO VIRAVIRA
Shrub Z8-10 H10-1 The finely divided leaves are carried on sprawling stems that eventually produce creamy, pompon flowers.
‡ 24in (60cm) ↔ 3ft (1m)

VERBASCUM BOMBYCIFERUM
Perennial

PLANTS FOR SPRING COLOR

Spring is a frantic time in the garden, and at times it seems that every plant is trying to flower. The earliest flowers are demure and adapted to survive any snows, sleet, and wind, but by April, flowers are bigger and bolder, and the yellows, white, and blues of the spring bulbs are joined by masses of pink cherry blossoms, showy magnolias, rhododendrons, clematis, and wisteria.

ACER PSEUDOPLATANUS
'BRILLIANTISSIMUM'
Tree   **page 37**

BERGENIA PURPURASCENS
Perennial Z3-8 H8-1 Bold, leathery leaves turn red in cold weather, and clusters of bright, purplish flowers open in spring.
‡ 18in (45cm) ↔ 12in (30cm)

CALTHA PALUSTRIS
Perennial   **page 99**

CAMELLIA × *WILLIAMSII* CULTIVARS
Evergreen shrubs   **pages 104–105**

CHAENOMELES SPECIOSA
'MOERLOOSEI'
Shrub   **page 115**

CLEMATIS ALPINA
Climber Z6-9 H9-6 The blue, bell-shaped flowers have white centers and are followed by fluffy seedheads.
‡ 6–10ft (2–3m)

CLEMATIS ALPINA 'FRANCES RIVIS'
Climber   **page 128**

CLEMATIS MACROPETALA
'MARKHAM'S PINK'
Climber   **page 128**

CLEMATIS MONTANA VAR. *RUBENS*
Climber   **page 128**

CORYDALIS SOLIDA
Bulbous perennial Z5-7 H7-5 Pink flowers are held above feathery, gray foliage.
‡ 10in (25cm) ↔ 8in (20cm)

CORYLOPSIS PAUCIFLORA
Shrub   **page 142**

DAPHNE TANGUTICA
Evergreen shrub Z7-9 H9-7 The tips of shoots are studded with fragrant, pink and white flowers in late spring.
‡ ↔ 3ft (1m)

DICENTRA 'LUXURIANT'
Perennial Z4-8 H8-1 Lobed leaves and clusters of red flowers over a long season.
‡ 12in (30cm) ↔ 18in (45cm)

DODECATHEON MEADIA
Perennial Z4-8 H8-1 A clump-forming plant with clusters of magenta-pink flowers that resemble cyclamen.
‡ 16in (40cm) ↔ 10in (25cm)

EPIMEDIUM × *RUBRUM*
Perennial   **page 184**

EPIMEDIUM × *VERSICOLOR*
'SULPHUREUM'
Perennial Z5-9 H9-1 Evergreen, clump-forming plant with divided leaves and pretty, pale yellow flowers.
‡ ↔ 12in (30cm)

EUPHORBIA × *MARTINII*
Evergreen subshrub   **page 202**

EUPHORBIA POLYCHROMA
Perennial   **page 203**

FORSYTHIA × *INTERMEDIA*
'LYNWOOD'
Shrub   **page 208**

FOTHERGILLA MAJOR
Shrub   **page 209**

HEPATICA NOBILIS
Perennial   **page 255**

MAGNOLIA CAMPBELLII 'CHARLES RAFFILL'
Shrub   page 332

MAGNOLIA 'ELIZABETH'
Shrub   page 332

MAGNOLIA × *LOEBNERI* 'MERRILL'
Shrub   page 332

MAGNOLIA × *SOULANGEANA* 'LENNEI'
Tree Z5-9 H9-5 Beautiful tree of spreading habit with large, deep purple flowers.
↕ ↔ 20ft (6m)

MAGNOLIA STELLATA
Tree   page 333

MALUS FLORIBUNDA
Tree   page 336

PIERIS JAPONICA 'MOUNTAIN FIRE'
Evergreen shrub Z6-8 H8-6 Acidic-soil--loving shrub with white flowers and red new growth becoming bronze then green.
↕ 12ft (4m) ↔ 10ft (3m)

PRIMULA VERIS
Perennial   page 419

PRIMULA VIALII
Perennial Z5-8 H8-5 Short-lived perennial with dense heads of lilac flowers blooming from contrasting red buds.
↕ 12–24in (30–60cm) ↔ 12in (30cm)

PRUNUS AVIUM 'PLENA'
Tree   page 424

PRUNUS GLANDULOSA 'ALBA PLENA'
Shrub   page 421

PRUNUS 'KANZAN'
Tree   page 424

PRUNUS PADUS 'COLORATA'
Tree   page 424

PRUNUS PADUS 'WATERERI'
Tree   page 424

PRUNUS 'PANDORA'
Tree   page 424

PRUNUS 'PINK PERFECTION'
Tree   page 425

PRUNUS 'SHIROFUGEN'
Tree   page 425

PRUNUS 'SHÔGETSU'
Tree   page 425

PRUNUS 'SPIRE'
Tree   page 425

PRUNUS × *SUBHIRTELLA* 'AUTUMNALIS ROSEA'
Tree   page 425

PRUNUS 'UKON'
Tree   page 425

PRUNUS × *YEDOENSIS*
Tree   page 425

PULMONARIA RUBRA
Perennial   page 428

RHODODENDRON SPECIES AND CULTIVARS
Shrubs   pages 438–444

SAXIFRAGA 'TUMBLING WATERS'
Alpine Z6-7 H7-6 Rosettes of silvery green leaves produce tall, arching stems bearing hundreds of tiny white flowers.
↕ 18in (45cm) ↔ 12in (30cm)

VIOLA 'MAGGIE MOTT'
Perennial Z5-7 H7-5 Dainty blue and white flowers on bushy plants.
↕ 6in (15cm) ↔ 10in (25cm)

WISTERIA FLORIBUNDA 'MULTIJUGA'
Climber   page 542

WISTERIA FLORIBUNDA 'ROSEA'
Climber Z5-9 H9-5 Long racemes of pale pink flowers cascade from this vigorous plant.
↕ 28ft (9m)

PLANTS FOR SUMMER COLOR

In gardens the summer months are often dominated by bedding, but there are many bright-flowered perennials at their best. There are fewer shrubs in flower in mid-summer than in spring,

but an important exception is the rose, without which gardens would be much poorer. There are roses for every part of the garden, from lofty climbers to spreading groundcovers.

ANCHUSA AZUREA
'LODDON ROYALIST'
Perennial   page **57**

AQUILEGIA VULGARIS
'NORA BARLOW'
Perennial   page **63**

BUDDLEJA DAVIDII 'DARTMOOR'
Shrub Z6-9 H9-3 The flowers, borne in unusually large, branched clusters, are a rich reddish purple.
‡ 10ft (3m) ↔ 15ft (5m)

BUDDLEJA GLOBOSA
Shrub   page **94**

CAMPANULA LACTIFLORA
'LODDON ANNA'
Perennial   page **107**

CLEMATIS 'BEES' JUBILEE'
Climber   page **129**

CLEMATIS × *DURANDII*
Perennial Z6-9 H9-6 Non-climbing hybrid that sprawls through other plants, with large, blue flowers.
‡ 3–6ft (1–2m)

CLEMATIS 'GIPSY QUEEN'
Climber Z4-9 H9-1 Velvety, purple flowers with red anthers throughout summer.
‡ 10ft (3m)

CLEMATIS 'PERLE D'AZUR'
Climber   page **133**

DEUTZIA × *HYBRIDA* 'MONT ROSE'
Shrub   page **170**

DICENTRA 'LANGTREES'
Perennial Z4-8 H8-1 Pale, pearly white flowers are held on glossy stems above the feathery gray foliage.
‡ 12in (30cm) ↔ 18in (45cm)

DIGITALIS LANATA
Perennial Z3-9 H9-1 Leafy stems with densely packed, small cream flowers.
‡ 24in (60cm) ↔ 12in (30cm)

ERICA CINEREA 'VELVET NIGHT'
Evergreen shrub Z6-8 H8-6 Dark foliage is highlighted by deep purple flowers.
‡ 24in (60cm) ↔ 32in (80cm)

ERICA VAGANS 'LYONESSE'
Evergreen shrub   page **189**

ERICA VAGANS 'MRS D. F. MAXWELL'
Evergreen shrub   page **189**

EUPHORBIA SCHILLINGII
Perennial   page **203**

FUCHSIA HARDY TYPES
Shrubs   page **212**

FUCHSIA 'PHYLLIS'
Shrub Z8-10 H10-8 The semidouble cerise flowers are freely carried on an upright, hardy plant.
‡ 3–5ft (1–1.5m) ↔ 30–36in (75–90cm)

GENISTA TENERA 'GOLDEN SHOWER'
Shrub   page **224**

GERANIUMS, HARDY, LARGE
Perennials   pages **228–229**

HEBE 'GREAT ORME'
Evergreen shrub   page **241**

HEMEROCALLIS CULTIVARS
Perennials page 254

HEMEROCALLIS 'PINK DAMASK'
Perennial Z3-11 H12-1 Large, dark salmon-pink flowers held above arching leaves.
‡3ft (1m)

HYDRANGEA SERRATA 'BLUEBIRD'
Shrub page 268

HYPERICUM 'HIDCOTE'
Shrub page 269

BEARDED IRIS
Perennials pages 284–287

IRIS 'ARCTIC FANCY'
Perennial White petals heavily edged with deep violet.
‡20in (50cm)

IRIS 'BLUE-EYED BRUNETTE'
Perennial Z5-8 H8-5 Large flowers are pale brown with a lilac-blue mark by the base of the beard.
‡3ft (90cm)

IRIS LAEVIGATA
Perennial page 278

JASMINUM HUMILE 'REVOLUTUM'
Shrub Z7-9 H9-7 Fragrant, bright yellow flowers are set against divided foliage for most of summer.
‡8ft (2.5m) ↔ 10ft (3m)

LATHYRUS LATIFOLIUS 'WHITE PEARL'
Climber Z5-9 H9-5 This herbaceous perennial has pure white, scentless flowers.
‡6ft (2m)

OENOTHERA FRUTICOSA 'FYRVERKERI'
Perennial page 354

PENSTEMON CULTIVARS
Perennials pages 378–379

PHOTINIA × FRASERI 'RED ROBIN'
Evergreen shrub page 396

PHYGELIUS AEQUALIS 'YELLOW TRUMPET'
Evergreen shrub page 396

PLATYCODON GRANDIFLORUS
Perennial page 406

POTENTILLA 'GIBSON'S SCARLET'
Perennial page 411

ROSA 'JUST JOEY'
Hybrid tea rose page 449

ROSA 'MANY HAPPY RETURNS'
Floribunda rose page 451

ROSA 'MOUNTBATTEN'
Floribunda rose page 451

ROSA 'SWEET DREAM'
Patio rose page 457

ROSA 'TEQUILA SUNRISE'
Hybrid tea rose Z5-9 H9-5 Bright yellow flowers heavily edged with scarlet.
‡30in (75cm) ↔ 24in (60cm)

ROSES, OLD GARDEN
Deciduous shrubs pages 460–1

ROSES, RAMBLER
Deciduous climbers pages 454–5

SALVIA × SYLVESTRIS 'MAINACHT'
Perennial page 479

THALICTRUM DELAVAYI 'HEWITT'S DOUBLE'
Perennial page 510

TRADESCANTIA × ANDERSONIANA 'J. C. WEUGELIN'
Perennial page 517

TRADESCANTIA × ANDERSONIANA 'OSPREY'
Perennial page 518

Plants for Autumn Color

Autumn is a season of great change in the garden, and although many annuals and perennials continue their summer display, it is the colors of leaves and fruits (see also pp.502–3) that most

capture the imagination. This should be the most spectacular time of all in the garden, as borders erupt in fiery orange and red shades before the more somber displays of winter.

ACER GROSSERI VAR. *HERSII*
Tree   page 32

ACER PALMATUM 'BLOODGOOD'
Small tree   page 34

ACER PALMATUM 'GARNET'
Shrub   page 34

ACER PALMATUM 'OSAKAZUKI'
Shrub or small tree   page 35

ACER RUBRUM 'OCTOBER GLORY'
Tree   page 38

AMELANCHIER LAMARCKII
Large shrub   page 56

ANEMONE HUPEHENSIS
'HADSPEN ABUNDANCE'
Perennial   page 59

ANEMONE HUPEHENSIS
'SEPTEMBER CHARM'
Perennial Z4-8 H8-1 Pale pink flowers on neat growth.
‡ 24–36in (60–90cm) ↔ 16in (40cm)

ASTER AMELLUS 'KING GEORGE'
Perennial   page 72

ASTER ERICOIDES 'PINK CLOUD'
Perennial Z5-8 H8-5 The bushy plants are covered with small, pink flowers.
‡ 3ft (1m) ↔ 12in (30cm)

ASTER LATERIFOLIUS 'HORIZONTALIS'
Perennial   page 73

BERBERIS WILSONIAE
Shrub   page 87

CEANOTHUS X *DELILEANUS*
'GLOIRE DE VERSAILLES'
Shrub   page 113

CLEMATIS 'ALBA LUXURIANS'
Climber   page 132

CLEMATIS 'DUCHESS OF ALBANY'
Climber   page 132

CLEMATIS X *TRITERNATA*
'RUBROMARGINATA'
Climber Z4-9 H9-1 Strong shoots bear masses of small, cross-shaped deep pink and white flowers.
‡ 15ft (5m)

CORNUS KOUSA VAR. *CHINENSIS*
Tree   page 139

CORTADERIA SELLOANA
'SUNNINGDALE SILVER'
Ornamental grass   page 141

COTONEASTER MICROPHYLLUS
Evergreen shrub Z6-8 H8-6 An arching shrub with pinkish red berries in autumn.
‡ 3ft (1m) ↔ 5ft (1.5m)

DAHLIA CULTIVARS
Perennials   pages 162–163

EUCRYPHIA X *NYMANSENSIS*
'NYMANSAY'
Evergreen tree   page 198

EUONYMUS ALATUS
Shrub   page 198

EUONYMUS EUROPAEUS
'RED CASCADE'
Shrub   page 199

FUCHSIA 'MRS. POPPLE'
Shrub page **212**

GENTIANA SEPTEMFIDA
Perennial page **225**

GINKGO BILOBA
Tree Z5-9 H9-2 This deciduous conifer has broad leaves that turn butter yellow before they drop in autumn.
‡ to 100ft (30m) ↔ 25ft (8m)

HELIANTHUS 'LODDON GOLD'
Perennial page **249**

HIBISCUS SYRIACUS 'OISEAU BLEU'
Shrub page **256**

INDIGOFERA AMBLYANTHA
Shrub Z7-9 H9-7 Slender stems bear feathery leaves and upright stems of tiny pink flowers.
‡ 6ft (2m) ↔ 8ft (2.5m)

LIRIODENDRON TULIPIFERA
Tree page **320**

LIRIOPE MUSCARI
Perennial page **321**

MALUS 'JOHN DOWNIE'
Tree page **336**

NANDINA DOMESTICA
Shrub page **345**

NYSSA SINENSIS
Tree page **353**

NYSSA SYLVATICA
Tree page **353**

PARTHENOCISSUS TRICUSPIDATA
Climber page **369**

PHYGELIUS CAPENSIS
Shrub page **396**

PRUNUS SARGENTII
Tree page **425**

PRUNUS × *SUBHIRTELLA* 'AUTUMNALIS ROSEA'
Tree page **425**

PSEUDOLARIX AMABILIS
Tree Z5-9 H9-5 A deciduous conifer that is grown for its attractive conical shape and golden autumn color.
‡ 50–70ft (15–20m) ↔ 20–40ft (6–12m)

RHUS TYPHINA 'DISSECTA'
Shrub page **445**

RUDBECKIA FULGIDA VAR. *DEAMII*
Perennial Z4-9 H9-1 Daisylike flowers of orange, with black centers.
‡ 24in (60cm) ↔ 18in (45cm)

RUDBECKIA 'GOLDQUELLE'
Perennial page **468**

SALVIA ULIGINOSA
Perennial page **479**

SCHIZOSTYLIS COCCINEA 'MAJOR'
Perennial page **486**

SEDUM 'RUBY GLOW'
Perennial page **488**

SEDUM SPECTABILE 'ICEBERG'
Perennial Z4-9 H9-1 Fleshy, pale-leaved plant with pure white flowers.
‡ 12–18in (30–45cm) ↔ 14in (35cm)

SORBUS REDUCTA
Shrub page **499**

SORBUS VILMORINII
Shrub or small tree page **500**

TRICYRTIS FORMOSANA
Perennial Z6-9 H9-6 Erect stems with glossy leaves, and pale pink, starry flowers with darker spots.
‡ 32in (80cm) ↔ 18in (45cm)

VIBURNUM PLICATUM 'MARIESII'
Shrub page **536**

VITIS COIGNETIAE
Climber page **540**

PLANTS FOR WINTER INTEREST

Gardeners who do not think that anything happens in gardens in winter miss out on some of the most exciting plants of all: some bear flowers; others have highly attractive bark in winter; and many evergreens come into their prime. Many grow happily in shady positions, and this is the ideal place to plant a winter garden, preferably by a door or from where it can be viewed.

ACER GRISEUM
Tree   page 32

ACER PENSYLVANICUM
'ERYTHROCLADUM'
Deciduous tree   page 36

ASPLENIUM SCOLOPENDRIUM
CRISTATUM GROUP
Evergreen fern Z6-8 H8-6 Erect, leathery fronds with broadened, irregular tips, which look bold in winter.
‡ 18in (45cm) ↔ 24in (60cm)

AUCUBA JAPONICA 'CROTONIFOLIA'
Evergreen shrub   page 78

BERGENIA 'BALLAWLEY'
Perennial   page 88

CALLUNA VULGARIS 'ROBERT CHAPMAN'
Heather   page 98

CHAMAECYPARIS OBTUSA
'NANA AUREA'
Conifer Z4-8 H8-1 This dwarf conifer is rounded with a flat top and yellow foliage.
‡ 6ft (2m)

CHIMONANTHUS PRAECOX
'GRANDIFLORUS'
Shrub   page 120

CLEMATIS CIRRHOSA VAR.
BALEARICA
Climber Z7-9 H9-7 This evergreen climber has pale cream, bell-shaped flowers that are fragrant.
‡ 8–10ft (2.5–3m)

CORNUS ALBA 'SIBIRICA'
Shrub   page 137

CORNUS MAS
Shrub or small tree   page 139

CORNUS MAS 'AUREA'
Shrub Z5-8 H8-5 Masses of tiny yellow flowers in winter followed by chartreuse spring foliage that turns green in summer.
‡ ↔ 15ft (5m)

CYCLAMEN CILICIUM
Tuberous perennial   page 157

CYCLAMEN COUM PEWTER GROUP
Bulb   page 158

DAPHNE BHOLUA 'GURKHA'
Shrub   page 164

ERICA CARNEA 'ANN SPARKES'
Evergreen shrub   page 187

ERICA CARNEA 'PINK SPANGLES'
Evergreen shrub Z5-7 H7-5 This bright heather has pink flowers that are pink and white as they first open.
‡ 6in (15cm) ↔ 18in (45cm)

ERICA CARNEA 'VIVELLII'
Evergreen shrub   page 187

ERICA × DARLEYENSIS 'FURZEY'
Evergreen shrub Z7-8 H8–7 Small shrub with dark foliage and deep pink flowers.
‡ 12in (30cm) ↔ 24in (60cm)

ERICA × DARLEYENSIS 'J. W. PORTER'
Evergreen shrub Z7-8 H8-7 Deep green foliage tipped with cream and red in spring, and deep pink flowers.
‡ 12in (30cm) ↔ 24in (60cm)

HAMAMELIS X *INTERMEDIA*
CULTIVARS
Shrubs pages **238–239**

HELLEBORUS ARGUTIFOLIUS
Perennial page **252**

HELLEBORUS FOETIDUS
Perennial page **253**

HELLEBORUS NIGER
Perennial page **253**

HELLEBORUS X *NIGERCORS*
Perennial Z4-8 H8-1 Clump-forming plant
with short, branched stems of white
flowers, flushed green and pink
‡ 12in (30cm) ↔ 3ft (1m)

ILEX AQUIFOLIUM 'GOLDEN
MILKBOY'
Tree page **273**

ILEX X *MESERVEAE* 'BLUE PRINCESS'
Shrub page **274**

IRIS UNGUICULARIS
Perennial page **289**

JUNIPERUS COMMUNIS 'REPANDA'
Conifer Z2-6 H6-1 The foliage of this
ground-hugging conifer is often bronze in
winter.
‡ 8in (20cm) ↔ 3ft (1m)

LONICERA X *PURPUSII*
'WINTER BEAUTY'
Shrub page **325**

MAHONIA X *MEDIA*
'LIONEL FORTESCUE'
Evergreen shrub Z8-9 H9-8 Divided leaves
with leaflets like holly leaves and upright
spikes of bright yellow flowers.
‡ 15ft (5m) ↔ 12ft (4m)

MAHONIA X *MEDIA* 'WINTER SUN'
Evergreen shrub Z8-9 H9-8 The appeal of
this prickly, upright shrub is its scented
yellow winter flowers.
‡ 15ft (5m) ↔ 12ft (4m)

PULMONARIA RUBRA
Evergreen perennial page **428**

RUBUS THIBETANUS
Shrub page **467**

SALIX BABYLONICA VAR. *PEKINENSIS*
'TORTUOSA'
Tree page **469**

SALIX HASTATA 'WEHRHAHNII'
Shrub page **470**

SKIMMIA JAPONICA 'NYMANS'
Evergreen shrub Z7-9 H9-7 This spreading
shrub is female and bears good clusters of
red berries.
‡ 3ft (1m) ↔ 6ft (2m)

STACHYURUS PRAECOX
Shrub page **503**

SYMPHORICARPUS X *DOORENBOSII*
'WHITE HEDGE'
Shrub Z4-7 H-7-1 Suckering shrub of
upright habit with white berries.
‡ 6ft (2m) ↔ indefinite

VIBURNUM X *BODNANTENSE* 'DAWN'
Shrub page **534**

VIBURNUM FARRERI
Shrub page **535**

VIBURNUM TINUS 'EVE PRICE'
Evergreen shrub page **537**

BERRYING PLANTS

If birds do not enjoy the feast as soon as they ripen, berries can enhance the garden for many months. Red berries are most common, but there are black, white, yellow, pink, blue, and even purple berries, to be included in almost any garden. Pale berries look best against a dark background such as an evergreen hedge, and red berries are attractive against a wintery, sunny sky.

ACTAEA ALBA
Perennial Z4-9 H9-1 Clump-forming plant with divided leaves and fluffy flowers followed by pearly, white berries with black eyes.
‡ 36in (90cm) ↔ 18–24in (45–60cm)

ARBUTUS UNEDO F. *RUBRA*
Evergreen tree Z7–9 H9-7 The pink flowers and red, globular fruits are both at their best in autumn.
‡ ↔ 25ft (8m)

ARUM ITALICUM 'MARMORATUM'
Perennial Z6-9 H9-6 Evergreen, marbled foliage and spikes of red berries in autumn when the leaves die down.
‡ 12in (30cm) ↔ 6in (15cm)

BERBERIS DICTYOPHYLLA
Shrub Z6-9 H9-6 This deciduous shrub is at its best in winter when the white shoots are studded with red berries.
‡ 6ft (2m) ↔ 5ft (1.5m)

BERBERIS X *STENOPHYLLA*
'CORALLINA COMPACTA'
Evergreen shrub   page **85**

BERBERIS VERRUCULOSA
Evergreen shrub   page **87**

CALLICARPA BODINIERI VAR.
GIRALDII 'PROFUSION'
Shrub   page **96**

CELASTRUS ORBICULATUS
Climber Z4-8 H8-1 Strong-growing climber with yellow autumn color and yellow fruits opening to reveal red seeds.
‡ 46ft (14m)

CLERODENDRON TRICHOTOMUM
VAR. *FARGESII*
Shrub Z7-9 H9-7 Fast-growing plant with fragrant white flowers and turquoise berries set against red calyces.
‡ ↔ 15ft (5m)

CORIARIA TERMINALIS VAR.
XANTHOCARPA
Shrub Z9-10 H10-9 Arching subshrub with small leaves and clusters of translucent yellow berries.
‡ 3ft (1m) ↔ 6ft (2m)

CORNUS 'NORMAN HADDEN'
Evergreen tree Z7-9 H9-7 Some leaves turn yellow and drop each autumn, when the cream and pink flowers are followed by large red fruits.
‡ ↔ 25ft (8m)

COTONEASTER CONSPICUUS
'DECORUS'
Evergreen shrub   page **146**

COTONEASTER 'ROTHSCHILDIANUS'
Evergreen shrub Z6-8 H8-6 An arching shrub with golden yellow berries in autumn after white flowers in summer.
‡ ↔ 15ft (5m)

EUONYMUS PLANIPES
Shrub Z5-9 H9-5 The foliage is bright red in autumn and falls to reveal red capsules containing orange seeds.
‡ ↔ 10ft (3m)

GAULTHERIA MUCRONATA
'WINTERTIME'
Evergreen shrub   page **220**

HIPPOPHAE RHAMNOIDES
Shrub   page 257

HYPERICUM KOUYTCHENSE
Shrub   page 270

ILEX AQUIFOLIUM & CULTIVARS
Evergreen shrubs   pages 272–273

ILEX × MESERVEAE 'BLUE ANGEL'
Evergreen shrub Z5-9 H9-5 Compact, slow-growing shrub with glossy, dark, bluish green leaves and red berries.
‡ 12ft (4m) ↔ 6ft (2m)

ILEX VERTICILLATA 'WINTER RED'
Shrub Z5-8 H8-3 Deciduous shrub with white flowers in spring and masses of small red berries in winter.
‡ 8–10ft (2.5–3m) ↔ 10ft (3m)

LEYCESTERIA FORMOSA
Shrub Z9-10 H10-9 Tall, arching stems tipped with white flowers within maroon bracts, followed by purple berries.
‡↔ 6ft (2m)

LONICERA NITIDA 'BAGGESEN'S GOLD'
Evergreen shrub   page 323

LONICERA PERICLYMENUM 'GRAHAM THOMAS'
Climber   page 324

PHYSALIS ALKEKENGI
Perennial Z5-8 H8-5 Creeping plant with upright stems: orange lanterns containing orange berries follow white flowers.
‡ 24–30in (60–75cm) ↔ 36in (90cm)

PYRACANTHA 'CADROU'
Evergreen shrub Z7-9 H9-7 Spiny shrub with white flowers and red berries, resistant to scab.
‡↔ 6ft (2m)

ROSA 'FRU DAGMAR HASTRUP'
Shrub rose   page 464

ROSA MOYESII 'GERANIUM'
Shrub rose Z4-9 H9-1 Arching, prickly stems
with neat red flowers and large, long red hips.
‡ 8ft (2.5m) ↔ 5ft (1.5m)

ROSA 'SCHARLACHGLUT'
Shrub rose Z4-9 H9-1 Vigorous long-stemmed rose that can be trained as a climber, with showy scarlet flowers and bright scarlet hips.
‡ 10ft (3m) ↔ 6ft (2m)

SAMBUCUS RACEMOSA 'PLUMOSA AUREA'
Shrub Z3-7 H7-1 Divided yellow leaves in summer and clusters of small, red berries.
‡↔ 10ft (3m)

SKIMMIA JAPONICA 'FRUCTU ALBO'
Evergreen shrub Z7-9 H9-7 Neat evergreen with white flowers and bright, white fruits.
‡ 24in (60cm) ↔ 3ft (1m)

SORBUS ARIA 'LUTESCENS'
Tree   page 498

SORBUS HUPEHENSIS VAR. *OBTUSA*
Tree   page 498

TROPAEOLUM SPECIOSUM
Perennial climber   page 521

VIBURNUM DAVIDII
Evergreen shrub   page 535

VIBURNUM OPULUS 'XANTHOCARPUM'
Shrub   page 536

CONIFERS FOR SMALL GARDENS

Conifers provide an amazing range of shapes, sizes, colors, and textures. They can be used to give upright accents in borders, as dense screens, and for evergreen groundcover. They tolerate most soils but most, except yew, need sun. Many change color with the seasons and are especially brilliant in early summer when new growth contrasts with older foliage.

ABIES BALSAMEA F. *HUDSONIA*
Conifer Z3-6 H6-1 This very dwarf form grows into a rounded shrub and does not bear cones.
‡ 24in (60cm) ↔ 3ft (1m)

ABIES KOREANA 'SILBERLOCKE'
Conifer Z5-6 H6-5 Attractive twisted foliage that reveals the silver reverse to the needles, and attractive cones.
‡ 30ft (10m) ↔ 20ft (6m)

ABIES LASIOCARPA 'COMPACTA'
Conifer Z5-6 H6-5 Slow-growing conical tree with blue-gray leaves.
‡ 10–15ft (3–5m) ↔ 6–10ft (2–3m)

ABIES NORDMANNIANA
'GOLDEN SPREADER'
Conifer Z4-6 H6-1 Dwarf, slow-growing plant with bright gold foliage.
‡ 3ft (1m) ↔ 5ft (1.5m)

CHAMAECYPARIS LAWSONIANA
'CHILWORTH SILVER'
Conifer Z5-9 H9-5 Slow-growing conical shrub with silver-gray foliage.
‡ 5ft (1.5m)

CHAMAECYPARIS LAWSONIANA
'ELLWOOD'S GOLD'
Conifer   page **117**

CHAMAECYPARIS OBTUSA
'NANA GRACILIS'
Conifer   page **118**

CHAMAECYPARIS OBTUSA
'TETRAGONA AUREA'
Conifer   page **119**

CRYPTOMERIA JAPONICA
'ELEGANS COMPACTA'
Conifer   page **155**

CRYPTOMERIA JAPONICA
'VILMORINIANA'
Conifer Z6-9 H9-6 Forms a tight ball of foliage that is green in summer but bronze in winter.
‡ ↔ 18in (45cm)

JUNIPERUS CHINENSIS 'BLAAUW'
Conifer Z3-9 H9-1 Forms a dense, upright shrub with blue-gray leaves.
‡ 4ft (1.2m) ↔ 3ft (1m)

JUNIPERUS CHINENSIS 'OBELISK'
Conifer Z3-9 H9-1 Grows slowly into an interesting, upright shape with bluish green leaves.
‡ 8ft (2.5m) ↔ 24in (60cm)

JUNIPERUS COMMUNIS 'COMPRESSA'
Conifer   page **293**

JUNIPERUS X *PFITZERIANA*
'PFITZERIANA'
Conifer   page **293**

JUNIPERUS PROCUMBENS 'NANA'
Conifer   page **294**

JUNIPERUS SCOPULORUM
'BLUE HEAVEN'
Conifer Z 4-7 H7-1 Neat in habit, with blue leaves and a conical shape.
‡ 6ft (2m) ↔ 24in (60cm)

JUNIPERUS SQUAMATA 'BLUE STAR'
Conifer   page **294**

JUNIPERUS SQUAMATA 'HOLGER'
Conifer Z5-8 H8-4 Spreading evergreen
with bluish foliage that contrasts with the
yellowish new growth.
↕ ↔ 6ft (2m)

MICROBIOTA DECUSSATA
Conifer Z3-7 H7-1 Spreading conifer with
fine foliage that turns bronze in winter
sun.
↕ 3ft (1m) ↔ indefinite

PICEA ABIES 'NIDIFORMIS'
Conifer Z3-8 H8-1 This slow-growing plant
grows outward to form a "nest" in the
center of the plant.
↕ 5ft (1.5m) ↔ 10–12ft (3–4m)

PICEA GLAUCA VAR. *ALBERTIANA*
'CONICA'
Conifer page **400**

PICEA MARIANA 'NANA'
Conifer page **401**

PICEA PUNGENS 'KOSTER'
Conifer page **401**

PINUS MUGO 'MOPS'
Conifer page **404**

PINUS PARVIFLORA
'ADCOCK'S DWARF'
Conifer Z6-9 H9-6 A dwarf cultivar of the
Japanese white pine, with grayish leaves.
↕ 6ft (2m)

PINUS SYLVESTRIS 'BEUVRONENSIS'
Conifer Z3-7 H7-1 A rounded, dwarf
cultivar of the Scots pine.
↕ 3ft (1m)

TAXUS BACCATA 'DOVASTONII AUREA'
Conifer page **509**

TAXUS BACCATA
'FASTIGIATA AUREOMARGINATA'
Conifer Z7-8 H8-7 Upright accent plant
with leaves margined in yellow, and red-
fleshed (poisonous) berries.
↕ 10–15ft (3–5m) ↔ 3–8ft (1–2.5m)

TAXUS BACCATA 'FASTIGIATA'
Conifer page **510**

TAXUS BACCATA 'REPENS AUREA'
Conifer Z7-8 H8-7 This spreading form of
yew has golden leaves.
↕ ↔ 3–5ft (1–1.5m)

THUJA OCCIDENTALIS 'HOLMSTRUP'
Conifer page **511**

THUJA OCCIDENTALIS 'RHEINGOLD'
Conifer page **512**

THUJA OCCIDENTALIS 'SMARAGD'
Conifer Z2-7 H7-1 A dwarf, conical bush
with bright green leaves.
↕ 3ft (1m) ↔ 32in (80cm)

THUJA ORIENTALIS 'AUREA NANA'
Conifer page **512**

THUJA PLICATA 'STONEHAM GOLD'
Conifer page **513**

TSUGA CANADENSIS 'JEDDELOH'
Conifer page **521**

TREES FOR SMALL GARDENS

Trees add shade and character to gardens, but large forest trees should never be planted in small gardens or too near homes. Beech, oaks, and ash may be cheap to buy, but it is best to look for small trees that will give interest over a long period during the year. Consider the shade they will cast: dense evergreens can create areas that are dry and dark, where little will grow.

ACER DAVIDII 'ERNEST WILSON'
Deciduous tree Z5-7 H7-5 Unlobed leaves turn orange in autumn before falling to show the green, white-streaked branches.
$\updownarrow$ 25ft (8m) ↔ 30ft (10m)

ACER PALMATUM CULTIVARS
Deciduous trees or large shrubs
pages 34–35

AMELANCHIER × *GRANDIFLORA* 'BALLERINA'
Deciduous tree page 55

BETULA UTILIS VAR. *JACQUEMONTII*
Deciduous tree page 90

CERCIS SILIQUASTRUM
Deciduous tree page 115

CORNUS 'EDDIE'S WHITE WONDER'
Deciduous tree Z5-8 H8-5 Multistemmed tree that bears deep purple, small flowers surrounded by large white bracts.
$\updownarrow$ 20ft (6m) ↔ 15ft (5m)

CRATAEGUS LAEVIGATA 'PAUL'S SCARLET'
Deciduous tree page 149

GENISTA AETNENSIS
Deciduous tree or large shrub page 223

GLEDITSIA TRIACANTHOS 'RUBYLACE'
Deciduous tree Z3-7 H7-1 Elegant divided foliage that is bright wine-red when young, becoming bronzed green.
$\updownarrow$ 40ft (12m) ↔ 30ft (10m)

LABURNUM × *WATERERI* 'VOSSII'
Deciduous tree page 300

LIGUSTRUM LUCIDUM
Evergreen tree or large shrub page 313

MAGNOLIA 'HEAVEN SCENT'
Deciduous tree Z6-9 H9-6 Goblet-shaped pink flowers, with white interiors, in spring and early summer.
$\updownarrow$ ↔ 30ft (10m)

MAGNOLIA × *LOEBNERI* 'LEONARD MESSEL'
Deciduous tree page 333

MALUS CORONARIA 'CHARLOTTAE'
Deciduous tree Z5-8 H8-5 Fragrant, semidouble, pale pink flowers in spring.
$\updownarrow$ ↔ 28ft (9m)

MALUS TSCHONOSKII
Deciduous tree page 337

PRUNUS SERRULA
Deciduous tree page 423

PYRUS CALLERYANA 'CHANTICLEER'
Deciduous tree page 431

SALIX CAPREA 'KILMARNOCK'
Deciduous tree page 470

SALIX 'ERYTHROFLEXUOSA'
Deciduous tree Z5-9 H9-5 Semi-weeping tree with twisted, orange-yellow shoots.
$\updownarrow$ ↔ 15ft (5m)

SORBUS 'JOSEPH ROCK'
Deciduous tree page 499

STYRAX JAPONICUS
Deciduous tree page 504

STYRAX OBASSIA
Deciduous tree page 504

HEDGE PLANTS WITH ATTRACTIVE FOLIAGE

Formal hedging plants must be tolerant of regular clipping. Those that have one flush of growth each year, such as yew, need clipping only once a season, unlike privet, which may require

trimming twice or three times. Evergreens are most popular, but deciduous plants still reduce wind speed, and are often cheap. Dimensions below are ultimate sizes.

BUXUS SEMPERVIRENS 'ELEGANTISSIMA'
Evergreen shrub   page **95**

BUXUS SEMPERVIRENS 'SUFFRUTICOSA'
Evergreen shrub   page **95**

CHAMAECYPARIS LAWSONIANA 'FLETCHERI'
Conifer Z5-9 H9-5 Dense, gray foliage on an erect, compact shrub.
↕ 40ft (12m)

CHAMAECYPARIS LAWSONIANA 'LANE'
Conifer   page **117**

CHAMAECYPARIS LAWSONIANA 'PEMBURY BLUE'
Conifer   page **117**

× *CUPRESSOCYPARIS LEYLANDII*
Conifer Z6-9 H9-6 Very vigorous plant that can be managed if trimmed at an early stage, and then regularly.
↕ 120ft (35m) ↔ 15ft (5m)

× *CUPRESSOCYPARIS LEYLANDII* 'HAGGERSTON GREY'
Conifer   page **156**

× *CUPRESSOCYPARIS LEYLANDII* 'ROBINSON'S GOLD'
Conifer Z6-9 H9-6 The best gold form, with foliage that is bronze when young.
↕ 120ft (35m) ↔ 15ft (5m)

FAGUS SYLVATICA
Deciduous tree Z5-7 H7-1 European beech and its purple form retain their dead leaves in winter if trimmed to 2m (6ft).
↕ 80ft (25m) ↔ 50ft (15m)

LIGUSTRUM OVALIFOLIUM 'AUREUM'
Evergreen shrub Z6-8 H8-6 Good choice where a bright yellow hedge is required, and regular clipping is possible.
↕ ↔ 12ft (4m)

PRUNUS × CISTENA
Deciduous shrub   page **421**

PRUNUS LAUROCERASUS
Evergreen shrub Z6-9 H9-6 Cherry laurel requires careful pruning but can be attractive, and withstands hard pruning well.
↕ 25ft (8m) ↔ 30ft (10m)

PRUNUS LAUROCERASUS 'OTTO LUYKEN'
Evergreen shrub   page **422**

PRUNUS LUSITANICA
Evergreen shrub Z7-9 H9-7 Pleasant evergreen with dark green leaves on red stalks, and white flowers if not clipped.
↕ ↔ 70ft (20m)

TAXUS BACCATA
Evergreen tree   page **509**

FLOWERING HEDGES

Flowering hedges add much more than structural elements and security to the garden: they can become a focus of attention. Many flowering shrubs that tolerate pruning can be used but,

because of the pruning required to maintain flowering at its best, they may not be suitable for dense, formal hedges, or for boundary hedges where year-round screening is required.

ESCALLONIA 'APPLE BLOSSOM'
Evergreen shrub page **194**

FORSYTHIA X *INTERMEDIA*
'LYNWOOD'
Shrub page **208**

FUCHSIA 'RICCARTONII'
Shrub page **212**

HEBE 'MIDSUMMER BEAUTY'
Evergreen shrub Z9-10 H10-9 Bright green leaves and purple flowers, fading to white, on short spikes in mid- to late summer.
‡ 3ft (1m) ↔ 4ft (1.2m)

HYPERICUM 'ROWALLANE'
Shrub Z7-9 H9-7 Semi-evergreen, bearing clusters of yellow, cupped flowers in summer on arching stems.
‡ 6ft (2m) ↔ 3ft (1m)

LAVANDULA ANGUSTIFOLIA
'HIDCOTE'
Evergreen shrub page **305**

OSMANTHUS X *BURKWOODII*
Evergreen shrub page **359**

PHILADELPHUS CORONARIUS
'AUREUS'
Shrub Z5-8 H8-5 Golden yellow foliage that may scorch in full sun on poor soil, and fragrant white flowers.
‡ 8ft (2.5m) ↔ 5ft (1.5m)

POTENTILLA FRUTICOSA
'PRIMROSE BEAUTY'
Shrub page **410**

PRUNUS X *CISTENA*
Shrub page **421**

PRUNUS LUSITANICA SUBSP. *AZORICA*
Shrub page **423**

RHODODENDRON 'HINO-MAYO'
Evergreen shrub page **436**

RIBES SANGUINEUM
'PULBOROUGH SCARLET'
Shrub page **446**

ROSA 'BUFF BEAUTY'
Modern shrub rose page **462**

ROSA 'CHINATOWN'
Floribunda rose page **450**

ROSA 'FELICIA'
Modern shrub rose page **462**

SPIRAEA X *VANHOUTTEI*
Shrub page **502**

SYRINGA PUBESCENS SUBSP.
MICROPHYLLA 'SUPERBA'
Shrub page **506**

VIBURNUM TINUS 'GWENLLIAN'
Evergreen shrub Z8-10 H10-8 Dense shrub with pinkish flowers that open from deep pink buds.
‡ ↔ 10ft (3m)

SPINY HEDGES

There are places in the garden, usually around the edges, where the physical barrier of a hedge is not enough, and plants with spines are needed to ensure privacy and prevent the access of animals. Though these plants have many advantages, pruning and clipping must be carefully done, and dropped twigs can cause more discomfort in the future when weeding at the base.

BERBERIS DARWINII
Evergreen shrub page 84

BERBERIS × OTTAWENSIS 'SUPERBA'
Shrub page 85

BERBERIS × STENOPHYLLA
Evergreen shrub Z6-9 H9-6 Long, arching shoots are covered with small orange flowers in spring, and spines all year.
‡ 10ft (3m) ↔ 15ft (5m)

BERBERIS THUNBERGII
Shrub Z5-8 H8-5 Spiny stems have purple leaves that turn red before falling.
‡ 3ft (1m) ↔ 8ft (2.5m)

CRATAEGUS MONOGYNA
Tree Z5-7 H7-5 The singleseed hawthorn forms a quick-growing spiny hedge, but is not as attractive as some.
‡ 30ft (10m) ↔ 25ft (8m)

ILEX AQUIFOLIUM & CULTIVARS
Evergreen shrubs pages 272–273

MAHONIA JAPONICA
Evergreen shrub page 334

MAHONIA × MEDIA 'BUCKLAND'
Evergreen shrub page 335

PONCIRUS TRIFOLIATA
Shrub Z5-9 H9-5 Angular green shoots with vicious spines, fragrant white flowers, and orange-like fruits in autumn.
‡ ↔ 15ft (5m)

PRUNUS SPINOSA
Tree Z5-9 H9-5 The blackthorn is a dense shrub, with white spring flowers and sloes in autumn.
‡ 15ft (5m) ↔ 12ft (4m)

PYRACANTHA 'ORANGE GLOW'
Evergreen shrub page 430

PYRACANTHA 'WATERERI'
Evergreen shrub page 431

ROSA GLAUCA
Species rose page 464

ROSA RUGOSA 'ALBA'
Species rose Z2-9 H9-1 Thickets of prickly stems with white flowers followed by large red hips.
‡ ↔ 3–8ft (1–2.5m)

ROSA RUGOSA 'RUBRA'
Species rose page 465

GROUNDCOVERS FOR SUN

Many plants with creeping, trailing, or clump-forming habits can be planted to form a groundcover in sunny gardens. However, most will only suppress new weeds, and very few will actively smother existing weeds, so clear the soil of all perennial weeds before you plant. When planting, mix different plants to create interest, and add a few taller plants to prevent a flat effect.

ALCHEMILLA MOLLIS
Perennial page **49**

ARTEMISIA STELLERIANA
'BOUGHTON SILVER'
Perennial Z3-7 H7-1 Divided, evergreen, silver foliage that forms dense mats.
‡ 6in (15cm) ↔ 12–18in (30–45cm)

CAMPANULA GLOMERATA 'SUPERBA'
Perennial page **106**

CEANOTHUS THYRSIFLORUS VAR. *REPENS*
Evergreen shrub page **113**

CORNUS CANADENSIS
Perennial page **138**

DICENTRA 'STUART BOOTHMAN'
Perennial page **176**

ERICA X *DARLEYENSIS* 'JENNY PORTER'
Evergreen shrub page **187**

GERANIUM 'JOHNSON'S BLUE'
Perennial page **227**

GERANIUM X *OXONIANUM* 'WARGRAVE PINK'
Perennial page **229**

HOSTA FORTUNEI VAR. *AUREOMARGINATA*
Perennial page **259**

JUNIPERUS SQUAMATA 'BLUE CARPET'
Conifer Z5-8 H8-5 Low-growing plant with shoots that lift from the ground at a gentle angle.
‡ 12–18in (30–45cm) ↔ 5–6ft (1.5–1.8m)

LAMIUM MACULATUM
'WHITE NANCY'
Perennial page **301**

OSTEOSPERMUM JUCUNDUM
Perennial page **360**

PERSICARIA VACCINIFOLIA
Perennial page **382**

PHALARIS ARUNDINACEA 'PICTA'
Perennial grass page **383**

PHLOMIS RUSSELIANA
Perennial page **386**

PHLOX SUBULATA 'MCDANIEL'S CUSHION'
Alpine Z3-8 H8-1 Mossy foliage is covered with starry, pink flowers in late spring.
‡ 2–6in (5–15cm) ↔ 20in (50cm)

POTENTILLA MEGALANTHA
Perennial page **411**

ROSA GROUNDCOVER TYPES
Shrubs pages **458–459**

ROSMARINUS OFFICINALIS
'SEVERN SEA'
Evergreen shrub Z8-10 H10-8 A mound-forming plant with arching branches and bright blue flowers.
‡ 3ft (1m) ↔ 5ft (1.5m)

SEMPERVIVUM CILIOSUM
Alpine page **492**

VERONICA GENTIANOIDES
Perennial page **532**

VIOLA 'NELLIE BRITTON'
Perennial page **539**

GROUNDCOVERS FOR SHADE

Shade is often considered to be a problem, but there are lots of plants to use as groundcovers that do not need full sun. However, the more dense the shade, the less choice there is. Luckily, those that tolerate the worst conditions are evergreen, though slow growing. In less hostile conditions, many of these plants will quickly spread: an excellent alternative to grass under trees.

ADIANTUM VENUSTUM
Fern page 44

AJUGA REPTANS 'CATLIN'S GIANT'
Perennial Z3-9 H9-1 Very large, purple leaves and tall, blue flower spikes.
‡ 8in (20cm) ↔ 24–36in (60–90cm)

BERGENIA 'SILBERLICHT'
Perennial page 88

CONVALLARIA MAJALIS
Perennial page 135

COTONEASTER DAMMERI
Evergreen shrub Z6-8 H8-6 Spreading shrub with white flowers and red berries.
‡ 8in (20cm) ↔ 6ft (2m)

EPIMEDIUM X PERRALCHICUM
Perennial page 184

EUONYMUS FORTUNEI 'EMERALD GAIETY'
Evergreen shrub Z5-9 H9-5 Bushy, with white-edged leaves tinted pink in winter.
‡ 3ft (1m) ↔ 5ft (1.5m)

EUPHORBIA AMYGDALOIDES VAR. *ROBBIAE*
Perennial page 200

GAULTHERIA PROCUMBENS
Evergreen shrub page 221

GERANIUM MACRORRHIZUM 'CZAKOR'
Perennial Z4-8 H8-1 Mats of scented foliage tinted with purple in autumn, and magenta flowers in summer.
‡ 20in (50cm) ↔ 24in (60cm)

GERANIUM SYLVATICUM 'ALBUM'
Perennial Z4-8 H8-1 Deeply lobed leaves and small, white flowers. For moist soil.
‡ 30in (75cm) ↔ 24in (60cm)

HEDERA HIBERNICA
Evergreen climber page 247

HEUCHERA 'RED SPANGLES'
Perennial page 256

HOSTA 'FRANCES WILLIAMS'
Perennial page 259

OMPHALODES CAPPADOCICA
Perennial page 355

PACHYSANDRA TERMINALIS
Perennial page 362

POLYSTICHUM SETIFERUM
Fern page 409

SANGUINARIA CANADENSIS 'PLENA'
Perennial Z3-9 H9-1 Large glaucous leaves and white, double flowers. For moist soil.
‡ 6in (15cm) ↔ 12in (30cm)

TIARELLA CORDIFOLIA
Perennial page 516

TOLMIEA 'TAFF'S GOLD'
Perennial page 516

TRACHYSTEMON ORIENTALIS
Perennial Z6-8 H8-6 Large, rough, heart-shaped leaves and borage-like flowers.
‡ 12in (30cm) ↔ 3ft (1m)

VINCA MINOR 'ARGENTEOVARIEGATA'
Perennial Z4-9 H9-1 Pale blue flowers among gray-green and cream leaves.
‡ 6in (15cm) ↔ 36in (1m)

PLANTS WITH SCENTED FOLIAGE

While flowers tend to have sweet, fruity perfumes, leaf scents tend to be more spicy or resinous, though some, especially scented geraniums, mimic other plants. Some plants waft their perfume onto the air, and others need gentle stroking. It is likely that these plants evolved their scents to make themselves less appealing to insect pests; gardeners find them irresistible.

ALOYSIA TRIPHYLLA
Shrub   page **54**

AMICIA ZYGOMERIS
Perennial Z8-10 H10-8 Unusual plant, related to beans, with gray-green foliage that smells of cucumber when crushed.
‡7ft (2.2m) ↔ 4ft (1.2m)

CALOCEDRUS DECURRENS
Conifer Z5-8 H8-5 Columnar tree with sweetly scented foliage when crushed.
‡70–130ft (20–40m) ↔ 6–28ft (2–9m)

CALYCANTHUS OCCIDENTALIS
Shrub Z6-9 H9-6 Large leaves with a spicy scent; brick red flowers that smell fruity.
‡10ft (3m) ↔ 12ft (4m)

CERCIDIPHYLLUM JAPONICUM
Tree Z4-8 H8-1 In autumn the leaves of this graceful tree turn orange and red and smell like caramel.
‡70ft (20m) ↔ 50ft (15m)

CHAMAEMELUM NOBILE
'TRENEAGUE'
Perennial Z6-9 H9-6 This non-flowering form of chamomile hugs the soil, and its foliage smells fruity when gently crushed.
‡4in (10cm) ↔ 18in (45cm)

CISTUS X HYBRIDUS
Evergreen shrub   page **127**

CISTUS LADANIFER
Evergreen shrub Z8-10 H10-8 The dark green leaves are sticky and fragrant; the flowers are white with a yellow eye.
‡6ft (2m) ↔ 5ft (1.5m)

HELICHRYSUM ITALICUM
Evergreen shrub Z7-10 H10-7 Narrow, silver foliage on a small shrub that smells of curry.
‡24in (60cm) ↔ 3ft (1m)

HOUTTUYNIA CORDATA
'FLORE PLENO'
Perennial Z6-11 H12-6 A rather invasive, creeping plant with purplish leaves that have a strong citrus smell when crushed.
‡6–12in (15–30cm) ↔ indefinite

LAVANDULA ANGUSTIFOLIA
'TWICKEL PURPLE'
Evergreen shrub   page **305**

LAVANDULA STOECHAS
Shrub Z8-9 H9-8 The purple flowerheads are topped with purple bracts.
‡↔ 24in (60cm)

MELISSA OFFICINALIS 'AUREA'
Perennial Z3-7 H7-1 Form of lemon balm with yellow splashes on the leaves.
‡3ft (1m) ↔ 18in (45cm)

MENTHA SUAVEOLENS 'VARIEGATA'
Perennial Z6-9 H9-6 Variegated apple mint has a pleasant fragrance and showy leaves.
‡3ft (1m) ↔ indefinite

MONARDA 'CAMBRIDGE SCARLET'
Perennial   page **342**

MONARDA 'SCORPION'
Perennial Z4-8 H8-1 Whorls of bracts and violet flowers on tall, leafy stems.
‡5ft (1.5m) ↔ 3ft (1m)

ORIGANUM LAEVIGATUM
Perennial   page **357**

ORIGANUM LAEVIGATUM
'HERRENHAUSEN'
Perennial   page 358

PELARGONIUMS, SCENTED-LEAVED
Perennials,   pages 372–373

PERILLA FRUTESCENS VAR. *CRISPA*
Annual   page 380

PEROVSKIA ATRIPLICIFOLIA
Shrub Z6-9 H9-1 The upright stems carry
tiny, blue flowers in autumn, but the
grayish leaves are fragrant all summer
‡4ft (1.2m) ↔ 3ft (1m)

PEROVSKIA 'BLUE SPIRE'
Subshrub   page 380

PROSTANTHERA CUNEATA
Evergreen shrub Z9-10 H10-9
Small, mint-scented leaves and
pretty white flowers in summer.
‡↔ 12–36in (30–90cm)

PROSTANTHERA ROTUNDIFOLIA
Shrub Z9-10 H10-9 Mint-scented leaves
are smothered in lilac flowers in spring.
↑6–12ft (2–4m) ↔ 3–10ft (1–3m)

PSEUDOTSUGA MENZIESII
Conifer Z5-7 H7-5 A large tree with
resinous foliage.
‡80–160ft (25–50m) ↔ 20–30ft (6–10m)

PTELEA TRIFOLIATA 'AUREA'
Tree Z5-9 H9-4 The gold foliage and bark
is strongly scented.
‡15ft (5m)

ROSA EGLANTERIA
Species rose Z4-9 H9-1 Very thorny,
arching shoots with small pink flowers,
and foliage that smells of apples when wet
or in high humidity.
‡↔ 8ft (2.5m)

ROSMARINUS OFFICINALIS 'SILVER
SPIRES'
Evergreen shrub Z8-10 H10-1 The culinary
rosemary, but with silver-variegated foliage
on an upright plant.
‡3ft (1m) ↔ 24in (60cm)

SALVIA DISCOLOR
Shrub   page 473

SALVIA OFFICINALIS 'ICTERINA'
Subshrub   page 476

SKIMMIA × *CONFUSA* 'KEW GREEN'
Evergreen shrub   page 494

PLANTS WITH SCENTED FLOWERS

Fragrance is too often forgotten when planting a garden. Yet there are as many shades of fragrance as there are of colors: they can affect mood, take you back to your childhood, or whisk you off to a far-off land with a single sniff. The most strongly scented flowers are often white or insignificant in appearance, but they have evolved to make their presence felt in other ways.

ABELIA CHINENSIS
Shrub Z7-9 H9-7 Spreading, with heads of small pale pink flowers in late summer.
‡ 5ft (1.5m) ↔ 8ft (2.5m)

BUDDLEJA ALTERNIFOLIA
Shrub   page 92

CAMELLIA 'INSPIRATION'
Evergreen shrub   page 99

CAMELLIA JAPONICA
'ADOLPHE AUDUSSON'
Evergreen shrub   page 100

CAMELLIA JAPONICA
'ELEGANS'
Evergreen shrub   page 100

CHIMONANTHUS PRAECOX
'GRANDIFLORUS'
Shrub   page 120

CHIMONANTHUS PRAECOX
'LUTEUS'
Shrub Z7-9 H9-7 Pale yellow flowers scent the late winter air.
‡ 12ft (4m) ↔ 10ft (3m)

CHOISYA TERNATA
Evergreen shrub   page 121

CHOISYA 'AZTEC PEARL'
Evergreen shrub Z9-10 H10-9 Narrowly divided, deep green leaves and white, pink-tinged flowers in spring and autumn.
‡ ↔ 8ft (2.5m)

CLEMATIS MONTANA
F. *GRANDIFLORA*
Climber   page 128

DAPHNE BHOLUA 'GURKHA'
Shrub   page 164

DAPHNE TANGUTICA RETUSA GROUP
Evergreen shrubs   page 165

DIANTHUS 'DORIS'
Perennial   page 172

ERICA ERIGENA
'GOLDEN LADY'
Evergreen shrub   page 187

HAMAMELIS (WITCH HAZELS)
Shrubs   pages 238–239

HOSTA 'HONEYBELLS'
Perennial   page 260

JASMINUM OFFICINALE
Climber Z9-10 H10-9 A strong, twining climber with white flowers in summer that have an intense, sweet scent.
‡ 40ft (12m)

JASMINUM OFFICINALE
'ARGENTEOVARIEGATUM'
Climber   page 292

LILIUM PINK PERFECTION GROUP
Bulb   page 317

LONICERA CAPRIFOLIUM
Climber Z6-9 H9-6 The Italian honeysuckle has pink and cream, fragrant flowers in summer.
‡ 20ft (6m)

LONICERA PERICLYMENUM 'BELGICA'
Climber Z5-9 H9-5 In early summer this honeysuckle produces creamy yellow flowers streaked with maroon.
‡ 22ft (7m)

LONICERA PERICLYMENUM 'GRAHAM THOMAS'
Climber

MAGNOLIA GRANDIFLORA 'GOLIATH'
Evergreen tree

MAHONIA × MEDIA 'CHARITY'
Evergreen shrub

OSMANTHUS DELAVAYI
Evergreen shrub

PAEONIA LACTIFLORA 'DUCHESSE DE NEMOURS'
Perennial

PHILADELPHUS 'BEAUCLERK'
Shrub

PHILADELPHUS 'BELLE ETOILE'
Shrub

PHLOX PANICULATA 'WHITE ADMIRAL'
Perennial Z4-8 H8-1 Large heads of pure white flowers with a sweet, peppery scent, borne in summer.
↕3ft (1m)

PITTOSPORUM TENUIFOLIUM
Evergreen shrub

PITTOSPORUM TOBIRA
Evergreen shrub or small tree

PRIMULA FLORINDAE
Perennial

ROSA 'ALBERTINE'
Rambler rose

ROSA 'ARTHUR BELL'
Floribunda rose

ROSA 'BLESSINGS'
Hybrid tea rose

ROSA 'COMPASSION'
Climbing rose

ROSA 'GRAHAM THOMAS'
Modern shrub rose

ROSA 'ICEBERG, CLIMBING'
Climbing rose Z5-9 H9-5 This fine rose has many pure white flowers all summer.
↕8ft (2.5m)

ROSA 'JUST JOEY'
Hybrid tea rose

ROSA 'MARGARET MERRIL'
Floribunda rose

ROSA 'PEACE'
Hybrid tea rose

ROSA 'PENELOPE'
Modern shrub rose

ROSA 'REMEMBER ME'
Hybrid tea rose

SARCOCOCCA HOOKERIANA VAR. *DIGYNA*
Evergreen shrub

SKIMMIA JAPONICA 'RUBELLA'
Evergreen shrub

SMILACINA RACEMOSA
Perennial

SYRINGA MEYERI 'PALIBIN'
Shrub

SYRINGA VULGARIS 'MME LEMOINE'
Shrub

ULEX EUROPAEUS 'FLORE PLENO'
Evergreen shrub Z6-8 H8-6 Spiny bush that has a few of its double flowers, scented of coconut, open almost all year.
↕8ft (2.5m) ↔6ft (2m)

VIBURNUM × BURKWOODII 'PARK FARM HYBRID'
Evergreen shrub Z4-8 H8-1 Upright shrub with bronze new leaves and deep pink, scented flowers in late spring.
↕10ft (3m) ↔6ft (2m)

VIBURNUM CARLESII 'AURORA'
Shrub Z5-8 H8-4 Pink flowers in late spring, opening from red buds.
↕↔6ft (2m)

PLANTS FOR PAVING

Plants help break up large expanses of paving or gravel. The clean surface also helps prevent the flowers of small plants from becoming splashed with soil and reflects heat back up.

Few plants tolerate being stepped on; use only the toughest, such as thymes and chamomile, where there is heavy foot traffic. Less busy areas can be home to dwarf shrubs and alpines.

ACAENA 'BLUE HAZE'
Perennial Z7-9 H9-7A vigorous, spreading perennial with divided, gray-blue leaves and round, white flowerheads followed by red burrs.
‡ 4–6in (10–15cm) ↔ 3ft (1m)

ACAENA MICROPHYLLA
Perennial   page **31**

ACHILLEA AGERATIFOLIA
Perennial   page **39**

ACHILLEA × LEWISII 'KING EDWARD'
Perennial   page **40**

AETHIONEMA 'WARLEY ROSE'
Shrub   page **46**

AJUGA REPTANS 'ATROPURPUREA'
Perennial   page **48**

ANTHEMIS PUNCTATA SUBSP.
CUPANIANA
Perennial   page **61**

ARENARIA MONTANA
Perennial   page **66**

ARMERIA JUNIPERIFOLIA
Subshrub   page **68**

CAMPANULA COCHLEARIFOLIA
Perennial   page **106**

CHAMAEMELUM NOBILE
'TRENEAGUE'
Perennial Z6-9 H9-6 This non-flowering form of chamomile hugs the soil, and its foliage smells fruity when gently crushed.
‡ 4in (10cm) ↔ 18in (45cm)

DIANTHUS 'PIKE'S PINK'
Perennial   page **173**

DIASCIA 'JOYCE'S CHOICE'
Perennial Z8-9 H9-8 Early-flowering, with long spikes of pale, apricot-pink flowers in summer.
‡ 12in (30cm) ↔ 18in (45cm)

ERIGERON KARVINSKIANUS
Perennial   page **190**

ERINUS ALPINUS
Perennial   page **190**

HELIANTHEMUM 'RHODANTHE
CARNEUM'
Evergreen shrub   page **248**

LYSIMACHIA NUMMULARIA 'AUREA'
Perennial   page **329**

PENSTEMON RUPICOLA
Dwarf shrub Z4-9 H9-1 Tiny compared to border penstemons: evergreen, with leathery leaves and small, tubular deep pink flowers in early summer.
‡ 4in (10cm) ↔ 18in (45cm)

PHLOX DOUGLASII 'CRACKERJACK'
Perennial   page **388**

PHLOX DOUGLASII 'RED ADMIRAL'
Perennial   page **388**

PRATIA PEDUNCULATA
Perennial Z5-7 H7-5 Mildly invasive creeping plant with tiny leaves and star-shaped, pale blue flowers in summer.
‡ ⅛in (1.5cm) ↔ indefinite

SAPONARIA OCYMOIDES
Perennial page **481**

SEDUM ACRE 'AUREUM'
Perennial Z4-9 H9-1 Rather invasive succulent with tiny shoots and leaves that are yellow when young, and yellow flowers.
↕ 2in (5cm) ↔ 24in (60cm)

SEDUM KAMTSCHATICUM
'VARIEGATUM'
Perennial page **488**

SEDUM SPATHULIFOLIUM
'PURPUREUM'
Perennial page **489**

SEDUM SPURIUM 'SCHORBUSER BLUT'
Perennial page **490**

SOLEIROLIA SOLEIROLII 'AUREA'
Perennial Z10--11 H10 1 A surprisingly vigorous plant with bright lime green, tiny leaves that form mounds and cushions.
↕ 2in (5cm) ↔ 3ft (1m)

THYMUS × *CITRIODORUS*
'BERTRAM ANDERSON'
Evergreen shrub page **514**

THYMUS × *CITRIODORUS*
'SILVER QUEEN'
Evergreen shrub Z6-9 H9-6 The leaves of this cultivar are variegated and look good with the lavender-pink flowers.
↕ 12in (30cm) ↔ 10in (25cm)

THYMUS 'PINK CHINTZ'
Perennial Z4-9 H9-1 Trailing stems that root as they grow, with grayish leaves and pink flowers loved by bees.
↕ 10in (25cm) ↔ 18in (45cm)

THYMUS POLYTRICHUS SUBSP.
BRITANNICUS 'ALBUS'
Subshrub Z5-9 H9-5 A mat-forming woody plant with hairy leaves and white flowers.
↕ 2in (5cm) ↔ 24in (60cm)

THYMUS SERPYLLUM VAR.
COCCINEUM
Subshrub page **515**

VIOLA 'JACKANAPES'
Perennial page **539**

ARCHITECTURAL PLANTS

Every garden needs plants that are larger than life, with the sort of shape or texture that cannot be ignored. Too many of these plants can be visually overwhelming, with their bold leaves and spiky shapes, but if carefully placed among less flashy plants, they become the focus of a view or a feature in a border. Make use of light and shade to emphasize bold silhouettes.

ACANTHUS SPINOSUS
Perennial page **31**

AESCULUS PARVIFLORA
Shrub page **46**

AGAVE AMERICANA
Succulent Z11 H12-10 Spiny plant with steel gray leaves in a magnificent rosette.
↕ 6ft (2m) ↔ 10ft (3m)

AILANTHUS ALTISSIMA
Tree Z4-8 H8-1 Widely considered weedy, this will produce divided leaves 4ft (1.2m) long if cut back hard every spring. Foliage smells strongly.
↕ 80ft (25m) ↔ 50ft (15m)

ARAUCARIA HETEROPHYLLA
Conifer page **64**

BETULA NIGRA
Tree page **89**

BETULA PENDULA 'YOUNGII'
Tree page **89**

CATALPA BIGNONIOIDES 'AUREA'
Tree Z5-9 H9-5 Spreading tree that can be pruned hard for large, gold leaves.
↕↔ 30ft (10m)

CHAMAECYPARIS NOOTKATENSIS 'PENDULA'
Conifer page **118**

CHAMAECYPARIS PISIFERA 'FILIFERA AUREA'
Conifer Z4-8 H8-1 A broad, arching shrub with whiplike, golden shoots.
↕ 40ft (12m) ↔ 15ft (5m)

CORYLUS AVELLANA 'CONTORTA'
Shrub page **143**

CROCOSMIA MASONIORUM
Perennial page **152**

CYCAS REVOLUTA
Palmlike tree page **157**

ERYNGIUM GIGANTEUM
Biennial Z5-8 H8-5 Rosettes of deep green leaves, and spiny, white stems and flowerheads in the second year.
↕ 36in (90cm) ↔ 12in (30cm)

EUCALYPTUS PAUCIFLORA SUBSP. *NIPHOPHILA*
Evergreen tree page **197**

EUPHORBIA CHARACIAS
Perennial page **201**

FAGUS SYLVATICA 'PENDULA'
Tree Z5-7 H7-5 A tree of huge proportions with horizontal and arching branches cascading to the ground.
↕ 50ft (15m) ↔ 70ft (20m)

FARGESIA NITIDA
Ornamental grass page **205**

GUNNERA MANICATA
Perennial page **233**

HELIANTHUS 'MONARCH'
Perennial page **250**

KNIPHOFIA CAULESCENS
Perennial page **297**

MACLEAYA × *KEWENSIS* 'KELWAY'S CORAL PLUME'
Perennial page **330**

MELIANTHUS MAJOR
Perennial   page 340

PAEONIA DELAVAYI
Shrub   page 363

PAULOWNIA TOMENTOSA
Tree   page 371

PHORMIUM COOKIANUM SUBSP.
HOOKERI 'CREAM DELIGHT'
Perennial   page 392

PHORMIUM TENAX
Perennial   page 393

PHORMIUM TENAX PURPUREUM
GROUP
Perennials   page 394

PHYLLOSTACHYS AUREA
Bamboo Z6-10 H10-6 The golden bamboo:
yellow-brown canes and yellow-green leaves.
↕ 6–30ft (2–10m) ↔ indefinite

PHYLLOSTACHYS AUREOSULCATA
'AUREOCAULIS'
Bamboo Z6-10 H10-6 Large bamboo with
bright, golden canes and narrow leaves.
↕ 10–20ft (3–6m) ↔ indefinite

PHYLLOSTACHYS NIGRA
Bamboo   page 398

PHYLLOSTACHYS NIGRA VAR.
HENONIS
Bamboo   page 399

PLEIOBLASTUS VARIEGATUS
Bamboo   page 407

PRUNUS 'AMANOGAWA'
Tree Z6-8 H8-6 Very slender, upright
growth, and semidouble pink flowers
in spring.
↕ 25ft (8m) ↔ 12ft (4m)

PRUNUS 'KIKU-SHIDARE-ZAKURA'
Tree   page 422

RODGERSIA AESCULIFOLIA
Perennial Z5-8 H8-5 Creeping rhizomes
produce clumps of large leaves like those
of horse chestnuts, and pink flowers.
↕ 6ft (2m) ↔ 3ft (1m)

SORBARIA TOMENTOSA VAR.
ANGUSTIFOLIA
Shrub Z8-10 H10-8 A spreading shrub with
feathery leaves, red stems and fluffy, white
flowerheads.
↕ ↔ 10ft (3m)

STIPA GIGANTEA
Ornamental grass   page 503

TRACHYCARPUS FORTUNEI
Palm Z9-10 H10-9 Slow-growing but rather
cold-tolerant palm with fan-shaped leaves
and a furry trunk with age.
↕ 70ft (20m) ↔ 8ft (2.5m)

VIBURNUM PLICATUM 'PINK BEAUTY'
Shrub Z4-8 H8-1 A spreading shrub with
horizontal tiers of branches, covered
with white flowers turning to pink.
↕ 10ft (3m) ↔ 12ft (4m)

WOODWARDIA RADICANS
Fern Z8-9 H9-8 A large, evergreen fern
with huge, arching fronds.
↕ 6ft (2m) ↔ 10ft (3m)

YUCCA FILAMENTOSA
Evergreen shrub Z5-10 H10-4 A clump-
forming, stemless plant with soft leaves
and spires of creamy flowers.
↕ 30in (75cm) ↔ 5ft (1.5m)

YUCCA FILAMENTOSA 'BRIGHT EDGE'
Shrub   page 543

YUCCA FLACCIDA 'IVORY'
Shrub   page 544

YUCCA GLORIOSA
Evergreen shrub Z7-10 H10-7 Erect trunks
with gray-green narrow, sharp-tipped
leaves, and large clusters of white flowers.
↕ ↔ 6ft (2m)

SHRUBS AND CLIMBERS FOR COLD WALLS

The coldest walls or fences are sunless nearly all year, but the even temperatures and often moist soil suits ivies, climbing hygrangeas, and some shrubs. Walls that receive only morning sun can be a problem in colder climates: rapid thawing can damage shoots and flowers, as with magnolias. However, this is the perfect site for some clematis, climbing roses, chaenomeles, and honeysuckles.

AKEBIA QUINATA
Semi-evergreen climber Z5-9 H9-4 Twining stems with dark green, divided leaves and scented, purple flowers in spring.
‡ 30ft (10m)

CAMELLIA × WILLIAMSII 'FRANCIS HANGER'
Evergreen shrub Z8-10 H10-8 Glossy leaves form a good foil to the white, golden-centered flowers.
‡ ↔ 5ft (1.5m)

CHAENOMELES SPECIOSA 'GEISHA GIRL'
Shrub Z5-8 H8-4 Bushy plant with semidouble flowers of pale apricot pink.
‡ ↔ 5ft (1.5m)

CLEMATIS 'CARNABY'
Mid-season clematis Z4-9 H9-1 Compact climber with large pink flowers, with a deeper center on each petal.
‡ 8ft (2.5m) ↔ 3ft (1m)

CLEMATIS ALPINA 'HELSINGBORG'
Early clematis Z4-9 H9-1 Masses of dainty, deep purple-blue flowers are followed by fluffy seedheads.
‡ 2–3m (6–10ft) ↔ 1.5m (5ft)

CLEMATIS 'HENRYI'
Mid-season clematis page 130

CLEMATIS 'MINUET'
Late-season clematis page 133

CLEMATIS 'NELLY MOSER'
Mid-season clematis page 130

CLEMATIS 'NIOBE'
Mid-season clematis page 131

CLEMATIS 'VENOSA VIOLACEA'
Late-season clematis page 133

CODONOPSIS CONVOLVULACEA
Perennial climber page 134

CORYLOPSIS PAUCIFLORA
Shrub page 142

COTONEASTER HORIZONTALIS
Shrub page 146

DAPHNE ODORA 'AUREOMARGINATA'
Evergreen shrub Z7-9 H9-7 Low-growing, mounded shrub with leaves edged with gold, and pale pink, fragrant flowers.
‡ ↔ 5ft (1.5m)

EUONYMUS FORTUNEI 'EMERALD 'N' GOLD'
Evergreen shrub page 199

FORSYTHIA SUSPENSA
Shrub page 209

GARRYA ELLIPTICA 'JAMES ROOF'
Evergreen shrub page 219

HEDERA CANARIENSIS 'GLOIRE DE MARENGO'
Evergreen climber Z7-10 H10-7 Silvery green leaves variegated with white, and tinged pink in winter.
‡ 12ft (4m)

HEDERA COLCHICA 'DENTATA'
Evergreen climber page 245

HEDERA COLCHICA
'SULPHUR HEART'
Evergreen climber   page 245

HEDERA HELIX 'GOLDHEART'
Evergreen climber Z-10 H10-5 Red stems
with deep green leaves marked with
a central gold splash.
‡25ft (8m)

HYDRANGEA ANOMALA SUBSP.
PETIOLARIS
Climber   page 264

JASMINUM HUMILE
Evergreen shrub Z9-10 H10-9 Sparsely
branched, arching shrub with bright yellow
flowers in summer.
‡ ↔ 8ft (2.5m)

JASMINUM NUDIFLORUM
Shrub   page 291

KERRIA JAPONICA 'PLENIFLORA'
Shrub Z4-9 H9-1 Vigorous, upright plant
with slender, green stems and double
orange/gold flowers.
‡ ↔ 10ft (3m)

LONICERA JAPONICA 'HALLIANA'
Evergreen climber Z4-10 H10-1 Strong-
growing climber with scented white
flowers that age to yellow.
‡30ft (10m)

MUEHLENBECKIA COMPLEXA
Climber Z8-10 H10-8 Masses of threadlike,
dark, twisting stems with tiny violin-
shaped leaves.
‡10ft (3m)

PARTHENOCISSUS HENRYANA
Climber   page 369

PARTHENOCISSUS QUINQUEFOLIA
Climber Z3-9 H9-1 Vigorous, deciduous
climber with leaves divided into five
leaflets that take on vivid red shades
in autumn.
‡50ft (15m)

PILEOSTEGIA VIBURNOIDES
Evergreen climber Z7-10 H10-7 Oblong,
dark green leaves and clusters of fluffy,
white flowers.
‡20ft (6m)

PYRACANTHA 'HARLEQUIN'
Evergreen shrub Z7-9 H9-7 Prickly shrub
with white-variegated leaves, white
flowers, and red berries.
‡5ft (1.5m) ↔ 6ft (2m)

ROSA 'ALBÉRIC BARBIER'
Rambler rose   page 454

ROSA 'DUBLIN BAY'
Climbing rose   page 452

ROSA 'HANDEL'
Climbing rose   page 453

ROSA 'MERMAID'
Climbing rose Z6-9 H9-6 Strong, thorny
climber with dark, shiny leaves and single,
primrose yellow flowers.
‡20ft (6m)

SCHIZOPHRAGMA INTEGRIFOLIUM
Climber Z5-9 H9-5 Large climber with
toothed, dark green leaves and showy
white flowers.
‡40ft (12m)

PLANTS FOR WARM WALLS

Reserve the warmest, sunniest garden walls to grow plants that are slightly tender in your climate. However, these sites can also be very dry, especially if the border is narrow and in the shadow of a roof, and it may be difficult to establish plants. Walls that receive only the morning sun are more gentle to plants, which may grow more quickly because there may be more moisture.

ESCALLONIA 'LANGLEYENSIS'
Evergreen shrub page 195

FREMONTODENDRON 'CALIFORNIA GLORY'
Shrub page 210

HEDYCHIUM GARDNERIANUM
Perennial Z9-10 H10-9 Large heads of spidery, sweetly scented cream flowers.
‡ ↔ 6–7ft (2–2.2m)

IPOMOEA INDICA
Climber page 277

JASMINUM × *STEPHANENSE*
Climber Z8-10 H10-8 Fast-growing, with clusters of pink, fragrant flowers in summer.
‡ 15ft (5m)

JOVELLANA VIOLACEA
Semi-evergreen shrub Z9-10 H10-9 Weak shrub with fine foliage and bell-like, pale violet flowers in summer.
‡ 24in (60cm) ↔ 3ft (1m)

LAPAGERIA ROSEA
Climber page 301

LONICERA × *ITALICA*
Climber page 323

LONICERA × *TELLMANNIANA*
Climber page 325

MAGNOLIA GRANDIFLORA 'EXMOUTH'
Evergreen shrub page 330

PASSIFLORA CAERULEA
Climber page 370

PHYGELIUS
Shrubs, pages 396–8

PITTOSPORUM TENUIFOLIUM 'SILVER QUEEN'
Evergreen shrub Z9-10 H10-9 Wiry black twigs support gray-green, white-edged leaves, and purple, scented flowers in autumn.
‡ 3–12ft (1–4m) ↔ 6ft (2m)

RHODANTHEMUM HOSMARIENSE
Subshrub page 435

RIBES SPECIOSUM
Shrub Z7-9 H9-7 Spiny shrub with bristly stems, small glossy leaves, and pendulous red flowers resembling fuchsias.
‡ ↔ 6ft (2m)

ROSES, CLIMBING
Deciduous climbers pages 452–453

SOLANUM CRISPUM 'GLASNEVIN'
Climber page 496

SOLANUM JASMINOIDES 'ALBUM'
Climber page 496

THUNBERGIA GRANDIFLORA
Climber page 513

TRACHELOSPERMUM JASMINOIDES
Evergreen climber page 517

VESTIA FOETIDA
Shrub Z8-10 H10-8 A short-lived plant with unpleasantly scented leaves and prolific, pendulous yellow flowers.
‡ 6ft (2m) ↔ 5ft (1.5m)

VITIS 'BRANT'
Climber Z5-9 H9-5 An ornamental grape with green leaves that turn red in autumn. Bears edible black grapes.
‡ 22ft (7m)

WISTERIA FLORIBUNDA 'ALBA'
Climber page 542

WISTERIA SINENSIS
Climber page 543

WISTERIA SINENSIS 'SIERRA MADRE'
Evergreen shrub Z5-8 H8-5 Attractive cultivar with bicolored, fragrant flowers.
‡ 28ft (9m)

ZAUSCHNERIA CALIFORNICA 'DUBLIN'
Perennial page 545

PLANTS FOR BEES AND BUTTERFLIES

Plants that will attract these fascinating and useful garden visitors usually have simple, tubular or daisylike flowers, especially in pinks and purples; avoid double-flowered varieties. Butterflies also like fruity scents. Remember that their caterpillar stage needs different food plants. For example, milkweed and some of its relatives in the genus *Asclepias* attract monarch caterpillars.

AJUGA REPTANS 'BRAUNHERZ'
Perennial Z3-9 H9-1 Creeper with glossy, purplish leaves and blue flowers in spring.
‡ 6in (15cm) ↔ 36in (90cm)

ALLIUM SCHOENOPRASUM 'FORESCATE'
Perennial Z3-9 H9-1 Ornamental chives with abundant heads of pink flowers.
‡ 24in (60cm)

ASCLEPIAS INCARNATA
Perennial Z3-8 H8-1 Thick, upright stems support small heads of curious pale pink flowers followed by interesting seedheads.
‡ 4ft (1.2m) ↔ 24in (60cm)

ASTER AMELLUS 'SONIA'
Perennial Z5-8 H8-5 Pale pink, yellow-centered flowers.
‡ 24in (60cm) ↔ 18in (45cm)

ASTER 'ANDENKEN AN ALMA PÖTSCHKE'
Perennial   page 72

ASTER × *FRIKARTII* 'MÖNCH'
Perennial   page 73

ASTER TURBINELLUS
Perennial Z4-8 H8-1 Wiry, stems with small leaves and lilac flowers in late summer.
‡ 4ft (1.2m) ↔ 2ft (60cm)

BUDDLEJA AURICULATA
Evergreen shrub Z6-9 H9-6 Small clusters of white and orange, scented flowers in autumn.
‡ ↔ 10ft (3m)

BUDDLEJA DAVIDII CULTIVARS
Shrubs   page 93

BUDDLEJA DAVIDII 'BLACK KNIGHT'
Shrub Z6-9 H9-6 Large spikes of deep purple flowers. Prune hard as growth begins.
‡ 10ft (3m) ↔ 15ft (5m)

BUDDLEJA 'LOCHINCH'
Shrub   page 94

CALLUNA VULGARIS 'WICKWAR FLAME'
Evergreen shrub Z5-7 H7-5 Gold leaves turn red in winter; pink flowers in summer.
‡ 20in (50cm) ↔ 26in (65cm)

CARYOPTERIS × *CLANDONENSIS* 'HEAVENLY BLUE'
Shrub   page 110

CEANOTHUS 'PUGET BLUE'
Evergreen shrub Z8-10 H10-8 Mass of fine foliage covered with mid-blue flowers.
‡ ↔ 2.2m (7ft)

CYTISUS × *BEANII*
Shrub   page 160

DAHLIA MERCKII
Perennial Z9-11 H12-1 Tuberous-rooted plant with slender, translucent stems and pale mauve, often nodding flowers.
‡ 6ft (2m) ↔ 3ft (1m)

DIGITALIS PURPUREA 'SUTTON'S APRICOT'
Biennial Z4-8 H8-1 Tall foxglove with pale apricot-pink flowers in summer.
‡ 3–6ft (1–2m)

ECHINACEA PURPUREA
Perennial Z3-9 H9-1 Large, daisylike flowers with pink petals and dark centers.
‡ 3ft (1m) ↔ 18in (45cm)

ECHIUM VULGARE 'BLUE BEDDER'
Annual Z3-8 H8-1 Bushy plant with bristly,
grayish green leaves and soft blue flowers.
↕ ↔ 18in (45cm)

ERICA VAGANS 'BIRCH GLOW'
Evergreen shrub   page **189**

ERICA VAGANS 'VALERIE PROUDLEY'
Evergreen shrub Z7-9 H9-7 Gold foliage;
white flowers in summer.
↕ 6in (15cm) ↔ 12in (30cm)

ERICA × VEITCHII 'EXETER'
Evergreen shrub   page **186**

ERYNGIUM PLANUM
Perennial Z5-9 H9-5 Steely blue, branched
stems with small, light blue, spiky flower
heads emerge from evergreen leaf rosettes.
↕ 36in (90cm) ↔ 18in (45cm)

HELIOTROPIUM 'PRINCESS MARINA'
Shrub   page **252**

HOHERIA GLABRATA
Tree   page **258**

HYSSOPUS OFFICINALIS
Evergreen shrub Z6-9 H9-6 Green leaves
and spikes of blue flowers in summer.
↕ 24in (60cm) ↔ 3ft (1m)

LAMIUM ORVALA
Perennial Z4-8 H8-1 A choice, clump-
forming plant that does not creep, with
large leaves and purplish flowers in spring.
↕ 24in (60cm) ↔ 12in (30cm)

LAVANDULA ANGUSTIFOLIA
'LODDON PINK'
Evergreen shrub Z5-8 H8-5 Compact shrub
with gray leaves and spikes of pale pink
flowers.
↕ 18in (45cm) ↔ 24in (60cm)

LUNARIA REDIVIVA
Perennial Z6-9 H9-6 Pale lilac, fragrant
flowers are followed by translucent
seedheads.
↕ 24–36in (60–90cm) ↔ 12in (30cm)

MENTHA LONGIFOLIA BUDDLEJA
MINT GROUP
Perennial Z6-9 H9-6 Tall stems of grayish
leaves and heads of pink flowers.
↕ ↔ 3ft (1m)

MONARDA 'CROFTWAY PINK'
Perennial   page **343**

ORIGANUM LAEVIGATUM
'HERRENHAUSEN'
Perennial   page **358**

PAPAVER ORIENTALE 'CEDRIC MORRIS'
Perennial   page **367**

PAPAVER RHOEAS 'MOTHER OF PEARL'
Annual H12-1 Easy to grow from seed,
with delicate flowers in pastel shades.
↕ 36in (90cm) ↔ 12in (30cm)

PENSTEMON 'SOUR GRAPES'
Perennial Z6-9 H9-6 Intriguing flowers in
shades of grayish blue, pink, and mauve
on spikes above large, green leaves.
↕ 24in (60cm) ↔ 18in (45cm)

PRUNELLA GRANDIFLORA
'LOVELINESS'
Perennial   page **420**

ROSMARINUS OFFICINALIS
'MISS JESSOP'S UPRIGHT'
Evergreen shrub   page **466**

SEDUM 'HERBSTFREUDE'
Perennial Z3-10 H10-1 Upright,
unbranched stems with pale green, fleshy
leaves, and deep pink flowers in flat heads
in late summer. Also sold as 'Autumn Joy'.
↕ ↔ 24in (60cm)

TAGETES 'NAUGHTY MARIETTA'
Annual H12-1 Bushy plants with single,
yellow flowers marked with red.
↕ 12–16in (30–40cm)

TRACHELIUM CAERULEUM
Perennial Z9-10 H10-1 Usually grown as an
annual, this upright plant produces flat
heads of small purple flowers in summer.
↕ 3ft (1m) ↔ 12in (30cm)

PLANTS TO ATTRACT GARDEN BIRDS

Native and visiting birds will visit gardens to feed on a wide variety of plants, especially those bearing berries and seeds (see also pages 586 and 615). Unfortunately, their feeding necessarily means that the food source – and the attractive autumn display – does not last long, so it is worth offering them a variety of plants and providing extra food on a regular basis.

ARBUTUS MENZIESII
Tree   page **65**

ATRIPLEX HORTENSIS VAR. *RUBRA*
Annual H12-1 Vigorous plant with deep red leaves that contrast well with other plants; its seeds are loved by birds.
$\updownarrow$ 4ft (1.2m) $\leftrightarrow$ 12in (30cm)

BERBERIS THUNBERGII
Shrub Z5-8 H8-5 Green leaves and small, yellow flowers in summer become red leaves and berries in autumn.
$\updownarrow$ 6ft (2m) $\leftrightarrow$ 8ft (2.5m)

CORTADERIA SELLOANA 'PUMILA'
Ornamental grass Z7-10 H10-7 A compact pampas grass with short flower spikes.
$\updownarrow$ 5ft (1.5m) $\leftrightarrow$ 4ft (1.2m)

COTONEASTER LACTEUS
Evergreen shrub   page **147**

COTONEASTER SIMONSII
Shrub   page **147**

CRATAEGUS × *LAVALLEI* 'CARRIEREI'
Tree   page **150**

CYNARA CARDUNCULUS
Perennial   page **159**

DAPHNE MEZEREUM
Shrub Z5-8 H8-5 Fragrant pink flowers in spring, red berries in autumn.
$\updownarrow$ 4ft (1.2m) $\leftrightarrow$ 3ft (1m)

HEDERA HELIX & CULTIVARS
Evergreen climbers   pages **246–247**
When ivy reaches its flowering stage the black berries are attractive to many birds; ivy also provides valuable nesting sites.

HELIANTHUS ANNUUS 'MUSIC BOX'
Annual H12-1 Multicolored sunflowers that produce heads of seeds that may be harvested to feed birds in later months.
$\updownarrow$ 28in (70cm) $\leftrightarrow$ 24in (60cm)

ILEX AQUIFOLIUM 'HANDSWORTH NEW SILVER'
Evergreen shrub   page **273**

LONICERA PERICLYMENUM 'SEROTINA'
Climber   page **324**

MAHONIA AQUIFOLIUM
Evergreen shrub Z7-9 H9-7 A suckering shrub with gently spiny leaves, and yellow flowers followed by black berries.
$\updownarrow$ 3ft (1m) $\leftrightarrow$ 5ft (1.5m)

MALUS × *ZUMI* 'GOLDEN HORNET'
Tree   page **337**

MISCANTHUS SINENSIS
Ornamental grass Z4-9 H9-1 This grass forms clumps of long, arching leaves and silver or pink flowerheads in late summer.
$\updownarrow$ 8ft (2.5m) $\leftrightarrow$ 4ft (1.2m)

ONOPORDUM NERVOSUM
Biennial Z7-9 H9-7 A large, silvery, prickly plant with thistlelike purple flowers.
$\updownarrow$ 8ft (2.5m) $\leftrightarrow$ 3ft (1m)

PAPAVER SOMNIFERUM 'WHITE CLOUD'
Annual H8-1 White, double flowers and pretty seedheads attractive to birds.
$\updownarrow$ 3ft (1m) $\leftrightarrow$ 12in (30cm)

PRUNUS PADUS
Tree Z4-8 H8-1 A spreading tree with
pendent spikes of small white flowers
followed by
black berries.
‡ 50ft (15m) ↔ 30ft (10m)

PYRACANTHA 'MOHAVE'
Evergreen shrub Z6-9 H9-6 Dense, spiny
growth with dark green leaves and bright
red berries.
↓ 12ft (4m) ↔ 15ft (5m)

RIBES ODORATUM
Shrub Z5-8 H8-4 Weakly branched shrub
with yellow clove-scented flowers in
spring, and black berries in late summer.
‡ ↔ 6ft (2m)

ROSA FILIPES 'KIFTSGATE'
Climbing rose   page **452**

ROSA PIMPINELLIFOLIA
Species rose Z3-9 H9-1 This very spiny
bush has single white flowers followed by
purplish black hips.
‡ 3ft (1m) ↔ 4ft (1.2m)

ROSA 'SCABROSA'
Shrub rose 2-9 H9-1 Deep pink flowers
and bright red hips on a mounded bush
with deeply veined foliage.
‡ ↔ 5½ft (1.7m)

SAMBUCUS NIGRA
'AURFOMARGINATA'
Shrub Z4-9 H9-1 Fast-growing plant for any
soil, with yellow-edged leaves, white
flowers, and heads of black elderberries.
‡ ↔ 20ft (6m)

SILYBUM MARIANUM
Biennial Z6-9 H9-6 Rosettes of spiny
leaves, veined with white, prickly mauve
seedheads and thistle seeds.
‡ 5ft (1.5m) ↔ 24–36in (60–90cm)

SORBUS AUCUPARIA 'FASTIGIATA'
Tree Z4-7 H7-1 Upright, with red berries in
late summer after white spring flowers.
‡ 25ft (8m) ↔ 15ft (5m)

VIBURNUM BETULIFOLIUM
Shrub Z5-8 H8-4 Spectacular displays of
red berries follow white flowers in summer
when several plants are grown together.
‡ ↔ 10ft (3m)

VIBURNUM OPULUS
Shrub Z4-8 H8-1 Strong-growing shrub
with white flowers in summer, bright
autumn color and red berries.
‡ 15ft (5m) ↔ 12ft (4m)

VITIS VINIFERA 'PURPUREA'
Climber   page **540**

FLOWERS FOR CUTTING

It is useful to be able to cut flowers from the garden, either to use on their own or to add to bought flowers. Many annuals are grown especially for cutting, but other garden plants can supply flowers for the house without spoiling the display. To produce many smaller stems for cutting, pinch out the shoots of free-branching plants such as asters and delphiniums in early summer.

ACHILLEA 'CORONATION GOLD'
Perennial page 39

ACONITUM 'BRESSINGHAM SPIRE'
Perennial page 42

ASTER 'LITTLE CARLOW'
Perennial page 74

ASTER PRINGLEI 'MONTE CASSINO'
Perennial Z4-8 H8-1 Thin stems of narrow, upright habit, forming a dense bush with needle-like leaves and small white flowers.
‡3ft (1m) ↔ 12in (30cm)

ASTILBE × *ARENDSII* 'FANAL'
Perennial page 74

ASTRANTIA MAJOR 'SHAGGY'
Perennial The bracts around the flower clusters are longer than usual.
‡12–36in (30–90cm) ↔ 18in (45cm)

BAPTISIA AUSTRALIS
Perennial page 79

CALLISTEPHUS MILADY SUPER MIXED
Annuals page 97

CAMPANULA LACTIFLORA 'PRICHARD'S VARIETY'
Perennial Z5-7 H7-5 Compact, with heads of violet-blue flowers in mid summer.
‡30in (75cm) ↔ 18in (45cm)

CAMPANULA PERSICIFOLIA 'CHETTLE CHARM'
Perennial Z3-8 H8-1 Deep green foliage and white, blue-tinted flowers.
‡3ft (1m) ↔ 12in (30cm)

CHRYSANTHEMUMS
Perennials pages 122–125

CLEMATIS 'VYVYAN PENNELL'
Climber page 109

CROCOSMIA × *CROCOSMIIFLORA* 'SOLFATERRE'
Perennial page 151

DELPHINIUM 'BELLAMOSUM'
Perennial Z3-7 H7-1 Well-branched stems with thin spikes of deep blue flowers.
‡1–1.2m (3–4ft) ↔ 45cm (18in)

DELPHINIUM 'BRUCE'
Perennial page 166

DELPHINIUM 'SUNGLEAM'
Perennial page 169

BORDER CARNATIONS (*DIANTHUS*)
Perennials page 171

DIANTHUS 'CORONATION RUBY'
Perennial Z5-9 H9-4 Laced pink with pink and ruby red flowers with a clove scent.
‡38cm (15in) ↔ 30cm (12in)

ERYNGIUM × *TRIPARTITUM*
Perennial page 192

GEUM 'MRS J. BRADSHAW'
Perennial Z5-9 H9-4 Hairy leaves, wiry branched stems, and double scarlet flowers.
‡40–60cm (16–24in) ↔ 60cm (24in)

KNIPHOFIA 'ROYAL STANDARD'
Perennial page 298

LATHYRUS ODORATUS (SWEET PEAS)
Annual climbers page 303

LEUCANTHEMUM × *SUPERBUM* 'WIRRAL SUPREME'
Perennial page 310

NARCISSUS 'MERLIN'
Bulb   page 349

NARCISSUS 'WHITE LION'
Bulb Z3-9 H9-1 Double, white flowers too
heavy to stand up outside; best when cut.
‡16in (40cm)

OSTEOSPERMUM 'WHIRLIGIG'
Subshrub   page 361

PAEONIA LACTIFLORA 'SARAH
BERNHARDT'
Perennial   page 364

PHLOX MACULATA 'ALPHA'
Perennial   page 390

PHLOX MACULATA 'OMEGA'
Perennial Z5-8 H8-5 Conical heads
of fragrant, small white flowers with
a deep pink eye.
‡3ft (90cm) ↔ 18in (45cm)

PHYSOSTEGIA VIRGINIANA 'VIVID'
Perennial   page 400

ROSA 'ALEXANDER'
Hybrid tea rose   page 448

ROSA 'ICEBERG'
Floribunda rose   page 451

ROSA 'ROYAL WILLIAM'
Hybrid tea rose   page 449

ROSA 'SILVER JUBILEE'
Hybrid tea rose   page 449

ROSES, MODERN SHRUB
Deciduous shrubs   pages 462–463

RUDBECKIA FULGIDA VAR.
SULLIVANTII 'GOLDSTURM'
Perennial   page 468

RUDBECKIA 'GOLDQUELLE'
Perennial   page 468

SCABIOSA CAUCASICA 'CLIVE GREAVES'
Perennial   page 485

SCHIZOSTYLIS COCCINEA 'SUNRISE'
Perennial   page 486

SOLIDAGO 'GOLDENMOSA'
Perennial   page 497

X *SOLIDASTER LUTEUS* 'LEMORE'
Perennial   This generic hybrid
produces heads of yellow daisylike
flowers.
‡3ft (90cm) ↔ 12in (30cm)

TANACETUM COCCINEUM 'BRENDA'
Perennial   page 508

TULIPA 'SORBET'
Bulb Z3-9 H9-1 Late blooms are pale pink
with carmine streaks and flashes.
‡24in (60cm)

VERONICA SPICATA SUBSP. *INCANA*
Perennial   page 533

FLOWERS FOR DRYING

Dried flowers prolong the beauty of summer throughout the year. Many are easy to grow and dry, by simply hanging them upside down in a shady, airy position. Many flowers can be used if dried in warm sand or silica gel, then kept in a dry atmosphere. Select young, unblemished flowers that are not fully open, then remove most of the leaves before tying them into bunches.

ACHILLEA FILIPENDULINA
'GOLD PLATE'
Perennial   page **40**

ACHILLEA 'MOONSHINE'
Perennial   page **41**

AMARANTHUS HYPOCHONDRIACUS
'GREEN THUMB'
Annual H12-1 Plants produce upright, branched spikes of pale green flowers.
‡ 24in (60cm) ↔ 12in (30cm)

ASTRANTIA MAXIMA
Perennial   page **76**

BRACTEANTHA BRIGHT BIKINI SERIES
Annuals   page **91**

CATANANCHE CAERULEA 'MAJOR'
Perennial Z3-8 H8-1 Cornflower-like flowers of papery texture on wiry stems above narrow, grayish leaves.
‡ 20–36in (50–90cm) ↔ 12in (30cm)

CENTAUREA CYANUS 'FLORENCE PINK'
Annual H10-1 Upright-growing annual with a bushy habit and pink flowers.
‡ 14in (35cm) ↔ 18in (45cm)

CONSOLIDA AJACIS GIANT IMPERIAL SERIES
Annual Z9-10 H9-1 Larkspur producing elegant spires of flowers: essentially annual delphiniums.
‡ 2–3ft (60–90cm) ↔ 14in (35cm)

CORTADERIA SELLOANA
'SUNNINGDALE SILVER'
Ornamental grass   page **141**

ECHINOPS RITRO
Perennial   page **181**

GOMPHRENA HAAGEANA
'STRAWBERRY FIELDS'
Annual   page **233**

HYDRANGEA MACROPHYLLA
CULTIVARS
Shrubs   page **266**

HYDRANGEA SERRATA 'BLUEBIRD'
Shrub   page **268**

LAGURUS OVATUS
Ornamental grass   page **300**

LIMONIUM SINUATUM 'ART SHADES'
Perennial Z8-9 H9-1 Usually grown as annuals, with crispy flowers in shades of pink, salmon, orange, pink, and blue.
‡ 24in (60cm) ↔ 12in (30cm)

LIMONIUM SINUATUM 'FOREVER GOLD'
Perennial   page **319**

NIGELLA DAMASCENA 'MULBERRY ROSE'
Annual H10-1 Feathery foliage and flowers in purplish pink, and inflated seed pods.
‡ 18in (45cm) ↔ 9in (23cm)

RHODANTHE MANGLESII
'SUTTON'S ROSE'
Annual Z10-11 H7-1 Wiry plants with grayish leaves and white or pink flowers with a strawlike texture.
‡ 24in (60cm) ↔ 6in (15cm)

SEDUM SPECTABILE 'BRILLIANT'
Perennial   page **490**

PLANTS WITH ORNAMENTAL SEEDHEADS

Although they may lack the bright colors of the flowers, there is much beauty in the seedheads of plants. Some may be cut and preserved to decorate the home, while others can be left in the garden to bring straw or bronze tones to the winter scene; they look especially good when covered with frost or snow until birds pull them apart in their hunt for food.

ALLIUM CRISTOPHII
Bulb page **51**

ASTILBE CHINENSIS VAR. *PUMILA*
Perennial Z3-8 H8-2 Pink flower spikes become rust-brown as they age.
‡ 10in (25cm) ↔ 8in (20cm)

CLEMATIS 'BILL MACKENZIE'
Climber page **132**

CLEMATIS MACROPETALA 'WHITE SWAN'
Climber Z6-9 H9-6 A very compact, early-flowering clematis with white blooms and silver seedheads.
‡ 3ft (1m)

COTINUS COGGYGRIA
Shrub Z5-8 H8-4 Green leaves in summer that turn scarlet in autumn, with feathery, smoke-like seedheads.
‡ ↔ 15ft (5m)

HYDRANGEA PANICULATA 'GRANDIFLORA'
Shrub page **267**

HYOSCYAMUS NIGER
Annual H9-1 Extremely poisonous plant with sinister, veined flowers and beautiful seedheads resembling shuttlecocks.
‡ 2–4ft (60–120cm) ↔ 3ft (1m)

IRIS FOETIDISSIMA
Perennial Z7-9 H9-7 Pale blue and brown flowers develop into green pods that split in autumn to reveal orange seeds.
‡ 12–36in (30–90cm) ↔ 12in (30cm)

IRIS FOETIDISSIMA 'VARIEGATA'
Perennial page **282**

IRIS 'SHELFORD GIANT'
Perennial Z6-9 H9-6 Sheaves of long, green leaves, tall spikes of yellow and white flowers, and distinctive ribbed seedheads.
‡ 6ft (1.8m) ↔ 24in (60cm)

NIGELLA ORIENTALIS 'TRANSFORMER'
Annual H8-1 Bushy annual with finely divided leaves and small yellow flowers that produce umbrella-like seed pods.
‡ 18in (45cm) ↔ 9–12in (22–30cm)

PAEONIA LUTEA VAR. *LUDLOWII*
Shrub page **365**

PAPAVER SOMNIFERUM 'HEN AND CHICKENS'
Annual H8-1 The single flowers are followed by curious pods that are surrounded by a ring of tiny pods.
‡ 14ft (.2m) ↔ 12in (30cm)

PHYSALIS ALKEKENGI
Perennial Z5-8 H8-5 Vigorous, suckering perennial with bright orange, "Chinese lantern" fruits in autumn.
‡ 24–30in (60–75cm) ↔ 3ft (90cm)

SCABIOSA STELLATA 'DRUMSTICK'
Annual H8-1 Wiry-stemmed, hairy annual with pale lilac flowers and round, crispy seedheads.
‡ 12in (30cm) ↔ 9in (23cm)

COTTAGE GARDEN-STYLE PLANTS

The idealized image of a cottage garden is in summer with bees lazily buzzing around roses, lilies, hollyhocks, and peonies, but in fact the authentic cottage garden was a glorious mixture because it contained old-fashioned plants discarded by wealthier gardeners. Cottage garden flowers are often scented, usually herbaceous, and always evocative of a gentler age.

ACONITUM 'SPARK'S VARIETY'
Perennial   page 42

ALCEA ROSEA 'NIGRA'
Biennial Z3-9 H9-1 The "black-flowered" hollyhock.
‡ 6ft (2m) ↔ 24in (60cm)

CALENDULA 'FIESTA GITANA'
Annual   page 96

CAMPANULA 'BURGHALTII'
Perennial Z4-8 H8-1 Mounds of mid-green leaves and tubular flowers of grayish blue.
‡ 2ft (60cm) ↔ 12in (30cm)

CAMPANULA PERSICIFOLIA 'WHITE CUP AND SAUCER'
Perennial Z3-8 H8-1 Pure white flowers are bell-shaped with a white, circular disk, like a saucer, below the bloom.
‡ 36in (90cm) ↔ 12in (30cm)

CAMPANULA PORTENSCHLAGIANA
Perennial   page 107

DELPHINIUMS
Perennials   pages 166–169

DIANTHUS 'GRAN'S FAVOURITE'
Perennial   page 172

DICENTRA SPECTABILIS
Perennial   page 175

ERYNGIUM ALPINUM
Perennial   page 191

ESCHSCHOLZIA CALIFORNICA
Annual   page 196

GERANIUM MACRORRHIZUM 'ALBUM'
Perennial Z4-8 H8-1 Scented, evergreen leaves and white flowers in summer.
‡ 20in (50cm) ↔ 24in (60cm)

GERANIUM × OXONIANUM 'A. T. JOHNSON'
Perennial Z4-8 H8-1 This clump-forming plant has silvery pink flowers.
‡ ↔ 12in (30cm)

GERANIUM SANGUINEUM 'ALBUM'
Perennial Z4-8 H8-1 A compact plant with divided leaves and white flowers.
‡ 8in (20cm) ↔ 12in (30cm)

GERANIUM SYLVATICUM 'MAYFLOWER'
Perennial   page 229

GEUM 'LADY STRATHEDEN'
Perennial   page 230

KNIPHOFIA TRIANGULARIS
Perennial   page 299

LAVATERA, ANNUALS
Annuals   page 308

LILIUM CANDIDUM
Bulb   page 314

LUPINUS POLYPHYLLUS 'BAND OF NOBLES'
Perennial Z7-9 H9-7 A good seed mixture with tall spikes of bicolored flowers.
‡ 5ft (1.5m) ↔ 30in (75cm)

LUPINUS 'THE CHATELAINE'
Perennial Z5-8 H8-5 Tall spires of bicolored flowers in deep pink and white.
‡ 36in (90cm) ↔ 30in (75cm)

LYCHNIS CHALCEDONICA
Perennial   page 327

PAEONIA LACTIFLORA
'BOWL OF BEAUTY'
Perennial   page 363

PAEONIA OFFICINALIS 'RUBRA PLENA'
Perennial   page 365

PAPAVER ORIENTALE 'BEAUTY OF
LIVERMERE'
Perennial   page 366

PAPAVER ORIENTALE 'MRS. PERRY'
Perennial Z4-9 H9-1 Salmon-pink flowers
with petals like satin above coarse foliage.
↕ 30in (75cm) ↔ 24–36in (60–90cm)

PAPAVER RHOEAS SHIRLEY MIXED
Annuals   page 367

PHLOX 'KELLY'S EYE'
Perennial   page 390

PHLOX PANICULATA CULTIVARS
Perennials   page 391

PRIMULA 'WANDA'
Perennial   page 407

ROSA 'BALLERINA'
Patio rose   page 456

ROSA 'FANTIN-LATOUR'
Old garden rose   page 461

ROSA 'GERTRUDE JEKYLL'
English shrub rose   page 463

ROSA XANTHINA 'CANARY BIRD'
Shrub rose   page 465

SAXIFRAGA × *URBIUM*
Perennial Z6-7 H7-6 Mats of evergreen leaf
rosettes and sprays of dainty, white flowers
in late spring.
↕ 12in (30cm) ↔ indefinite

SCABIOSA CAUCASICA
'MISS WILLMOTT'
Perennial   page 485

SCHIZOSTYLIS COCCINEA 'SUNRISE'
Perennial   page 486

VERBASCUM 'COTSWOLD BEAUTY'
Perennial   page 529

VERBASCUM 'PINK DOMINO'
Perennial Z5-9 H9-5 Dark green leaves
give rise to unbranched stems of rounded,
deep pink flowers.
↕ 4ft (1.2m) ↔ 12in (30cm)

VIOLA CORNUTA
Perennial   page 538

Plants for a Rock Garden

Rock gardens are good places to grow small plants, raising them closer to observers' eyes. But the raised beds also allow the soil to be tailored to suit these plants, which often require perfect drainage or specific soil mixes. Most of the plants below are easily grown and require no special treatment, making them yet more attractive: rock gardening can be an addictive hobby.

ADIANTUM PEDATUM
Fern page 43

ALLIUM MOLY
Bulbous perennial page 52

ANCHUSA CESPITOSA
Alpine Z5-7 H7-5 White-eyed blue flowers appear between narrow leaves in spring.
‡ 2–4in (5–10cm) ↔ 6–8in (15–20cm)

ANDROSACE CARNEA SUBSP. *LAGGERI*
Perennial page 57

ANDROSACE SEMPERVIVOIDES
Alpine Z5-7 H7-5 Leaf rosettes form loose mats, and pink flowers open in late spring.
‡ 1–2in (2.5–5cm) ↔ 6–8in (15–20cm)

ARENARIA MONTANA
Perennial page 66

ARMERIA MARITIMA 'VINDICTIVE'
Perennial Z3-9 H9-1 Hummocks of narrow leaves; slender stems of deep pink flowers.
‡ 6in (15cm) ↔ 8in (20cm)

AUBRIETA × *CULTORUM* 'BRESSSINGHAM PINK'
Perennial Z5-7 H7-5 Green cushions covered with double, pink flowers in spring.
‡ 2in (5cm) ↔ 24in (60cm)

AURINIA SAXATILIS
Perennial page 78

BERBERIS THUNBERGII 'BAGATELLE'
Shrub page 86

CAMPANULA 'BIRCH HYBRID'
Perennial Z4-7 H7-1 Spreading plant with deep blue bellflowers.
‡ 4in (10cm) ↔ 40in (50cm)

CAMPANULA CHAMISSONIS 'SUPERBA'
Alpine Z2-6 H6-1 The rosettes of pale green leaves disappear under pale blue flowers in early summer.
‡ 2in (5cm) ↔ 8in (20cm)

CROCUS CORSICUS
Spring bulb page 153

DAPHNE PETRAEA 'GRANDIFLORA'
Evergreen shrub page 164

DIANTHUS 'LA BOURBOULE'
Perennial page 173

DIASCIA BARBERAE 'RUBY FIELD'
Perennial Z8-9 H9-8 Mats of heart-shaped leaves are covered with deep salmon-pink flowers in summer.
‡ 10in (25cm) ↔ 24in (60cm)

DRYAS OCTOPETALA
Evergreen shrub Z3-6 H6-1 Mats of deep green leaves, with white flowers in spring, then fluffy seedheads.
‡ 4in (10cm) ↔ 36in (1m)

GENTIANA ACAULIS
Perennial page 224

GERANIUM CINEREUM 'BALLERINA'
Perennial page 226

GEUM MONTANUM
Perennial page 230

GYPSOPHILA 'ROSENSCHLEIER'
Perennial page 235

HELIANTHEMUM 'FIRE DRAGON'
Shrub page 247

HOT COLOR SCHEMES

A grouping of plants in warm, vivid colors looks best in full sunlight; if your garden can offer a really sunny spot, take care when choosing an assortment of plants that they will all enjoy the heat.

Mixing in some plants with dark bronze and purple foliage (see p.574) will heighten the fiery effect. Remember that hot colors jump toward the eye and can make spaces seem smaller.

ALONSOA WARSCEWICZII
Perennial   page **54**

ALSTROEMERIA LIGTU HYBRIDS
Perennial   page **55**

ARCTOTIS X *HYBRIDA* 'FLAME'
Perennial Z10 H7-1 Reddish gold daisy flowers with silver petal backs and silver-gray leaves. 'Mahogany' and 'Red Magic' are also recommended.
‡ 18–20in (45–50cm) ↔ 12in (30cm)

ASTILBE X *ARENDSII* 'FANAL'
Perennial   page **74**

BASSIA SCOPARIA F. *TRICHOPHYLLA*
Annual H10-1 Feathery leaves that start off green, then turn fiery red aging to purple over the summer.
‡ 1–5ft (0.3–1.5m) ↔ 12–18in (30–45cm)

BEGONIA 'ILLUMINATION ORANGE'
Perennial   page **82**

CALENDULA 'FIESTA GITANA'
Annual   page **96**

CALLISTEMON CITRINUS 'SPLENDENS'
Evergreen shrub   page **97**

CAMPSIS X *TAGLIABUANA* 'MADAME GALEN'
Climber   page **108**

CARTHAMUS TINCTORIA 'ORANGE GOLD'
Annual H12-1 Clusters of bright, thistlelike tufted flowers, good for drying.
‡ 12–24in (30–60cm) ↔ 12in (30cm)

CHRYSANTHEMUM 'AMBER YVONNE ARNAUD'
Perennial   page **122**

CHRYSANTHEMUM 'WENDY'
Perennial   page **124**

COREOPSIS TINCTORIA 'SUNRISE'
Annual H12-1 Upright stems among clumps of mid-green leaves bearing solitary, daisy-like flowers attractive to bees.
‡ 24in (60cm) ↔ 12in (30cm)

COREOPSIS VERTICILLATA 'GRANDIFLORA'
Perennial Z4-9 H9-1 Loose clusters of dark yellow flowers in early summer.
‡ 24–32in (60–80cm) ↔ 18in (45cm)

CROCOSMIA 'LUCIFER'
Perennial   page **152**

DAHLIA 'HAMARI GOLD'
Perennial   page **163**

DAHLIA 'ZORRO'
Perennial   page **163**

DIASCIA 'RUPERT LAMBERT'
Perennial Z8-9 H9-8 Mat-forming, with spikes of spurred, deep warm pink flowers from summer to autumn.
‡ 8in (20cm) ↔ 20in (50cm)

EMBOTHRIUM COCCINEUM 'NORQUINCO'
Shrub Z8-10 H10-8 Upright, with spidery scarlet flowers in early summer.
‡ 8in (20cm) ↔ 12in (30cm)

ESCHSCHOLZIA CALIFORNICA
Annual   page **196**

HELIANTHEMUM 'FIRE DRAGON'
Evergreen shrub page 247

HELIOPSIS 'GOLDGEFIEDER'
Perennial Z4-9 H9-1 Double daisylike
golden yellow flowerheads with a green
center, on stiff stems with coarse leaves.
‡ 36in (90cm) ↔ 24in (60cm)

IRIS 'APRICORANGE'
Perennial page 284

IRIS 'SUN MIRACLE'
Perennial page 287

KNIPHOFIA 'BEE'S SUNSET'
Perennial page 297

LIGULARIA 'GREGYNOG GOLD'
Evergreen shrub page 313

LONICERA ETRUSCA 'DONALD
WATERER'
Climber Dark, red-bloomed stems and
buds, bright orange berries.
‡ 12ft (4m)

LOTUS BERTHELOTII
Subshrub page 326

LYCHNIS CHALCEDONICA
Perennial page 327

MIMULUS CUPREUS 'WHITECROFT
SCARLET'
Perennial Z8-9 H9-8 Spreading stems with
tubular, scarlet summer flowers.
‡ 4in (10cm) ↔ 6in (15cm)

PAPAVER ORIENTALE 'AGLAIA'
Perennial Z4-9 H9-1 Salmon flowers with
cherry-pink shading at the petal bases.
‡ 18–36in (45–90cm) ↔ 24–36in (60–90cm)

PAPAVER ORIENTALE 'LEUCHTFEUER'
Perennial Z4-9 H9-1 Orange flowers with
black blotches at the petal bases, silvery
leaves.
‡ 18–36in (45–90cm) ↔ 24–36in (60–90cm)

PELARGONIUM 'VOODOO'
Perennial page 376

PENSTEMON 'CHESTER SCARLET'
Perennial page 379

PENSTEMON 'SCHOENHOLZERI'
Perennial page 379

PERSICARIA AMPLEXICAULIS
'FIRETAIL'
Perennial Z5-8 H8-5 Robust clump-forming
plant with tall, bright red "bottlebrush"
flower heads on upright stems.
‡ ↔ to 4ft (1.2m)

PHORMIUM 'SUNDOWNER'
Perennial page 393

PHYGELIUS × RECTUS 'DEVIL'S
TEARS'
Shrub page 397

POTENTILLA 'GIBSON'S SCARLET'
Perennial page 411

RHODODENDRON 'SPEK'S ORANGE'
Deciduous shrub page 439

ROSA, MANY

*RUDBECKIA FULGIDA VAR.
SULLIVANTII* 'GOLDSTURM'
Perennial page 468

SALVIA COCCINEA
'PSEUDOCOCCINEA'
Perennial page 473

STREPTOSOLEN JAMESII
Climber Z11 H12-7 Sprawling stems with
small dark green leaves and rounded
clusters of saucer-shaped orange flowers.
‡ 6–10ft (2–3m) ↔ 3–8ft (1–2.5m)

TROPAEOLUM MAJUS 'HERMINE
GRASHOFF'
Annual climber page 520

VELTHEIMIA BRACTEATA
Bulbous perennial page 528

COOL COLOR SCHEMES

Cool blues, purples, and creamy whites always look elegant and can be used to create an illusion of distance. As dusk falls, cool colors appear to glow in the fading light, a bonus in gardens used for evening entertaining. Mix in plenty of lush foliage to cool down summer heat still further, or for a lighter, brighter look, choose some plants with gray and silvery leaves (see p.576).

AEONIUM HAWORTHII
Succulent page 44

AGERATUM 'BLUE DANUBE'
Annual H12-2 Low, bushy plants covered in fluffy lavender-blue flowers. Deeper blue 'Blue Horizon' is also recommended.
‡ 8in (20cm) ↔ 12in (30cm)

ALLIUM CAERULEUM
Bulb page 50

ANCHUSA AZUREA 'LODDON ROYALIST'
Perennial page 57

ARUNCUS DIOICUS
Perennial Z3-7 H7-1 In moist ground, produces clumps of ferny leaves and feathery cream flower plumes.
‡ 8in (20cm) ↔ 12in (30cm)

BAPTISIA AUSTRALIS
Perennial page 79

CAMASSIA LEICHTLINII
Bulb Z4-10 H10-1 Bears spires of star-shaped, greenish white flowers in spring.
‡ 8in (20cm) ↔ 12in (30cm)

CAMPANULA GLOMERATA 'SUPERBA'
Perennial page 106

CENTAUREA CYANUS 'BLUE DIADEM'
Annual H10-1 Deep blue cornflower.
‡ 8–32in (20–80cm) ↔ 6in (15cm)

CONVOLVULUS SABATIUS
Trailing perennial page 136

CYANANTHUS LOBATUS
Perennial page 156

CYNARA CARDUNCULUS
Perennial page 159

DELPHINIUM 'GIOTTO'
Perennial page 167

DELPHINIUM 'LORD BUTLER'
Perennial page 168

DELPHINIUM 'THAMESMEAD'
Perennial page 169

ECHINOPS RITRO SUBSP. *RUTHENICUS*
Perennial Z3-9 H9-1 Metallic blue globe thistle with silvery, cobwebby leaves.
‡ 24–36in (60–90cm) ↔ 18in (45cm)

ERYNGIUM BOURGATII 'OXFORD BLUE'
Perennial Z5-9 H9-4 Silver-veined spiny leaves and branching stems of blue thistle flowers with silver bracts.
‡ 6–18in (15–45cm) ↔ 12in (30cm)

ERYNGIUM × *TRIPARTITUM*
Perennial page 192

GALTONIA VIRIDIFLORA
Bulb Z8-10 H10-8 In late summer, bears spires of snowdroplike greenish white flowers among gray-green straplike leaves.
‡ to 3ft (1m) ↔ 4in (10cm)

HEBE ALBICANS
Shrub page 240

HEBE HULKEANA 'LILAC HINT'
Shrub Z9-10 H10-9 Glossy green leaves and, in late spring and early summer, long sprays of lavender-blue flowers.
‡ ↔ 24in (60cm)

HELIOTROPIUM ARBORESCENS
Perennial Z11 H12-1 Popular summer bedding with purple, very fragrant flowers.
‡ 2–3ft (60–100cm) ↔ 12–18in (30–45cm)

HOSTA 'LOVE PAT'
Perennial   page **260**

IPHEION 'ROLF FIEDLER'
Bulb Z6-9 H9-6 Star-shaped blue flowers and blue-green leaves in spring.
‡ 4–5in (10–12cm)

IRIS 'ORINOCO FLOW'
Perennial   page **285**

IRIS SIBIRICA 'SMUDGER'S GIFT'
Perennial   page **279**

IRIS SIBIRICA 'UBER DEN WOLKEN'
Perennial   page **279**

LAVANDULA × *INTERMEDIA* DUTCH GROUP
Shrub   page **306**

LINUM NARBONENSE 'HEAVENLY BLUE'
Perennial Z7-9 H9-7 Forms clumps covered with saucer-shaped pale blue flowers, each lasting a single day.
‡ 12–24in (30–60cm) ↔ 18in (45cm)

MOLUCELLA LAEVIS 'PIXIE BELLS'
Annual H6-1 Pale green leaves and flower spires conspicuous for the pale green, shell-like calyces surrounding each tiny flower.
‡ 24–36in (60–90cm) ↔ 9in (23cm)

MYOSOTIS 'BOUQUET'
Annual Z10-11 H7-1 Floriferous, compact blue forget-me-not. The dwarf 'Ultramarine' is also recommended.
‡ 4–8in (12–20cm) ↔ 6in (16cm)

PHLOX PANICULATA 'LE MAHDI'
Perennial   page **391**

PULMONARIA SACCHARATA ARGENTEA GROUP
Evergreen perennial   page **428**

RUTA GRAVEOLENS 'JACKMAN'S BLUE'
Shrub Z5-9 H9-5 Gray-blue feathery leaves; the dull yellow flowerheads can be trimmed off to the benefit of the foliage. Be very careful when handling this plant: contact with foliage may cause an allergic sun-activated reaction.
‡ ↔ 24in (60cm)

SALVIA CACALIIFOLIA
Perennial   page **472**

SALVIA GUARANITICA 'BLUE ENIGMA'
Perennial   page **474**

SCABIOSA CAUCASICA 'CLIVE GREAVES'
Perennial   page **485**

TEUCRIUM FRUTICANS 'AZUREUM'
Shrub Z8-9 H9-8 White-woolly stem, gray-blue leaves and, in summer, short spires of whorled, deep blue flowers.
‡ 2–3ft (60–100cm) ↔ 6ft (2m)

THALICTRUM DELAVAYI 'HEWITT'S DOUBLE'
Perennial   page **510**

VERONICA 'SHIRLEY BLUE'
Perennial Z3-8 H8-1 Gray-green, hairy leaves and spires of saucer-shaped blue flowers from late spring to mid-summer
‡ ↔ 12in (30cm)

PLANTS FOR WHITE GARDENS

Single-color gardens are popular with many gardeners, and the most planted are white gardens, perhaps because so many white flowers are also scented. Consider also leaf color and foliage, including variegated, silver, and gray-leaved plants. To relieve the sameness of the scheme, it is often helpful to add a few cream or pale blue flowers – these will actually enhance the effect.

ANEMONE BLANDA 'WHITE SPLENDOUR'
Bulb page **58**

ANEMONE × *HYBRIDA* 'HONORINE JOBERT'
Perennial page **59**

ASTILBE 'IRRLICHT'
Perennial Z4-9 H9-1 The coarsely cut dark foliage is a good contrast to the upright, white, fluffy flowers.
↕ 18in (50cm)

CLEMATIS 'MARIE BOISSELOT'
Climber page **130**

COSMOS BIPINNATUS 'SONATA WHITE'
Annual page **144**

CRAMBE CORDIFOLIA
Perennial page **149**

CROCUS SIEBERI 'ALBUS'
Bulb page **153**

DAHLIA 'HAMARI BRIDE'
Perennial Z8-11 H12-1 This semi-cactus dahlia has pure white flowers and is popular for exhibition.
↕ 4ft (1.2m) ↔ 2ft (60cm)

DELPHINIUM 'SANDPIPER'
Perennial page **169**

DEUTZIA SETCHUENENSIS VAR. *CORYMBIFLORA*
Shrub Z6-8 H8-6 Masses of white flowers are produced on a bush with brown, peeling bark.
↕ 6ft (2m) ↔ 5ft (1.5m)

DICENTRA SPECTABILIS 'ALBA'
Perennial page **175**

DICTAMNUS ALBUS
Perennial page **176**

DIGITALIS PURPUREA F. *ALBIFLORA*
Biennial page **178**

ECHINACEA PURPUREA 'WHITE LUSTRE'
Perennial Z3-9 H9-1 The stiff stems have creamy white flowers with golden cones.
↕ 32in (80cm) ↔ 18in (45cm)

ERICA CARNEA 'SPRINGWOOD WHITE'
Evergreen shrub page **187**

ERICA TETRALIX 'ALBA MOLLIS'
Evergreen shrub page **189**

GILLENIA TRIFOLIATA
Perennial page **231**

GYPSOPHILA PANICULATA 'BRISTOL FAIRY'
Perennial page **234**

HOHERIA SEXSTYLOSA
Evergreen tree page **258**

HYDRANGEA ARBORESCENS 'ANNABELLE'
Shrub page **265**

HYDRANGEA PANICULATA 'FLORIBUNDA'
Shrub page **267**

HYDRANGEA QUERCIFOLIA
Shrub page **268**

IRIS 'BEWICK SWAN'
Perennial Z7-9 H9-7 The ruffled, white
flowers have bright orange beards.
‡ 36in (1m) ↔ 12in (30cm)

IRIS CONFUSA
Bulbous perennial   page 280

IRIS SIBIRICA 'CREME CHANTILLY'
Perennial   page 279

IRIS SIBIRICA 'HARPSWELL
HAPPINESS'
Perennial   page 279

IRIS SIBIRICA 'MIKIKO'
Perennial   page 279

JASMINUM POLYANTHUM
Climber   page 292

LUNARIA ANNUA VAR. *ALBIFLORA*
Biennial Z9-9 H9-5 The white-flowered
form of common honesty.
‡ 3ft (90cm) ↔ 12in (30cm)

MALVA MOSCHATA F. *ALBA*
Perennial   page 338

NARCISSUS 'EMPRESS OF IRELAND'
Bulb   page 348

PAEONIA OBOVATA VAR. *ALBA*
Perennial Z5-8 H8-5 A choice plant with
rounded, grayish leaflets and pure white
flowers, most attractive in bud.
‡ ↔ 24–28in (60–70cm)

PAPAVER ORIENTALE 'BLACK AND
WHITE'
Perennial   page 366

PARAHEBE CATARRACTAE
Subshrub   page 368

PHYSOSTEGIA VIRGINIANA
'SUMMER SNOW'
Perennial Z4-8 H8-1 Pure white flowers in
spikes on upright stems.
‡ 4ft (1.2m) ↔ 24in (60cm)

PULMONARIA OFFICINALIS
'SISSINGHURST WHITE'
Perennial   page 427

PULSATILLA VULGARIS 'ALBA'
Perennial   page 430

RANUNCULUS ACONITIFOLIUS
'FLORE PLENO'
Perennial   page 433

ROSA 'ICEBERG'
Floribunda rose   page 451

ROSA 'MADAME HARDY'
Shrub rose   page 461

ROSA 'MARGARET MERRIL'
Floribunda rose   page 451

ROSA 'RAMBLING RECTOR'
Rambler rose   page 455

RUBUS 'BENENDEN'
Shrub   page 467

TULIPA 'PURISSIMA'
Bulb Z3-8 H8-1 The compact stems carry
very large, pure white flowers in mid-
spring.
‡ 14in (35cm)

ZANTEDESCHIA AETHIOPICA
Perennial   page 544

PLANTS FOR CLAY SOIL

Clay soil is difficult to dig, either wet or dry. It is prone to harbor slugs, and it is slow to warm up in spring; it is often described as a cold soil. However, it is usually rich in nurients, and if plenty of

organic matter is added it can be very fertile. Plants to avoid are those from upland areas, such as alpines, or those on the borderline of hardiness in your climate.

CAMPANULA LATILOBA 'HIDCOTE AMETHYST'
Perennial Z4-8 H8-1 Mauve-purple, cup-shaped flowers in mid-summer.
‡ 36in (90cm) ↔ 18in (45cm)

CLEMATIS 'POLISH SPIRIT'
Climber Z5-9 H9-5 Small, single, purple flowers with red anthers. Late-flowering
‡ 15ft (5m) ↔ 6ft (2m)

CORNUS STOLONIFERA 'FLAVIRAMEA'
Shrub   page 140

COTONEASTER X WATERERI 'JOHN WATERER'
Evergreen shrub   page 148

DEUTZIA X ELEGANTISSIMA 'ROSEALIND'
Shrub   page 170

DIGITALIS GRANDIFLORA
Perennial   page 177

FILIPENDULA PURPUREA
Perennial   page 207

GERANIUM PSILOSTEMON
Perennial   page 229

HEMEROCALLIS 'STELLA DE ORO'
Perennial   page 254

HYDRANGEA PANICULATA 'KYUSHU'
Shrub Z4-8 H8-1 Erect cultivar with glossy leaves and large creamy white flowers.
‡ 10–22ft (3–7m) ↔ 8ft (2.5m)

IRIS SIBIRICA CULTIVARS
Perennials   page 279

LONICERA NITIDA 'SILVER LINING'
Evergreen shrub Z6-9 H9-6 Each small leaf of this mound-shaped shrub has a thin, white margin.
‡ ↔ 5ft (1.5m)

MAHONIA AQUIFOLIUM 'APOLLO'
Evergreen shrub   page 334

NARCISSUS 'JUMBLIE'
Bulb   page 347

PERSICARIA CAMPANULATA
Perennial Z5-8 H8-5 Small clusters of pink, bell-shaped flowers on spreading stems.
‡ ↔ 36in (90cm)

PHILADELPHUS 'MANTEAU D'HERMINE'
Shrub   page 385

POTENTILLA FRUTICOSA 'TANGERINE'
Shrub Z3-7 H7-1 Twiggy, with yellow flowers flushed red throughout summer.
‡ 3ft (1m) ↔ 5ft (1.5m)

ROSA 'AMBER QUEEN'
Floribunda rose   page 450

SPIRAEA JAPONICA 'ANTHONY WATERER'
Shrub   page 501

SYMPHYTUM 'GOLDSMITH'
Perennial Z5-9 H9-5 This spreading plant has heart-shaped leaves edged in gold, with pale blue, cream, and pink flowers.
‡ ↔ 12in (30cm)

SYRINGA VULGARIS 'KATHERINE HAVEMEYER'
Shrub   page 507

PLANTS FOR SANDY SOIL

The advantages of sandy soils include the ability to dig, hoe, and prepare them during much of the year because they drain quickly after rain. However, water drains through quickly, taking nutrients with it, so it is important to dig in organic matter to improve the soil structure, retain moisture, and improve fertility. Silver-leaved and slightly tender plants are very suitable.

BUDDLEJA DAVIDII 'WHITE PROFUSION'
Shrub page 93

CALLUNA VULGARIS 'DARKNESS'
Evergreen shrub page 98

CERATOSTIGMA WILLMOTTIANUM
Shrub page 114

ECHINOPS BANNATICUS 'TAPLOW BLUE'
Perennial Z5-9 H9-5 A robust, thistlelike plant with globular blue flowerheads.
‡ 4ft (1.2m) ↔ 2ft (60cm)

ERICA CINEREA 'EDEN VALLEY'
Evergreen shrub page 188

ERYNGIUM × *OLIVERIANUM*
Perennial page 191

ESCALLONIA 'PEACH BLOSSOM'
Evergreen shrub Z8-9 H9-8 Peach-pink and white flowers in late spring.
‡ ↔ 8ft (2.5m)

EUCALYPTUS DALRYMPLEANA
Evergreen tree Z10-11 H12-10 Green adult leaves and white bark.
‡ 70ft (20m) ↔ 25ft (8m)

GENISTA HISPANICA
Shrub Z7-9 H9-7 Small, spiny, covered with small yellow flowers in early summer.
‡ 30in (75cm) ↔ 5ft (1.5m)

GLADIOLUS COMMUNIS SUBSP. *BYZANTINUS*
Bulb page 232

KNIPHOFIA 'LITTLE MAID'
Perennial page 298

LAVATERA ARBOREA 'VARIEGATA'
BiennialZ8-10 H10-8 An evergreen, slightly tender, intensely variegated plant with purple flowers in the second year.
‡ 10ft (3m) ↔ 5ft (1.5m)

LAVATERA 'ROSEA'
Shrub page 307

LIMNANTHES DOUGLASII
Annual page 319

OENOTHERA MACROCARPA
Perennial page 354

PENSTEMON 'HIDCOTE PINK'
Perennial Z6-9 H9-6 Spikes of small, tubular, pink flowers. Good in bedding.
‡ 24–30in (60–75cm) ↔ 18in (45cm)

PENSTEMON PINIFOLIUS 'MERSEA YELLOW'
Evergreen shrub Z4-10 H10-1 Dwarf, spreading, with yellow flowers in summer.
‡ 16in (40cm) ↔ 10in (25cm)

PERSICARIA AFFINIS 'SUPERBA'
Perennial page 381

PERSICARIA BISTORTA 'SUPERBA'
Perennial page 381

POTENTILLA FRUTICOSA 'DAYDAWN'
Shrub page 410

POTENTILLA NEPALENSIS 'MISS WILLMOTT'
Perennial page 412

SANTOLINA ROSMARINIFOLIA 'PRIMROSE GEM'
Evergreen shrub page 481

PLANTS FOR ALKALINE SOILS

The majority of plants will grow in soil that is neutral or slightly alkaline, but some positively prefer more alkaline soil. These include plants that are just as important as the rhododendrons and camellias of acidic soils and include delphiniums, clematis, and dianthus. But quality of soil is important: it must be improved with organic matter, and poor, thin soils are difficult to plant.

AQUILEGIA VULGARIS 'NIVEA'
Perennial   page **62**

BUDDLEJA DAVIDII 'PINK DELIGHT'
Shrub Bright pink flowers are produced on thick, conical spikes.
‡ 10ft (3m) ↔ 15ft (5m)

BUDDLEJA DAVIDII 'ROYAL RED'
Shrub   page **93**

BUDDLEJA X WEYERIANA 'SUNGOLD'
Shrub Z6-8 H8-6 Spikes of golden yellow flowers in summer.
‡ 12ft (4m) ↔ 10ft (3m)

CERCIS SILIQUASTRUM
Tree   page **115**

CHAENOMELES SPECIOSA 'NIVALIS'
Shrub Z5-8 H8-5 A variety of Japanese quince with pure white flowers in spring.
‡ 8ft (2.5m) ↔ 15ft (5m)

CLEMATIS 'COMTESSE DE BOUCHAUD'
Climber   page **133**

CLEMATIS X JOUINIANA 'PRAECOX'
Climber Z4-9 H9-1 This unusual hybrid is a scrambler, with a frothy mass of tiny white and blue flowers.
‡ 6–10ft (2–3m)

CLEMATIS 'MISS BATEMAN'
Climber   page **130**

CONVALLARIA MAJALIS VAR. *ROSEA*
Perennial Z2-7 H7-1 This lily of the valley has dusky pink flowers; familiar sweet scent.
‡ 9in (23cm) ↔ 12in (30cm)

COTONEASTER STERNIANUS
Evergreen shrub   page **148**

DELPHINIUM 'BLUE NILE'
Perennial   page **166**

DEUTZIA SCABRA 'PRIDE OF ROCHESTER'
Shrub Z6-8 H8-6 The stems have attractive, peeling, brown bark, but the chief merit is the scented, double, pale pink flowers.
‡ 10ft (3m) ↔ 6ft (2m)

DIANTHUS ALPINUS
Perennial Z3-8 H8-1 Cushions of gray foliage and scented flowers in pink shades.
‡ 3in (8cm) ↔ 4in (10cm)

DIANTHUS DELTOIDES
Perennial Z3-10 H10-1 Mats of deep green leaves are covered with small pink flowers for several weeks in summer.
‡ 8in (20cm) ↔ 12in (30cm)

DIANTHUS 'MONICA WYATT'
Perennial   page **173**

EUONYMUS EUROPAEUS 'RED CASCADE'
Shrub   page **199**

FRAXINUS ORNUS
Tree Z6-9 H9-6 Bushy, round-headed tree with showy white flowers and bright, purple autumn color.
‡ ↔ 50ft (15m)

FUCHSIA 'HEIDI ANN'
Shrub Z11 H12-10 An upright, bushy plant with double lilac and cerise flowers.
‡ ↔ 18in (45cm)

FUCHSIA 'PROSPERITY'
Shrub Z11 H12-10 A vigorous plant with
crimson and pink double flowers.
‡↔ 18in (45cm)

GALANTHUS 'MAGNET'
Bulb page **218**

HELIANTHEMUM 'JUBILEE'
Shrub Z6-8 H8-6 Small shrub with bright
green leaves and double yellow flowers.
‡ 8in (20cm) ↔ 12in (30cm)

HELLEBORUS ORIENTALIS
Perennial Z4-9 H9-1 Nodding flowers in
shades of pink, white, and green are
produced in early spring.
‡↔ 18in (45cm)

ILEX AQUIFOLIUM 'SILVER QUEEN'
Evergreen tree page **273**

MAGNOLIA × *KEWENSIS*
'WADA'S MEMORY'
Shrub page **333**

MAGNOLIA 'RICKI'
Shrub page **333**

MAGNOLIA SALICIFOLIA
Shrub page **333**

MAGNOLIA × *SOULANGEANA*
'RUSTICA RUBRA'
Shrub page **333**

MAGNOLIA WILSONII
Shrub page **333**

MORUS NIGRA
Tree Z5-9 H9-5 The black mulberry is a
long-lived, picturesque tree with tasty fruit.
‡ 40ft (12m) ↔ 50ft (15m)

PHILADELPHUS 'SYBILLE'
Deciduous shrub Z5-8 H8-5 Arching shrub
with cup-shaped, intensely fragrant white
flowers in early summer.
‡ 4ft (1.2m) ↔ 6ft (2m)

PRUNUS 'OKAME'
Tree page **424**

PRUNUS 'TAIHAKU'
Tree page **425**

PRUNUS TENELLA 'FIRE HILL'
Shrub Z6-8 H8-6 Deep pink, single flowers
cover the upright branches in spring.
‡↔ 5ft (1.5m)

PULSATILLA VULGARIS
Perennial page **429**

SYRINGA VULGARIS
'CHARLES JOLY'
Shrub page **506**

VERBASCUM 'COTSWOLD BEAUTY'
Perennial page **529**

PLANTS FOR ACIDIC SOIL

Acidic soils contain low quantities of calcium, a plant nutrient found in limestone, but some of the most beautiful plants, including rhododendrons, heathers, and pieris, have adapted to grow well only in soils where it is deficient. Most also benefit from light shade and rich soil. Where soil is not ideal, grow plants in large pots or other containers of acidic soil.

ACER JAPONICUM 'ACONITIFOLIUM'
Shrub   page 33

ACER PALMATUM VAR. *DISSECTUM*
Shrub Z5-8 H8-2 The finely cut leaves turn yellow in autumn, on a mounded shrub.
‡ 6ft (2m) ↔ 10ft (3m)

ACER PALMATUM 'SEIRYU'
ShrubZ5-8 H8-2 An upright shrub with divided leaves that turn orange in autumn.
‡ 6ft (2m) ↔ 4ft (1.2m)

CAMELLIA 'LEONARD MESSEL'
Evergreen shrub   page 102

CAMELLIA SASANQUA 'NARUMIGATA'
Evergreen shrub   page 103

CAMELLIA × *WILLIAMSII* 'DEBBIE'
Evergreen shrub Z8-10 H10-8 The semidouble flowers are deep pink.
‡ 6–15ft (2–5m) ↔ 3–10ft (1–3m)

CASSIOPE 'EDINBURGH'
Evergreen shrub   page 111

CRINODENDRON HOOKERIANUM
Evergreen shrub   page 150

DABOECIA CANTABRICA 'BICOLOR'
Evergreen shrub   page 161

DABOECIA CANTABRICA 'WILLIAM BUCHANAN'
Evergreen shrub   page 161

ENKIANTHUS CAMPANULATUS
Shrub   page 183

ERICA ARBOREA VAR. *ALPINA*
Evergreen shrub   page 186

ERICA ARBOREA 'ESTRELLA GOLD'
Evergreen shrub Z9-10 H12-9 Fragrant white flowers appear among the lime green foliage and yellow shoot tips.
‡ 4ft (1.2m) ↔ 30in (75cm)

ERICA CILIARIS 'CORFE CASTLE'
Shrub   page 188

ERICA CILIARIS 'DAVID MCLINTOCK'
Shrub   page 188

ERICA CINEREA 'C. D. EASON'
Shrub   page 188

ERICA CINEREA 'FIDDLER'S GOLD'
Shrub   page 188

ERICA CINEREA 'WINDLEBROOKE'
Shrub   page 188

ERICA ERIGENA 'W. T. RATCLIFF'
Evergreen shrub   A compact plant with green foliage and white flowers.
‡ 30in (75cm) ↔ 22in (55cm)

EUCRYPHIA NYMANSENSIS 'NYMANSAY'
Evergreen shrub   page 198

HAMAMELIS × *INTERMEDIA* 'PALLIDA'
Shrub   page 239

HYDRANGEA MACROPHYLLA 'BLUE WAVE'
Shrub Z6-9 H9-2 This lacecap provides a delicate but showy display, with large and small blue flowers in each head.
‡ 5ft (1.5m) ↔ 6ft (2m)

IRIS DOUGLASIANA
Perennial   page 281

RHODODENDRON 'GINNY GEE'
Dwarf rhododendron Z6-9 H9-6 A compact plant bearing pink flowers that fade almost to white with age.
‡↔ 24–36in (60–90cm)

RHODODENDRON IMPEDITUM
Dwarf rhododendron Z5-8 H8-5 Gray-green leaves are almost hidden by lavender-blue flowers in spring.
‡↔ 24in (60cm)

PLANTS FOR POOR SOIL

While it is true that most plants grow better in well-prepared soil, there are some that grow well in poor soil that has not had much preparation or cultivation. Many annuals evolved to take advantage of open sites, disappearing as the soil improves and larger plants invade the area, so they are a good choice, but there are shrubs and perennials that will also survive.

ACHILLEA 'MOONSHINE'
Perennial   page **41**

ARTEMISIA ABROTANUM
Shrub Z5-8 H8-5 Small shrub with green, finely divided, pleasantly fragrant leaves.
‡ ↔ 3ft (1m)

BUDDLEJA DAVIDII 'EMPIRE BLUE'
Shrub   page **93**

CEANOTHUS 'BLUE MOUND'
Evergreen shrub   page **112**

CYTISUS PRAECOX 'ALLGOLD'
Shrub   page **160**

CYTISUS PRAECOX 'WARMINSTER'
Shrub Z6-9 H9-6 Arching shoots, thickly set with creamy yellow flowers in spring.
‡ 4ft (1.2m) ↔ 5ft (1.5m)

CISTUS × *PURPUREUS*
Evergreen shrub   page **127**

ERYSIMUM CHEIRI 'HARPUR CREWE'
Perennial   page **193**

ESCHSCHOLZIA CAESPITOSA
'SUNDEW'
Annual H12-1 Neat, low-growing, with divided grey leaves and yellow flowers.
‡ ↔ 6in (15cm)

FALLOPIA BALDSCHUANICA
Climber   page **204**

FESTUCA GLAUCA 'BLAUFUCHS'
Ornamental grass   page **207**

GAILLARDIA 'DAZZLER'
Perennial   page **217**

GENISTA LYDIA
Shrub   page **223**

HEBE OCHRACEA 'JAMES STIRLING'
Evergreen shrub   page **242**

IBERIS SEMPERVIRENS
Evergreen shrub   page **270**

KOLKWITZIA AMABILIS 'PINK CLOUD'
Shrub   page **299**

LATHYRUS LATIFOLIUS
Climber   page **302**

LAVANDULA ANGUSTIFOLIA
'TWICKEL PURPLE'
Evergreen shrub   page **305**

LAVATERA, SHRUBS
Shrubs   page **307**

PHLOMIS FRUTICOSA
Evergreen shrub   page **386**

POTENTILLA FRUTICOSA 'ELIZABETH'
Shrub   page **410**

ROBINIA HISPIDA
Shrub   page **446**

SANTOLINA CHAMAECYPARISSUS
'LEMON QUEEN'
Evergreen shrub Z6-9 H9-6 Silver, feathery foliage; small, round, pale yellow flowers.
‡ ↔ 12in (60cm)

THYMUS VULGARIS 'SILVER POSIE'
Evergreen shrub Z4-9 H9-1 Thyme with variegated leaves and pink flowers.
‡ 6–12in (15–30cm) ↔ 16in (40cm)

PLANTS FOR WET SOIL

Waterlogged, badly drained soils are inhospitable places for most plants. Roots need to breathe, and if all the air spaces within the soil are filled with water, most roots rot and only marginal or aquatic plants can survive. However, if the soil is permanently moist, there are many beautiful plants that will thrive, and they may survive flooding if it is only for a few days.

PLANTS FOR HOT, DRY SITES

As problems of water supply become more acute, consider plants that have low water requirements. Often, these have silvery or small leaves, and some are fragrant, so the garden can still be interesting through the year. They look attractive growing through gravel, an effective mulch to retain soil moisture. In addition, many establish quickly and are evergreen and low maintenance.

ABUTILON VITIFOLIUM 'VERONICA TENNANT'
Shrub   page 30

ACHILLEA TOMENTOSA
Perennial   page 41

AGAVE VICTORIAE-REGINA
Perennial   page 48

ALLIUM HOLLANDICUM
Bulb Z4-10 H10-1 Round heads of small purple flowers in early summer.
‡ 3ft (1m)

ALSTROEMERIA LIGTU HYBRIDS
Perennial   page 55

ARMERIA JUNIPERIFOLIA 'BEVAN'S VARIETY'
Perennial   page 68

ARTEMISIA 'POWIS CASTLE'
Perennial   page 70

ARTEMISIA SCHMIDTIANA 'NANA'
Perennial Z5-8 H8-5 An evergreen that forms a feathery, silver carpet with small yellow flowerheads in summer.
‡ 3in (8cm) ↔ 12in (30cm)

BALLOTA PSEUDODICTAMNUS
Evergreen shrub   page 79

CEANOTHUS ARBOREUS 'TREWITHEN BLUE'
Shrub   page 111

CEANOTHUS 'CASCADE'
Evergreen shrub Z9-10 H10-9 The arching branches bear masses of powder blue flowers in late spring.
‡ ↔ 12ft (4m)

CEDRONELLA CANARIENSIS
Perennial Z11 H8-1 The slightly sticky leaves are aromatic; produces small clusters of mauve flowers in late summer.
‡ 4ft (1.2m) ↔ 24in (60cm)

CERATOSTIGMA PLUMBAGINOIDES
Perennial   page 114

CISTUS X *AGUILARII* 'MACULATUS'
Evergreen shrub   page 126

CONVOLVULUS CNEORUM
Evergreen shrub   page 136

CYTISUS BATTANDIERI
Shrub   page 159

CYTISUS X *KEWENSIS*
Shrub Z6-8 H8-6 Arching stems are covered with cream flowers in spring.
‡ 12in (30cm) ↔ 5ft (1.5m)

CYTISUS MULTIFLORUS
Shrub Z7-8 H8-7 An upright shrub at first, then spreading, with masses of small white flowers.
‡ 10ft (3m) ↔ 8ft (2.5m)

DIANTHUS 'HAYTOR WHITE'
Perennial   page 172

DICTAMNUS ALBUS VAR. *PURPUREUS*
Perennial   page 177

DIERAMA PULCHERRIMUM
Perennial Z8-10 H10-8 Clumps of grasslike leaves produce arching stems of pendent, pink, bell-shaped flowers.
‡ 3–5ft (1–1.5m) ↔ 24in (60cm)

ERYNGIUM BOURGATII
Perennial Z5-9 H9-5 Silver-veined spiny
leaves form clumps with branching stems
of steely blue prickly flowerheads.
‡6–18in (15–45cm) ↔ 12in (30cm)

ERYSIMUM 'BOWLES' MAUVE'
Evergreen shrub   page **192**

ERYSIMUM 'WENLOCK BEAUTY'
Perennial   page **193**

ESCHSCHOLZIA CAESPITOSA
Annual   page **196**

EUPHORBIA CHARACIAS
Perennial   page **201**

EUPHORBIA CHARACIAS SUBSP.
WULFENII 'JOHN TOMLINSON'
Perennial   page **201**

EUPHORBIA MYRSINITES
Perennial   page **202**

GAURA LINDHEIMERI
Perennial   page **221**

GERANIUM MADERENSE
Perennial Z8-9 H9-8 Large plant with
divided leaves and a colorful display of
mauve flowers in summer.
‡↔ 24in (60cm)

GYMNOCALYCIUM ANDREAE
Cactus   page **234**

× *HALIMIOCISTUS SAHUCII*
Evergreen shrub   page **236**

× *HALIMIOCISTUS WINTONENSIS*
Evergreen shrub Z7-9 H9-7 Pale cream
flowers with maroon centres are produced
in clusters above woolly leaves.
‡24in (60cm) ↔ 36in (90cm)

HALIMIUM LASIANTHUM
Evergreen shrub   page **237**

HEBE MACRANTHA
Evergreen shrub   page **242**

HEBE RAKAIENSIS
Evergreen shrub   page **243**

HIBISCUS SYRIACUS 'WOODBRIDGE'
Shrub   page **257**

LAVANDULA STOECHAS SUBSP.
PEDUNCULATA
Evergreen shrub   page **306**

PARAHEBE PERFOLIATA
Evergreen shrub   page **368**

ROSMARINUS OFFICINALIS
'BENENDEN BLUE'
Evergreen shrub Z8-10 H10-8 Upright
branches with deep green leaves and vivid
blue flowers.
‡↔ 5ft (1.5m)

SPARTIUM JUNCEUM
Shrub   page **500**

TULIPA LINIFOLIA
Bulb   page **522**

TULIPA TARDA
Bulb Z3-9 H9-1 Each bulb produces a
cluster of yellow and white flowers on
short stems.
‡6in (15cm)

VERBASCUM 'GAINSBOROUGH'
Perennial   page **530**

VERBASCUM DUMULOSUM
Perennial   page **530**

VERBASCUM 'HELEN JOHNSON'
Perennial   page **531**

PLANTS FOR DAMP SHADE

A border that has damp soil and is in shade for much of the day is a useful place to grow woodland plants without having to plant a woodland. Without the drying effect of the trees the soil will support a greater range of plants, and plants from the Himalayas and South America should thrive, especially if the soil is acidic. It is also a good site for hellebores, lilies, and ferns.

ANEMONE NEMOROSA
'ROBINSONIANA'
Perennial   page 60

ANEMONE RANUNCULOIDES
Perennial   page 60

ATHYRIUM FILIX-FEMINA
Fern   page 77

CARDIOCRINUM GIGANTEUM
Perennial   page 108

DIGITALIS × *MERTONENSIS*
Perennial   page 178

DODECATHEON MEADIA F. *ALBUM*
Perennial   page 179

EPIMEDIUM × *YOUNGIANUM*
'NIVEUM'
Perennial   page 185

GALANTHUS (SNOWDROPS)
Bulbs   pages 217–219

GENTIANA ASCLEPIADEA
Perennial   page 225

HACQUETIA EPIPACTIS
Perennial Z5-7 H7-5 A woodland plant;
small ruffs of leaves surround clusters of
yellow flowers.
‡ 2in (5cm) ↔ 6–12in (15–30cm)

HEPATICA TRANSSILVANICA
Perennial Z5-8 H8-5 Spring pastel flowers.
‡ 6in (15cm) ↔ 8in (20cm)

HYDRANGEA ASPERA VILLOSA GROUP
Shrub   page 265

IRIS GRAMINEA
Perennial   page 283

MAHONIA JAPONICA
Shrub   page 334

ONOCLEA SENSIBILIS
Fern   page 356

POLYGONATUM × *HYBRIDUM*
Perennial   page 408

POLYSTICHUM ACULEATUM
Fern   page 409

PRIMULA SIEBOLDII
Perennial Z3-8 H8-3 Pink or white.
‡ 24in (60cm) ↔ 3ft (1m)

PULMONARIA 'LEWIS PALMER'
Perennial   page 426

SARCOCOCCA CONFUSA
Evergreen shrub   page 482

THALICTRUM FLAVUM SUBSP.
GLAUCIUM
Perennial   page 511

TIARELLA CORDIFOLIA
Perennial   page 516

TOLMEIA 'TAFF'S GOLD'
Perennial   page 516

TRILLIUM LUTEUM
Perennial   page 519

TROLLIUS × *CULTORUM* 'ORANGE
PRINCESS'
Perennial   page 520

UVULARIA GRANDIFLORA
Perennial   page 526

VIBURNUM × *CARLCEPHALUM*
Shrub   page 534

PLANTS FOR DRY SHADE

The dry shade under trees is not a hospitable place for most plants. Those that survive best are spring-flowering bulbs that disappear underground in summer before the soil dries out.

Some evergreens and winter-flowering plants also survive. Even these require good soil preparation and careful watering and feeding for several seasons until they are well established.

ASPLENIUM SCOLOPENDRIUM
Fern   page 71

AUCUBA JAPONICA 'ROZANNIE'
Evergreen shrub Z6-10 H10-4 Cultivar with green leaves; the flowers are bisexual and self-fertile, resulting in many red berries.
‡3ft (1m)

BERGENIA CORDIFOLIA
Perennial Z3-8 H8-1 The large, rounded, evergreen leaves make a good ground-cover; pink flowers in spring are showy.'
‡24in (60cm) ↔ 30in (75cm)

DRYOPTERIS FILIX-MAS
Fern   page 179

EUONYMUS FORTUNEI 'EMERALD 'N' GOLD'
Evergreen shrub   page 199

GALANTHUS NIVALIS 'FLORE PLENO'
Bulb   page 218

GERANIUM MACRORRHIZUM 'INGWERSEN'S VARIETY'
Perennial   page 228

HEDERA HELIX 'LITTLE DIAMOND'
Evergreen climber   page 246

HEDERA HIBERNICA 'SULPHUREA'
Evergreen climber Z5-10 H10-5 Ivy with gold-edged leaves; good groundcover.
‡10ft (3m)

HELLEBORUS FOETIDUS 'WESTER FLISK'
Perennial Z6-9 H9-6 Deep red stems, dark green, finely divided leaves, and red-edged green flowers.
‡24in (60cm) ↔ 3ft (1m)

IRIS FOETIDISSIMA
Perennial Z7-9 H9-7 Purple and brown flowers, and orange seeds in winter.
↓12–36in (30–90cm)

IRIS FOETIDISSIMA 'VARIEGATA'
Perennial   page 282

KERRIA JAPONICA 'GOLDEN GUINEA'
Shrub   page 296

LAMIUM GALEOBDOLON 'HERMANN'S PRIDE'
Perennial Z4-8 H8-1 Arching stems marked silver, and pale yellow flowers.
‡18in (45cm) ↔ 3ft (1m)

RHODODENDRON 'CECILE'
Shrub   page 438

RUBUS TRICOLOR
Evergreen shrub Z7-9 H9-7 The creeping stems are covered with decorative red bristles, and the leaves are deep green.
‡24in (60cm) ↔ 6ft (2m)

RUSCUS ACULEATUS
Perennial Z7-9 H9-7 No leaves, but the flattened, green and spiny stems are evergreen, and red berries are sometimes produced.
‡30in (75cm) ↔ 3ft (1m)

RUSCUS HYPOGLOSSUM
Perennial Z7-9 H9-7 Arching stems are glossy and evergreen, without spines.
‡18in (45cm) ↔ 3ft (1m)

VINCA MINOR 'ATROPURPUREA'
Perennial   page 538

PLANTS FOR EXPOSED SITUATIONS

Gardens exposed to strong winds, especially cold ones, make gardening difficult. Choose compact varieties that require less staking, and avoid large-leaved plants that may be damaged.

Late-flowering cultivars will not be caught by spring frosts. Protect plants with netting when planting and in winter to reduce damage, and plant hedges and screens as windbreaks.

ASTER ALPINUS
Perennial page **71**

BERBERIS THUNBERGII
'GOLDEN RING'
Shrub Z5-8 H8-5 A spiny shrub with purple leaves edged with a thin gold band.
‡ 5ft (1.5m) ↔ 6ft (2m)

CALLUNA VULGARIS 'KINLOCHRUEL'
Evergreen shrub page **98**

CHAENOMELES × *SUPERBA*
'PINK LADY'
Shrub page **116**

DEUTZIA × *HYBRIDA* 'MONT ROSE'
Shrub page **170**

DIANTHUS GRATIANOPOLITANUS
Perennial Z4-9 H9-1 Low-growing mats of gray foliage and solitary pink flowers.
‡ 6in (15cm) ↔ 16in (40cm)

ERICA CARNEA 'VIVELLI'
Evergreen shrub page **187**

ERICA × *WATSONII* 'DAWN'
Evergreen shrub page **189**

HYPERICUM OLYMPICUM
Shrub Z6-8 H8-6 Compact, deciduous shrub with gray leaves and yellow flowers.
‡ 10in (25cm) ↔ 12in (30cm)

PHILADELPHUS 'VIRGINAL'
Shrub Z5-8 H8-5 Scented, double white flowers in clusters on upright branches.
‡ 10ft (3m) ↔ 8ft (2.5m)

POTENTILLA FRUTICOSA
'ABBOTSWOOD'
Shrub page **410**

SALIX GRACILISTYLA
'MELANOSTACHYS'
Shrub Z5-8 H8-5 An upright shrub with gray leaves, and black catkins with red anthers in early spring.
‡ 10ft (3m) ↔ 12ft (4m)

SALIX RETICULATA
Shrub Z2-6 H6-1 A low-growing shrub with glossy leaves and erect, yellow and pink catkins in spring.
‡ 3in (8cm) ↔ 12in (30cm)

SAMBUCUS NIGRA 'GUINCHO PURPLE'
Shrub page **480**

SPIRAEA JAPONICA 'SHIROBANA'
Shrub Z4-9 H9-1 Mounds of foliage are dotted with both pink and white flowerheads throughout the summer.
‡ 24in (60cm) ↔ 36in (90cm)

SPIRAEA NIPPONICA 'SNOWMOUND'
Shrub page **502**

TAMARIX TETRANDRA
Shrub page **508**

VIBURNUM OPULUS 'ROSEUM'
Shrub Z4-8 H8-1 Erect, fast-growing shrub with globular heads of white flowers in summer.
‡ ↔ 12ft (4m)

PLANTS FOR COASTAL GARDENS

Coastal gardens are windy (see facing page) and, nearer the shore, plants may also need to cope with winds laden with salt. Silver plants and evergreens often thrive, and if the winds can be lessened, a wide range of plants should do well. Hydrangeas in particular are often the pride of coastal gardeners.

AGAPANTHUS CAULESCENS
Perennial   page **47**

ARBUTUS UNEDO
Evergreen tree   page **66**

BERBERIS DARWINII
Evergreen shrub   page **84**

BUDDLEJA GLOBOSA
Shrub   page **94**

CHOISYA TERNATA
Evergreen shrub   page **121**

CRAMBE MARITIMA
Perennial Z6-9 H9-6 Silver-blue leaves, giant heads of white flowers followed by seed pods.
‡ 24in (60cm)

ELAEAGNUS X EBBINGEI 'GILT EDGE'
Evergreen shrub   page **182**

ERICA X WILLIAMSII 'P. D. WILLIAMS'
♀ **Shrub**   page **189**

ESCALLONIA 'DONARD RADIANCE'
Evergreen shrub Z8-9 H9-8 Pink flowers in summer.
‡ 8ft (2.5m)

ESCALLONIA 'IVEYI'
Evergreen shrub   page **195**

X *FATSHEDERA LIZEI*
Shrub   page **205**

FUCHSIA 'MRS. POPPLE'
Shrub   page **212**

FUCHSIA 'TOM THUMB'
Shrub   page **212**

X *HALIMIOCISTUS WINTONENSIS* 'MERRIST WOOD CREAM'
Evergreen shrub   page **236**

HEBE 'ALICIA AMHERST'
Evergreen shrub Z9-10 H12-9 Mid-green leaves and dark violet flowers.
‡ ↔ 4ft (1.2m)

HEBE CUPRESSOIDES 'BOUGHTON DOME'
Shrub   page **240**

HEBE X FRANCISCANA 'VARIEGATA'
Evergreen shrub   page **241**

HEBE 'LA SÉDUISANTE'
Evergreen shrub Z9-10 H10-9 Leaves tinted purple; purple-red flowers in late summer.
‡ ↔ 3ft (1m)

HYDRANGEA MACROPHYLLA 'ALTONA'
Shrub   page **266**

HYDRANGEA MACROPHYLLA 'GEOFFREY CHADBUND'
Shrub Z6-9 H9-6 Lacecap; deep red flowers.
‡ 3ft (1m) ↔ 5ft (1.5m)

LEPTOSPERMUM RUPESTRE
Shrub   page **309**

LUPINUS ARBOREUS
Shrub   page **326**

MATTHIOLA CINDERELLA SERIES
Biennial   page **339**

OLEARIA MACRODONTA
Evergreen shrub   page **355**

SENECIO CINERARIA 'SILVER DUST'
Biennial   page **493**

HARDINESS ZONES

This map, produced by the United States Department of Agriculture, is based on average annual minimum temperatures. A hardiness zone range is given for every plant in this book, except tender plants and annuals.

Although useful as an indicator of a plant's dependability in a given area, a hardiness zone range is not the only indicator of the possible success of a plant. Many factors, including heat tolerance, soil type and fertility, soil moisture and drainage, humidity, and exposure to sun and wind determine a plant's success or failure.

See p. 8 for a more detailed discussion on hardiness, including the AHS heat zones.

°F	ZONES	°C
BELOW -50°	1	BELOW -46°
-50° TO -40°	2	-46° TO -40°
-40° TO -30°	3	-40° TO -34°
-30° TO -20°	4	-34° TO -29°
-20° TO -10°	5	-29° TO -23°
-10° TO 0°	6	-23° TO -18°
0° TO 10°	7	-18° TO -12°
10° TO 20°	8	-12° TO -7°
20° TO 30°	9	-7° TO -1°
30° TO 40°	10	-1° TO 4°
ABOVE 40°	11	ABOVE 4°

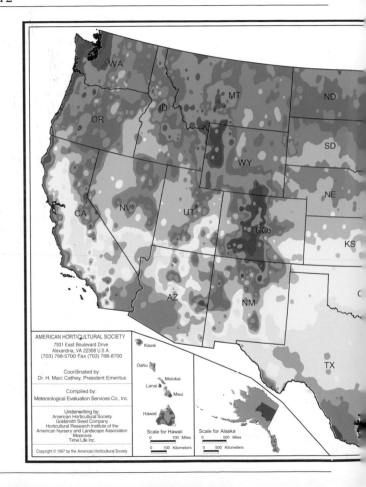

WA

ID

MT

ND

OR

SD

WY

NE

CA

NV

UT

CO

KS

AZ

NM

AMERICAN HORTICULTURAL SOCIETY
7931 East Boulevard Drive
Alexandria, VA 22308 U.S.A.
(703) 768-5700 Fax (703) 768-8700

Coordinated by:
Dr. H. Marc Cathey, President Emeritus

Compiled by:
Meteorological Evaluation Services Co., Inc.

Underwriting by:
American Horticultural Society
Goldsmith Seed Company
Horticultural Research Institute of the
American Nursery and Landscape Association
Moorovia
Time Life Inc.

Copyright © 1997 by the American Horticultural Society

Kauai

Oahu

Molokai

Lanai

Maui

Hawaii

TX

Scale for Hawaii

0   100 Miles

0   100 Kilometers

Scale for Alaska

0   500 Miles

0   500 Kilometers

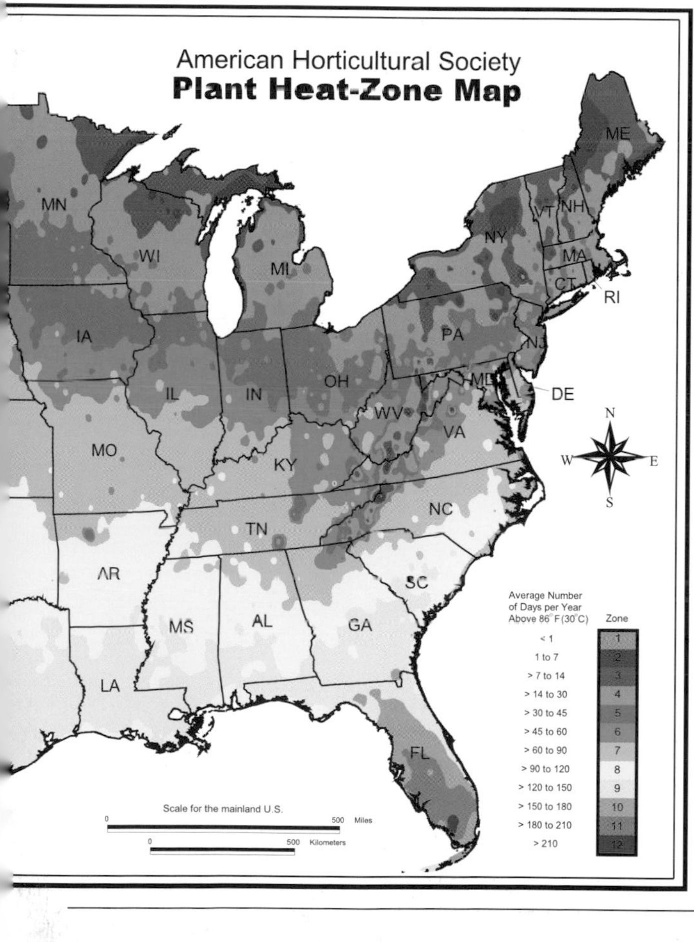

American Horticultural Society
Plant Heat-Zone Map

Average Number
of Days per Year
Above 86°F (30°C)

Zone	
1	< 1
2	1 to 7
3	> 7 to 14
4	> 14 to 30
5	> 30 to 45
6	> 45 to 60
7	> 60 to 90
8	> 90 to 120
9	> 120 to 150
10	> 150 to 180
11	> 180 to 210
12	> 210

Scale for the mainland U.S.

Miles 0 500
Kilometers 0 500

INDEX

ACKNOWLEDGEMENTS

The publisher would like to thank the following for their kind permission to reproduce the photographs:

l=left, r=right, c=center; a=above, b=below:

A–Z Botanical 252d, Anthony Cooper 312d; Geoff Kidd 212br, 228br; Malcolm Richards 538l; Gillian Beckett 31tr; Neil Campbell-Sharp 72tl, 144tl, 330bl, 336tl; Garden Picture Library Brian Carter 47br, 144bl; 320l, 422tl, 480bl, 493br, John Glover 6, 56bl, 150d, 219br, 338d, 312d, 409br, 511br, 515tr, Sunniva Harte 72bl, Neil Holmes 94bl, Lamontagne 119br, 181br, Jerry Pavia 264tl, Howard Rice 32tl, 77br, 365br; David Russel 508l, 509r, JS Sira 402d; Derek Gould 148br; Diana Grenfell 259d; Photos Horticultural 55br, 514bl, 53tr; Andrew Lawson 26, 205tr, 337br; Clive Nichols 113br, 193br, 263tr, 271tr, 289br, 325tr, 466tl; RHS Garden, Wisley 12; Eric Sawford 92tr; Harry Smith Collection 47tr, 49tr, 63tr, 68bl, 69tr, 95tr, 110bl, 117l, 118bl, 126d, 248d, 300d, 304tl, 310bl, 319br, 334l, 344bl, 383tr, 420bl, 481tr, 520bl, 529br.

Dorling Kindersley would also like to thank:

Text contributors and editorial assistance
Geoff Stebbings, Candida Frith-Macdonald, Simon Maughan, Andrew Mikolajski, Sarah Wilde, Tanis Smith and James Nugent, at the Royal Horticultural Society; Vincent Square; Susanne Mitchell, Karen Wilson and Barbara Haynes
Design assistance Wendy Bartlet, Ann Thompson
DTP design assistance Louise Paddick
Additional picture research Charlotte Oster, Sean Hunter; special thanks also to Diana Miller, Keeper of the Herbarium at RHS Wisley
Index Ella Skene